leak

leak

Why Mark Felt Became
Deep Throat

Max Holland

 University Press of Kansas

Published by the
University Press of
Kansas (Lawrence,
Kansas 66045), which
was organized by
the Kansas Board
of Regents and is
operated and funded
by Emporia State
University, Fort Hays
State University,
Kansas State
University, Pittsburg
State University, the
University of Kansas,
and Wichita State
University

© 2012

by Max Holland

Library of Congress Cataloging-in-Publication Data

Holland, Max.
Leak : Why Mark Felt became Deep Throat / Max Holland.
    p. cm.
Includes bibliographical references and index.
ISBN 978-0-7006-1829-3 (cloth : alk. paper)
1. Felt, W. Mark, 1913–2008. 2. Watergate Affair,
1972–1974—Biography. 3. United States. Federal Bureau of
Investigation—Officials and employees—Biography. I. Title.
E860.H65 2012
973.924092—dc23
[B]
2011046025

British Library Cataloguing in Publication Data is available.

Printed in the United States of America

10 9 8 7 6 5 4 3 2

The paper used in this publication is recycled and contains
30 percent postconsumer waste. It is acid free and meets
the minimum requirements of the American National Standard
for Permanence of Paper for Printed Library Materials z39.48-1992.

For Tamar, who believes

Contents

Cast of Characters

Frederick C. LaRue: special consultant

Robert C. Mardian: political coordinator; former assistant attorney general

Powell Moore: director of press and information

Robert C. Odle, Jr.: director of administration and personnel

Herbert L. "Bart" Porter: director of scheduling

DeVan L. Shumway: director of public affairs

Hugh W. Sloan, Jr.: finance committee treasurer

Watergate Burglars and Co-conspirators

E. Howard Hunt, Jr.: White House consultant; "plumber" and former CIA officer

G. Gordon Liddy: finance counsel, CRP; "plumber" and former FBI agent

James W. McCord, Jr.: burglar; chief of security, CRP; former CIA officer

Alfred C. Baldwin III: lookout; security guard, CRP; former FBI agent

Bernard L. Barker: burglar

Virgilio R. Gonzalez: burglar

Eugenio R. Martinez: burglar

Frank A. Sturgis: burglar

Department of Justice

Richard G. Kleindienst: attorney general

Elliott L. Richardson: attorney general

Henry E. Petersen: assistant attorney general, Criminal Division

Donald E. Santarelli: associate deputy attorney general

Federal Judges

George E. MacKinnon: U.S. Court of Appeals, Washington, D.C.

John J. Sirica; chief judge, U.S. District Court, Washington, D.C.

Federal Prosecutors

Harold H. Titus, Jr.: U.S. attorney for the District of Columbia

Earl J. Silbert: assistant U.S. attorney, chief Watergate prosecutor

Donald E. Campbell: assistant U.S. attorney

Seymour Glanzer: assistant U.S. attorney

Watergate Special Prosecution Force

Archibald Cox: special prosecutor

Leon Jaworski: special prosecutor

Federal Bureau of Investigation, Headquarters, 1969–1972
John Edgar Hoover: director
Clyde A. Tolson: associate director

Cartha D. "Deke" DeLoach: deputy associate director
William Mark Felt: deputy associate director
John P. Mohr: assistant director, Administration
Alex Rosen: assistant director, Investigations
William D. Soyars, Jr.: assistant to W. Mark Felt
William C. Sullivan: deputy associate director

Federal Bureau of Investigation: Headquarters, 1972–1973
L. Patrick Gray III: acting director
William D. Ruckelshaus: acting director
Clarence M. Kelley: director
William Mark Felt: acting associate director

Daniel M. "Mack" Armstrong: special assistant to Gray
Charles W. Bates: assistant director, General Investigative Division
Thomas E. Bishop: assistant director, Crime Records Division
Charles Bolz: chief, Accounting and Fraud Section, General
    Investigative Division
Wason G. Campbell, assistant to W. Mark Felt
Jack L. Conmy: aide to Ruckelshaus
Dwight Dalbey: assistant director, Office of Legal Counsel
Paul V. Daly: special agent
Robert E. Gebhardt: assistant director, General Investigative Division
Barbara L. Herwig: special assistant to Gray
David D. Kinley: executive assistant to Gray
Richard E. Long: chief, Accounting and Fraud Section, General
    Investigative Division
Edward S. Miller: assistant director, Domestic Intelligence Division
Charles A. Nuzum: supervisor, Accounting and Fraud Section,
    General Investigative Division
William D. Soyars, Jr.: assistant director, Computer Systems Division
Leonard M. "Bucky" Walters: assistant director, Inspection Division
Federal Bureau of Investigation, Washington Field Office, 1972–1973
Robert G. Kunkel: special agent in charge
John J. "Jack" McDermott: special agent in charge
Angelo J. Lano: case agent, Watergate

Robert E. Lill: special agent
Paul P. Magallanes, special agent
Daniel C. Mahan: special agent
John W. Mindermann: special agent

Central Intelligence Agency
Richard M. Helms: director
Vernon A. "Dick" Walters: deputy director

Congress
Sam J. Ervin, Jr.: senator (D–North Carolina); chairman, Select
  Committee on Presidential Campaign Activities (Watergate
  Committee)
Howard H. Baker, Jr.: senator (R-Tennessee); ranking member,
  Watergate Committee
Robert C. Byrd: senator (D–West Virginia); member, Judiciary
  Committee
Lucien N. Nedzi: representative (D-Michigan); chairman, Special
  Subcommittee on Intelligence, Armed Services Committee

Samuel Dash: majority counsel, Watergate Committee
Fred D. Thompson: minority counsel, Watergate Committee
Scott Armstrong: investigator, Watergate Committee
Terry F. Lenzner: investigator, Watergate Committee

Journalists
Jack Anderson: syndicated columnist
E. J. Bachinski: police reporter, *Washington Post*
David Beckwith: correspondent, *Time* magazine
Carl Bernstein: reporter, *Washington Post*
Benjamin C. Bradlee: executive editor, *Washington Post*
Richard M. Cohen: reporter, *Washington Post*
Patrick Collins: reporter, *Washington Daily News*
John M. Crewdson: reporter, *New York Times*
Leonard Downie, Jr.: deputy metro editor, *Washington Post*; later,
  executive editor
Rowland Evans, Jr.: syndicated political columnist
Hays Gorey: correspondent, *Time* magazine
Richard C. Harwood: national editor, *Washington Post*
Seymour Hersh: reporter, *New York Times*

Robert L. Jackson: reporter, *Los Angeles Times*
William G. Lambert: investigative reporter, *Life* magazine
John A. Limpert: editor, *The Washingtonian* magazine
Brendan Lyons: reporter, Albany (NY) *Times Union*
James Mann: reporter, *Washington Post*
Jack Nelson: reporter, *Los Angeles Times*
Robert D. Novak: syndicated political columnist
Jeremiah O'Leary: reporter, *Washington Star*
Ronald J. Ostrow: reporter, *Los Angeles Times*
Robert H. Phelps: Washington editor, *New York Times*
Harry M. Rosenfeld: metro editor, *Washington Post*; editor, Albany
    (NY) *Times Union*
Walter F. Rugaber: reporter, *New York Times*
Howard Simons: managing editor, *Washington Post*
Sandy Smith: correspondent, *Time* magazine
John F. Stacks: news editor, Washington bureau, *Time* magazine
Laurence Stern: reporter, *Washington Post*
Barry Sussman: city editor, *Washington Post*; special Watergate editor
Tad Szulc: reporter, *New York Times*
Sanford J. Ungar: reporter, *Washington Post*
Bob Woodward: reporter, *Washington Post*

Nongovernment Lawyers
Joseph A. Califano, Jr.: outside counsel, the *Washington Post* and the
    Democratic National Committee; name partner, Williams, Connolly
    & Califano
John F. Dowd: in-house editorial counsel, *Time* magazine
J. Alan Galbraith: attorney, Williams, Connolly & Califano
Roswell L. Gilpatric: partner, Cravath, Swaine & Moore
Herbert W. Kalmbach: personal attorney to President Nixon
Kenneth W. Parkinson: counsel, CRP
Stephen H. Sachs: counsel to L. Patrick Gray III
John P. Sears: former deputy counsel, White House
Donald H. Segretti: attorney hired by Dwight Chapin for campaign
    "dirty tricks"
Edward Bennett Williams: outside counsel, the *Washington Post*; name
    partner, Williams, Connolly & Califano

leak

Introduction

With a story as enticing, complex, and competitive and quickly unfolding as Watergate, there was little tendency or time to consider the motive of our sources. What was important was whether the information checked out and whether it was true. . . . The cliché about drinking from a fire hose applied. There was no time to ask our sources, Why are you talking? Do you have an ax to grind? Why don't you blow the whistle publicly, stand up there and tell all you know? This was the case with Mark Felt.

. . . His words and guidance had immense, at times even staggering, authority. The weight, authenticity and his restraint were more important than his design, if he had one.

—Bob Woodward, The Secret Man

What motivated W. Mark Felt, a.k.a. "Deep Throat," to leak to a cub reporter at the *Washington Post?* Nearly forty years after the Watergate break-in, Felt's "design" is the only significant question unresolved.

When *All the President's Men* introduced the public to Deep Throat, in the spring of 1974, authors Bob Woodward and Carl Bernstein fostered an impression of his motive: Deep Throat was a selfless, high-ranking official intent on exposing the lawlessness of the Nixon White House. He "was trying to protect the office [of the presidency]," they wrote, "to effect a change in its conduct before all was lost." This depiction of Mark Felt as a principled whistle-blower became practically indelible after Hal Holbrook's "neurotically loaded" portrayal of Deep Throat in the 1976 screen adaptation of the book.[1]

One of the more telling aspects of *The Secret Man*, Woodward's 2005 portrait of his relationship with Felt, was how he backed away from that Hollywoodized depiction. In his second take on Deep Throat, Woodward wrote that Felt "never really voiced pure, raw outrage to me about Watergate or what it represented." Woodward was able to parse Felt's motive only after the Watergate "fire hose" had petered out—that is, after Nixon's resignation. At that point, he deduced that Felt's motive was more pedestrian than principled: Far from defending the office of the presidency, Felt leaked because he "believed he was protecting the [FBI]" from the Nixon White House. Felt's disclosures, in other words, helped create the public and political pressure necessary to hold the president and his staff accountable, while insulating Felt's revered FBI from a White House determined to manipulate and control it—as evinced by the appointment of L. Patrick Gray III, an alleged Nixon crony, to succeed J. Edgar Hoover as FBI director in May 1972.[2]

There has long been a third, less honorable, explanation of Felt's motive: that he acted neither out of principle nor institutional pride, but out of pure pique. According to this view, he was a deeply embittered man, coldly furious at Nixon for having passed him over for the FBI directorship when Hoover died, and at the White House in general for what it was trying to do to the organization Hoover had built over four decades. The Watergate break-in, which occurred just a few weeks after Gray's appointment, was serendipitous for someone seeking retaliation.[3]

None of these competing explanations has ever really taken hold to the exclusion of the others. Even on the surface, each seems less than totally persuasive, and, on closer inspection, each has a flaw sufficient to discount it entirely.

The problem with the Hollywoodized explanation is that Felt himself authorized illegal, surreptitious entries into the homes of people associated with the Weather Underground, a domestic terrorist group, during 1972–1973. At the same time that he was supposedly mortified by the White House's law breaking, he was busy sanctioning similar behavior by FBI agents.[4]

Woodward's 2005 explanation has defects as well. Although Hoover's death gave Richard Nixon a rare opportunity to put his own man at the top of the FBI, the notion that the White House would thereafter be able to manipulate the Bureau at will is preposterous. Hoover's FBI was notoriously hidebound and could not be remade overnight. Indeed, forty years later we are still living with the Bureau's insular, peculiar, and highly resistant culture. Nor did Felt have to act to protect the integrity of the FBI's Watergate investigation. Although very early on Nixon tried to rein it in by making unfounded claims about national security and CIA equities, that effort quickly collapsed and the Bureau's investigation was never circumscribed thereafter, despite some improprieties by the then-acting director, Pat Gray. Not even Felt ever publicly subscribed to the notion that the White House had interfered successfully with the Bureau's probe, though, to be sure, it hindered the inquiry insofar as possible and exploited several courtesies to further the cover-up. In his 1979 memoir, Felt asserted that the attacks on the FBI for "dragging [its] feet" on the Watergate inquiry were unfair. "No one," wrote Felt, "could have stopped the driving force of the investigation without an explosion in the Bureau—not even J. Edgar Hoover."[5]

The revenge theory, for its part, not only seems borrowed from a bad Washington potboiler, but also assumes that Felt was willing to risk his career for an intangible, rather insignificant reward. Leaking put Felt in a dangerous position, as Woodward observed in *The Secret Man*: "Technically, it was illegal to talk about grand jury information or FBI files; or it could have been made to look illegal." As a lawyer, Felt surely understood the adage that the wheels of justice may grind slowly, but they grind extremely fine. If he wanted revenge, why act before the criminal and civil processes had played themselves out, possibly achieving his ends for him?[6]

Contrary to the widely held perception that the *Washington Post* "uncovered" Watergate, the newspaper essentially tracked the progress of the FBI's investigation, with a time delay ranging from weeks to days, and published elements of the prosecutors' case well in advance of the trial. Keeping the story in the news was meaningful and important, of course, especially when that newspaper was the *Post*. Owing to its prized readership, it had an influence that far outstripped its circulation. Every important official in Washington and every reporter based there read the *Post*, which meant the newspaper was an elite publication in that it helped define the news in and coming out of Washington. Its articles surely had an impact on Judge John J. Sirica, in whose courtroom the burglars were tried in January 1973 and the cover-up conspirators in October 1974. The stories also undoubtedly influenced the U.S. Senate, which in January 1973 formed a select committee, chaired by Sam Ervin (D–North Carolina), to probe the 1972 campaign. Perhaps most significantly, the Nixon administration reacted initially to the *Post*'s stories by denying and dissembling, creating an epic credibility gap with the media and eventually the public from which the White House never recovered.[7]

Still, the main effect of Deep Throat's leaks was merely to accelerate the scandal by perhaps six months or a year, as former White House counsel Leonard Garment once observed. Felt helped the *Post* print "eye-popping stories, preceding disclosures by law enforcement . . . that built momentum and drew in the rest of the press at a time when Watergate might otherwise have faded from public view." But unless Felt's judgment was impaired by sheer rage, he took an extraordinary risk for an inordinately small payoff—and one that contradicted his politics to boot. Any disclosures before November 1972 stood to benefit only George McGovern, and Felt harbored nothing but disdain for the Democrat dubbed the candidate of "acid, amnesty, and abortion."[8]

By 2010, Woodward had begun to ascribe "multiple motives" to Felt, apparently in recognition of the uncertainty and contradictions that have simmered since 2005. This new admixture is one part principle; one part personal pique over having been passed over for the directorship; and one part outrage over the White House's efforts to control and abuse the FBI. Felt "knew there was a cover-up . . . and did not trust the acting FBI director, Pat Gray. He knew the Nixon White House was corrupt. At the same time, he was disappointed that he did not get the directorship." But merely combining three weak explanations does not result in a credible one.[9]

What, then, can possibly explain Felt's urgency and the risks he took? Woodward maintains that Felt was a "secret man," impenetrable and unfathomable. Yet now that Deep Throat's identity is beyond dispute, going back to find his motive is imperative. And there exists a tried and true technique for doing so. When counterintelligence officers suspect a person of being a double agent, they fashion a ledger of everything that person knew, when, and how that person acted on the information. At the end there is a final tally, and that is supposed to reveal in whose interests the suspected double agent was genuinely working all along.

This book is akin to Felt's ledger, because understanding his design, even at this late date, matters greatly to our historical understanding. As Christopher Hitchens wrote in his review of *The Secret Man,* Watergate "ranks as the single most successful use of the news media by an anonymous unelected official with an agenda of his own." Without a consensus about what that agenda was, there is a gaping hole at the center of the narrative.[10]

The story of the break-in at the Democrats' headquarters and the subsequent cover-up are terrific yarns. But the meta-narrative about the forces at work *behind* the scandal that brought Nixon down, as *The Washingtonian*'s John Limpert once pointed out, "tells you an awful lot more about how things happen in Washington."[11]

CHAPTER ONE

A Forced Departure

May 1973

Heroes don't lurk in shadows for 33 years.
—*Jack McDermott, SAC of the Washington Field Office*

A sensible answer about why Deep Throat leaked begins with the circumstances of his resignation from the FBI in June 1973.

According to *The Secret Man*, Mark Felt retired quietly and without fanfare. This bland explanation is unchanged from the original AP story that appeared in the *Post* and elsewhere ("FBI's No. 2 Man to Retire") and is consistent with Felt's 1979 ghost-written memoir, *The FBI Pyramid*. That the cover story has persisted so long is striking, given the interest in deconstructing Deep Throat's motive and the ease of ascertaining the true circumstances of his departure. It should have struck a false note with anyone who believed that Felt's overriding motive was to protect the FBI: were that true, the last thing Felt would have done was abandon his post at a moment of unprecedented turmoil for the Bureau, and at a time when he was still publicly considered a candidate for the directorship.[1]

Felt was only sixty in the spring of 1973; he had five years before mandatory retirement. More to the point, the FBI was facing its biggest crisis since the Teapot Dome scandal fifty years earlier. The still-unfolding Watergate revelations had "brought egg to [the FBI's face] and demoralization to its ranks," as a *Post* article asserted on the first anniversary of the break-in. The acting director, Patrick Gray, had just resigned, "heavily discredited for his role in the investigation and the subsequent White House cover-up," and the stain had spread to the Bureau as a whole.[2]

In fact, Felt did not casually resign—he quit abruptly rather than subject himself to a leak investigation. Although parts of this story appeared in print as early as 1976, it is told here in full for the first time.[3]

The events that precipitated Felt's resignation began on May 11. That morning the *New York Times* published a story by John M. Crewdson about the wiretapping of several reporters and some former aides to Henry Kissinger, the president's national security adviser, over a two-year period beginning in 1969. Crewdson was not the first to disclose the wiretaps' existence; that scoop belonged to *Time* magazine's Sandy Smith, an investigative reporter known for his law-enforcement sources. In late February Smith had written that the White House ordered the FBI in 1969 to institute electronic surveillance of "six or seven reporters" suspected of receiving leaks of classified information, along with "an undisclosed number of White House aides."[4]

But until Crewdson's article appeared there was little detail about the wiretaps and no accurate mention of the names of those who were tapped. The stories that had been published elsewhere were full of errors, whereas Crewdson's was right on the money. His sources included a former FBI official directly involved in funneling the results from the wiretaps to the White House (though he was not identified as such), and so Crewdson was able to name some names: William Beecher and Hedrick Smith, both *New York Times* reporters; Henry Brandon from the *Sunday Times* of London; and Morton Halperin, a former staff member of the National Security Council.[5]

The day Crewdson's article appeared, William D. Ruckelshaus, the interim FBI director after Pat Gray, received a telephone call from a man who introduced himself as John Crewdson. The caller said that he was not ordinarily in the business of revealing an anonymous source, but he was going to make an exception. Mark Felt had supplied him with the details about the wiretaps, "Crewdson" declared. Moreover, Felt had said that he was in the running to be the next FBI director—making it seem as if the leak were a down payment for editorial support in the near future from the *Times*.[6]

Taken aback, Ruckelshaus asked "Crewdson" why he was identifying his source. The man replied that he was "just very concerned about the situation in the country," Ruckelshaus told me in a 2007 interview. "He thought things were kind of falling apart and that I ought to know this."[7]

Surprised by the reporter's ostensible breach of confidentiality but satisfied that the information was accurate, Ruckelshaus took immediate action. The Bureau, of course, often leaked information to the media. But there was a vast difference between official or authorized leaks and Felt's unsanctioned behavior. It "violated everything": the Bureau's regulations, decent conduct, perhaps even the law. Ruckelshaus was particularly incensed because he had ordered an urgent investigation, still ongoing, into the wiretaps, and believed that Crewdson's scoop undercut him. It denied the Bureau the opportunity to begin rebuilding its credibility by telling the story first.[8]

Felt was visiting his son in California on the day the story appeared. But Ruckelshaus confronted him immediately upon his return to headquarters, on May 14. The acting director said he had "very good information that [Felt] was the source" of the leak to Crewdson. Ruckelshaus did not want to betray a supposed confidence, but at the same time he wanted to impress Felt with the quality of his information. So instead of disclosing exactly how he had come by the information, Ruckelshaus used a ruse: he claimed that a fraternity brother of his worked as an editor at the *Times*. This friend had supposedly been somewhat skeptical about the story when it came in and had insisted on learning the name of Crewdson's primary source. Subsequently he had called his old frat brother (Ruckelshaus) to confirm that Felt was an FBI employee and in a position to know such information.[9]

Ruckelshaus accused Felt of undermining him at every opportunity, and at a time when he was trying to mend the Bureau's badly tattered reputation. Felt vehemently denied the accusation. Initially he denied having any contact with Crewdson but then relented and admitted he had had a brief conversation with the reporter while out in California. But he had only tried to correct information that Crewdson already knew, Felt insisted to Ruckelshaus; at one point, Felt also suggested that William C. Sullivan, a former high-ranking official who had had a bitter falling out with Hoover, was the true culprit. The two men quarreled, and Ruckelshaus remembers thinking that not only was Felt "willing to leak, but he was willing to lie about it." The conversation ended with Ruckelshaus saying he would decide overnight what he was going to do. In the meantime, he asked for and received Felt's keys to the director's office.[10]

When Ruckelshaus arrived in his office the next morning, he found a letter of resignation from Felt. He took this to mean that Felt believed Ruckelshaus might back down if the ante were raised, given the acting director's inexperience and the enormous problems on his desk. To Felt's apparent surprise, Ruckelshaus instantly accepted the resignation, completely confident that Felt was the leaker. "If he hadn't done it," Ruckelshaus recalls thinking, "I don't think he would [be resigning]." Felt was allowed to stay on until June 12 to finish some projects, and it was agreed that his official records would reflect a "voluntary retirement." The flowery letters of resignation and acceptance that were publicly released made no mention of a confrontation between the two men. Instead, the press dutifully reported that Felt wanted to take advantage of a "bonus being offered government workers who retire during June."[11]

I asked Crewdson about the matter in 2008, and he vigorously denied that he had called Ruckelshaus to disclose that Felt was leaking. "I mean, if [Ruckelshaus] told you that, he told you that. But that's totally bizarre," he said. "It's certainly not true." He added, "Not only would I *not* call the head of the FBI to tell him who my source was, I wouldn't call the head of the FBI to *lie* about who my source was." Moreover, Felt had not been Crewdson's anonymous source. "My source was . . . not even in the FBI," Crewdson told me.[12]

Both Ruckelshaus and Crewdson have stellar reputations. Ruckelshaus was one of the few high-level Nixon appointees to come through Watergate with his reputation not only intact but enhanced (recall that he resigned from the Justice Department rather than carry out Nixon's order to fire the first special prosecutor, Archibald Cox). And Crewdson is a highly respected journalist who won a Pulitzer Prize in 1981. The contradiction between their accounts has three possible explanations. Either Ruckelshaus or Crewdson was not being truthful—or both were telling the truth as they knew it.

If the last scenario is correct, whoever gave the wiretap details to Crewdson also arranged for the call to Ruckelshaus. (Ruckelshaus had been the interim FBI director for less than a month; although he knew who Crewdson was, he would not have recognized his voice.) And whoever called Crewdson, besides being privy to the information about the wiretaps, would have had to know that Felt could be plausibly blamed for the leak. This point is crucial: knowledge of the wiretaps was very tightly held in the FBI, and only a very few persons were even remotely aware of it, much less the details. None of the records had been indexed and all had been personally controlled by William C. Sullivan, one of the Bureau's highest-ranking officials, when the surveillance was conducted.[13]

When I asked him in 2008 if the passage of time might allow him to divulge his source, Crewdson initially responded that "it has always been my position that confidential source relationships are to be protected, even after the source in question has been dead for many years." But he later wrote to say that he "continue[d] to respect confidential source-reporter relationships even in cases where the source was killed in a hunting accident many years ago." That description can mean only one thing: Crewdson's source was William Sullivan, who famously died in a 1977 hunting accident in New Hampshire. Sullivan was considered Hoover's most likely successor until October 1971, when he was summarily fired for disloyalty and insubordination. At the time of Crewdson's article, however, he was making an unlikely comeback, and some outside observers considered him Felt's strongest rival for the Bureau's directorship.[14]

William Sullivan framed Mark Felt: This is the thread, if pulled, that unravels the mystery of Deep Throat's motive.

In *The Wars of Watergate* (1990), historian Stanley I. Kutler argued that the scandal encompassed a number of festering conflicts—institutional, political, ideological, and personal. One of the most prominent was the "War of the FBI Succession," a phrase he first heard from an anonymous source in 1973 or 1974. More than any other single factor, the desperate, no-holds-barred war of succession explains why Mark Felt did what he did, and to a considerable extent, why the scandal played out in the media as it did. The contest to succeed Hoover was perceived as a once-in-a-generation opportunity, and it brought out the worst in the Bureau and Mark Felt.[15]

When Pat Gray presided over his first meeting in the Bureau's inner sanctum in May 1972, several officials present believed they were far better qualified to run the FBI. One was John P. Mohr, the assistant to the director for administrative matters, a self-described "hard-headed Dutchman." Although Mohr was almost completely unknown to the public, inside the Bureau he was one of the most powerful men the FBI had ever known, and many insiders considered him the most capable of the senior executives. Alex Rosen, the assistant to the director for investigative matters and a Hoover stalwart since World War II, was also not without ambition. The two were relatively open about their disenchantment over Gray's ascension and disappointed about not gaining the opportunity to serve as director. Rather than feign loyalty while working to undermine Gray, both men quit within a month of his appointment.[16]

Not so with Mark Felt. He stayed at the Bureau and worked for almost a year on what might be called his own psychological warfare plan. Felt's private counterintelligence program (or COINTELPRO, in FBI parlance) was designed to disrupt and confuse his adversaries and manipulate those in power. Pat Gray and Bill Sullivan were the intended victims. The White House, and to a lesser extent, Congress, were the targets of his manipulations, and the press was his instrument of choice.

The bulk of Felt's effort would consist of trying to prove to the White House, through anonymous leaks to the media, that Gray was dangerously incompetent and incapable of running the Bureau. Felt was supremely confident that because of his extensive counterintelligence experience, he could keep his hand invisible. But the plan was too clever by half: by late October 1972, Nixon learned about Felt's leaks. Despite the president's inclination to exact swift retribution, Nixon shied away from firing Felt because he feared the consequences. Felt lasted until May 1973, when he was finally outwitted by his bitter rival and another FBI master of deception, Bill Sullivan. In the ultimate irony, an instance when Felt was *not* the leaker proved to be his undoing.[17]

The portrait of Felt that emerges when we follow this thread does not resemble any of Bob Woodward's depictions. Felt held the news media in contempt and was neither a high-minded whistle-blower, nor was he genuinely concerned about defending his institution's integrity. He was not even hopelessly embittered—just calculating. A single-minded determination to succeed Hoover drove him, even as his chances, slim to begin with, evaporated.

John McDermott was the special agent in charge of the FBI's Washington Field Office from October 1972 onwards. He later rose to the number three position in the Bureau before retiring in 1979. Soon after Felt uncloaked himself in 2005, McDermott wrote,

> Felt had not a scintilla of evidence that the Bureau's investigation was being *effectively* [emphasis in the original] impeded or thwarted by the White House, the Justice Department, or [Pat] Gray. . . . In assessing [Felt's] actions . . . let us not be distracted now by his frail circumstance, but remember him as he was in 1972: a healthy, ambitious, 59-year-old. . . . Some have called Felt a hero, but heroes don't lurk in shadows for 33 years. . . .[18]

Later, he added in a private letter:

> . . . I personally challenge any person, in or out of the FBI, to document any information that was suppressed or any diversion of the investigation from unlimited, impartial probity. Absent any such "fact," all other arguments seeking to justify Felt's actions are trash.
>
> Felt was the Bureau's Benedict Arnold. . . . Arnold betrayed his oath, his country, and his fellow citizen-soldiers to pursue his own ambitions. Felt did no less to the Bureau and his fellow agents.[19]

Felt's last year at the FBI coincided almost exactly with the first year of the Watergate scandal. In reconstructing what he did during that year and why, it's important not only to recall events in the proper order, but also to view them as they were actually lived—that is, without over-interpretation based on hindsight. Too often, speculations about Deep Throat's motive have been influenced by Watergate's seemingly inexorable endgame. But the scandal did not start out as a mortal threat to Nixon's presidency, and its history should not be written as if it did.

Watergate metastasized into a "cancer on the presidency," in John Dean's memorable phrase, but it started out as an operable tumor. A key part of the argument here is that Mark Felt had no thought of bringing Nixon down. The first seven months of the scandal were dominated not by the cover-up but by the crime, and the notion that "the cover-up is worse than the crime" took nearly a year to become conventional wisdom. It wasn't until the summer of 1973, when the Senate Watergate hearings transfixed the nation, that the groundswell for impeachment began.

Nixon's downfall was an entirely unanticipated result of Felt's true and only aim.

CHAPTER TWO

The "War of the FBI Succession"

1969–1972

Anybody who wanted to be director of the FBI was willing to do some mighty strange things. It was interesting to see the lengths to which an otherwise decent human being would go.
—*Anonymous FBI official, quoted in Sanford Ungar's* FBI

Long before the dénouement, several observers remarked that Watergate might have played out very differently had J. Edgar Hoover not chosen an inopportune time to die: May 2, 1972, just seven weeks before the break-in at the Democratic Party headquarters. The profundity of that observation was never sufficiently appreciated. If Nixon had managed a dignified exit for Hoover and installed a new permanent director before the break-in, he just might have saved his presidency. Alternately, Hoover was the kind of director with enough gumption to walk into the Oval Office and tell the president face-to-face that some of his most trusted advisers had been implicated in a crime and had to be fired.[1]

In 1969, when Nixon took office, he expected that his administration would be entirely in sync with Hoover's Bureau. Although Hoover had initially been wary of Nixon when he first came to Washington, the two men began to be friendly after then-Representative Nixon went out of his way to praise the FBI's investigation of Alger Hiss, whom Nixon exposed in 1948 as a Soviet spy while serving on the House Committee on Un-American Activities. After Nixon became vice president in 1953, Hoover became not only a source of invaluable information to the up-and-coming politician, but also a trusted adviser. He cultivated Nixon even during Nixon's "wilderness years," 1963 to 1966, when he was out of electoral politics altogether. Of all the people Nixon had met in public life, he considered Hoover one of his closest friends.[2]

Initially the relationship between the president and the director was seamless. Nixon extended the special presidential order that had allowed Hoover to remain in office past the mandatory retirement age of sixty-five, and he gave Hoover direct access to the Oval Office. The director responded with a program code-named INLET, under which the FBI regularly forwarded reports about the personal and political associations of the president's critics. The Bureau also provided, upon request, information about illicit sexual activity by members of the Washington press corps.[3]

By February 1971, however, relations between the White House and the FBI had soured, largely unbeknownst to the press. The president had come to believe that Hoover—whom Chief of Staff H. R. "Bob" Haldeman considered a "real character out of [the] days of yore"—was being singularly uncooperative. The White House perceived itself and the nation as under siege from a motley collection of home-grown white radicals, militant black nationalists, and antiwar protesters. Yet Hoover was still fixated on the Communist menace and prone to taking two-hour afternoon naps in his office. His FBI seemed stuck in time, unwilling or unable to take effective countermeasures.[4]

Nothing had eroded Hoover's standing more than his objections to the so-called "Huston plan" in July 1970. The proposal for a White House–coordinated counterintelligence effort against radical and antiwar elements went down in flames because of his opposition. "At some point, Hoover has to be told who is president," noted the proposal's frustrated author, White House aide Tom Charles Huston. "He has become totally unreasonable and his conduct is detrimental to our domestic intelligence operations."[5]

By 1971 Nixon had decided that a dignified way for Hoover to step down had to be found before the November 1972 elections. He didn't want to run the risk of having a Democratic president appoint a new director, for Nixon considered the appointment equivalent to nominating a new chief justice of the U.S. Supreme Court. Nonetheless, the president could not bring himself to force Hoover to step aside. The situation became much more complicated in the spring of 1971, when Hoover came under unprecedented attack—not only from his usual foes, but from quarters that normally provided unflinching support. The precipitating event was a March 8 raid by antiwar activists on the FBI's office in Media, Pennsylvania. In one fell swoop FBI surveillance of dissidents was exposed and the Bureau's carefully nurtured mystique destroyed. Far from being invincible, the FBI appeared merely petty, obsessed with monitoring what seemed to be, in many cases, lawful dissent.[6]

In May the pollster Lou Harris began surveying Americans about whether J. Edgar Hoover should resign. The public was evenly divided: 43 percent said yes, 43 percent said no, and the rest were undecided. Although Hoover had never been free of attacks, he was now on the receiving end of an unusual number of brickbats. The columnist Jack Anderson published an exposé alleging that Hoover had personally profited from books written by FBI employees on government time. The Bureau's usually staunch supporters were thrown on the defensive and left wondering if Hoover had finally lost his touch. As one historian later wrote, "It was all rather embarrassing for an institution that had once been the object of envy and unstinting admiration. The Bureau was becoming a caricature of itself."[7]

Nixon did not want to create the impression that his longtime friend had been forced to resign under pressure, so he postponed his plans for a showdown. When it finally occurred, on September 20, 1971, the president, who was notorious inside the White House for an inability to deliver bad or difficult news personally, could not make his decision stick in a face-to-face meeting with Hoover. It was "no go," Nixon reported to Haldeman, seemingly embarrassed by his inability to dislodge the wily man aptly described as the "No. 1 Sacred Cow of American Politics."[8]

Not even evidence of mounting turmoil within the Bureau was sufficient to move Nixon to act. In the end, he simply had too much history in common with Hoover. They shared the same enemies: the Old Left and the New Left, black militants and antiwar activists, and most of all, the liberal elites who dominated the major newspapers and television networks. Hoover hated the press almost as much as Nixon did and delighted the president with his frequent references to reporters as "skunks" or "jackals." Ultimately, Nixon resigned himself to ousting Hoover but only after the 1972 election. Indeed, he decided to turn his defeat by the director into a political bargaining chip. It would be another argument for why Nixon had to have four more years: only he could be entrusted with making such an important appointment.[9]

These White House maneuvers were not lost on the FBI executives who hoped to succeed Hoover and were watching very carefully. Yet within the Bureau, the struggle for power was unlike any that normally took place at a federal entity—in large part because a cult of personality dominated the FBI. Hoover was, effectively, the only director the Bureau had ever known, a fixture ever since his appointment in May 1924 at the age of twenty-nine. He demanded, and with a few notable exceptions received, a servile kind of loyalty.

As his powers and grip on power began to loosen, the internal scheming resembled what happened inside the Kremlin whenever a superannuated Soviet leader was nearing the end of his reign. It was crucial to be in the right place at the right time, but too much naked careerism was also dangerous. As one former FBI agent later recalled, "If you wanted to ruin somebody's career in the FBI, all you had to do [was] leak it to somebody in the press that so-and-so [was] being groomed as Hoover's successor."[10]

Although a number of senior FBI officials saw a potential director when they looked in the mirror during their morning shave, only three names were commonly bandied about in the press: Cartha D. "Deke" De-Loach, William C. Sullivan, and W. Mark Felt. They were all in their fifties and had joined the Bureau during its rapid war-time expansion. Each had taken a slightly different path, but they had one thing in common: all had spent the bulk of their careers at the "seat of government," as FBI headquarters was immodestly called. That meant maximum exposure to the Bureau's Byzantine ways and the cult of Hoover.

For years Deke DeLoach had been several lengths ahead of any conceivable rival. A smooth-talking Georgian, he had held the number three post in the Bureau in the late 1960s, below J. Edgar himself and Clyde Tolson, Hoover's alter ego. He was the Bureau's liaison with President Lyndon Johnson, and the two southerners grew so close that DeLoach was considered a shoo-in to replace Hoover after LBJ's expected re-election in 1968. But then LBJ abruptly declined to run, and their close association proved to be DeLoach's undoing. Nixon blamed DeLoach (much more so than Hoover) for allegedly putting the 1968 GOP campaign under electronic surveillance at Johnson's order. (LBJ had believed that the Republicans were urging the South Vietnamese government to boycott his peace negotiations and promising Saigon that it would get a better deal under Nixon.) The surveillance was in fact never implemented to the extent LBJ had demanded, although Nixon refused to accept that reality, having heard about the effort from Hoover himself.[11]

An able reader of political tea leaves, DeLoach retired from the Bureau in June 1970, taking a lucrative job at Pepsi-Cola. Nonetheless, he wasn't entirely eliminated from consideration. He still had staunch friends and advocates within and without the administration who intended to put his name forward at the right moment. DeLoach cultivated, in particular, Richard Kleindienst (initially the deputy attorney general, then attorney general) during Hoover's descendancy. But what had been almost a foregone conclusion now became an open competition.[12]

With DeLoach's departure, William C. Sullivan assumed the inside-pole position. His mercurial, intense, and secretive personality had earned him the sobriquet "Crazy Billy," and his office was in a constant state of upheaval, which was most un-Hoover-like. Yet the director regarded Sullivan almost like a son. The standard measure for where subordinates stood with Hoover was his method of addressing them. If he called someone "Miller" rather than "Mr. Miller," that person had achieved a high level of familiarity with Hoover. Sullivan's was the highest of all: he was "Bill" in person, and "Dear Bill" whenever Hoover dashed off a memo.[13]

Sullivan shared the title of assistant director and the number three ranking with John P. Mohr, but was presumed to have an edge because of his expertise in counterintelligence and domestic security—critical areas at a time when the White House was fixated on antiwar activists, radicals, and black militants who were carrying out acts of violence and terrorism. Sullivan managed the Bureau's most sensitive counterintelligence program (COINTELPRO) operations, including surveillance and disruption of the Old and the New Left; the Klan and other white supremacist organizations; black nationalist groups; and Soviet bloc espionage.[14]

His new proximity to Hoover did not cement Sullivan's status as heir apparent. In fact, in the new position the feisty Sullivan began to chafe at being constantly corrected or second-guessed by the director over managerial decisions and substantive issues, such as whether the U.S. Communist Party was instrumental in fomenting racial and antiwar unrest. Memos exchanged between them suddenly acquired a sarcastic and fiery tone. Sullivan also had a fatal character flaw in that he was impatient. While every other contender sought to wrap himself in Hoover's mantle, Sullivan came to believe that by leveraging the White House's disenchantment with Hoover, he might be able to hasten the director's departure.

As late as April 1971, when the aging director came under widespread attack in the wake of the Media, Pennsylvania, break-in, Sullivan was still expressing his unwavering support in private. But by June, after consulting several trusted FBI executives and agents, Sullivan consciously decided to pursue what he knew would be a "collision course." Soon he began openly criticizing the Bureau's ossified leadership with the quiet support of some like-minded Justice Department officials, including the deputy attorney general, Richard G. Kleindienst, and the assistant attorney general in charge of the Internal Security Division, Robert C. Mardian. On August 28, 1971, Sullivan sent Hoover a letter in which he said bluntly that Hoover had lost his grip and the Bureau was suffering as a result.[15]

Hoover soon fired Sullivan for disloyalty, insolence, and insubordination, but not before a confrontation that instantly became part of FBI lore.

In October, Sullivan returned from his annual leave to find he had been physically displaced from the Domestic Intelligence Division by Edward S. Miller, a man loyal to the Bureau's new number three official, W. Mark Felt, who himself had been abruptly promoted as the Sullivan-Hoover relationship rapidly deteriorated. Even the locks on the file cabinets in Sullivan's former office had been changed. This touch had been Felt's idea, and the two men exchanged harsh words. Felt accused Sullivan of being a "Judas," and the rumpled, bantam-sized Sullivan challenged the dapper, six-foot-tall Felt to a fist fight.[16]

In Sullivan's 1979 memoir, he expressed regret about his impatience. If he had only known that the "egomaniacal old rogue [Hoover] was going to die less than a year after our quarrel," he wrote, "I would not have allowed our differences to surface." This was wisdom acquired through hindsight. At the time, Sullivan's rebellion polarized the Bureau to an unprecedented degree. Even though many executives and rank-and-file agents would have readily agreed, if asked in private, that Hoover's best days were long past, Sullivan's behavior was considered unforgivable. It's hard to know what Hoover's acolytes considered worse: Sullivan's disloyalty to the director, who had treated him like a son, or his indiscretion in making his differences with Hoover public and aligning himself with forces outside the FBI.[17]

With Sullivan's exit, the new internal heir apparent became Mark Felt, every bit as smooth as Sullivan had been rough-edged, and known for his impenetrable, if not icy, demeanor. Reporters who covered the Bureau regarded him as a man who was eager to rise, for he wore his ambition on his well-tailored sleeves and seemed to invite notice. This was in marked distinction to most FBI executives, who deliberately sought to appear colorless and almost interchangeable. "He had this quite flamboyant hair" for an FBI official, recalled Nicholas Horrock, who covered the FBI for *Newsweek* in the early 1970s. "And the other thing I remember is that he had a better class of suits. . . . Mark dressed well and it was noticeable." Also noticeable was the three-room suite reserved for Felt, his principal assistant William Soyars, Jr., and their secretaries, as he ascended to the number three position. The newly remodeled offices were right across the hall from Hoover's suite.[18]

One of the qualities that differentiated Felt from the earlier heir apparents, however, was that he had almost no champions outside the Bureau, either in the Justice Department or White House itself. Both DeLoach and Sullivan were just as ambitious for the directorship, of course, but unlike Felt, they didn't go to great lengths to pretend otherwise. DeLoach, for his part, was egotistical, played fast and loose, and was also kind of a rascal. Yet he knew he was a rascal, he told you he was a rascal, and he enjoyed being a rascal. There was nothing covert about it, but when he employed that thick-as-molasses Georgia drawl, he was so disarming that all was forgiven. Similarly, Sullivan's intense, opinionated personality was on display for everyone to see: there was no space between the private and public man. While he had many detractors, who considered him too eccentric, he also inspired considerable loyalty.

Felt was decidedly different in his approach, and engendered distrust as a result. He was not just egotistical like DeLoach, but vain, too, and self-serving in an unattractive way. He was consumed with a concern for his own career and what he believed was his rightful inheritance, as Hoover's natural legatee. Unlike his putative rivals, he played things "too close to the vest" for a man who was an insider and "did not interact with credibility." He was too hidden, even among his peers in the Bureau and Justice Department. Felt never seemed to engage with anyone, and because he was so unreadable, he would not create administration advocates for his appointment.[19]

During the nine months Felt served as the number three man, he effectively functioned as the FBI director. Hoover's age had taken a great toll on his powers of concentration and memory, and Tolson, whose close attention to detail had helped make Hoover a bureaucratic powerhouse, was in even worse shape, having suffered two strokes. Insofar as he could, Felt tried to replace Tolson as Hoover's best friend and confidant; amid the crush of public criticism, Hoover was "not himself, seemed alone, and needed a friend." Felt also did everything he could think of to curry favor with those who would determine the next director, short of being frank about his ambition. Aware of Nixon's fixation on campus unrest and antiwar protests, he made regular reports to the White House about events as benign as a high school cafeteria fight.[20]

Hoover was clearly nearing the end of his tenure, and Felt's positioning seemed as impeccable as his dress. Felt had devoted his entire adult life to the Bureau and made lasting personal sacrifices, often putting his work before anything else. Now he was close enough to the top of the FBI pyramid that he could practically touch it.

Hoover's body was discovered on the morning of May 2, after his FBI chauffeur arrived to take him to work. When hundreds of executives, agents, and former agents came to the funeral home to pay their respects they were stunned by what they saw. There in the coffin lay a gray-haired, frail-looking, small man. The mortician had washed his hair and all the dye had come out—from his eyebrows, too.[21]

Attorney General Richard Kleindienst was one of the first persons outside of the Bureau to hear the news. He informed Bob Haldeman, and then called Deke DeLoach. "I'm going to recommend to President Nixon that you be appointed interim director," Kleindienst said. "It's important that we have somebody of your experience and stature." For the next three hours DeLoach was under the impression that he was about to be named acting director, and that having left the FBI for Pepsi-Cola hadn't damaged his chances.[22]

For an even longer period—exactly 26 hours and 10 minutes—Mark Felt envisioned himself stepping effortlessly into Hoover's shoes. "The thought more than crossed my mind that I might receive the appointment," he wrote in his 1979 memoir. He had ample reason to think so. Besides functioning as the Bureau's director in all but title, he had managed to convey to Haldeman that he was ambitious and willing to cooperate on matters of importance to the White House. Felt lacked DeLoach's political acumen and had lulled himself into thinking that Nixon would simply pluck the next person in the ranks. Yet the president was determined to make a clean break if he could, and only the need for a sudden decision led him to contemplate appointing an insider at all.[23]

Haldeman's handwritten notes reflect the prospects that were tossed around as a possible successor during a meeting at the White House. John Ehrlichman, the White House's liaison to the FBI, and Dick Moore, a special counsel, bandied about several names with Haldeman, while the president repeatedly interrupted the discussants by phone to ask if they were making any progress. Some candidates proposed were predictable, others surprising.

> Clyde Tolson: "can be trusted and p[resident] knows him, but
>   probably too sick"
> Mark Felt: "perfectly competent"
> Vernon Walters: "prob[lem]—not a lawyer; military"[24]

John Mohr, Al Rosen, and Lou Nichols, all longtime Bureau executives, also cropped up, as did DeLoach. Mohr and Rosen were apparently thought too insular and tied to the past, while Nichols, a good friend of the president's, had entered the private sector years before and was not keen to come back into government. The reference to DeLoach had nothing to do with offering him the job; the president wanted him approached because he presumably knew where Hoover kept his fabled secret files. "Get Deke DeLoach to find out what's there . . . who controls it . . . where skeletons are," Haldeman noted down. Bill Sullivan's name was notable for being absent, although his friends were busy lobbying White House staffers, like Chuck Colson, who were presumably going to have some influence over the president's selection. In fact, Nixon never sought Colson's advice on the matter.[25]

Nixon kept suggesting the appointment of Tolson as a holding action, but everyone else was against that idea because of his age and health (nor would he have accepted the post). Finally Nixon decided on a dark horse that "everybody agreed" with: a Justice Department official named L. Patrick Gray III. He was the preferred candidate of former attorney general John Mitchell, who believed that anyone promoted from within the FBI might prove to be just as self-directed and independent of the White House as Hoover had been. Mitchell, like many attorneys general before him, desired to bring an end to the day when the Bureau functioned as a virtually autonomous institution, answerable only to itself. As Haldeman noted in his handwritten memo,

> Rec: Pat Gray as acting director
> Guts—ability & loyalty
> Easy to confirm after election
> otherwise have
> Felt—Mohr or [Al] Rosen
> best to do it today[26]

There was also one other consideration involved in the decision to elevate an outsider to the directorship. If an insider were selected, and eventually nominated, that would in all likelihood open up a huge can of worms having to do with Hoover's sclerotic management, his supposed secret files, wiretaps on such notables as the Reverend Martin Luther King, Jr., and the Bureau's COINTELPROS. Putting an outsider in avoided this forseeable problem, which not only had the potential to sully Hoover's name but might result in a major confirmation battle and even defeat for the administration.

For DeLoach, it was just a minor disappointment when Kleindienst called back to explain that the president had decided on another man. But when Felt got the news, hours later—indeed, along with the public— it was an unexpected, terrible blow, and not only to him. Felt's wife, Audrey, was widely known to harbor the same ambition for her husband, even pushing him to achieve it. And within the Bureau generally, from rank-and-file agents up to Hoover's inner circle, few had doubted that Mark Felt would be sitting in the director's chair. To be sure, he was far from popular. Agents who knew him referred to the "ice water" that seemed to course through Felt's veins, and supervisors often recalled a "trademark sneer" that Felt wore while conducting reviews of field offices when he was head of the Inspection Division. Many executives, who could themselves lay some claim to Hoover's legacy, could not stomach Felt's preening and semi-concealed ambition; some had dubbed him "the white rat" for his thick mane of white hair and tendency to squeal whenever he thought it might help his own agenda. Still, after Sullivan's fall everyone had more or less conceded the internal race. Felt did not anticipate that the inside position would prove the wrong place to be.[27]

Felt might have been mollified if the appointee was a person of stature or national renown. But the president had elected to appoint a virtual unknown, a man who seemed as colorless as his name, known primarily for his almost slavish loyalty to Nixon. No one had seen it coming, except perhaps Gray himself, who had been quietly asked by Mitchell if he would like to be considered when Nixon first contemplated easing Hoover out, in the spring of 1971. One of the few times Gray had attracted any attention as a Justice Department official occurred that April, when he joined the chorus of Nixon appointees who were criticizing the then-dominant TV networks and newspapers for coverage that was "often inaccurate, biased, and grossly unfair."[28]

Gray's main qualification seemed to be that he was one of Nixon's old friends; as the New York Times editorialized, it was "abundantly clear that the president has chosen a highly political and professionally unqualified crony to direct this powerful and semisecret police agency." In fact, the two were not friends and had never socialized together, even though they had known one another for a long time. What really mattered was that Gray was loyal to Nixon personally and might even put the president's interests and desires above the Bureau's.[29]

One factor that may have given Gray the nod over Felt was the role the former had just played in a political controversy over a large corporate donation from International Telephone & Telegraph (ITT) to the Republican Party. A corporate memo, allegedly written by Dita Beard, ITT's Washington lobbyist, made it appear as if a $400,000 donation ($2.2 million in 2011 dollars) from the conglomerate had resulted in a favorable settlement of ITT's antitrust problems with the Justice Department. It was in the administration's interest to have the FBI declare the memo a forgery, but the lab examination had been inconclusive and Hoover was immovable, as only he could afford to be. Felt might have been inclined to curry the White House's favor, but his hands had been tied by Hoover's refusal to color the lab's findings.

By contrast, Gray had managed to get the original memo released from the Bureau despite an agreement between the Justice Department and the Senate Judiciary Committee that this would not be done. He had then made it available to John Dean, White House counsel to the president, and eventually document experts retained by ITT had been able to examine the memo and declared it fraudulent. Thus Gray had proven his mettle during a recent episode that was deeply embarrassing to the administration and still on everyone's mind. Years later, Felt would devote a whole chapter in his memoir to the ITT episode, calling the pressure from the White House "a prelude to Watergate."[30]

While tough-minded, loyal, and a hard-line Nixon supporter, Pat Gray was nonetheless something of an ingénue in Washington. He really didn't understand the nature of politics—with a small "p"—as played inside the government, bureaucratic politics that were far more treacherous than the overt Republican/Democrat divide. The waters in Washington were shark-infested, and nowhere more so than at the FBI. Gray's formative experience was as a submariner, and he still operated by the ethos of the submarine service: the captain is king and the crew completely loyal and dependent. It had to be that way, because a lack of loyalty or conflicting goals could prove disastrous. And he would not have a clue about how to adjust his life's major experience to a new and hostile environment. Gray's major problem was that he had no inkling of what he did not know.[31]

The most important facet of Nixon's decision, although it seemed unremarkable at the time, was to designate Gray as *acting* director, meaning that Gray would only serve through November. Nixon wanted to avoid a messy confirmation fight—the first one ever for the post, as the law making it subject to Senate confirmation had only been passed in 1968. Liberal Democrats were likely to turn any hearings during an election year into an indictment of the Bureau's tactics and techniques and, by extension, the administration's. By waiting until after the election, which Nixon seemed poised to win, the ultimate appointee would surely have an easier path to confirmation. Then, too, after six months of seasoning, Gray would presumably be a more acceptable nominee, no longer an "unqualified crony." He was not promised the job, just an inside track to it if he performed creditably.[32]

This bit of political calculation would have worked well if applied to any federal agency *but* the FBI. It completely disregarded the machinations awaiting any outsider who had the misfortune to come in after Hoover's forty-eight-year rule. Gray would command almost no loyalty within the so-called seat of government. He was earnest and intelligent, if a bit plodding, but most of all he was naïve and trusting and blind to what was happening around him. He stood little chance of surviving a den of intrigue. An FBI director has a number of constituencies, from the president and Congress to the press and the public. Gray would never have the support of the most important one of them all—the FBI itself.[33]

Lou Nichols, the president's closest Bureau friend apart from Hoover, was furious when he heard about the decision, and not just because his preferred candidate, Deke DeLoach, had been removed from consideration. He understood, as only an insider could, the fate that awaited any outsider imposed on the Bureau, especially one coming from the Justice Department. The FBI director was nominally part of the Justice Department and under the attorney general, yet no AG had ever been able to rein in Hoover's FBI. Given that Gray's only Washington experience was in main Justice, his appointment suggested that Nixon was going to at least try to assert greater control over the Bureau via his political appointees in the Justice Department. Few things were more likely to incite executives in the seat of government than an appointee from Justice, and Nichols knew better than to try. "This is doom," he told Nixon.[34]

Still, in the larger scheme of things, Gray's acting appointment might not have mattered that much—except that seven weeks later, during the wee hours of June 17, 1972, five men were caught breaking into the Democratic National Committee (DNC) offices at the recently completed Watergate complex in Washington. By mid-morning, once it was determined that the burglars had been carrying electronic eavesdropping devices, the FBI assumed the lead role in investigating the burglary, the purpose of which was not to steal money, but information. The case was assigned to two young agents in the Bureau's Washington Field Office: thirty-three-year-old Angelo J. Lano and his twenty-nine-year-old partner, Daniel C. Mahan.

As CIA Director Richard Helms would later observe, in sympathy with Gray, "Can you imagine the predicament of a new FBI director coming into office and having this thing break over his head?" But for someone who still yearned to succeed Hoover, who thought Nixon was educable about the need to elevate an FBI insider, the break-in was serendipitous. It meant that the president might be persuaded to "see the light," correct his mistake, and eventually nominate a permanent director from within the ranks—to appoint Mark Felt.[35]

CHAPTER THREE

Felt's Private COINTELPRO

June 1972

Someone in the FBI is talking about the details of the investigation.
—*L. Patrick Gray's June 23 note to himself*

There did not appear to be much Felt could do about Pat Gray's appointment initially. Felt's best, if not his only, recourse seemed to be to ingratiate himself with the acting director and hope that he would stumble—perhaps with a little strategic push. Meanwhile, it would be best if Gray believed that Felt was fully behind him and had an attitude of "complete cooperation." If Gray lost the president's confidence, as Felt hoped, it nonetheless might help to have Gray's strong endorsement when it came time to name a replacement.[1]

Felt did not hesitate to implement this strategy. Gray gave an im-promptu, twenty-minute talk during his first full day in office to the Bu-reau's top hierarchy, the so-called Executive Conference—a gathering of all the barons who ran the FBI like a series of feudal fiefdoms. These were men still reeling from Hoover's death and in shock over the abrupt imposition of an outsider. Afterwards Gray met with Nixon in the Oval Office and proudly told the president that Felt had called him right after to say it had been a "hell of a session" and that the acting director had done a "magnificent job." Some FBI officials had been talking seriously about resigning in protest, according to Felt, but after the meeting the consensus was, "With this kind of guy, we can serve." Of course, "[these same executives] may be some of the fellows that you want to go," Felt had added, probably with John P. Mohr and Alex Rosen in mind. As Gray conveyed this anecdote to the president, Nixon nodded his head affirma-tively: A "house cleaning" was long overdue at the FBI. But "it should not come now," he told Gray, "because we can't have any flaps about that."[2]

Gray regarded Felt as his unswerving ally from that day on: an indis-pensable, pragmatic lieutenant, lined up on his side against the Hoover men on the Executive Conference who would never accept an outsider or new ways. Gray would entrust Felt with running the Bureau's day-to-day operations and became so at ease with his "executive officer" that he gave Felt the keys to the director's office so that he could come and go as he pleased. All the while, Felt would project quite another image to high-level Bureau personnel, presenting himself as the FBI's defender against the unwelcome Gray. A rare picture of the Executives Conference that appeared in the *New York Times* on May 12, 1972—just ten days after Hoover's death—spoke volumes. The assembled assistant directors clearly resented being props in the public relations campaign Pat Gray was already mounting to smooth his path to the permanent appointment.[3]

The Watergate break-in altered Felt's initial calculus. He immediately recognized that the crime posed a real dilemma for Gray. If the acting director pressed the investigation, he risked alienating those with the power to decide whether to nominate him for the permanent directorship. But if he tried to curtail the probe, or showed any signs of being politically influenced, he would almost certainly fail to win confirmation from what was sure to still be a Democrat-dominated Senate. Gray was between the proverbial rock and a hard place.[4]

Felt could have hung back, taking comfort in the notion that someone of Gray's inexperience was not likely to navigate such a difficult situation successfully. Gray was bound to do *something* wrong, and then the directorship would (presumably) fall to Felt.

The problem with being patient, of course, was that Felt had tried that tack once, to no avail. Achieving the right position under Hoover at exactly the right time had not produced the desired result. And simply hanging back left open the possibility, however slight, that Gray just might thread the needle and satisfy both the White House and Senate Democrats. The latter might decide that Gray was as good as anyone the president might put forward, and perhaps better than most. Felt was apparently unwilling to take that risk.

Instead, he decided to treat the break-in as an unusually good opportunity to school the president in an important fact: that only an insider could be entrusted with the delicate task of running the Bureau. If Gray could not exercise Hoover-like control over the FBI on a matter of great sensitivity to the White House, he would appear to be a hapless, risky choice. And the easiest way to prove Gray's ineptitude would be to leak sensitive information from the FBI's investigation to the media. Given what Felt knew of the administration's fury over leaks, nothing was more likely to get Gray in trouble, and more swiftly. Turning the Bureau into a sieve would almost certainly open the way for a true "professional" to be given the reins.[5]

Felt would not be doing anything particularly foreign to either himself or the Bureau. During the Hoover era, the FBI had perfected the art of the leak, becoming one of the most feared purveyors of strategically placed information in town. It had its own stable of trusted journalists—reporters such as Jeremiah O'Leary at the *Washington Star* and Walter Trohan at the *Chicago Tribune*—who could be depended upon to give prominent play to whatever information the FBI fed them. Of course, that almost never included information that would generate adverse headlines for an incumbent president, so Felt would be taking the tactic a large and risky step farther.[6]

It was one thing, moreover, to leak with official sanction and in the supposed interests of the Bureau as a whole, and quite another to use leaks to advance a personal agenda. In effect, Felt would be following in the footsteps of Bill Sullivan. Two 1971 columns by Rowland Evans and Robert Novak, both of which scathingly criticized the aged Hoover, had aroused great ire among Bureau loyalists. No executive inside the FBI doubted for a moment that Sullivan, seeking to create a political groundswell against Hoover, had supplied the details that made the columns authoritative, and their convictions were correct.[7]

Leaking in order to thwart Gray's permanent appointment would be highly dangerous. But from Felt's perspective, the reward appeared commensurate with the risk. He had consummate confidence in his ability to pull it off, and frankly, there was no better alternative. If Gray became the permanent director, Felt would be past the mandatory retirement age by the time a new administration took power. Of equal import, the Watergate "caper," as it was being called initially, did not appear to be a serious problem for the White House. Leaks might greatly discomfit the administration and incite the president, but they seemed unlikely to change the political equation. This fact was of the utmost importance. Felt stood no chance of becoming director if George McGovern, the Democrats' putative nominee, won in November.

On June 19, two days after the break-in, Felt took his first step down the road of leaking to discredit Pat Gray. The precipitating event was a telephone call from a hard-working and ambitious thirty-year-old journalist who had met Felt in the summer of 1969 and persisted in keeping up with him despite the FBI official's chilly demeanor at times.[8]

That 1969 encounter, in a National Security Council anteroom, had already paid dividends for Bob Woodward, a cub reporter on the *Wash-*

ington Post's metropolitan staff. In May 1972, when Arthur Bremer shot Alabama Governor George Wallace in a Maryland shopping center, Felt had given Woodward valuable information from the FBI's investigation, enabling Woodward to write some A-section stories. During his first nine months on the paper he had accumulated more front-section bylines than anyone else on the metro staff, yet Woodward was going to need even more of those clippings if he was ever going to "graduate" to the newspaper's prestigious national staff. From the FBI's perspective, the Wallace leak had been the kind of sanctioned release of information the Bureau (and Felt) excelled in. Both the White House and the FBI wanted it known that Bremer had acted alone, although the White House desired to go even further and portray Bremer as a left-winger.[9]

There had been only one problem with Woodward's reporting, from Felt's point of view: the leak was poorly disguised. He mildly chastised Woodward for this failing, and the reporter realized that he "might as well have raised a flag that said 'FBI—senior official reviewing investigative reports is talking.'" Felt was not about to write Woodward off for one infraction, though. As he had written in a November 1971 letter to Hoover, there was an outstanding need to "develop good contacts and friends among some of the younger, but up-and-coming, members of the news media. This is vital to protect the Bureau's interests."[10]

Now, in mid-June 1972, Woodward was contacting Felt again, this time about the perplexing burglary at the DNC headquarters. One of those caught red-handed, James W. McCord, Jr., was a former CIA technician who now ran a private security company and had been hired as such by the Nixon campaign. The Committee for the Re-election of the President (CRP) was insisting that McCord's involvement in the break-in was completely coincidental and unsanctioned. "This man and the other people were not operating either on our behalf or with our consent," read the official statement issued under the name of CRP director John Mitchell, Nixon's first attorney general and a trusted adviser. The entire statement was untrue, of course, but McCord's arrest, in particular, was embarrassing and had come as an unwelcome jolt. No one who provably worked for the CRP was supposed to participate directly in the actual break-in.[11]

Woodward and other reporters were racing to find additional links between the burglars and the Nixon campaign—or the *other* organization that could be behind the crime, the CIA. Yet there was a Keystone Kops quality to the break-in that suggested it was political in nature, and not CIA-related. Agency operatives would hardly have left incriminating address books lying around. A "cutout"—an intermediary using a false name—would have recruited the burglars. And in case of capture, all they would have been able to give police would have been a sterilized telephone number and a physical description of the cutout, who would have vanished the moment the burglars were arrested.[12]

Nonetheless, it was hard to be sure which way the case would break, and one very promising lead led both ways simultaneously. It involved a man called E. Howard Hunt, Jr., whose name had been found inside two address books belonging to the burglars. By making a few telephone calls, Woodward had established that Hunt worked for the CIA from 1949 to 1970. At the same time—and perhaps this was more important, Woodward could not be sure—Hunt had subsequently worked at the White House with Charles W. Colson, a special counsel to the president. Was all this happenstance, or was Hunt connected with the break-in? And if so, via which connection? Woodward did not want to publish a story sensationalizing a White House link that might be mere coincidence.

During the second of two telephone calls Woodward made to Felt about the burglary, the FBI's number two official gave Woodward a small but crucial piece of information: The Bureau considered Hunt a "prime suspect" for he represented a "productive line of inquiry." A check bearing Hunt's name had been found among the belongings left in the burglars' hotel rooms across the street, and the FBI deemed neither the check nor the address book entries coincidental. Indeed, an agent had already spoken to Hunt at his home about the check on the afternoon of June 17. Hunt had acknowledged that it was his but then refused to answer any more questions.[13]

Felt's detailed knowledge of where the investigation stood early on was not a given, of course. As it happened, though, Gray was in Palm Springs, California, and someone at the top needed to be fully briefed in his absence. Attorney General Richard Kleindienst had called Gray at 7:30 a.m. Pacific time to notify him that "sometime today or possibly tomorrow RN is going to want to talk to [you]." Consequently, Gray had designated Felt to brief him so that he would be fully prepared when the president called.[14]

Woodward later described Felt as nervous and rushed during these conversations. Felt did not like having Woodward call him at the office; he hung up abruptly during the first call, having said that the investigation was about to "heat up." But when Woodward called back, Felt provided, off the record, the "critical and substantial buttress" for what would be a June 20 *Post* story headlined "White House Consultant Linked to Bugging Suspects," divulging information known only by the FBI at that time. In the story Woodward attributed the information to "Federal sources close to the investigation," recalling his lesson from the George Wallace article. Felt would voice no complaints.[15]

The significance of this first scoop is hard to exaggerate. The *Post*'s managing editor, Howard Simons, considered it the initial stepping-stone that "widen[ed] the story *way* beyond just a normal burglary." And Woodward's piece startled the White House. Although the press secretary, Ron Ziegler, observed contemptuously that he would not be commenting on a "third-rate burglary attempt," the administration immediately became obsessed with Watergate leaks. "Pick up that God-damn *Washington Post* and see that guilt by association!" special counsel Charles Colson roared to the president the day the article appeared. Colson had a special reason to fear that kind of logic, as the person responsible for hiring Hunt in the first place. And superficially, the scheme seemed like something a so-called political "hatchet man" might cook up, though Colson's ignorance of the break-in plan was genuine. "Where the hell are all these leaks from our side coming from?" Nixon wondered in response. Bob Haldeman complained to Attorney General Kleindienst, who replied defensively that the leaks had to be coming from the local police, not the FBI. And they would be staunched very soon, he asserted; because of the apparent violation of federal wiretapping statutes, the Bureau was assuming jurisdiction over the entire investigation.[16]

It will never be known for certain whether Felt's initial disclosure arose spontaneously out of a predisposition to help a dogged young reporter who had aggressively curried his favor, or whether other factors were already in play. In either case, it is apparent that Felt quickly realized that he might harness the Watergate story to his personal advantage. The near-violent reaction of the White House to Woodward's story (and to a similar one, using a Miami-based source, that appeared in the *New York Times*) could not have been lost on him. It was as if the stories had touched an exposed nerve—which, of course, they had. As John Ehrlichman put it, "(1) a burglar is doing a campaign job on the Democrats and (2) he carries Hunt's phone number; (3) Hunt is close to [White House adviser Charles] Colson, who is (4) close to Richard Nixon. (5) Hunt does jobs for Colson and (6) Colson does jobs for Nixon."[17]

Woodward's article represented a turning point for the administration, too, although it was not recognized as such at the time. If the White House ever had the slightest inclination to come clean, admit some responsibility, and dismiss the culpable parties—and there is no evidence it did—that possibility evaporated once the June 20 story appeared. Taking their lead from the president, the White House staff began to "stonewall it." The strategy of toughing every incremental exposure out, as White House counsel John Dean later described it, was followed

> from the very top of the administration to the bottom. It was also ad hoc, developed in small reactions to the flurry of each day's events. There was not time to take stock of the whole case or to plan a careful defense in the meticulous fashion of trial lawyers. Instead, we found ourselves trying to hold a line where we could.[18]

Regardless of whether the first leak to Woodward was spontaneous or calculated, inciting the White House against Gray was only half of Felt's plan. The other half involved giving Senate Democrats fodder against the acting FBI director in case he was nominated. Consequently, the next significant leak would insinuate that Gray was being less than professional about the investigation now under his purview. In a way, this information was even more sensitive than the leak about Hunt. And so it would not be fed to Woodward, whose discretion and ability to get a story published were still largely unproven, but to a renowned journalist: *Time*'s Sandy Smith.[19]

Smith had an enormous reputation within the Bureau, from the highest echelons down to the field offices. He was a grizzled and fearless reporter who had gotten his start in 1942 with the *Chicago Tribune* and specialized in exposing organized crime. A strapping man at 6 feet and more than 200 pounds, Smith, fifty-three, was known for staking out mob hangouts and crashing their parties; it was said that he knew the Mafia's pecking order better than most of its members, not to mention the police. He had joined the Time, Inc., conglomerate in 1967, after twenty years at the *Tribune*, and initially wrote about racketeering for *Life* magazine for two years. In 1969, the respected journalist Frank McCulloch became bureau chief for the Time-Life News Service, and organized an investigative "dream team" that featured Smith as one of its integral members. A 1971 editor's note observed that the "towering, jovial Smith has exposed much of organized crime's invisible empire, and in the process has become one of the best-known crime reporters in the nation." He was known, in particular, for an uncanny ability to find the threads that tied disparate data together, and his inviolable relationships with confidential sources. Indeed, a clause written into Smith's contract with Time-Life expressly permitted him to keep his sources secret, even in libel cases.[20]

When McCulloch left as bureau chief in early 1972, however, the "Blue

Team," as they were officially known (or "flying squad of muckrakers" unofficially), lost the one executive in the Time, Inc., hierarchy who championed investigative journalism, which was expensive. The team annually cost hundreds of thousands of dollars in salaries and expenses, and had provoked $80 million worth of libel suits; moreover, *Life* magazine was dying. Smith landed first in *Time*'s New York bureau, before eventually moving to the magazine's Washington office. There his reputation as a reporter who protected his sources, and kept attention focused on his stories, rather than himself, only grew. Legend had it that Smith used the public telephone booths nearby to communicate with his most sensitive sources rather than risk using the phones in the bureau. In those days *Time* rarely awarded bylines, and the distinction was highly sought after because otherwise the correspondent responsible for a story might actually be known to very few people. Yet whenever editors in New York, where all *Time* copy was edited, wanted to identify Smith with a particular story, his explicit instruction was, "First and foremost, pls delete the byline. Thanks, but no thanks, on this one.'" John Stacks, the Washington bureau's news editor, regarded Smith as "the best pure reporter I've ever seen."[21]

Smith's relationship with the FBI had been instrumental to his success. With the knowledge of Bureau higher-ups, agents in the field would leak to him raw information about public corruption, for example, from their files. The information might not constitute legal proof, or it might have been acquired by illegal means and thus be inadmissible in court. But the agents preferred to see it used in some way rather than simply gather dust. And Smith could be relied upon to "smoke-screen" especially sensitive information, such as a detail captured on a wiretap, by conducting so many interviews that no one could trace the information to its source. That level of trust toward Smith existed at practically every level of the Bureau. And now he was about to become *Time*'s principal correspondent on Watergate, working out of New York during the first six months of the scandal.[22]

Just before 6 p.m. on Friday, June 23, Smith contacted Pat Gray's office to ask the acting director some probing questions about his "personal actions" in the six days since the break-in. Smith said he had some "adverse information" that affected Gray but not the FBI, which he held in high regard. Allegedly, Gray had refused an agent's request to check Charles Colson's long-distance telephone records, although Colson had hired Hunt; Gray had also discussed the burglary right after it occurred with John Mitchell, the head of the president's reelection effort; and lastly,

Gray had been overheard boasting that the FBI's investigation would be wrapped up in "24 to 48 hours," the clear inference being that it would be a whitewash.[23]

Gray returned Smith's call shortly after 9 p.m. and denied each charge. No agent had requested to see Colson's toll calls; he hadn't discussed the arrests with Mitchell; and no, he had not said anything about wrapping up the case within two days. In fact, during a June 21 meeting with some of his top executives—Mark Felt, Charlie Bates (the assistant director in charge of the General Investigative Division), and Robert Kunkel (the special agent in charge of the Washington Field Office)—Gray had agreed that "the FBI's reputation was at stake" in the case and that "the investigation should be completely impartial, thorough, and complete."[24]

Gray struggled to remain cordial and businesslike while talking with Smith, but inside he was seething. When he had met with Nixon to accept the acting directorship, the president had spent what seemed an inordinate amount of time warning him about the press, especially Time-Life. "Never see anybody from Time-Life," Nixon had advised him. "Never, never, never . . . they're really out to get us." Yet these false allegations stunned Gray, not only because they had come so quickly, but from Sandy Smith of all reporters. Obviously someone in a responsible position inside the Bureau was leaking erroneous and derogatory information. A journalist of Smith's caliber and experience would not be asking such questions unless the allegations came from someone he knew, trusted, and firmly believed was in a position to know. An inveterate and meticulous note-taker, Gray wrote down in all caps, "SOMEONE IN THE FBI IS TALKING ABOUT THE DETAILS OF THE INVESTIGATION."[25]

Although the next day was a Saturday, Gray insisted that everyone from the Washington Field Office who was actively involved in the Watergate probe assemble in the director's conference room at 11 a.m. Most of the agents didn't know what was up. Told to don their best "FBI uniform" (a white shirt, conservative tie, and dark blue suit), many actually believed they were about to receive a commendation and monetary bonus for their work one week into the case. As the twenty-seven agents filed into the room, their names were checked off on a roster, which suddenly gave the meeting a forbidding tone. Felt's presence was not required, so he was not in attendance.

Gray walked in briskly, firmly grabbed both sides of a lectern, and immediately lit into the group. Looking distressed and angry, he accused the agents of suffering from flap-jaw, his voice rising in volume as he spoke. "Gentlemen, I had a call from Sandy Smith last night, [from] *Time* magazine, and he wanted to know and wanted to verify certain information that he had. He wanted me to deny or admit for publication whether or not the information was true."[26]

Gray said that Smith's information could only have come from Washington Field Office agents, and "we are here today with this group to find out exactly which agent or agents leaked this information." He demanded that the "yellow-bellied sniveling agents" responsible take a step forward and accept discipline. When no one did, Gray became even more incensed. "I demand that any agent or agents who leaked information to Sandy Smith or anybody else take one step forward immediately!" he shouted. Robert Kunkel, the special agent in charge of the Washington Field Office, broke ranks and tried to speak in defense of his agents' integrity, but he was brusquely interrupted. "Mr. Kunkel, did you leak the information?" Gray demanded. "No, I did not," Kunkel said. "Take one step back then," Gray ordered.[27]

After a few moments of strained silence, Gray erupted in a tirade that few if any of those present would ever forget. "You—you will not fool me," he shouted, his face almost crimson with anger.

> I will get to the bottom of this. . . . I have conducted many investigations in the navy and I know how to conduct an investigation. I will find out who leaked the information to Sandy Smith. You group of men are nothing but a bunch of caterwauling individuals who do not have the guts or courage to come forward.

Gray then turned to Assistant Director Charlie Bates, who was holding the clipboard with the roster of attendees. If "I catch one [agent on this roster] in the act of leaking to the press or anywhere else," he declared, "that agent will be brought before me and dismissed immediately." With that, the twenty-minute tongue-lashing was over. Agents who had served for decades under Hoover knew what it was like to be treated harshly and summarily. But none had ever been treated so rudely in person.[28]

As they walked back to the Washington Field Office at 12th Street and Pennsylvania, the agents were simmering with anger. Gray's demeaning accusations made them even more determined to get to the bottom of the break-in. They subsequently referred to the dressing-down as the "Saturday morning massacre," even though no one had been fired. And although Gray's tirade prompted a full-blown investigation by the Inspection Division, the FBI's internal policing unit, that effort proved futile. The only purpose the event served was to harden rank-and-file agents like Bob Lill against Pat Gray personally, and make them even more determined to pursue the Watergate case by the book, regardless of where it led.[29]

When the *Time* story actually appeared, on June 26, the allegations were not remotely in the form in which Smith had leveled them over the phone—or, as Gray put it, the piece was "trimmed of its falsehoods." The only specific charge that made it into print was the undeniable fact that during the weekend of the burglary, Mitchell and Gray happened to be staying in the same Newport Beach, California, hotel, although "both denied seeing the other man there." Smith had apparently been unable to corroborate the original allegations to his or his editors' satisfaction— which was hardly surprising, since none of them were true.[30]

Smith, who died in 2005, was famous for never discussing his sources. He believed that self-promotion at the expense of his contacts would ruin his information network, which he prized above all else. He would never write one word about how he had gone about his work, much less his sources, despite what must have been ample and attractive opportunities. Thus, it will be never known precisely how Smith came across what he clearly assumed was good, inside information about the politicization of the FBI.[31]

Yet the allegations Smith presented to Gray emanated from Felt or someone—most likely Charlie Bates—whom Felt had designated to leak. In Felt's original memoir, published in 1979, he singled out Smith's June 26 story, although it was not a remarkable article at the time or even in light of later developments, and alluded approvingly to its innuendo about a "White House effort," allegedly involving Gray, to "whitewash the case." Subsequently, Felt's revised memoir, published in 2006 with coauthor John O'Connor, was even more explicit. An editor's note states that "correspondent Sandy Smith of *Time* magazine, who was well connected to the FBI's upper echelons, was the recipient of this leak. . . . The leak probably came from Felt himself, [as a] warning [to] Gray that if he allowed a Watergate whitewash, his career would be in public tatters."[32]

A week after the break-in, Felt had every reason to be pleased with his handiwork. He had managed to incite the White House all over again regarding leaks; plant a seed of doubt inside the administration about Gray's grip on the FBI; engender distrust between Gray and virtually the entire Washington Field Office; and almost place a story in *Time* about a supposed whitewash orchestrated by Gray. (It is true, of course, that the administration wanted a cursory investigation, but Smith's reporting at the time had no facts to back up this insinuation.) Over the next several months White House counsel John Dean would call Pat Gray numerous times about Watergate; nearly half of the conversations were about leaks of FBI information to the press—and this doesn't include the number of times Dean complained to Felt because Gray was out of town.[33]

Mark Felt probably thought there was more work to be done, but in fact he was already on the verge of destroying whatever chances Pat Gray had of becoming director. The leaks so mortified Gray that he was about to make a pivotal decision that in ten months' time would prove fatal to his nomination and reputation.[34]

On the afternoon of June 28, Gray was meeting with his top two Watergate lieutenants, Mark Felt and Charlie Bates, to discuss the latest developments in the investigation. John Ehrlichman, the president's domestic policy adviser and chief liaison to the FBI, had asked him to stop by for a chat later in the day, he informed Felt and Bates. The meeting was not likely to be pleasant. Indeed, Gray was going to be on the receiving end of the kind of heat he had recently put on his agents. Ehrlichman intended to convey the president's displeasure about "many rumors and allegations about leaks from the FBI" in the eleven days since the break-in, with Woodward's June 20 story about Hunt being the most damaging.[35]

Gray arrived at around 6:30 p.m., knowing he was probably in for a brusque lecture. The president's men were capable of talking tough when they wanted to make a point. To Gray's surprise, he found John Dean waiting in Ehrlichman's office, holding two manila envelopes. Ehrlichman explained that the envelopes contained documents from E. Howard Hunt's office that were "political dynamite" and needed to be safeguarded. Because the papers had nothing to do with Watergate—they were "national security documents [that] should never see the light of day," Dean said—they had not been included in the material handed over to FBI agents from Hunt's safe two days earlier. Gray asked why they were being given to him, and Dean replied that the White House needed to be able to say that all of Hunt's office files were in the FBI's possession.[36]

There was no mention of the fact that Ehrlichman had previously suggested to Dean that he "deep-six" the documents by throwing them into the Potomac. Dean's legal antennae had quivered over the prospect of being responsible for destroying documents found in Hunt's safe. After pondering the problem for several days, he had come up with what seemed like a better solution—secretly give the politically explosive documents to Gray, while keeping, and eventually disposing, of sensitive Watergate-related papers.[37]

Ehrlichman then pointed out that the reason Dean was giving the envelopes to Gray *personally* was so that "the contents didn't get leaked by [Gray's] subordinates at the FBI." The meeting lasted another ten minutes or so, during which Gray assured Ehrlichman that "he had spoken to all of the agents assigned to the case and was quite confident these leaks had not come from the FBI." Privately, Gray believed differently—but he was hardly going to level with Ehrlichman about his inability to keep discipline at the Bureau.[38]

Gray wanted the FBI job badly and was inclined to do whatever was asked of him, within certain bounds. He was on probation, in effect, which made it unusually hard to say "no." The leaks that had already occurred on his watch only compounded the situation. Now he was seemingly being offered a chance to make amends by helping to safeguard documents that were politically embarrassing but had "nothing" really to do with the Watergate break-in or other criminal activities. Gray apparently thought that at the rarefied level at which he was now operating, political expediency and hard-ball sometimes had to trump the strict letter of the law.[39]

The acting director accepted the documents and vowed they would never be compromised. The unorthodox transfer would be an inviolable secret; he would tell no one, not even trusted members of his personal staff. Gray interpreted Dean's remarks to mean that the documents should be destroyed—a task he would eventually carry out six months later, over Christmas, unwittingly sealing his fate. The entire matter of the papers from Hunt's safe remained a secret until it exploded in the press in late April 1973.[40]

Felt had no way of knowing that Gray had taken the first, fateful step that would end in ignominy and disgrace. The acting director shared almost everything with his executive officer, but not such delicate matters. And so Felt pressed ahead with his plan.

In light of Kleindienst's and Gray's vigorous demurrals, which were halfway believable, Felt decided to orchestrate a third leak before June was out—one that would prove to the White House that the FBI had to be the source of the embarrassing disclosures appearing in the press. The evidence that Deep Throat arranged this leak comes from an unimpeachable source: Felt himself. In his 1979 memoir, he wrote that "of course" Deep Throat orchestrated the leak that resulted in a June 30 scoop in the *Washington Daily News*.[41]

At that time the *Daily News*—a tabloid, and the smallest and scrappiest of the capital's three dailies—had a reputation as a "reporter's newspaper." The journalist who would break the story, Patrick Collins, was even younger than Woodward, and, like Woodward, was vigorously pursuing the Watergate story. Leaking to him rather than to a more seasoned reporter was a shrewd move, for it greatly reduced the chance that the story could be traced to Felt. No one would imagine that there was a pipeline from the FBI's top echelon to a cub reporter like Collins.

The leak consisted of the FBI's June 26 report about the contents of E. Howard Hunt's safe (minus, of course, the documents John Dean had secretly passed to Gray, and the others that he kept in his own safe). This kind of standard report was known inside the FBI as an "FD-302" or just a "302," after the number on the form. Leaking the report to Collins immediately resulted in a front-page tabloid headline, "Searchers Turn Up Map of Dem Watergate HQ in Nixon Aide's Desk."[42]

The actual contents of the safe were of little consequence; what really mattered was the fact the story appeared at all. To anyone versed in the detection of sources, every indication from the article was that the information could only have come from the Bureau's 302. That's because, aside from Hunt himself, the only other people with knowledge of the safe's contents were John Dean and Fred Fielding, an associate in Dean's office. Given that Dean was becoming the desk officer for the cover-up, his office was not a likely source of the information. That left the FBI as the only plausible candidate.

Dean was apparently the first person in the White House to express outrage over the story—ironically enough, to Mark Felt, since Gray was out of town. "JWD [Dean] is upset by the innuendo in the *Washington Daily News* article," Felt eventually reported to Gray. "He insists this information had to leak from [the] FBI." Posing as a determined investigator of the leak, Felt added that he had ordered a full inquiry into this latest embarrassment. "I'm looking into this," he told Gray. "I don't believe the leak was in [the] Bureau. [The] article [was] written by a police reporter who covers [the] Metropolitan Police Department—[and] there are some inaccuracies in the story."[43]

When Dean eventually reached Gray to convey his disgust directly, the acting director was well prepared with responses provided by Felt. Gray denied that the leak had come from the FBI and "pointed out inaccuracies" in the story; Gray assured the White House counsel, moreover, that Felt had already looked into the matter "very, very thorough[ly] and was quite positive that no information . . . had leaked from the FBI." Important people in the White House did not believe this explanation, including Dean and Bob Haldeman, the president's chief of staff. The news "apparently leaked out of the Bureau," Haldeman told Nixon in mid-afternoon, several hours after the newspaper had hit the stands.[44]

The article was the first and last Watergate scoop to appear in the *Washington Daily News*—in fact, it was the publication's last scoop ever. The tabloid abruptly closed down on July 12, selling its assets to the *Washington Star* and leaving Washington a two-newspaper town—and really only a one-newspaper town when it came to Watergate. (The *Star*, with a staunchly Republican owner, was noticeably half-hearted in its Watergate coverage in 1972, more or less publishing stories only when developments made it absolutely necessary.)[45]

The other newspaper that all Washington journalists read, of course, was the *New York Times*. Yet it was an unlikely port for Felt. Any self-respecting Hoover man despised the *Times*, and in addition, its Justice Department reporter, Robert M. Smith, was considered rather adoring of Pat Gray. That left Felt with two main outlets: the *Washington Post* and, for a particularly sensitive story, *Time* magazine. That is not to say he would not also be a source for the two dozen or so other investigative reporters who eventually became drawn to the Watergate story. But the *Post* and *Time* would suffice for the purpose he had in mind.[46]

A crucial element in Felt's ability to leak would be his familiarity with the details of the investigation. Even though he was the Bureau's number two official, that didn't mean he would automatically know almost everything there was to know. But like so many other aspects of the matter, this one, too, broke in his favor.

When he took over as acting director, Gray had decided that the best way to get to know its personnel and disarm resistance to an outsider was to visit as many field offices as he could, and as quickly as possible. He saw no reason to change this plan six weeks later merely because of an odd caper involving Democratic Party headquarters. Consequently, during the crucial months before the November election, Gray would be absent from Washington about as often as he was there—leading Felt to refer to him derisively as "three-day [a week] Gray." Gray never perceived his ambitious travel schedule as a problem; after all, he had an effective, loyal subordinate running day-to-day operations in his stead. But, as it turned out, his self-promotional visits to far-flung field offices played nicely into Felt's hand.

For one, it heightened the distrust of Gray that already existed among the assistant directors who comprised the Executive Conference. They feared that Gray was going into the field to build an independent base of support amongst rank-and-file agents. Presumably, at some future point, he was going to leverage that support and purge everyone in the seat of government (FBI headquarters) who didn't agree with him or his new ways. The field visits also underscored a perception Felt wanted to foster at the White House: that of a director who was not only incapable of stopping the leaks, but less than attentive to the damage they were causing—or at least unwilling to change his schedule enough to get a grip on the problem.[47]

In Gray's absence, Felt, Charlie Bates (the assistant director in charge of the General Investigative Division), and Robert Kunkel (the special agent in charge of the Washington Field Office) formed a troika that oversaw the probe and reviewed every piece of significant information developed by agents in the field. Later, as the White House's involvement became increasingly clear, Gray recused himself because of his relationship with Nixon, leaving the investigation entirely in Felt's hands. Consequently, something that might have been problematic for Felt—exhibiting a little too much interest in the investigation—was never an issue. And his knowledge wasn't limited to the reports and summaries that crossed his desk; he was also briefed orally about developments.[48]

Felt, moreover, had the advantage of cooperation in his covert plan to impugn Gray, i.e., a number of active collaborators. He had not directly leaked the "302" about the contents of Hunt's safe; it was someone acting at his instruction, most likely Robert Kunkel. After the *Washington Daily News* printed the story, Angelo Lano, the FBI's Watergate case agent, recalled seeing the tabloid's reporter, Patrick Collins, in Kunkel's office.[49]

The notion that Deep Throat had help has been a point of speculation ever since *All the President's Men* revealed Deep Throat's existence. For starters, the signaling methods Woodward and Felt began using later in the summer suggested that Deep Throat had co-conspirators. Felt was much too busy and prominent a man to circle page 20 of Woodward's home-delivered *New York Times* (the signal when Felt wanted a meeting) or monitor the movement of a red-flagged flower pot on the balcony of Woodward's apartment (the signal when Woodward wanted one). Those mundane tasks were probably entrusted to reliable agents, possibly one or more of Felt's aides.[50]

But long before the signaling system was established, the leaks that occurred in June and July indicate that Felt never acted alone (save for his very first leak to Woodward) and had a group of collaborators from the outset.[51]

After Felt unmasked himself in 2005, firm evidence about the extent of the cooperation emerged. Paul V. Daly, a retired special agent in charge who once headed the Albany Field Office, confirmed to an Albany *Times Union* reporter that he knew as early as 1978 that Felt had headed "a clandestine group of high-ranking agents who agreed to leak information about the Watergate break-in" for a "noble purpose." The core group consisted of the Felt-Bates-Kunkel troika, according to Daly, who said he learned about the effort in 1978 from Richard E. Long, who had replaced Charlie Bolz as the chief of the FBI's Accounting and Fraud (or "white-collar crimes") Section in January 1973. That promotion had put Long squarely into the Watergate reporting chain at FBI headquarters.[52]

Long reportedly told Daly that the disclosures were made "so that the [FBI's] investigation into Watergate wouldn't be contained. . . . The news media . . . would create an atmosphere that would allow the investigation to go forward." A more realistic and discerning scenario is that these men constituted a Bureau faction that was conspiring to oust Gray and have Felt installed in his place. If Felt moved up, they would, too.[53]

For Felt to have his own faction, of course, was hardly unique. From the outside, the public impression of the FBI was that of a giant but unified monolith. In truth, particularly during Hoover's later years, it was not centrally run but a collection of rival fiefdoms run by assorted dukes and barons, all of whom inspired their own set of loyalists and maintained their favored coteries. Out in the field, a special agent in charge was often identifiable by the "rabbi" who protected him and represented his interests at the seat of government back in Washington.

Tracing the evolution of the Felt faction and its activities is impossible at this juncture; the alleged chief members are all deceased. Questions abound: were they eagerly on board as a group from the very start? If not, how soon after the June 17 break-in were they brought into Felt's scheme? Did he gain their cooperation through appeals to their loyalty to the Bureau, by arguing that an admittedly distasteful task (leaking) was the only way to rid the FBI of a rank outsider and amateur (Gray)? Did these men realize they were being used to achieve Felt's ambition all along, or did it only gradually dawn on them?[54]

There is reason to believe the faction's involvement began with the attempt to insert false information in *Time* magazine, just after Felt's first leak to Woodward on June 19. It did not escape notice, among rank-and-file agents like Angelo Lano, that Charlie Bates was known to be close to Sandy Smith. "So when [Gray] is telling us about this guy, Sandy Smith [during the Saturday morning massacre on June 24] . . . [someone later said], 'Gee, isn't it a coincidence: Sandy Smith comes to Washington at the same time [as Bates]. Oh, and he's got FBI stories [in *Time*].'" Bates had been special agent in charge of the Chicago Field Office for seventeen months before coming to the seat of government in October 1971, as part of the reshuffling that occurred after the purge of William Sullivan. That promotion alone meant he was solidly on Felt's side of the great internal divide. And the attempted leak to *Time,* of course, had been followed quickly by Kunkel's role in the June 30 leak to the *Washington Daily News.*[55]

That perceptions of self-interest, rather than a principle, motivated the Felt faction can also be understood by what *didn't* happen. When counterintelligence officers draw up a ledger on a suspected double agent, counterfactual history—or what did not occur—can be just as important in deducing an agent's true loyalties as what did happen. Given the selfless motives attributed to Felt and his faction, it seems appropriate to ask: what genuine information about the break-in were they privy to in July, but chose *not* to leak?[56]

CHAPTER FOUR

To Leak or Not to Leak?

July 1972

We're having problems with the Bureau.
—*Haldeman to Nixon on June 30*

There is no doubting that Nixon's campaign organization, the Committee for the Re-election of the President (CRP), dragged its feet, sent agents chasing after false leads, and otherwise sought to impede the Bureau's investigation in the summer of 1972. These efforts did not really abate until the cover-up fell apart.

The spectacle astonished most of the capital's FBI agents, who were generally from less-privileged backgrounds than staffers in the campaign. As John Mindermann, one of the Washington Field Office "street" agents recalled,

> All these fine, pedigreed young men who were highly educated, graduated from the finest universities, familially and politically well-connected, and dressed in custom-fitted, expensive suits, began traipsing into the WFO headquarters in the Old Post Office Building [just blocks east of the White House]. In they came, unable, each one of them, when the chips were down, to take a stand for what was right; to be willing or able to stand alone, dissent from what happened, to stand apart from the acceptable, corrupt norm of your peers. They were gutless and completely self-serving.[1]

Still, the effort to hinder the investigation that would eventually cause President Nixon the most trouble—it would prompt two counts in the first article of impeachment drawn up in July 1974—occurred over a period of fourteen days in late June and early July, and it had nothing to do with the CRP's well-scrubbed young men. That this effort even happened stemmed, in large part, from the unfamiliarity of several key actors with one another in the wake of J. Edgar Hoover's death in early May. In the two months since then, CIA Director Richard Helms had not had enough time to take Pat Gray's measure, and vice versa. Each man knew better than to put too much stock in newspaper clippings; nonetheless they were influenced by them.[2]

Helms had grown accustomed to dealing with Hoover, who, while irascible, wily, and stubborn, had the quality of being at least predictable. By contrast, Helms knew little about Gray, other than that his appointment reportedly rested on his being one of the president's cronies. Moreover, Helms, a keen student of leaks, had already come to the conclusion that Gray's Bureau was leaking badly. What he couldn't quite fathom was why, and to what end. All Helms could see was that the game was being played in a different manner than what happened during Hoover's reign, when most every leak was directed, purposeful, institutional—in short, understandable.

Pat Gray, for his part, could not help but be influenced by the Agency's reputation for secrecy, deception, and compartmentalization. Before becoming acting director, he had little interaction with the CIA, other than to know that it supposedly operated on a "need to know" basis, and thus the left hand did not always know what the right hand was doing. In addition, there was a long history of animosity and distrust between the two entities, and it was not unusual for FBI agents' questions to be met with denials and obfuscations. Together with Gray's lack of familiarity with Helms, the bottom line was that the acting FBI director did not really know if he could take the CIA director at his word.[3]

The vapors suggestive of CIA involvement in the break-in were, from Nixon's point of view, extremely fortuitous. He didn't like the Agency or the Ivy Leaguers who he believed overpopulated it, and had few scruples about trying to use it to impede the Bureau's investigation into aspects of Watergate that were politically embarrassing. On the morning of June 23, during what would later become known infamously as the "smoking gun" conversation, the president and his chief of staff adopted a scheme—allegedly suggested by John Mitchell and Robert Mardian, with John Dean's concurrence—to falsely invoke CIA equities so that the FBI would stand down from certain "productive areas" of its investigation. One was the transfer of large political donations to the CRP through Mexico, by way of one of the burglar's bank accounts. This same burglar, Bernard L. Barker, had also deposited a $25,000 check originally made out to Kenneth Dahlberg, a major Nixon fund-raiser in the Midwest. Although these monies had not directly financed the break-in, because they had been commingled, they indubitably established that, like James

McCord, Barker was closely connected to the president's reelection apparatus. Naturally, the White House preferred that culpability begin and end with the five suspects who had been arrested. There was also another element to these donations that concerned the White House in equal measure: it wasn't entirely clear (at first) that they were lawful, and in any case, they were supposed to be kept anonymous and secret, or so the donors had been promised.[4]

The White House expected Gray to do the heavy lifting at the Bureau. In a telephone call to John Dean, Gray had warned the White House counsel that the FBI "was out of control." He didn't know how to deflect the probe of what the White House was calling a "third-rate burglary" from areas that were definitely politically embarrassing and perhaps tangential to the break-in itself. As Haldeman subsequently explained the situation to the president, there was no doubt Gray wanted to be a team player and help contain the investigation. His problem was that he did not quite know how to achieve the desired result. But if the White House gave the proper instructions, Haldeman thought, it could all work out. Gray would turn to Felt for expert advice, and Felt would go along with the plan. "Felt wants to cooperate," Haldeman told the president, "because he's ambitious."[5]

The compliant counterpart at CIA was to be Lieutenant General Vernon A. Walters, the newly appointed deputy director. A capable and respected career army officer, "Dick" Walters was regarded as "Nixon's man" at the CIA. Working as an interpreter, the multilingual Walters had accompanied then–Vice President Nixon during his 1958 visit to Venezuela—an ill-fated trip marked by a notorious riot. Ever since then there had been a close bond between the two men.

And it was precisely that friendship that made Walters's appointment to the CIA unusual. Normally the number two man at the CIA, responsible for running the Agency on a day-to-day basis, was a virtual unknown, a career intelligence or military officer with no political connections and with no interests save the usual bureaucratic ones. In this instance, however, even if the goal wasn't to give Walters a little seasoning before naming him CIA director outright, his ties to the president were far closer than Helms's. That gave Walters an unprecedented amount of room to maneuver should he choose to exercise it. Whether his institutional loyalty to the Agency would outweigh his political loyalty to the White House was an open question.[6]

Blunting the FBI's probe in certain areas by dragging in the CIA wasn't going to be easy. Helms had called Gray promptly on the evening of June

17 to disavow any CIA involvement whatsoever, notwithstanding the per-petrators' eyebrow-raising backgrounds. Five days later, just after the Bu-reau established that Barker had received $89,000 from a Mexican law-yer named Manuel Ogarrio and had also deposited in his bank account a check made out to Dahlberg, Gray called Helms to advise him that the FBI might be "poking around" some sensitive matters. According to what was known as the "delimitation" agreement between the two agencies, the Agency was supposed to be informed promptly of any FBI investigation that might touch upon CIA operations so that sources and methods could be protected. According to Gray's notes, Helms reiterated that "he had been meeting on this [Watergate break-in] every day with his men—they knew the people [involved]—but they cannot figure out this one—there is no CIA involvement." Gray was noncommittal in response.[7]

Nonetheless, the very next day, June 23, the White House commenced its efforts to use the CIA. There was a fair degree of confidence that the Agency would cooperate, albeit perhaps with some reluctance. At Ehr-lichman's order, and long before the break-in, the CIA had once supplied Howard Hunt and Gordon Liddy with some logistic support, not know-ing what it was going to be used for. Eventually the assistance was termi-nated. But now that Hunt and Liddy were soon to be entangled legally in the Watergate break-in, the White House presumed the CIA would be at least as eager as the administration to keep the entire connection under wraps, if not more so.[8]

That morning Haldeman went over the plan with President Nixon, in what would become known in August 1974 as the "smoking gun" conver-sation. Shortly after their meeting concluded, Helms and Walters were invited to meet with John Ehrlichman—an unusual request that set the CIA director's political antennae quivering, as he had never been asked specifically to bring a deputy director to the White House before. Helms's wonderment increased when, at precisely 1 p.m., just as the meeting was about to begin, Haldeman marched in and took charge.

With typical briskness Haldeman got right to the point, declaring that "it has been decided to have General Walters go to see Pat Gray." Walters was to tell Gray not to push the FBI's inquiry any further, "especially in Mexico," because it might lead to the exposure of certain CIA assets and channels for handling money. Helms was still certain the Agency was not implicated in Watergate and remonstrated against the proposal. None of the FBI's investigative leads so far had touched upon covert CIA projects, in Mexico or anywhere else. Why, just the day before he had told Pat Gray *again* that the Agency was not involved.[9]

Haldeman would not budge. He asserted that Gray "would be receptive as he was looking for guidance in the matter." When Helms stood his ground, Haldeman hinted that if the FBI continued its investigation of money transfers to and from Mexico it would ultimately unravel secrets about the Agency's 1961 Bay of Pigs invasion. The mention of the CIA's greatest debacle caused Helms to lose the even manner he was famous for. Baffled and exasperated by this red herring, he responded, with uncharacteristic fire, "The Bay of Pigs hasn't got a damned thing to do with this. And what's more, there's nothing about the Bay of Pigs that's not already in the public domain."[10]

Despite Helms's protests, Haldeman's report to the president about the twenty-minute meeting was optimistic. "We didn't in any way say we had any political interest or concern or anything like that," he told Nixon, and the chief of staff predicted that both Walters and Helms would cooperate. But Helms didn't think that Haldeman knew more about CIA equities and funding channels than he did, and the reference to the Bay of Pigs had left him nonplussed. After years of exposure to the feints and maneuvers of White House aides, he was alarmed about being drawn into a trap.[11]

Helms found it exceedingly suspicious that Nixon's staffers wanted Walters to convey this message, given that he owed his job to the White House. Why hadn't Pat Gray been invited to the meeting, too, and the request put before him directly? Why was it necessary to dispatch an administration-friendly executive from the CIA, as if it were the Agency's idea? Helms offered Walters some advice about his scheduled meeting that Friday afternoon with Gray. He cautioned him to stick to reminding the FBI director about the delimitation agreement, which required the FBI to notify the CIA whenever it ran into an Agency connection during the course of a criminal investigation.[12]

Walters did not regard the White House meeting, nor his marching orders from Haldeman, with anything near Helms's level of alarm. Having come from the military, he was used to carrying out instructions without asking too many questions. Haldeman's allusion to the Bay of Pigs may have had a "devious, hard-nosed White House smell" to Helms, but Walters regarded the request as legitimate and reasonable. "It simply did not occur to me that the chief of staff to the president might be asking me to do something that was illegal or wrong," Walters later wrote. At least so far, his fidelity to Nixon trumped his loyalty to his new institution.[13]

Walters met with Gray at 2:30 and conveyed Haldeman's message. While no ongoing covert projects had yet been jeopardized, he said, continuing the probe "might lead to some projects." And since the five burglars were already under arrest, the CIA deputy director continued, "it would be best to taper the matter off there." This was not unwelcome news to Gray, who did not relish an investigation that might well lead straight to John Mitchell, his former Justice Department boss and benefactor, the man more responsible than anyone for his appointment as acting director. Watergate was a "most awkward matter to come up during an election year," Gray understatedly observed. He did not want to believe that Mitchell might be deeply implicated in the break-in.[14]

Over the weekend, Helms's view of the matter hardened considerably. It seemed clear that Haldeman and Ehrlichman wanted to stem an aspect of the FBI's investigation without appearing to do so. Helms grew even more determined to keep as much distance as possible between the Agency and the aftermath of Watergate. The CIA would have to continue taking its lumps in the press for its past connections with the burglars, but it would end there.

On Monday, June 26, John Dean asked Walters to come to the White House, saying that he had been authorized to discuss further the matter raised on Friday. After checking with Ehrlichman, Walters complied with Dean's request and found that the protective net was being cast even wider. Dean said that one of the FBI's working theories was that the CIA *was* involved in Watergate, which was an accurate statement. Dean implied that the Agency therefore had a stake in sharply limiting the entire investigation, not just the Mexican angle mentioned on Friday. When Walters reiterated Helms's denial, Dean replied that the CIA might be involved without Walters's knowledge.[15]

When Walters later reported the conversation to Helms, the CIA director's fears about an attempt to draw in the Agency rose exponentially. Walters was beginning to have reservations, too, but his loyalty to the president still overrode other considerations. He expressed a desire to meet the White House's request at least halfway and offered to take the flak if the effort backfired. "I've had my ticket punched," he told Helms, "and I've got a great place to live in Florida." That remark took the CIA director aback. Walters didn't understand, thought Helms, that there was no way he personally could accede to White House demands without permanently damaging the Agency.[16]

So Helms proclaimed:

> I want it to be clearly understood between us that you are not to agree to anything that will in any way besmirch this Agency. I don't

care whether you are prepared to be a scapegoat or anything else, that is not the point. The Agency is not the Army or Navy or some big institution like that. It can hurt it badly by having somebody act improperly who was in the line of command, and I don't want you to acquiesce in a single thing that will besmirch this Agency.[17]

The next day Dean asked Walters to visit his office again. This time the president's counsel, under orders from Ehrlichman, put out a feeler that surprised even Walters. The Watergate burglars could not afford money for bail and were beginning to "wobble," so Dean wanted to know if it were possible for the Agency to bail them out using its unvouchered, covert funds. They would also need the money to support themselves and their families until the trial, and for the duration of their presumed sentences.

That was out of the question, Walters responded. Doing so would implicate the CIA deeply in something it was not party to. Besides, if the Agency were to provide bail, such a disbursement would have to be cleared with the House and Senate oversight committees; in the current atmosphere of leaks, such financial support was bound to become public. Walters said that if he were given such an order, he would resign and insist upon explaining his reasons directly to the president. He cautioned Dean not to turn the Watergate caper—currently a "medium-sized political explosion"—into a "multi-megaton" controversy.[18]

When Helms heard about this expanded request, he was naturally upset. But in a way, the point of maximum danger had passed; Walters was no longer amenable to meeting the White House even halfway. From this point on he would comport himself like a normal deputy director, one whose first loyalty was to the Agency. Sensing that he might someday need a record of what had transpired, Walters began dictating memos about every meeting since the extraordinary June 23 session with Haldeman and Ehrlichman.

Walters met for a third and last time with Dean the next day; during this meeting, the White House counsel exuded gloom. What promised to be an elegant solution to several of the White House's mounting problems had proved to be a nonstarter. Walters tried to leaven Dean's mood by suggesting that "scandals had a short life [span] in Washington, and another newer [and] spicier one would soon replace [Watergate]." Don't become "unduly agitated" by this affair, Walters advised. There was a ready scapegoat: just blame the Cubans, a scenario that had already been put forward by *New York Times* reporter Tad Szulc in a series of five articles. The break-in "had a strong Cuban flavor"—skilled professionals were already on record as deploring the amateurish job—and everyone knew that the exile community was conspiratorial and would go to great lengths to learn the policies of both political parties toward Fidel Castro. Pinning responsibility on the Cubans "might be costly but it would be plausible," Walters offered in parting.[19]

During this same period, June 23 to June 28, Dean monitored the FBI to make sure it was keeping up its side of the bargain. On June 23, fifteen minutes after the Helms/Walters meeting with Haldeman, Dean had advised Gray that Walters would soon be calling on him. Immediately after the two met, Gray had briefed Dean on the result. The FBI agreed to "work around" any possible CIA operations in Mexico or elsewhere, and an order blocking agents from interviewing Manuel Ogarrio was issued that afternoon. It was going to be trickier to forestall an interview with Dahlberg; FBI agents in Minneapolis were already hot on his trail.[20]

But keeping everyone on the same page without revealing the White House's intense interest proved difficult. The same morning Dean asked Walters about possibly using covert CIA funds for the burglars' bail, Gray called Helms to ask specifically if the Agency had "any interest" in Ogarrio. When Helms called back a few hours later with a definite "no," the two directors agreed to convene a high-level meeting, something the Justice Department's Henry Petersen had strongly been urging. It was to include Gray, Felt, Helms, and Walters, and presumably the gathering would settle the matter of CIA exposure in the Watergate investigation.[21]

When Gray told Dean about what in normal circumstances would have been a relatively routine meeting, Dean passed along the information to Ehrlichman. This was not part of the scenario. The CIA and FBI were supposed to be obedient and discreet, and the White House's script did not include high-level meetings between the two agencies to discuss the matter. They might realize that the impetus for invoking the delimitation agreement was coming primarily from the White House. Ehrlichman intervened; he called Gray and ordered him to cancel the session immediately. "There is no reason at all to hold that meeting," Ehrlichman said. Gray so informed Helms, but in keeping with the wary relationship between them, he made no mention of Ehrlichman's edict.[22]

Now it was Gray who began to waffle. In lieu of the cancelled meeting, he met with Mark Felt and Charlie Bates to discuss the supposedly mixed CIA messages. Bates argued that the Bureau should not back away from any aspect of the investigation without forcing the CIA to "reveal completely their interest in this matter." Felt seconded Bates, and Gray agreed. That evening the acting director lifted the restriction on interviewing Ogarrio, which had been in place for five days. But the next morning, Gray abruptly reversed himself. He had had another telephone conversation with Dean, and he was again prohibiting field agents from contacting Ogarrio.[23]

Meanwhile, at the Bureau's lower levels, concern began to mount over the sand being thrown in the gears of the FBI's investigation. The first to speak up was Angelo Lano, the Watergate case agent. On June 29, he sent a teletype to headquarters complaining, in effect, about days of inaction and vacillation at headquarters over several issues, one of which was the Ogarrio interview. The next day, the chief prosecutor, Earl Silbert, also called Mark Felt (in Gray's absence) to express his keen interest in pursuing the Ogarrio and Dahlberg leads, among others. Silbert claimed his boss, Harold Titus, was on his back, pressing for the interviews to get done.[24]

Lano's teletype was regarded as so explosive that Robert Kunkel, under whose name it was nominally sent out, never signed it. Nor did Felt initial it when it reached his desk—that would constitute proof that he had read the sharply worded communication, which laid out several specific instances of actual, inexplicable delays. If word or the gist of the teletype leaked out, and eventually it became known that pressure was being exerted on the FBI to circumscribe parts of its investigation, the press might instantly regard Watergate as something much more than a mere "caper."

The matter rested there until Gray returned to headquarters the first week in July and held another meeting about the investigation's progress with all the key executives and agents involved. He picked up Lano's teletype and waved it over his head. Who had the audacity to send this communication to the acting director? he asked. Lano admitted to authorship, explaining that it seemed necessary "to light a fire in headquarters" about the inexplicable delays he was encountering. Requests to move the investigation ahead had been stalled for days, he complained.[25]

Much as Gray disliked Lano's temerity, the teletype, along with pressure from the federal prosecutors, had the desired effect. Gray, ultimately, had a keen interest in an investigation that could pass political muster. Late on the evening of July 5, he called Vernon Walters (Helms was out of the country) and asked him to put in writing the CIA's supposed equities concerning Ogarrio and Dahlberg. Otherwise, Gray said, the FBI would have no alternative but to press ahead. When Walters came to Gray's office the next morning figuratively empty-handed, the White House effort to embroil the CIA in Watergate was effectively finished—at least until the Senate Watergate hearings commenced.[26]

Walters not only refused to extend the charade but expressed annoyance at having been approached in the first place. Without going into details—he did not mention Haldeman or Ehrlichman by name, or disclose Dean's request to provide the burglars' bail—he told Gray about the effort from his perspective. Walters emphasized his long association with Nixon and said he was as mindful as anyone could be about protecting the president. But "he did not believe that a letter from the Agency asking the FBI to lay off this investigation on the spurious grounds that it would uncover covert operations would serve the president."[27]

Impressed by this relative frankness, Gray went into a semiconfessional mode, too. He explained that he had told Haldeman, Ehrlichman, Dean, and even Attorney General Kleindienst that he could not control the FBI probe. He was purposely avoiding John Mitchell, who had just resigned as CRP director, because he wanted to be able to say at any confirmation hearings that he had never talked to him about Watergate. He thought the president needed protection from his ostensible protectors—a notion Walters enthusiastically seconded, telling Gray he "wasn't going to let those kids [primarily Dean] kick him around any more." He advised Gray to express his concerns directly to Nixon.[28]

Meanwhile, even before this climactic meeting, word had begun trickling back to the White House that its scheme wasn't going to work. "We're having problems with the Bureau," Haldeman told Nixon on June 30. "That's what we were talking about with Dean and Mitchell before our meeting with you. . . . Gray doesn't know how to turn them off and neither does Felt." The president and his chief of staff briefly weighed the idea of sending Mitchell in to see both Kleindienst and Gray, to tell them that "your people are investigating stuff that must not be investigated." But they soon dropped that idea. As Haldeman noted in his diary entry for July 6, "Walters apparently has finked out and spilled the beans to Pat Gray, which complicates the [problem] substantially." No one at the White House knew quite what to do with the FBI now.[29]

All told, this fourteen-day episode left Gray feeling queasy. On the one hand, the investigation was moving forward again, which was very desirable, for he wanted it finished as soon as humanly possible. Yet Gray was also unnerved by the curious episode he had just been party to. Lacking in cunning and guile, he couldn't decide whether the confusion and mixed signals were normal, given heightened political sensitivities in an election year, or whether they masked something ominous. He was sufficiently worried that he wanted to do what Walters had urged—tell Nixon personally he didn't think the presidency was being well served.

Gray was still shy, however, about exercising the prerogatives that Hoover had taken for granted, such as contacting the president directly whenever it suited him. Instead, Gray asked Clark MacGregor, a former congressman who had just succeeded Mitchell as the head of CRP, to pass along his concerns. MacGregor talked to Nixon on the morning of July 6, and about thirty minutes later Nixon called Gray. It was the first time they had spoken in months. After a few niceties, Gray blurted out his fears. Without identifying anyone by name, he said there were "people on your staff" who were "using the CIA and FBI," and "confusing the question of CIA interest in, or not in, people the FBI wishes to interview." After a perceptible pause, Nixon replied, "Pat, you just continue to conduct your aggressive and thorough investigation."

Gray instantly regretted having said anything about the matter, if only because it suggested that maybe he was not a team player after all. And in the run-up to the election, he would publicly deny ever having had "one single bit of pressure put upon" him in connection with the Bureau's Watergate investigation.[30]

Mark Felt was not a central actor in the June 23–July 6 effort to channel the Watergate investigation away from areas the White House believed the FBI had no business investigating. Still, he was close enough to the action to realize Haldeman was trying to entangle the CIA, and by doing so impede the FBI's probe into aspects of Watergate. When Felt wasn't running the Bureau in Gray's absence, he participated in meetings with Gray, Charlie Bates, and Robert Kunkel to discuss the probe nearly every day the acting director was in town. Felt surely recognized how irregular the exercise with the CIA had been. White House staffers seldom, if ever, concerned themselves with the delimitation agreement, much less enforcing it. With the possible exception of Helms, no one was more likely than Felt to recognize that the effort reeked of politics and had nothing to do with genuinely protecting Agency sources or methods.[31]

If Felt's primary motivation was some principle—whether defense of the presidency, the law, or concern for his own institution's integrity—then presumably he would have found some way to disclose this attempt to contain the FBI's investigation—if not to Woodward, who was still a relatively untested reporter, then to the tried-and-true Sandy Smith. But the *Time* reporter never wrote such a story, and Woodward, when asked if Felt ever mentioned the attempted obstruction, replied, "Not that I recall." Consequently, it took almost a full year before the effort to entangle the CIA became public knowledge. Only belatedly, in mid-May 1973, did Felt confirm to Woodward that Haldeman had ordered Helms and Walters to participate in an attempt to set limits on the FBI's probe. Woodward, apparently, did not wonder why Felt had neglected to raise it earlier. When asked later in 1973 how it happened that the *Post* completely missed the story of the cover-up, Woodward only observed, somewhat inaccurately, "It was too high. It was held too close. Too few people knew. We couldn't get that high."[32]

Even the most principled whistle-blower, to be sure, rarely discloses everything he or she knows. And Felt may have believed that the effort was known to so few people—only a handful of high officials—that any contemporaneous disclosure would have been extraordinarily risky. Still, in the context of his other leaks, it's far more plausible that the decisive factor for Felt was how disclosure would—or wouldn't—advance his personal goal. And the bottom line is that Felt never divulged to Woodward in a timely manner information about the CIA aspect of the cover-up, which ultimately turned out to be a defining and decisive element in the Watergate scandal writ large. Or as Barry Sussman later observed to David Halberstam, "The word *cover-up* did not appear in our paper until after January 1973."[33]

There are grounds for believing that Felt was playing a tricky double game here. He consistently urged Gray to keep the investigation moving, and not let it be derailed by trumped-up claims of CIA involvement. Yet he knew that doing so ran counter to White House wishes and that the acting director would likely pay the price for not being able to contain the FBI's probe. Pushing Gray to do the right thing, in other words, cost Felt nothing but was bound to hurt Gray. And there is some evidence that Felt was simultaneously communicating to the White House that everything would be different if *he* were the director—that he could accomplish what Gray was either unwilling or incapable of doing.

The clearest suggestion that Felt was playing such a double game came some two weeks after the White House effort fell apart. On July 22, Haldeman and Nixon were discussing the latest Watergate developments; in particular, whether it would be better to have the burglars indicted by a federal grand jury before or after the November election. They began musing about whether an FBI insider—specifically Felt—would have served their needs better than Gray. Nixon observed that the administration didn't have a real "Bureau man" working with it on Watergate. Haldeman responded, "Well, this guy [Felt] is pushing to try and be our boy, obviously, because . . . "—but before he could explain what he meant by that, Nixon interrupted.

"You know, I want one [Bureau official] as our boy," he said. Perhaps "we ought to throw some tests at Felt," Haldeman replied. "We could put some real sticky wickets to him and see how he bounces." For the first but not the last time since Hoover's death, the White House was musing about whether an FBI insider, rather than an outsider, might best serve its interests. Haldeman and Ehrlichman never got around to administering those tests, according to John Dean. Yet something Felt communicated had left Haldeman believing, both on June 23 and for weeks afterward, that Felt was potentially more valuable to the White House than Pat Gray. The most plausible explanation is that Felt managed to convey that he would have succeeded precisely at the point where Gray let the White House down.[34]

Another probable element in Felt's decision to keep entirely mum about the evidentiary straw that broke Nixon's back was his perception, by early July, that enough had been done already to torpedo Gray's chances of winning the permanent appointment. Why gild the lily? Indeed, after the flurry of leaks to the *Post*, *Time* magazine, and the *Washington Daily News* in mid- to late June, the Felt faction was almost completely dormant in July. Nor did there seem to be a reason to do much more. Gray was in a nearly impossible position already and digging his own hole deeper by the day through a series of bad decisions that were bound to get him into trouble in a Democrat-controlled Senate—that is, if by some miracle he got nominated. These ill-advised actions were the kinds of things an inexperienced or too-eager-to-please director would do, and loyal subordinates would have cautioned against—but then, Gray had no truly loyal executives under him, or at least too few of them. Felt merely watched with icy detachment as Gray made several choices that would eventually call his probity into question.[35]

One of the worst decisions was Gray's agreement to regard John Dean as the agent of the nation's chief law enforcement officer—the president—and regularly share the raw fruits of the FBI's investigation with him. Robert Mardian, the former assistant attorney general in charge of the Internal Security Division, had suggested this approach to Dean just after the break-in. There was some precedent for White House access to FBI information during sensitive investigations, but nothing quite akin to what happened in the aftermath of Watergate. The notion that Dean was ostensibly conducting an investigation for the president helped justify the largely unprecedented action, as did Gray's presumption of regularity in his dealings with the White House counsel. Dean's access to FBI teletypes and investigative reports was somewhat helpful in managing the cover-up, although it mostly served to convey to him the remarkable scope of the Bureau's investigation. Nonetheless, Gray would soon have a hard time explaining why he agreed to share the documents, not only to the U.S. Senate, but his own field agents.[36]

As day after day passed in July without any meaningful scoops, Howard Simons, the *Washington Post*'s managing editor and the driving force behind its investigation, became convinced that "the story was getting away" from the newspaper. "It really was," he later told Bernstein and Woodward. "We were drifting." On July 10, just after city editor Barry Sussman returned from a beach vacation, Simons expressed his anger over a Tad Szulc article in the *New York Times* about the expensive legal talent being assembled to represent the burglars. Simons thought Szulc's earlier series of five stories were all wrong; they had inadvertently promoted the White House's preferred line, that the break-in had been organized by former CIA officers and right-wing Cubans. Simons considered that "horse-shit, pure and simple." Still, where was the *Post*? It was not coming up with anything better.[37]

Simons grabbed Sussman and said, "Goddamit, we've gotta do more on Watergate. . . . It's a great story and we've got to go after it. I want an investigative team full-time and I don't care who you put on it. Just full-time on it and nothing else." Sussman suggested that Simons formalize what had been an ad hoc arrangement: put Woodward and Carl Bernstein on the story full-time, with Sussman closely overseeing their work.[38]

The *Post*'s Watergate team, soon to become known internally as "Woodstein," had been formed. Author J. Anthony Lukas would later term it a "bizarre hybrid, a kind of journalistic centaur with an aristocratic Republican head and runty Jewish hindquarters."

> Bob Woodward was a tall, good-looking Yale graduate whose face *Vogue* magazine was later to call "as open as a Finnish sandwich." . . . Bernstein was a rumpled, pock-marked, shaggy-haired dropout from the University of Maryland who occasionally wrote about rock music for the *Post* and reminded Woodward of "those counterculture journalists" [he] despised.[39]

Internally, their reputations were even more mixed than that. Although he had only been with the *Post* for nine months, that was long enough for the stolid Woodward to establish a reputation of being something of an editors' pet, deferential in manner, conservative in dress, and sober in habits—unlike many of his young male colleagues at the newspaper, who wore beards and reeked of marijuana. Some reporters resented his habit of poaching their beat in search of an A-section story. His writing was often awkward, and he had trouble mastering the inverted pyramid style that was the fall-back formula for most news stories. But he compensated for his lack of writing skills with doggedness and a willingness to put in long hours.[40]

Bernstein, by comparison, was something of a throwback to the days when reporters were made—or broken—in the newsroom, not minted in journalism schools or culled from Ivy Leaguers who had decided against becoming bankers or lawyers. He had started out, like so many others before him, as a lowly copyboy at the *Washington Star* and worked his way up the newspaper ladder from there. He was the superior writer by far and would fashion many of the "ledes" that appeared under their joint byline. Indeed, fundamental to their relationship was the fact that Woodward was generous enough to recognize that Bernstein improved his drafts.

Bernstein was also a throwback in another sense, and that was not serving him particularly well at the *Post*, which hankered to be an elite newspaper. Brash, combative, erratic, and infamous for abusing expense accounts, in six years at the paper Bernstein had been caught deceiving his editors more than once. That lent credence to complaints from news sources that he had "misquoted them, misrepresented their positions, or written things they said they had told him off the record." In fact, one instance of the latter had occurred with no one less than Tom Bishop, an FBI assistant director, in a news story about President Johnson's 1967 appointment of Walter E. Washington as D.C. mayor.[41]

Despite their different personalities and skills, and suspicions of one another (Bernstein thought Woodward was "a prima donna and an ass-kisser," while Woodward subscribed to the newsroom's rap on Bernstein as lazy and irresponsible), the duo turned out to be strangely comple-mentary—especially once Bernstein attained equal status on the story, rather than being regarded, as he was initially, as Woodward's tempo-rary sidekick. While Bernstein smoothed out Woodward's chunky prose, Woodward often served as a brake on Bernstein's tendency to overreach and push the story farther than the facts would allow. They both exhib-ited traits of resourcefulness and persistence, if not relentlessness, and the synergy between the two young reporters produced a better result than they could have managed working separately. Besides, they shared the single most important quality: a zest for the story and complete devotion to it.[42]

Well afterwards, Ben Bradlee would marvel at the accidental pairing that turned Bernstein and Woodward into the newspaper's primary reporters on Watergate. He had always thought of Bernstein as a guy "who was not always running at top speed . . . who had extraordinary talents that [he] didn't always use." He had hardly earned the right to be assigned to a story of historic significance; indeed, he was far closer to being fired. As for Woodward, while he reminded Bradlee of himself when he began in the business, any sound editor would have judged Woodward "hopelessly inexperienced" to tackle something like the Watergate scandal. How could Bradlee possibly rationalize giving "the biggest story in journalism to a guy who's been in the daily newspaper business nine months"?[43]

CHAPTER FIVE

Special Agent Woodward

August 1972

I suspect that in [Felt's] mind I was his agent.
—Bob Woodward, The Secret Man

One weekend in early August, aware of Felt's reluctance to talk on the telephone, a frustrated Bob Woodward drove uninvited to the FBI executive's comfortable suburban home on Wynford Drive in Fairfax, Virginia.

Woodward was at his wits' end. Despite his editors' commitment to covering Watergate, the *Post* had little to show for its efforts since June. The one exception was a major scoop on August 1, when, because of Bernstein's doggedness, the paper caught up with and passed (for good, as it turned out) Walter Rugaber of the *New York Times*. The *Post* broke the news that $25,000 found in the bank account of one of the Watergate burglars had been traced to Kenneth H. Dahlberg, Nixon's campaign finance chairman for the Midwest. It would be one of the most important "follow the money" stories Bernstein and Woodward ever produced. Jerry Landauer, an investigative reporter for the *Wall Street Journal* and something of a mentor to Woodward, told him, "I would have given my left testicle for that Dahlberg story." But apart from that scoop the trail had gotten cold.[1]

As Woodward sat in Felt's living room, the reporter expressed his certainty that Watergate was "one hell of a story"—and his *uncertainty* about how to proceed. He wanted to improve his working relationship with Felt, who, he realized, could be a better if not his best source. Since Felt's first significant leak to Woodward, on June 19, the FBI executive had been circumspect.[2]

The stone wall Woodward and Bernstein had come up against was not unlike what the FBI had initially encountered. Yet by mid-July, the fourth week of the probe, a series of big breaks had left WFO agents convinced that the burglars' trail led to the Nixon re-election campaign, with

E. Howard Hunt and G. Gordon Liddy, a CRP counsel, as the controllers of the operation. The investigation had "settled down" and ceased to be confusing. The CRP, not the CIA, was behind the conspiracy to break into the Democrats' headquarters. Learning precisely how high the conspiracy went was another matter. So far agents were unable to determine whether Hunt, Liddy, and James McCord had undertaken a rogue operation using CRP funds or had acted on behalf of higher-ups. But it seemed just a matter of time before the FBI would be able to determine whether or not the break-in had been conceived and sanctioned by the president's re-election apparatus, possibly even with the approval of the White House.[3]

Although they had much less information to work from, Woodward and Bernstein were on the edges of the same breakthrough. Bernstein had established a relationship with a confidential source, John P. Sears, who was proving invaluable in limning the lines of authority—and, just as important, the fierce rivalries—within the Nixon administration, and between it and the re-election committee. At the tender age of twenty-eight, Sears had played a critical role in overseeing Nixon's delegate count at the 1968 GOP convention, and the president-elect had regarded him favorably. But John Mitchell considered the political boy wonder too brash and overtly ambitious, and Sears did not get the White House job he had hoped for after the inauguration. He had had to settle for a lesser job as deputy counselor, a position from which he nonetheless proceeded to antagonize Ehrlichman and Haldeman too. Sears was one of the first White House aides wiretapped in 1969, and he had left the administration after only ten months. The "brilliant strategist" had flamed out like a shooting star.[4]

Still, some members of the administration appreciated his talents and sympathized with his plight. Among them was Rose Mary Woods, Nixon's longtime personal secretary. She nursed her own resentments toward aides like Haldeman, whose sense of self-importance had swelled enormously after the inauguration. Thus, although Sears had left the White House long before the break-in, his insights and information about the administration remained current. Moreover, one of his favorite pastimes was sharing trenchant opinions and political gossip with reporters.

Bernstein had first contacted Sears on June 21, and found him a willing source. Backgrounding Watergate stories was a perfect way to exact revenge against those who had thwarted his aspirations, chiefly Mitchell, Ehrlichman, and Haldeman. Their decline might even pave the way for him to return to a position of influence and power. Sears gave Bernstein details about the structure of the president's fund-raising juggernaut, for which the groundwork had been laid in 1969. This information would prove crucial in exposing the link between the campaign and the burglars. Indeed, right after the break-in, Sears provided Bernstein with details about the campaign's "security" fund. And Bernstein's third Watergate story, published on June 22, had been a Sears-inspired article exposing the CRP's network of dummy campaign committees erected to funnel money from business interests to the Nixon campaign.[5]

From the outset Sears held a firm, consistent opinion about the ultimate architect of the break-in: it "would have to be somebody who doesn't know about politics but thought he did. . . . Anybody who knew anything wouldn't be looking over there [Larry O'Brien's office] for real political information. They'd be looking for something else . . . scandal, gossip." He thought the most likely culprit was Chuck Colson, who had gotten the appointment as political counselor that Sears coveted. On the other hand, "Mitchell wouldn't let go of a decision like that," he told Bernstein. "Mitchell would decide, with advice from somebody who knew something about security."[6]

Thus it had primarily been Sears, not Felt, who initially persuaded the *Post* reporters that the break-in was a CRP-financed and sanctioned affair, however hare-brained. Sears also kept them on the right track early on, steering them away from false leads. After the explanation about right-wing Cubans acting independently failed to gain traction in the press, Sears told Bernstein that the White House was concocting a new scenario. The CRP was going to admit to having a large security fund controlled by G. Gordon Liddy, money that was set aside to prevent disruptions at the Republican convention. But then the CRP was going to maintain that Liddy, acting alone, had used these funds to finance the Watergate burglary. The CRP was counting on the perception that Liddy was just "strange enough to have pulled Watergate off on his own." The *Los Angeles Times* and *Washington Star* published stories along this line, but thanks to Sears, Bernstein and Woodward had not taken the bait.[7]

For all of Sears's undoubted value, however, he was not in a position to produce the critical investigative breakthroughs that were necessary to advance the story. He could take the reporters only so far. And so Woodward had decided to appeal to Felt in person.

Though discomfited by the unexpected visit, Felt was receptive to Woodward's initiative. The FBI executive had not sought the *Post* reporter out—it was quite the reverse—but another pipeline to the media could not help but come in handy. And who would suspect that such a neophyte reporter had the Bureau's number two man as a source? Felt had also been impressed by the enterprise Woodward and Bernstein had shown in breaking the Dahlberg story. But if he were going to provide information, Felt finally declared, he was going to have to insist on certain rules.[8]

In the most forbidding manner he could muster, Felt spelled out the risks. The FBI and the White House were already concerned about leaks to the press. Woodward and Bernstein might be followed and their telephones tapped. The administration, Felt emphasized, saw the stakes as "much higher than anyone [on the] outside perceived." He made vague allusions, which Woodward did not understand, to a connection between Watergate and national security.[9]

The two then ironed out the ground rules that would supposedly govern their relationship, although the letter of the arrangement lasted barely three months. Not surprisingly, given Felt's experience in counterintelligence, the system they came up with drew heavily on well-established protocols from the spy tradecraft. A signaling system was devised and a meeting place designated: column 32D in a nondescript parking facility at 1401 Wilson Boulevard in Arlington, Virginia, across the river from downtown Washington. Their relationship, Felt said, was to be "a compact of trust; nothing about it was to be discussed or shared with anyone." Felt would provide only "deep background" information to Woodward. Felt's identity and position inside the government were never to be divulged to anyone. Nothing he said was to be quoted ever. All their discussions "would be only to confirm information that had been obtained elsewhere and to add some perspective." Felt wanted "the greatest detachment—full deniability" from the stories that were to come.[10]

Unbeknownst to the *Post* reporter, he had also just drafted an FBI executive who had a much-better-than-average understanding of how the White House was organized and its competing power centers, separate and apart from Felt's access to information about Watergate. During the first year of the Nixon presidency, J. Edgar Hoover had informed Nixon that damaging allegations were being circulated about a "ring of homosexualists [*sic*] [operating] at the highest levels of the White House," a ring said to include chief of staff Bob Haldeman and John Ehrlichman, then the president's counsel. When Nixon reluctantly agreed to an investigation, Hoover had assigned Mark Felt, whom he described as one of his "most discreet executives," to the probe. After conducting several interviews, Felt had promptly concluded there was nothing to the allegation and the investigation was closed. In the process, however, the FBI executive had gained first-hand knowledge about how the Nixon White

House worked, its personalities, and its lines of power. Now he would couch his Watergate-related disclosures inside credible insights into the administration's leading personalities—Haldeman, Ehrlichman, Colson—all of whom were of intense interest to Woodward. The overall effect would be to heighten immeasurably Felt's already high face value as an irreplaceable source.[11]

If, from Woodward's perspective, he was negotiating a relationship that would enable him to scoop the *Post*'s competitors, from Felt's perspective the relationship was designed to serve an altogether different purpose. Felt would be Woodward's case officer, essentially, in the FBI executive's own covert operation. And if the operation worked, no one outside the Felt faction—arguably, not even Woodward—would ever know.

Felt was making a grave error in agreeing to the deep background arrangement. Although he had no way of knowing, his scheme was on the brink of success; all that was required on his part was a little more patience. On August 1, President Nixon and Haldeman had engaged in a long discussion about Watergate. Despite the disappointing end to the White House's effort to involve the CIA in early July, everything seemed to be going according to plan now. The burglars—even Howard Hunt—seemed satisfied with their payments; the indictments would be handed down in mid-September, and no one outside of Hunt, Liddy, and the five burglars were going to be accused of wrongdoing; finally, it appeared most unlikely that the actual trial would occur before the election.[12]

Political containment of Watergate, in other words, seemed to be working as well as could possibly be expected, and that apparently prompted Nixon and Haldeman to be more generous in their assessment of Pat Gray—but only up to a point. "I don't think, Bob, we should lay anything on Gray," observed the president. "He is in a *very* difficult position. He cannot . . . he just can't do it." Haldeman chimed in, "He doesn't have any control . . . he doesn't know how to do these [things]." Then Nixon declared that, after the election, "I don't believe that we oughta have Gray in that job. . . . I don't think it's the right thing, he's too close to us." But if they could get Mark Felt appointed director, Nixon surmised—"he's a good man"—then the White House would have someone both effective and loyal in the post. Haldeman, too, thought well of promoting Felt based on all the hints left by the FBI executive. "If you put him in, he'll *be your guy*," said the chief of staff.[13]

Felt would never know that his plan had in fact succeeded as of August 1 because of Gray's inability to navigate the Watergate investigation to Nixon's satisfaction. The president had done an about-face and decided that someone who knew how to control all the knobs and levers at the Bureau ought to be in charge after all. But with no outward sign that Nixon had soured on his acting director and now preferred an insider, and lacking any private signal from Haldeman, Felt decided there was more undermining of Gray to be done. The discretion he had exercised throughout July was over.

In embarking on a new series of leaks, Felt would not only overreach and expose himself—thus eliminating his very good chance of succeeding Gray—he would also help lay the foundation for the destruction of the only president willing to help him reach the Bureau's pinnacle.

Beginning in late August, and escalating from mid-September through to the November election, the deep background arrangement paid enormous dividends for the *Post*. The newspaper far outpaced the competition, which wrote about Watergate passively when it wrote about it at all. The *Post* had every other newspaper "outsourced," as Robert Phelps, the Washington editor of the *New York Times*, later acknowledged. Felt provided vital guidance, imparted knowledge, suggested leads, and gave Woodward (and by extension, Bernstein) confidence that they were on the right track. He sharpened and expanded upon information they had already gathered, and, on occasion, supplied raw information, known only to the FBI, that could be popped into a piece virtually unchanged. He nurtured one front-page story after another, allowing the *Post* reporters to replicate the FBI's investigation in several respects. It was later said that Woodward and Bernstein "believed in what they were doing" at a time when reporters at other prestigious outlets were at sea about what Watergate meant. The reason for that was Mark Felt.[14]

All the while Felt gave Gray (whom he had taken to calling "Boss") the impression that he considered Gray a worthy successor to J. Edgar Hoover. Felt was at his unctuous best when he thanked Gray for an autographed picture that September. "I am rearranging the pictures in my office so that yours will occupy the most prominent spot," he wrote.[15]

Of the many ironies that cropped up after the deep background arrangement was reached, none would surpass the fact that Felt, because of Gray's frequent absences, as often as not bore the brunt of the White House's ire over leaks, along with Henry Petersen, head of the Criminal Division. A lesser man than Felt might have felt trepidation after repeated scoldings from a White House counsel, even one as obviously lacking in gravitas as the young John Dean. But Felt was a cool customer, and often able to turn his dual identity as the leaker and the recipient of complaints to his advantage.

One tactic was to show the White House alternate ways in which Woodward and Bernstein might have gotten the information at issue. Felt also endeavored to point out details in the *Post* articles that could not have come from the FBI. Because of the enormous effort Woodward and Bernstein invested in their stories, few of them pivoted entirely around his information or guidance, leaving him shielded. On one occasion, Felt even instigated an ostentatious internal investigation into a particular leak that he knew had not come from the Bureau, which only served to muddy the waters.[16]

This kept the White House off balance and uncertain about its own judgments. From the president on down, the administration was almost certain the leaks were coming from the Bureau, but they lacked that last measure of certainty. Felt's qualifiers, alternate—and seemingly plausible—explanations, and flat denials saw to that. He did a masterful job of feigning outrage over the leaks while running one misdirection play after another.[17]

As he recounted his role in his 1979 memoir,

> Numerous times when Gray was out of the city, John Dean called me, demanding that [new] steps be taken to silence the leakers. I refused to take such action and frequently I was able to point out to him that some of the leaks could not possibly have come from the Bureau, since they included information to which we were not privy. This did not mollify Mr. Dean.[18]

Aside from his ability to thwart the FBI's internal leak investigations—which are difficult under the best of circumstances—the lack of political fallout from the scandal greatly aided Felt. Although this element was largely beyond his control, it was nonetheless crucial.

Weeks after the break-in, and in spite of the *prima facie* evidence linking the burglars with Nixon's campaign, Watergate was still not an election issue. The president maintained a steady 60 percent approval rating, and the intrinsic weakness of the liberal Democratic nominee had everything to do with this. Just as many predicted, George McGovern was proving to be a perfect foil for Nixon; as the president told his chief of staff just after the Democratic convention in July, "we have the candidate we want now as our opponent."[19]

John Dean, the cover-up's desk officer, was himself struck by this odd phenomenon. As he later wrote, "public consciousness of the scandal was light-years removed from the reality" he was living every day. He was scrambling, occasionally frantically, to keep the scandal under wraps. Meanwhile, the American public was remarkably unimpressed by the break-in, writing it off as something both parties indulged in, or as such a bungled effort that it could not possibly involve the president. The bottom line was that Felt never had to worry about the consequences at the ballot box of his actions, a liberating fact. He could leak with near impunity, taking only the precautions he needed to protect himself and his faction.[20]

Exactly as Felt had intended, the drumbeat of disclosures served chiefly, if not only, to incite the White House against Pat Gray. But just when everything seemed to be proceeding smoothly, the unexpected resurgence of his old antagonist, Bill Sullivan, complicated Felt's plans.

Sullivan had all but disappeared after his abrupt dismissal in September 1971, his chances of succeeding Hoover seemingly nil. Like many former high-ranking FBI officials, he had found a comfortable job far from Washington—in New Haven, Connecticut, as assistant director of the Insurance Crime Prevention Institute. But several influential supporters and friends, many of them outside the FBI, had not given up on the idea of having him lead the Bureau, particularly once Hoover was not just gone but dead. These supporters included such influential figures as Jay Lovestone, a labor union leader, and both Baroodys: William J. Baroody, Sr., a friend of the president's and the head of AEI, a conservative think-tank in Washington, and his son, William J. Baroody, Jr., then an aide to Secretary of Defense Melvin Laird. They and others plotted Sullivan's return and heavily lobbied White House officials, like Chuck Colson, who were presumed to have some input into the decision. Sullivan himself badly wanted revenge against those FBI executives (most prominently Mark Felt) who had helped bring about his fall from Hoover's grace, or so Sullivan believed. He turned down lucrative offers from several publishers to write an exposé about Hoover. That would burn more bridges, and he was consumed with finding some way to return triumphantly. The most he was willing to do in public was make occasional remarks about the "fossilized bureaucratic traditions and obsolete policies" that were hampering the FBI.[21]

In mid-July 1972, six weeks after Hoover's death, Attorney General Richard Kleindienst offered Sullivan a prestigious new post: director of the newly established Office of National Narcotics Intelligence in the Justice Department. If Sullivan rejoined Justice, it meant he was likely to be considered when it came time to name a permanent FBI director. In fact, Felt's leaks to damage Gray's reputation had the unintended consequence of boosting Sullivan's chances: like Felt, he was an "insider" who could presumably rediscipline the FBI. On Friday, August 4, less than a year after his inglorious departure from the Bureau, Sullivan arrived at Justice to report to work—and the FBI rumor mill went into overdrive.[22]

Sullivan's presence in the capital set off reverberations within FBI circles and gave the administration another line into the Bureau itself. Ensconced in an office just a few floors away from the division he once commanded, Sullivan began hiring agents and officials who had also left the Bureau after arousing Hoover's displeasure. He was like a leader-in-exile. Men who had once worked for him, who were now out in the field as special agents in charge (SACs) or assistant SACs, would visit his office discreetly, seeking his advice or just to say hello. It was a way of hedging their bets in case he returned to power.[23]

Felt, naturally, was very apprehensive about his erstwhile rival's return to Washington. It might take a while for Sullivan to identify the source and catch on to the purpose of Watergate-related leaks, but as an old COINTELPRO hand himself he would soon realize they were fast eroding the chances that Gray's appointment would be made permanent. Indeed, soon after his arrival Sullivan began inundating his old administration ally on internal security issues, Robert Mardian, who had moved with John Mitchell from Justice to the CRP, with letters extolling his own qualifications and ideas for the Bureau's top job.[24]

The possibility that Sullivan might yet triumph was also heightened because Gray was actually contemplating whether to bring him back into the Bureau in some capacity. Ever since taking office as acting director, Gray had been encouraged to reach out to Sullivan, and the two first met privately on July 6, just before Sullivan accepted Kleindienst's offer. Never at a loss for ideas, Sullivan gave Gray a host of suggestions about everything from reorganizing the Bureau's divisions to guidelines for the discipline of individual agents. He openly advocated the resumption of "black-bag jobs," that is, surreptitious and illegal searches by FBI agents, telling Gray the Bureau had some "very good talent" in that regard. Nor was that the last meeting between Gray and the eager-for-redemption Sullivan, who was not above engaging in some Hoover-like flattery of the acting director.[25]

In short, Felt had gathered enough intelligence and scuttlebutt to recognize, as he later declared, that there was "a whole scenario here of a man by the name of Sullivan, trying to take over the directorship." So he expanded his plan to take this unexpected development into account. Now he would carry out two psychological warfare operations, the second one even more sensitive than the first. It was one thing to leak particulars about the break-in that were meant only to infuriate the White House and prove Pat Gray inept. It would be another to foment disclosures aimed at discrediting William Sullivan. That task would involve divulging the administration's innermost secrets, including the real reason why the White House considered it so necessary to cover up the Watergate burglary.[26]

President Nixon's fury over leaks to the news media—an anger stoked by national security adviser Henry Kissinger—had actually first manifested itself in 1969. Over the next two years, at the direct order of the White House, the FBI wiretapped a total of thirteen administration officials and four newspapermen who were suspected of leaking or receiving classified information. The wiretaps, along with Hoover's general lack of enthusiasm for leak investigations, failed to produce the desired results and were discontinued by February 1971. But then, just five months later, the White House faced unauthorized publication of the so-called Pentagon Papers. One evening in the Oval Office, when the president was expressing his frustration to Chuck Colson and Bob Haldeman about the government's inability to recover the stolen documents, he asked his chief of staff, "Whatever happened to that plan that we had that we would have some people here who could do those jobs for us that no one else would do?"[27]

The White House decided to take matters into its own hands. It established a Special Investigations Unit (SIU), also known as the "Room 16 Group," after their office in the Old Executive Office Building, to go after leakers much more vigorously than Hoover was willing to do at the time. This meant carrying out black-bag jobs in pursuit of supposedly damaging evidence.[28]

In September 1971, this leak-chasing unit, which had whimsically dubbed itself the "plumbers," burglarized the Los Angeles office of the psychiatrist who had treated Daniel Ellsberg, the man primarily responsible for disclosing the Pentagon Papers. Because four operatives (Howard Hunt, G. Gordon Liddy, Bernard Barker, and Eugenio Martinez) were involved in both the Ellsberg and the Watergate break-ins, peeling back the latter threatened to expose the former. If Hunt or Liddy started talking, their revelations could lead to the unraveling of an entire skein of illegal, unethical, and politically explosive behavior by the Nixon White House.[29]

When John Mitchell learned about the plumbers' activities for the first time, just after the Watergate burglars were apprehended, the former attorney general fittingly dubbed them the "White House horrors." The intertwined issues and personnel—or "various lines of interlinkage," as Haldeman understatedly described the problem in his diary—was the fundamental reason why the White House's initial policy of political containment over the break-in had morphed into obstruction of justice within a matter of days. Or as Watergate prosecutor Earl Silbert would later observe,

> In trying to assess the obstruction—who was involved, who wasn't, and the like—the motive seemed weak [at first]. Why would they want to cover up . . . this burglary into the Democratic National Committee headquarters. . . .
>
> [But] when Dean said that Hunt, and Liddy, and [the] Cubans . . . had [also] been involved in a break-in into the office of Ellsberg's psychiatrist, that was like a bombshell. . . .
>
> It was the *same people* . . . that had to be what was bothering the White House. Because it's one thing, in the public eye, to break into a Democratic National Committee headquarters . . . [because] political skullduggery goes on. It's another thing to break in and obtain a psychiatrist's file on an individual. That, if disclosed . . . would have a far more significant political impact. . . . That became a driving force for the cover-up.[30]

Felt did not know about the 1969–1971 wiretaps at the time. Inside the Bureau, only Sullivan and Hoover had contemporaneous knowledge of the coverage and reasons for it. Felt had learned about the surveillance only upon becoming the Bureau's number three man, when a question arose about custody of these "special files," which were then missing from Sullivan's office. While several high administration officials were implicated in the highly secret operation (particularly Kissinger and John Mitchell), Sullivan's complicity was the one thing that mattered to Felt. Hoover had made Sullivan the liaison to the White House for the 1969–1971 wiretaps, and Sullivan had also been the FBI's contact with the plumbers (whose activities Felt had become privy to contemporaneously). The slightest leak about either effort, however vague, was bound to diminish Sullivan's viability as a candidate for the directorship. The

White House simply could not afford to nominate anyone from the FBI actively involved in activities that would be enormously embarrassing to the administration, if disclosed.[31]

Unlike leaks directly related to the Watergate break-in, Felt would divulge information about the wiretaps and/or the plumbers to a reporter known for his ability to get hard-to-confirm information published, and with an impeccable record of never revealing his sources— *Time*'s Sandy Smith. Felt would readily confirm Smith's stories for Woodward once they had been published (though even then Felt tended to drag his feet), but he would not give the information to the *Post* first.[32]

Smith was hungry, too, for he had not had a Watergate scoop either for some time. Reporting for a weekly magazine put him at something of a disadvantage. *Time* had more space to devote to a subject that really caught its interest, and something of a leg up on newspapers when it came to providing a coherent narrative. But genuine scoops were hard to achieve without daily publication. The last time Smith had been close to publishing one was in July, when he was the first reporter to learn that G. Gordon Liddy had been fired from the CRP on June 28 for refusing to answer the FBI's questions. When Smith called DeVan Shumway, the CRP's director of public affairs, on July 21—a Friday, and the deadline for anything in the following week's issue—Shumway confirmed the scoop. But in the meantime, a reporter named Judith Bender had heard about Liddy from a trusted source whose relative worked at the CRP. *Newsday*, a Long Island newspaper, broke the story on Saturday.[33]

There was no such problem with the revelation Felt now passed on to Smith, and thus it was on August 7, that *Time* magazine introduced the American public to the existence of the Room 16 Group and its connection to the Watergate break-in. "Before they apparently moved into political surveillance," the article revealed, "[G. Gordon] Liddy and [E. Howard] Hunt were part of a White House team known as 'the plumbers,' because they were assigned to investigate the source of leaks to the press like that of the Pentagon Papers." Two weeks later, on August 21, another Smith-reported article in *Time* put forward a fundamental, but at the time, greatly unappreciated truth. The mentality of the Watergate burglars, and most of their manpower, could be traced back directly to the plumbers. *Time*, which like most of the media had started out by calling Watergate a "caper," now began to cover the break-in as if it were the scandal of the year.[34]

Many months would pass before Watergate came into proper focus as part of a larger mosaic of unprecedented activities conducted by the

Nixon White House. In the meantime, the import of Smith's August scoops was all but lost. The White House's official response to the stories was to stiff-arm reporters, its only statement being "No comment." Within the administration, though, the stories were profoundly alarming—a warning of just how close to exposure the "White House horrors" were. The lid was still on, but barely. And under the circumstances, as Felt had hoped and expected, the notion of nominating Sullivan for the directorship became a nonstarter. Naming him would be akin to giving Senate Democrats the opener to a can of worms.[35]

In the weeks that followed, *Time* displayed a *Post*-like devotion to Watergate. Stories on the break-in appeared in nine of the thirteen issues published from August 7 to October 30—an extraordinary commitment for a newsweekly. The magazine's coverage mirrored the *Post*'s in tenor, treating the break-in as part of a complex, secret program that might have had its origins in the White House or even the Oval Office. Indeed, *Time*'s reporting and analysis were well ahead of the *Post*'s in some respects, such as when it linked Hunt and Liddy to the plumbers. More than once Woodward or Bernstein had a Sunday "shot to hell" because of a new angle that was about to appear in *Time* and thereby required the *Post* to have its own story ready the following day.[36]

As Barry Sussman, the *Post*'s special Watergate editor, observed in his 1974 history of the scandal, in the summer and fall of 1972 "*Time* magazine, with a reporter who had superb contacts at the Justice Department, was perhaps the leading provider of Watergate scandal news aside from the *Post*."[37]

The reason for this is now plain: *Time* was the *Post*'s closest competitor because Deep Throat was leaking to both. They were the twin prongs of Felt's personal counterintelligence operation against Pat Gray and Bill Sullivan.[38]

CHAPTER SIX

Retracing the Bureau's Steps

August–October 1972

Oh my God. That's my interview!
—FBI agent Paul Magallanes

Here's how the story goes in the popular imagination: Deep Throat leaked in the late summer and fall of 1972, Woodward and Bernstein did a little legwork, and the *Post* published another front-page scoop that rattled the White House. It was as if Woodward "did little more than show up with a bread basket that Deep Throat filled with goodies," as one *Post* editor later put it mockingly.[1]

In reality the relationship was far more nuanced and complicated. No two Watergate scoops came about in exactly the same way, though Felt played a role in several of the significant ones. Sometimes Woodward and Bernstein got their initial tip from an entirely unexpected source, and Felt served only to corroborate the story. On other occasions, Felt provided the initial guidance that enabled the reporters to replicate the Bureau's ongoing investigation. And sometimes, Felt, in his eagerness to impugn Gray, broke the deep background rules he himself had set. All these variations were clearly in evidence in September 1972 as the *Post* duo followed the FBI's investigative footsteps.[2]

But another part of the story, again, is the help Felt could have offered to Woodward but declined to extend. It wasn't because this information was about the cover-up, rather than the crime, and too closely held—as had been the case with the effort to involve the CIA, which Felt had said nothing about in July. The information outlined below was strictly about the break-in itself. And while no whistle-blower is under an obligation to divulge everything he knows, Felt's conspicuous failure to do so in this instance underscores again that his agenda was something other than exposure of the parties behind the Watergate break-in.

Early on the morning of June 17, the day of the break-in, Joe Califano, the legal counsel to the Democratic National Committee (DNC), called his good friend Howard Simons, the *Post*'s managing editor, to alert him about the arrests. In hindsight, the *Post* would have latched onto the story without Califano's tip, especially once James McCord's role had been ferreted out. But that was not obvious initially, and so the telephone call was deemed very sensitive. This was because Califano was not just the DNC's counsel; he was also the *Post*'s chief outside counsel, and the paper's editors feared that its coverage of Watergate would be seen as reflecting a bias toward the Democrats. So the Califano heads-up was obscured for many years.[3]

The potential for a conflict of interest escalated dramatically on June 20, when Califano announced that Williams, Connolly & Califano would be representing the DNC in a million-dollar civil lawsuit against the burglars, the CRP, and "unnamed others" for conspiring to violate the civil and constitutional rights of the Democrats. Standing with Califano at the news conference was the DNC chairman, Larry O'Brien, who stated without hesitation that the White House, if not the president, would ultimately be found responsible for the break-in. This assertion guaranteed that media coverage of Watergate would be politically charged, and especially for the *Post*, given its relationship with the law firm and its reputation as a liberal-leaning newspaper.[4]

Edward Bennett Williams, one of the law firm's founding partners, had an exceptionally relaxed notion, however, about what constituted a conflict of interest. As Califano later wrote in a memoir, Williams "always stretched to the limit the number of clients we could represent in a particular matter without finding a conflict." Almost any other law firm would have handed the suit off to another firm to avoid jeopardizing the prestige (and billable hours) that came from representing the *Post*. Califano practically worked *pro bono* for the DNC, and the lawsuit might not even be a paying proposition.[5]

The Republicans' lawyers were quick to point out the overlapping interests involved. In late June, at the first court hearing on the civil suit, CRP attorney Kenneth W. Parkinson immediately raised the issue of a possible conflict of interest. "I . . . understand that there is some relationship between Mr. Williams's firm and the Washington Post Newspaper Company," he understatedly observed. Thereafter, as the newspaper's commitment to the story deepened, GOP circles became increasingly suspicious that Williams, Connolly lawyers were fueling the *Post*'s coverage, or that a symbiotic relationship had developed. According to this scenario, the reason the *Post* was still digging into Watergate when the rest of the media had largely given up was that Williams was funneling information gained through the lawsuit to the paper's editors, and vice versa. As Kansas Senator Bob Dole eventually asked, "Does it not seem strange that Mr. E. B. Williams, the Democrats' unpaid attorney in the Watergate civil trial, is also the attorney for the *Washington Post*?"[6]

Washington Post executive editor Ben Bradlee consistently denied, both then and later, that there was any cross-pollination between the lawsuit and the newspaper's pursuit of the story; an impermeable wall supposedly separated the two efforts. "I didn't get anything out of him," Bradlee told a Williams biographer. "I thought 'Holy God, we'll get everything. Ed is finally going to pay off.'" But Williams refused on principle to give the *Post* any inside information from the suit, according to Bradlee.[7]

For the most part this assertion was true. But on at least one occasion, shortly after Labor Day, Williams did order an attorney at his firm to leak an important development to Bernstein and Woodward, conflict of interest be damned. Mark Felt would serve as an important backstop to the disclosure, verifying the essential truth of the information. Yet this same episode also raises the question: why didn't Felt *himself* tell Woodward two months earlier about a former FBI agent named Alfred C. Baldwin III who had served as a lookout the night of the break-in?

On August 5 Williams sent one of the attorneys in his firm, J. Alan Galbraith, to Connecticut to interview Baldwin, the only participant in the break-in who was cooperating with the federal prosecutors. Williams was acting on a tip from Baldwin's attorney, John Cassidento, a Democrat prominent in Connecticut state politics. James McCord had recruited Baldwin to monitor the electronic bugs in DNC headquarters and prepare notes from the conversations, summaries that eventually wound up in the in-box of Jeb Magruder, the CRP deputy director. Baldwin, who had begun secretly cooperating with the FBI in early July, promised to be a star witness at the trial because he could offer eyewitness proof of Hunt's and Liddy's complicity in the break-in. He also supplied a crucial factual correction: on June 17, the burglars had entered DNC premises for the *second* time.[8]

Galbraith gave Williams a detailed memo about his meeting with Baldwin. When Califano learned its contents, he "wanted [DNC chairman Larry] O'Brien to go public immediately with Baldwin's explosive revelations. But Ed Williams discouraged [him]." One of Williams's favorite maxims was "leak things slowly," in the belief that letting information dribble out maximized the benefits of a damaging disclosure.

Consequently, O'Brien went public with only part of Baldwin's story on August 15 and revealed a little more of it on September 7, but on neither occasion did he disclose Baldwin's identity. Still, both statements generated significant press coverage.[9]

Then, around September 10, "on Ed's instruction," Galbraith leaked information about Baldwin to Bernstein and Woodward. Despite the authority of the source, the reporters were intent on verifying the information with Felt. "They told me they'd corroborate [Baldwin's story] with their source at the FBI," Galbraith explained in 2009. The *Post* duo was not always as discreet as they later claimed when referring to Woodward's special source during this period. By this time, Bernstein had become privy to Deep Throat's true identity, notwithstanding Woodward's initial pledge to Felt; moreover, Woodward had been mentioning for weeks the existence of his highly placed source to other colleagues at the newspaper. According to James Mann, a *Post* reporter who co-wrote several Watergate-related stories with Woodward early on, Woodward would refer to Felt as "'my source at the FBI' or 'my friend at the FBI' . . . making it plain that this was a special, and unusually well-placed, source."[10]

The result of Galbraith's leak was another front-page scoop for Bernstein and Woodward. Appearing on September 11, it disclosed, without naming Baldwin, that a "self-described participant has [given] Democratic investigators" (namely Galbraith) a detailed account of the electronic surveillance of DNC headquarters. Bernstein and Woodward would later play down the significance of this particular scoop, presumably because of the sensitivity of its source, but at the time it certainly did not go unnoticed.[11]

Federal prosecutors, alarmed that their case was being aired in public, believed the revelations must have come from Baldwin's lawyer. They contacted Cassidento, who professed ignorance. The White House, too, recognized that the scoop was a real breakthrough. The article precipitated one of the longest and most detailed discussions about Watergate so far among the president and his closest advisers, who shrewdly deduced that the Democrats were "building their case on . . . Baldwin. . . . [The] feeling is that he's been immunized by the prosecutors, and that because he has . . . Democratic lawyers . . . that he's spilled the beans to them."[12]

The September 11 article made real the conflict of interest at the *Post* that had existed only in theory since late June. But even before the Baldwin story was published, there was a growing recognition at the newspaper that it was becoming very problematic, both legally and journalistically, for the same firm to represent the DNC and the *Post*—especially once Williams, Connolly began taking depositions from CRP officials. The situation risked giving credence to Republican charges that when it came to Watergate, the *Post* was essentially an appendage of the Democratic Party. Similar criticisms were already being made internally, most notably by Richard C. Harwood, the national editor and a "conservative-leaning cynic."[13]

Consequently, in early September, the *Post* decided to recuse Williams, Connolly from vetting any more Watergate stories as outside counsel until the case was settled. Edward L. Smith, a lawyer in New York who advised *Newsweek*, would be brought down or consulted via telephone in the interim. The irrepressible Edward Bennett Williams would continue to play a role, but primarily as Bradlee's informal sounding board. As Bradlee wrote in his 1995 memoir about a Watergate development, "I had no idea what to do except—as usual—talk with Ed Williams." More than once Williams would buck Bradlee up when the editor expressed private doubts (always behind closed doors) about where the coverage was going, or even concern that it all might be an elaborate hoax. At one point Williams reportedly said, "Ben, the kids [Bernstein and Woodward] have got to be right because otherwise why are the Nixon people lying so goddamn much? If they're clean why don't they show it? Why are there so many lies? I'll tell you why. Because you've got them."[14]

This was the very reason Williams was considered the best criminal attorney in town by a wide margin. "Ed had wonderful antennae," recalled Galbraith, the lawyer who had been dispatched to interview Baldwin. As an example, Galbraith recalled in 2009 a conversation he had had with Williams in late 1972. The legendary criminal lawyer assured Galbraith then that Nixon and his top aides were "talking about us in the Oval Office . . . [and] basically, what he told me they were saying about us was what turned out to be on the [Nixon] tapes, to my astonishment."[15]

Apart from illustrating that Republicans' suspicions about Williams and the *Post* were not entirely unfounded, the most telling aspect of how the Baldwin story got into the newspaper was the role that Felt did *not* play. When Baldwin began cooperating with the government in early July, his statement put an end to any suspicion among federal investigators that the break-in was a CIA operation rather than a CRP effort. Three months later, in early October, the *Los Angeles Times* would break the story wide open, publishing Baldwin's first-person account in what was rightly regarded as one of the most important Watergate stories of the entire year. It was not a story attributed to anonymous sources and unnamed officials. As *Los Angeles Times* reporter Jack Nelson later noted, it finally "put a face on the Watergate story." And Baldwin's later trial testimony would represent the most compelling evidence, at the time, of the link between the break-in and the president's campaign.[16]

Yet Felt, in the words of one Watergate historian, had "entirely failed" to tell Woodward about Baldwin. Nothing better illustrated the fact that Felt, all along, had a separate and distinctly self-serving agenda.

When asked in 2011 why Felt never told him about Baldwin, Woodward responded, "The answer is, I don't know why."[17]

Woodward and Bernstein's biggest achievement in the two months left before the election was to replicate results from the FBI's investigation into the CRP. Felt exercised notable influence here, notwithstanding his refusal to tip them off to Alfred Baldwin.

Because of these stories, FBI agents working the case would always suspect that Bernstein and Woodward had obtained their FD-302s (a "302" being the standard FBI interview reporting form) from a source within the Bureau and used them as the basis for their articles. Field agents generally had a dim view of reporters, doubting their enterprise and energy. It did not occur to them that an article might appear to have come from a 302 because the same person interviewed in the 302 had also talked to reporters, and said the same thing.

Bernstein and Woodward's September 11 story on Baldwin prompted just this kind of thinking at the FBI—that is, that the reporters had simply cribbed from the twenty-five-page-long 302 on Baldwin. Felt saw this assumption as a serendipitous opportunity for more mischief and misdirection. In an internal memo about leaks allegedly emanating from the Bureau, he wrote,

> The article which appeared in the *Washington Post* this morning appears to have been taken from the FD-302 of our interview with former S[pecial] A[gent] Baldwin. . . . I personally contacted SAC Kunkel to point out that it appeared the *Washington Post* or at least a reporter had access to the Baldwin FD-302. I told him he should forcibly remind all agents of the need to be most circumspect in talking about this case with anyone outside the Bureau.[18]

Four days later a federal grand jury returned its indictments in the Watergate break-in. The White House was relieved at their limited scope, and even deceived itself into believing (for a time) that the "Watergate problem" was destined to fade away, especially after the election. The narrowness of the indictments—only the five burglars and their two direct overseers, E. Howard Hunt and G. Gordon Liddy, were found culpable—stood in striking contrast to the wider conspiracy suggested by the press coverage. Indeed, the indictments seemed to confirm the official administration/campaign version of events as enunciated by John Mitchell. Notwithstanding the links between the campaign and the perpetrators, he had insisted that the burglars "were not operating on either [the CRP's] behalf or with our consent." Presenting Liddy and Hunt as the "big men" in the affair, of course, was an attempt to draw a line, and prevent the political fallout that would result if anyone higher up were implicated.[19]

It was a mistake, however, albeit an understandable one, to think that the press really was ahead of the Bureau or federal prosecutors in its understanding of the case. The parties ultimately responsible were not known, and the reasons for the activity were still shrouded—but this was not for lack of trying. The investigation had been given the highest priority. No resources had been spared, especially manpower in the Washington Field Office, where agents had been diverted from other responsibilities to assist in the Watergate investigation. Every lead had been followed vigorously, thoroughly, and imaginatively, and absolutely no limits had been placed on the investigation's scope since early July.[20]

Based on the information they already had, the prosecutors believed that the conspiracy went higher. But unless Hunt, Liddy, or McCord cracked, nothing could be proved in court, and they had to present the case and evidence they had developed before a jury, not what they *thought* was true. Their strategy, therefore, was to convict those who had been indicted and trust that the prospect of serious prison time would prompt them to talk. Their only deviation from this path would occur about ten days before the election, when they made a last-ditch, "special pitch" to the lawyers for McCord, judged the defendant most likely to break ranks first.[21]

If there was a flaw in this strategy, at least in terms of public perception, it was that Watergate was not a normal case. No one in the Justice Department recognized, much less factored in, the consequences from the FBI's largely covert war of succession. Over the next several weeks, Felt's guidance and leaks to the media would help open a yawning gap between the narrow legal case brought against the defendants, and perceptions about what the case truly involved and signified. The relentless disclosures in the *Post*—the symbiosis of Woodward/Bernstein's tireless legwork and Felt's assistance—would actually do little more than repli-cate the FBI's nonpublic findings, for they would be drawn from the same CRP informants who had contributed to the Bureau's understanding of the case. Nonetheless, the stories would heighten, if not create, the per-ception that the newspaper was far out in front of the government—that it was more interested in justice than was the Justice Department.[22]

The accelerated pace of disclosures served Felt's ends in two respects. Despite Nixon's seemingly impregnable lead in the polls, the weeks lead-ing up to the election would be highly sensitive. To politicians, only one poll really mattered—the one on election day—and so headline-grabbing revelations about Watergate would incite the White House even more in October than they had before Labor Day—especially since now that the narrow indictments had been issued, the story was supposed to dis-appear insofar as the White House was concerned. Pat Gray would be blamed, perhaps more than ever before, for failing to impose the disci-pline needed to keep the story out of the news. Simultaneously, the public impression—no matter how incorrect—would be fostered that the FBI's investigation had been less than thorough. That was bound to lessen Gray's chances of being nominated, or, if he were nominated, of being confirmed.

In any reasonably foreseeable scenario, Felt stood to win.

For the FBI agents working the case, the most disturbing disclosures began on Sunday, September 17—three days after Carl Bernstein knocked on the front door of a modest home on Montauk Street in Bethesda, Maryland.

Woodward and Bernstein had been working their way methodically through the CRP's employee roster—about 100 names—since mid-August, just after Woodward's meeting with Felt at his home; they tried to talk to those on the roster one by one. When doors weren't slammed in their faces they sometimes picked up a tidbit or two, but had come up with nothing to significantly advance the story.[23]

Their luck began to change when Bernstein realized that Millicent "Penny" Gleason had a security job with the CRP. Like Bernstein, Glea-son had grown up in the middle-class D.C. suburb of Silver Spring, Maryland, although their family backgrounds could hardly have been more different. Bernstein's parents were (as Bernstein himself once called them) "atheistic Jewish Communists" for whom Nixon was a *bête noire*. Penny came from a large Catholic family; her father, James Gleason, was a locally prominent Republican, and working for Nixon was a family tradition. Her father's first job after graduating law school, in 1951, had been as a research assistant to then-Senator Nixon. Penny wanted to be a police officer, an ambition that had led to a job under the CRP's director of security, James McCord.[24]

James Gleason was known for being plain-spoken and candid, and Penny shared these traits. When Bureau agents had first interviewed her at the CRP office, on June 30, with a CRP lawyer present, she had given only monosyllabic answers: yes or no. But the next morning she contacted the same agents to arrange a confidential interview. "I really have a lot to say [but] I couldn't say anything in front of the . . . [CRP] lawyer," she told them. Agents Charles Harvey and Paul Magallanes debriefed her for a total of seven hours, first in Magallanes's own car, and then in a Holiday Inn on Connecticut Avenue. The result was forty-seven pages of handwritten notes.[25]

Gleason disclosed that the CRP's initial attitude toward the FBI investigation was almost lighthearted. The organization assumed that the investigation would be a whitewash, and that the FBI was going through the motions only because the burglars had been caught in the act. But this complacency turned to panic once it became obvious the FBI intended to probe in depth. Gleason described the actions of a number of high-ranking CRP officials soon after the burglary, including the frantic purge of McCord's office files that had taken place. She said that some CRP employees, including Robert Odle, the director of administration, were not telling the truth in their interviews and were giving agents "busy work" leads they knew to be dead ends.[26]

Perhaps Gleason's most important contribution was to point the agents to another source. If you think I have a lot of information, she told Magallanes at the end of the session, "my friend [Judy Hoback] has even more information. She is the accountant for the CRP and is really frustrated as to what is happening." Hoback had been interviewed twice in the company of a CRP lawyer, but had said little. About a week after speaking with Gleason, Magallanes, along with agent John Mindermann, began reinterviewing Hoback. That first session took place in her Montauk Street home in Bethesda on July 18. It resulted in a nineteen-page FD-302.[27]

Along with the information provided by Alfred Baldwin and Hugh Sloan to federal prosecutors, Hoback's revelations represented some of the most direct information about the links between the burglars and the Nixon reelection effort. A petite thirty-five-year-old woman just 5 feet tall, newly widowed with a baby daughter to support, Hoback seemed an unlikely candidate to speak out given the pressure being exerted on CRP employees to remain silent. But she believed she was partly responsible for enabling criminal behavior and was deeply ashamed about her unwitting role. The least she could do was tell the truth.

Hoback said unequivocally that she believed campaign funds had been used for unlawful activities, such as the burglary. How do you know? the agents asked. "Because I'm the accountant," she replied. "I know what goes on here . . . where this money goes and to whom it's paid . . . McCord and Liddy." Hoback confirmed that large sums had gone to Liddy. By the time their investigation was over, Bureau agents would interview her privately on six separate occasions—more so than any other CRP employee.[28]

Now Bernstein began to follow the investigative trail blazed by FBI agents months earlier. In early September he had lunch with Gleason, who later reported back to the Bureau that Bernstein claimed to have access to FBI interviews and reports. About ten days later, on September 14, the *Post* reporter showed up on the doorstep of the home Hoback shared with her sister. It had been just over two months since her extensive debriefing by FBI agents, and it was the day before the indictments were to be handed down.[29]

When Hoback realized who Bernstein was, she blanched. "Oh, my God," she said, "you're from the *Washington Post*. You'll have to go, I'm sorry." Bernstein was not a large man, but Hoback found his presence overwhelming. He told her he knew that some CRP employees had gone back to the FBI after their initial sterile interviews, and that he thought Hoback was among them. "Where do you reporters get your information anyhow?" she asked. "That's what nobody at the [CRP] can figure out." By this time Bernstein had bummed a cigarette from Hoback's sister, who then offered him a cup of coffee. Curiosity started to get the better of Hoback. "Somebody is certainly giving you good information if you knew I went back to the prosecutors," she said.[30]

She then told him, often word for word, what she had disclosed to the FBI beginning in mid-July. And her revelations had the same impact on him as they had had on the agents. Here was a knowledgeable witness with direct evidence about the link between the break-in and the president's reelection apparatus.[31]

Woodward had had few direct meetings with Felt since their early August discussion in Felt's living room. But now was no time to start the cumbersome signaling system they had agreed on. Utilizing it would delay everything by at least a full day, and Woodward was too anxious to get Hoback's story into the paper to wait. He broke the rule about telephone contact and called Deep Throat to read him the entire draft of the article Bernstein and Woodward intended to submit. Based largely on Hoback's disclosures, it revealed that high CRP officials had been involved in funding the burglars. Felt seemed nervous, but when Woodward was finished reading, he told him the story was "too soft," adding, "You can go much stronger." As Woodward excitedly confided in fellow reporter James Mann, "I just talked to my friend at the FBI. I think we're on to a whole new level on this thing." The result, published on Sunday, September 17, and titled "Spy Funds Linked to GOP Aides," was one of Bernstein and Woodward's most important articles. It indicated that the federal indictments had not pierced the conspiracy and that the answers were to be found at the CRP.[32]

When Paul Magallanes picked up his copy of the *Post* that day and read the page-one story, he felt a chill run up and down his back. "Oh my God," he thought. "That's my interview!" It was as if his 302 had been printed in the paper. About the only thing left out, he thought, was that he had interviewed Hoback on such-and-such a date. None of the agents working on the Watergate case had ever experienced anything like this before.[33]

And Magallanes's reaction was muted when compared to the response at the White House. The indictments handed down on September 15 had left the White House feeling like it had dodged a bullet; no less an authority than the Reverend Billy Graham had assured Nixon that the Democrats were "overplaying" the break-in. "It's too clouded," he told the president. "People think the Democrats placed it themselves." But now the *Post* had virtually issued a declaration that it wasn't going to back off the story.[34]

Woodward and Bernstein were already preparing a sequel before the ink was dry on the first Hoback-sourced article. They went back to her home on Sunday afternoon, and she reluctantly let them in; it was better than having them seen camped on her doorstep. She admitted that the indictments disturbed her. "I went down in good faith to the grand jury and testified, and obviously the results are not there," she said. "My feeling is that the FBI turns the information in and it goes upstairs."[35]

She added an interesting tidbit concerning Hugh Sloan, the former CRP treasurer. Sloan had abruptly and inexplicably resigned after the break-in. Now Hoback disclosed why. He "wanted no part of what he then knew was going on," she told the reporters. Her words appeared verbatim, though anonymously, in their next story.[36]

Once the reporters were back in the newsroom, Woodward retreated to make another call to Felt. There was a certain amount of circularity in Woodward and Felt's dealings. Bernstein and Woodward had used information and perspective gleaned from Deep Throat to question Hoback. That fact seemed to give her some psychological comfort: She was merely confirming or denying information the reporters already had, rather than going into long exegeses that dealt with new territory. She could honestly say that she hadn't *told* Bernstein and Woodward anything they didn't already know—sort of. Indeed, whenever possible the pair adopted a casual stance and tried to create the impression they were only seeking clarification of a few points—you know, in the interests of accuracy and precision; after all, it wasn't in anyone's interest to have incorrect facts presented to the public. Then Woodward would go back to Felt to corroborate, and sometimes expand on, what Hoback had confirmed.[37]

But this time Felt was testy. For the second time in as many days the *Post* reporter was paying no heed to the signaling system that had been set up. That cavalier disregard of the safeguards they had supposedly agreed on put Felt at risk. After Woodward identified himself there was a long pause, and Felt said that this would be their last telephone conversation. In the wake of Sunday's story, the White House would be redoubling its effort to find the source of the *Post*'s information. Still, Felt went on to confirm—actually, to recorroborate—Hoback's information.[38]

After Woodward hung up, he was sorry he had made the call. As he later wrote, "His friend was displeased, even angry at him." Felt, as if to telegraph his annoyance, initially said that from now on, he would not go beyond "confirming and perhaps clarifying information . . . that they were already reasonably sure of." At the very end of their talk, though, he had softened a bit. If Woodward absolutely had to arrange a prompt meeting, Felt told him, he could call—but he was not to identify himself on the phone. "Just say something or ask for someone else," Felt said. He would recognize Woodward's voice and go to the parking garage that night.[39]

Despite Felt's irritation at Woodward's disregard for proper tradecraft, he never cut off the relationship. Indeed, his enthusiasm for the operation sometimes got the better of him, leading him to do much more than confirm information acquired elsewhere. One such occasion concerned an October 6 *Post* story about campaign funds being laundered through Mexico.

The nature of an investigative series demands that each story push the envelope a little further; thus the *Post* was competing against itself in some sense. As *Time* and other publications began devoting resources to Watergate, that only ratcheted up the pressure to be the first with exclusives. And then, in early October, the *Los Angeles Times* soundly beat the *Post* to what was considered one of the most important stories at the time: the eyewitness account of Alfred C. Baldwin.

Baldwin's name had been circulating widely among reporters ever since the *Post*'s September 11 article, which conveyed the gist of his story without disclosing his identity. Subsequently, Baldwin's name was leaked to a *Newsweek* correspondent—probably the result of Edward Bennett Williams acting on his own adage to "leak things slowly"—and articles reporting the *Newsweek* scoop appeared on September 17 in the *Los Angeles Times, Washington Post,* and *New York Times.* A reporters' scrum soon formed around Baldwin and his lawyers; everyone wanted to be the first to run an account that quoted him directly. There were even rumors of movie rights being dangled for exclusive access to his story. "Ugly fuckers, you reporters," Baldwin's lawyer told Woodward as he vied, among others, for the prized interview. On October 5, Jack Nelson and Ronald J. Ostrow of the *Los Angeles Times* won the coveted interview, to Bradlee's great and obvious chagrin. He hated being scooped, and even Woodward and Bernstein had to admit it was the "most vivid piece of journalism" published to date about Watergate. "I would like to have had that one," Bradlee said to them the day the story appeared.[40]

As if to reassert its clear lead on media coverage of Watergate, the *Post* then did something that was practically unheard of. On October 6, its front page featured three Watergate-related stories. Two were Bernstein and Woodward originals and the third was a republication of the *Los Angeles Times* piece on Baldwin from the day before, which Bradlee had vetoed from running in the *Washington Star,* which had wanted to publish it.[41]

Woodward and Bernstein, naturally, were anxious to get back on top by publishing something dramatic. One of their stories hastily followed up the Baldwin scoop with a supposedly new wrinkle (which turned out to be woefully wrong, making the article the reporters' first major mistake). The other story was a Felt special: with Deep Throat's assistance, they had been able to garner some striking new details about the Mexico money train story.[42]

The money-laundering article had been conceived well before the Baldwin interview broke, as one in a remarkable string of *Post* scoops that began in mid-September and lasted for some six weeks. Many of the pieces concerned fund-raising at the CRP and a "slush fund" used to finance the break-in. The *Post's* editors considered this line of inquiry crucial to breaking the back of the CRP's cover story, and by extension, the narrowness of the indictments. If they kept hammering away at how the funds were raised and who controlled the purse strings, they could eventually demonstrate that the claim that Liddy had diverted money for his own unauthorized use was dubious, even laughable.[43]

The *Post's* October 6 Mexican-money article cited "FBI sources," "government law enforcement sources," and FBI "findings" for most of the information about how $89,000 of a $100,000 contribution from the Gulf Resources and Chemical Corporation had wended its way from Houston to Mexico City the previous April before finally ending up with Bernard L. Barker, one of the burglars. Although Woodward obtained corroboration from Richard Haynes, an attorney for Gulf Resources, whose president, Robert Allen, was Nixon's chief Texas fund-raiser, Felt supplied the spine of the story. Some aspects of the transaction were already public knowledge via articles in the *New York Times* by Walter Rugaber and could be found in reports by the General Accounting Office and the House Banking Committee. But no one had gotten all the details nailed down. Deep Throat gave Woodward a step-by-step description of the activities during a garage meeting at 3 a.m. in early October. It had taken Woodward an inordinate amount of time to find a taxi that night—he had left his apartment at 1:30—but Felt waited patiently for him.[44]

Deep Throat was "considerably more talkative than usual" when Woodward explained that he and Bernstein were "particularly interested in doing a story about the $89,000" that had flowed from Gulf Resources to the CRP. Felt, without any prodding, began outlining the money trail.[45]

It had been a very convoluted transaction, and because Felt, as usual, would not allow any note taking, Woodward had to ask him to go over the steps a second time. The *Post's* account included names of companies and corporate officers, dollar amounts, and dates that were seemingly drawn straight from the FBI's investigative files.[46] Specifically:

- The first two steps Felt outlined to Woodward constituted the article's first FBI finding—that Gulf Resources had transferred $100,000 to its defunct Mexican subsidiary in April.
- The next two provided the basis for the article's second FBI

finding—that the Mexican subsidiary then passed the $100,000 to attorney Manuel Ogarrio as an inflated payment for "legal services" rendered.

- Steps five and six formed the basis for the article's third finding—that Ogarrio converted the funds to four cashier's checks and $11,000 in cash, all of which was sent to Texas initially and then rushed to Washington. The checks were subsequently deposited in Barker's Florida bank account.[47]

Last, the article cited Felt's summary finding—that the laundered funds linked the burglars with the re-election committee but "didn't finance the Watergate operation directly"—almost verbatim, but attributed it to "one knowledgeable Republican source," in keeping with Woodward's promise never to quote Felt, even anonymously, or attribute information to him.[48]

Felt's contribution, in this instance, revealed an occasional willingness to override the parameters he himself had set in early August. Supplying raw information developed by the FBI, of course, only underscored that the leaks had to be coming from the Bureau, notwithstanding Gray's assurances to the contrary.

One of the many common misrepresentations that would later arise was that Felt's most valuable piece of advice to Woodward was "follow the money," a line made famous by the film version of *All the President's Men.* He never actually said that, at least according to Woodward's contemporaneous notes, and it now appears likely that this useful thought was actually dispensed by Henry E. Petersen, or possibly Edward Bennett Williams. But Felt did advise Woodward to keep digging, and he provided valuable tools with which to dig. In the period between the break-in and the 1972 election, front-page stories about Watergate appeared seventy-nine times in the *Washington Post,* versus thirty-three times in the *New York Times,* with no other newspapers even close. Still, the public perception was that the *Times* almost wasn't covering the story at all, it was so cautious. At the time, Robert Phelps, the newspaper's Washington editor, believed that Woodward and Bernstein were erecting faulty "bridges" between the evidence they gathered and implications they drew from it. "The editors at the *Post* should have stopped the Watergate reporters from going on too long without hard facts," Phelps said in February 1973, just before the Watergate cover-up burst open.[49]

Unwittingly, Phelps was echoing criticisms that were being made internally at the *Post,* most often by Richard Harwood. A close friend of

Bradlee's, Harwood reportedly argued that the story—if true—was too big for the two metro reporters who had nurtured it. Alternately, he worried that Woodward and Bernstein were taking the newspaper on a giant joy ride. Why were so many of their sources anonymous? As the story ballooned in the late summer and early fall, Bradlee contemplated turning it over to the national desk, where many of the reporters thought, like Harwood, that it was just too big for metro. But Rosenfeld and Simons resisted, and the story stayed with "Woodstein."[50]

One reason that Simons thought the story should remain with metro was because whenever he attempted to add another reporter or two to the investigation, all they were able to produce were analyses or thumb-sucking articles. They could not advance the story because they had no real sources, and Woodward and Bernstein jealously guarded their painstakingly developed sources—above all, Deep Throat. To anyone with experience in newsrooms, this smacked of a familiar tactic employed by reporters when they want to protect their investment in a story, and keep other reporters away and their editors off balance: invent a "secret source" who only talks to them. Of course, in this instance it conveniently happened to be true.[51]

Indeed, there was a reason Woodward and Bernstein "believed in what they were doing," and continued to build their bridges amid so much doubt from their peers, internally and externally, and despite the public's apathy: that reason was Mark Felt.

It was during this same period, the late summer/early fall of 1972, when utilization of Felt was at its height, that managing editor Howard Simons irreverently dubbed Woodward's secret source with a "sexy moniker," borrowed from the first X-rated film to cross over to mainstream theaters. Despite the familiarity suggested by a nickname, the three editors working most closely with Woodward and Bernstein—Simons, metro editor Harry Rosenfeld, and city editor Barry Sussman (essentially the Watergate editor)—remained almost completely in the dark about who Deep Throat was or his exact position. That made it impossible for them to plumb his motives and meant they were wholly reliant on Woodward's cues. Nor were they informed that Bernstein knew who Deep Throat was.

In a 1973 interview with Woodward and Bernstein, Simons explained why he decided not to insist on knowing Deep Throat's identity, even though he routinely asked his reporters for the names of their sources. "Because you [Woodward] really didn't want to tell us," he said. Similarly, Harry Rosenfeld once asked Woodward, and "we agreed he would not tell me." The editors knew, at most, that Deep Throat was a high official in the Justice Department (although in October 1972 Ben Bradlee would insist upon learning a bit more). This description, of course, was true, but only technically. It was also misleading, because it led naturally to the presumption that Deep Throat was a principled Justice Department lawyer rather than an FBI executive involved in a once-in-a-generation struggle for power.[52]

With Woodward under the illusion that Felt's motive was altruistic, little wonder that Barry Sussman, for one, operated under the belief that Deep Throat was "thoroughly disgusted by Watergate."[53]

CHAPTER SEVEN

Richard Nixon's Own "Deep Throat"

October 1972

Now why the hell would he do that?
—*Richard Nixon, upon learning that Mark Felt was leaking*

As Watergate-related stories continued unabated, Gray surely sensed the permanent appointment slipping from his grasp. He faced problems on two fronts: the public perception that the FBI's investigation had been less than rigorous and/or exhaustive, despite his efforts to claim otherwise, and the White House's perception that he could not stem the leaks. He might be able to successfully rebut the first charge, as senators did not always believe what they read in the newspapers. But there seemed to be no way around the second. The White House continually badgered him about leaks, but nothing he tried worked.

His most drastic step, aside from ordering multiple internal investigations, was to remove Robert Kunkel as special agent in charge of the Washington Field Office in late September. The ostensible reason for the demotion was that Kunkel had failed to write a truthful report about an incident involving an undercover agent who was stripped of his gun during a protest by antiwar demonstrators. Gray said he wanted to send a message: that lying about an episode (as was common during the Hoover years) would get agents in trouble, not the event itself. In an editorial, the *Washington Post* praised Gray for showing little toleration for "lies being sent in from the field." It was long past time for the Bureau to get over its fetish about never being embarrassed in public.[1]

To be sure, Kunkel was guilty of the infraction as charged. But the underlying reason he was being transferred to the far less prestigious field office in St. Louis was that he had fallen into disfavor. Gray had come to believe that either Kunkel was leaking, or else he could not control the leaks coming out of the Washington Field Office. The new special agent in charge was John J. "Jack" McDermott, a twenty-two-year veteran who had been running the Bureau outpost in Alexandria, Virginia. Unlike the unpopular Kunkel, who was known for treating subordinates badly while behaving obsequiously to higher-ups, McDermott had a reputation as a straight shooter who was widely admired by the rank-and-file. Perhaps a greater sense of cohesion and loyalty within the field office would yield better results—at least Gray hoped so.[2]

There would be no noticeable effect from this diminishment in power of the Felt faction, as the *Post* kept up its reporting of Watergate. Around this time, however, Felt's scheme ran into a glitch. In late October, the White House discovered, in a roundabout manner no one could have foreseen, that Felt was the prime leaker. Whatever slim chance he had of becoming the director evaporated; indeed, Nixon's aides were barely able to persuade the president not to fire Felt immediately.

The chain of events that led to Felt's unmasking began on September 28, when Bernstein received a telephone call from a man who identified himself only as a "government lawyer." He told Bernstein that he had nothing to do with Watergate but that a friend of his, another lawyer, had been approached in June 1971 to do undercover political work for the Nixon campaign. After some digging, Bernstein was able to come up with the name of the recruiter: Donald Segretti, a thirty-one-year-old lawyer then living in Los Angeles. Bernstein checked with two of the prosecutors, Earl Silbert and Donald Campbell, and the FBI's Watergate case agent, Angelo Lano. Bernstein was startled to learn that Segretti's name had surfaced in the investigation, but none of the three would say how except that Segretti was not directly linked to the break-in. What did this new wrinkle mean? Woodward, who had initially been skeptical about the tip, agreed with Bernstein that a meeting with Deep Throat was in order.[3]

At the time, the *Post* was still feeling the sting of having been beaten soundly on the Baldwin interview and was hunting for a dramatic scoop. There were just a few weeks to go before the election, which meant only a little time remained to get the Watergate story out to the electorate and show that the break-in was no "third-rate burglary." But what did it really signify? Everyone from Bradlee on down to Bernstein and Woodward had been wrestling with the larger meaning of the scandal for months. Things didn't add up. In itself the bugging made little sense, especially given Nixon's impregnable lead in the polls. Yet scattered bits and pieces suggested it might have been part of a larger scheme. E. Howard Hunt's activities while on the White House payroll, including his stint as a "plumber," were not even close to being fully accounted for. And then there was the infamous "Canuck letter," which had badly damaged the candidacy of Senator Edmund Muskie (D-Maine), Nixon's toughest potential opponent. Published in the *Manchester Union Leader* on February 24, 1972, less than two weeks before the New Hampshire primary, the letter-to-the-editor alleged that Muskie had used an ethnic slur to refer to Americans of French-Canadian descent (many of whom, of course, lived in New Hampshire). Where had it come from?[4]

In the wee hours of October 9, Woodward and Felt held their longest-ever garage meeting, a grueling session that lasted from 1:30 to 6 a.m. The meeting, which was described in detail in *All the President's Men*, was the strangest one yet between the two men. "We really need help on this one," Woodward pleaded. He described everything Bernstein had developed about Segretti, including interviews with three of his former army buddies, all lawyers, who all said that he had tried to hire them in 1971 as undercover agents working for Nixon's re-election. Yet no one Bernstein or Woodward had spoken with could, or would, explain how Segretti fit in.

Fortunately, Deep Throat was in a relatively expansive mood. He offered a means of looking at the big picture. "'There is a way to untie the Watergate knot,'" he said. "'Everything points in the direction of what was called 'offensive security.'" By that Felt meant the standard techniques intelligence services like the CIA and the FBI used against adversaries or threats, which included the distribution of mis- and disinformation. Woodward did not realize that Felt was now using these same techniques on him. For interspersed in the "big picture" Felt now painted would be some plain untruths—things Felt didn't know because the FBI didn't know them; exaggerations or misrepresentations of facts the Bureau had developed; and falsifications of what Felt knew to be the truth.[5]

At first Felt demurred when asked about Segretti specifically. "'I don't know about Segretti, I just don't know,'" he said. "'I can't tell you anyway.'" The FBI, in fact, had known about him since June, but had lost interest because Segretti's misdemeanors had no connection to the Watergate break-in. "'Maybe you turned up' a nut," Felt told Woodward. "They [i.e., the White House] hate the news media and will set you up." Yet even if Felt had forgotten about this minor character after June, he had just received a reminder on October 7, two days before this latest rendezvous with Woodward. The memo referred to the fact that Carl Bernstein was known to be asking around about Segretti, who had been "hired by White House staff members to harass Democratic candidates." Felt was plainly dissembling.[6]

Nonetheless, Deep Throat still intimated that he knew everything there was to know about Nixon's electoral sabotage. What he said stoked

Woodward into believing there had been a massive effort to injure and subvert the Democrats, with Segretti as the point man. It was all one big ball of wax, Felt suggested, and everything was connected—the break-in, E. Howard Hunt and the plumbers, the disparate reports of dirty tricks on the campaign trail. After all, the FBI doesn't do 1,500 interviews (the number given publicly as evidence of the thoroughness of the investigation) and come up empty-handed, Felt said. The White House had sought to subvert the electoral process through the use of "more than 50" undercover operatives. "Not one of the 'games' [undercover operations] we unearthed was free-lance," Felt claimed. "This is important: every one was tied in."[7]

There was no question that Segretti's actions, instigated and financed by the White House, were an enormous political embarrassment. Yet the moon-faced lawyer was, as John Dean memorably put it, a "prankster who wore Weejuns," not the "point man of a brown-shirt horde." Segretti was supposed to be the Republicans' answer to Dick Tuck, a practical joker for Democrats who had been pulling devilish stunts on Nixon since his 1950 Senate campaign. One of the reasons Segretti only approached lawyers initially was that he did not want his hired hands to do anything illegal; those were Segretti's marching orders from his college roommate, Dwight Chapin, the White House appointments secretary (and former advance man) who was responsible for hiring Segretti at Haldeman's and Nixon's request.

Only after being turned down by his army buddies did Segretti seek out eager young Republicans willing to act as hecklers or plant stink bombs at Democratic rallies. His so-called "black advance" schemes—some of which were funny, others cruel, and some merely tasteless—barely rose to the level of being misdemeanors in some states and did not violate federal statutes. His small, amateurish network—never more than twenty-two operatives, half of whom received less than $50 ($240 in 2011 dollars) for one-time services—was no match for the Democrats' uncanny capacity for self-inflicted wounds during the 1972 campaign.[8]

Apart from lumping in the Segretti matter, most of Felt's distortions in the 4½-hour conversation with Woodward did not make it into print in the *Post* article that would be published the next day; either they were beside the point, or they resisted quick corroboration. One instance of the latter was Felt's patently false claim that the plumbers' mission was "not really to check leaks to the news media but to give them out; recipients include[d] . . . [columnists] Jack Anderson, Rowland Evans and Robert Novak, the *Washington Post, New York Times,* and *Chicago Tribune*." Another example was Felt's allusion to a "Hunt-like set-up" involving Jack Anderson's allegation about Senator Thomas Eagleton. In July 1972, the muckraking columnist had written an article asserting that Eagleton, then the Democratic vice presidential nominee, had been arrested for drunk driving in his home state of Missouri. In fact, E. Howard Hunt had nothing whatsoever to do with the story; Anderson's source had been True Davis, a Missouri Democrat who had run unsuccessfully against Eagleton in the primary contest for the senatorial nomination in 1968.[9]

What Felt had to say about the Canuck letter, however, did get published.

Toward the end of the marathon session, Woodward began to get frustrated by the vagueness of much of what Felt was saying. He was offering up generalities; the *Post* needed specifics. "What about the Canuck letter?" the reporter asked as Felt was walking away. This was Felt's reaction, as described in *All the President's Men* (as distinct from Woodward's contemporaneous typewritten notes, which contain no such quote): "Deep Throat stopped and turned around. 'It was a White House operation—done inside the gates surrounding the White House and the [Old] Executive Office Building. Is that enough?'" Deep Throat then gave Woodward some parting advice—"'Write what you can provide evidence for in court'"—along with a standard reminder: "Don't quote any of that . . . 'not one word' in [the] paper . . . 'this is just for your background.'"[10]

Felt had no basis for making the assertion about the Canuck letter, as the FBI had simply never investigated it. His claim about it, moreover, was false.[11]

Exactly why Felt chose this encounter to begin disinforming and informing Woodward in equal parts is not completely clear, even with the benefit of hindsight. On the other hand, there is no reason to believe that Felt would perpetually treat a cub reporter better than he had Sandy Smith, who had been told plausible falsehoods as early as June. The truth was, Felt had nothing but boundless contempt for the fourth estate. "I don't like newspapers," he had once admitted openly to Woodward, expressing disdain for their inexactitude and shallowness. Felt might as well have added the ease with which they could be manipulated in their quest for a story.[12]

Felt's delivery of false as well as true information on October 9 underscores the differences in how he and Woodward regarded their relationship. Woodward believed that Felt invariably told less than he knew, which was frequently exasperating. But what he did disclose, Woodward thought, was solid and authoritative—he "seemed committed to the best version of the obtainable truth," as *All the President's Men* later claimed. Moreover, Woodward believed that he and Felt were on the same side, allies in the struggle to expose the facts and larger truth. For Felt, however, their relationship was simply a means to the end of becoming FBI director. If that end was best served by salting the information he gave Woodward with details that had only a casual relationship with the facts, so be it.[13]

Felt could not be certain the Watergate stories would continue to fall on a deaf or uninterested electorate. Where was the tipping point? He probably saw himself treading a narrow path. Gray's unsuitability for the directorship had already been demonstrated, probably indelibly. That meant Felt's interest in having more Watergate-related stories in the press was correspondingly diminished. Yet he could not very well abruptly withdraw from a tenacious reporter, like Woodward had proven to be, and say, in effect, never mind. Watergate coverage had become a juggernaut at the *Post*, and Woodward had become deeply invested. Felt could influence (but not control) Woodward's interest in featuring Segretti. But by exaggerating the White House's sophomoric attempts at sabotage, and by misleadingly including the Canuck letter in the scheme, Felt was simultaneously providing the administration with ammunition to refute the story. The allegations would be made, a forceful rebuttal issued, the *Post* would stand behind its story, and the bottom line would be a confusing miasma of charges and countercharges—all of which would leave the White House steaming at Gray, and the electorate unsure about what, if anything, to make of Watergate.

That was a classic counterintelligence technique.

The Bernstein and Woodward article appeared the next day, October 10—exactly four weeks before the election. Occupying the prestigious upper-right quadrant of the front page, it was boldly headlined "FBI Finds Nixon Aides Sabotaged Democrats." It claimed the Bureau had established that the break-in "stemmed from a massive campaign of political spying and sabotage conducted on behalf of President Nixon's re-election" by officials in the White House and CRP. The overall thrust was derived wholly from information that Felt had provided or confirmed.[14]

In its official analysis of the article, the FBI deemed the bulk of it "pure conjecture." Its conclusions were hyperbolic, and it contained many untrue assertions, including the statement that federal investigators had found that the sabotage effort involved "leaking false and manufactured items to the press." The FBI had developed no such information, and the claim that it had uncovered "at least 50 undercover Nixon operatives" was also bogus. The Bureau's investigation of Segretti had not turned up any of his recruits; indeed, the *Post*'s description of his attempt to bring aboard his three army buddies was far more detailed than what the FBI knew about the matter.[15]

The *Post*'s editors didn't view the article, however, as a detour that mixed two unrelated things together. Everyone involved in reporting the Watergate story regarded it as the "centerpiece" of the newspaper's preelection coverage. It was not based on hearsay, as the *Columbia Journalism Review* later noted, for "the conclusions, and the frame of reference, were clearly attributed to FBI agents." It seemed to tie together the scandal's disparate strands and to finally put the break-in into context. Everything could be traced to what the Nixon campaign called "offensive security," the article alleged, quoting Felt in the guise of an "investigator." Both then and later Woodward and Bernstein considered the "assault on democracy" story their single most important Watergate article, as did newsmen outside the *Post*. Even Robert Phelps—the rival *Times* editor who had been deeply skeptical about the *Post*'s coverage—acknowledged that the seemingly seminal story "cemented" his arch-rival's lead. "From then on, Watergate was rightly regarded as Woodward and Bernstein's story," he later wrote.[16]

The article—also described as the "seminal story that changed everything"—had a decisive impact internally as well. The day it appeared, Bradlee decided to invite Bernstein and Woodward to lunch at the opulent Madison Hotel nearby. The time had come to learn more about his young reporters' sources, including the one mischievously dubbed "Deep Throat" by Howard Simons. As Bradlee explained to Woodward (Bernstein had to attend a funeral), "our cocks are on the chopping block now and I just want to know a little more about this. . . . Tell me again you're sure, and that Carl is sure, and that these are people who have no big ax to grind on the front page of the *Washington Post*." Woodward then described how the stories had been put together, and when he came to the matter of Deep Throat identified him by his "job, experience, access, and expertise." That was sufficient to satisfy Bradlee. Either he did not sense a need to probe Felt's motive, or Woodward persuaded him of his own view—that Felt's design was an entirely honorable one.[17]

Gray—again—was out of town when the article appeared and did not get a briefing about it until the following day. Although the White House was livid, Felt downplayed the article when he told Gray about it over the telephone. The *Post* is "talking about [an] anonymous letter sent to [the] *Manchester [Union Leader]*," he said. This statement reflected the central role the Canuck letter had assumed in the article. After the garage meeting with Felt, Woodward and Bernstein had established to their satisfaction that Ken Clawson, the deputy director of White House communications, was the likely culprit behind the Canuck letter, despite his vehement denial. And so they had written, "Law enforcement sources"—including Felt—"said that probably the best example of the sabotage was the fabrication—by a White House aide—of a celebrated letter . . . alleging that . . . Muskie condoned a racial slur." When conveying the details to Pat Gray, Felt accurately noted, "The FBI has *nothing in their reports* [emphasis added] on this." That was true. The Bureau had never investigated the incident because it had nothing whatsoever to do with Segretti, much less the break-in.[18]

When Gray returned to Washington on October 12, John Dean called to complain bitterly about the "apparent FBI leaks" in the piece. Upon reading it, Gray himself had been struck by the article's claim that much of the information came from FBI files, and he told Dean that an internal investigation was already in the works. The acting director had marked up a copy of the article and asked Charlie Bates—from the Felt faction—to answer ten specific questions about the piece. The fact that the article misrepresented what was supposedly in the Bureau's files made it easy for Bates to "prove" that no one from the FBI could have been involved. His most frequent answers to Gray's scribbled questions were "We developed no such information" and "The foregoing statement is absolutely false."[19]

Under normal circumstances, it would have been a cinch for the White House to discredit the article convincingly (and to be sure, CRP spokesman DeVan Shumway tried to disparage it, calling the story "not only fiction but a collection of absurdities"). Yet overall, the White House was constrained from launching a counterattack. Clawson's denial of authorship of the Canuck letter was included in the article, so that specific issue had already been countered. And if the White House made Segretti available to rebut the allegations of a massive scheme to disrupt Democrats, it would have to explain why it wasn't being equally forthcoming about the break-in. The White House, moreover, could not afford to have Segretti's paymaster, Herbert Kalmbach—the president's personal attorney—dragged into the public eye and scrutinized. By this time Kalmbach had personally raised $220,000 (more than $1.1 million in 2011 dollars) in "hush money" for the Watergate burglars since their arrest in June.

With no other option available to the White House, it simply continued to stonewall. Press secretary Ron Ziegler said to discuss the charges, or even to deny them, would give them an undeserved dignity. The most revealing administration comment on the October 10 article came from John Ehrlichman, during an appearance on one of the Sunday news shows. It was important to distinguish between the Watergate bugging, "which involved a crime," he said, and pranks or acts of intelligence gathering, like "finding out the other fellow's schedule."[20]

Time magazine weighed in on October 16 with a piece by Sandy Smith that marginally advanced the Segretti angle but didn't endorse the sweeping claims made by the *Post*. "Information in the Justice Department's files establishes a direct link between the White House and a Los Angeles attorney named Donald H. Segretti" who had been paid to subvert and disrupt Democratic campaigns, Smith reported. He presented several new details that probably came from the Felt faction, including how and when the Bureau had stumbled across Segretti; who had hired him (Dwight Chapin); and the fact that Kalmbach had paid him. The *Time* account prompted a follow-up Woodward and Bernstein article stating (without any basis) that *Time* was "apparently using different sources than the *Post*."[21]

Afterwards, both publications continued trying to advance the Watergate story incrementally in the days remaining before the election. *Time* published another lengthy article on October 23, which caused almost as much consternation in the White House as the *Post*'s October 10 story had. The story also prompted an exchange between Gray and Felt that was beyond ironic. The acting director turned to Felt and asked him who he thought was leaking to *Time*. Felt replied, "[Charlie Bates] says [Sandy Smith's] source is someone in the Department of Justice and it's the same as Bernstein and Woodward's."[22]

The leapfrogging *Post* and *Time* articles helped make Watergate a story of national importance, and the all-important national evening news programs began to stir. Over two nights in late October, the *CBS Evening News* devoted an extraordinary twenty-two minutes to the scandal, thus validating the *Post*'s months-long devotion. Although CBS did not supply any new information, as Ben Bradlee later observed, "The Great White Father, Walter Cronkite, the most trusted man in America . . . blessed the story by spending so much time on it." Since there were no documents to display, several of the visuals in Cronkite's broadcasts consisted entirely of montages of *Washington Post* front pages.[23]

The new sabotage and subversion angle not only raised the ante on media coverage, however. It also led to Felt's unmasking. Nine days after the *Post*'s "centerpiece" article appeared, White House chief of staff Bob Haldeman advised the president that he had received a reliable report by way of John Dean about the ultimate source. "Gray doesn't know who the leak is," he said, "[but we do]. . . . and it's very high up—Mark Felt." Just a few days earlier, Haldeman and the president had decided this latest leak could only have come from the FBI, Justice Department, or grand jury, but they could not settle on the culprit, although the FBI seemed the most likely by far. But now they finally knew for certain.[24]

Henry E. Petersen, the head of the Criminal Division at the Justice Department, had given this precious information to Dean. Nor was it the first time he had been useful, or "darn good" to the administration, as Haldeman had put it in August. From the very onset of the Watergate investigation, Petersen had made a point of being helpful and mindful of the White House's interests. One of the first FBI teletypes after the burglary had noted that "Petersen is closely following investigation . . . and desires all new infor[mation] developed furnished to him for passage to White House." Subsequently, he had given Dean regular reports about the status of the criminal case from the Justice Department's perspective, including the gist of testimony before the grand jury—something expressly forbidden. Because many of the investigative advances in the case were made inside the confines of the grand jury, no single stream of information was more important to Dean in his role as the Watergate desk officer; Petersen, in effect, was an unwitting enabler of the cover-up.[25]

Petersen had also worked hard to make sure the prosecutors kept their legal focus as narrow as possible—namely, on the break-in itself. As early as June 20, three days after the break-in, Dean had warned him that the White House "could not withstand a wide-open investigation." And although Petersen was a career official, a Democrat, and not a Nixon loyalist, he had done everything to heed that warning. With two decades of experience at Justice, he knew that a criminal case can only be limited before an investigation commences; after that point it becomes virtually impossible to stop the wheels from turning. He was, at bottom, instinctually and overly deferential to whomever occupied the White House, for he simply could not conceive that a felony would be hatched in the Oval Office. And so, in keeping with his general cooperativeness, Petersen now told the White House what he had learned confidentially from an unidentified lawyer affiliated with the offending publication: Mark Felt was the leaker.[26]

Nixon was stunned. For weeks he had been attributing the leaks to some "low-level shit-ass," some closet liberal at the Justice Department probably, or perhaps a government secretary. But Mark Felt? "Now why the hell would he do that?" Nixon asked Haldeman, sounding genuinely bewildered—almost as if Felt should have known the president was going to dispense with Gray, and probably appoint Felt in his stead. Haldeman, too, had had enough dealings with Felt to recognize his obvious ambition, and that seemed entirely incongruous with the allegation. Just three weeks earlier, Felt had offered to plant a story with a friendly reporter on the West Coast after the California office of Nixon's longtime physician, Dr. John C. Lungren, was burgled and Nixon's file rifled through. The White House had thought that drawing attention to the California break-in might help offset the Watergate burglary, and the FBI executive had been only too happy to help. Now the president was being told that he was the wellspring of the Watergate leaks. What was going on? What did Felt figure to gain?[27]

"It's hard to think what would make him do that, but there may be bitterness over there that we didn't put Felt in the top spot," Nixon speculated. Haldeman countered, more accurately, "I think he *wants* to be in the top spot," to which Nixon said only, "That's a helluva way." Although they had hit squarely on Felt's motive after just a few minutes of rumination, the insight didn't take hold. Haldeman went on to talk about Felt acting in "reprisal" for not getting the directorship. Later, the president and his chief of staff wondered if Felt were Jewish; all American Jews were presumed to be liberal Democrats and therefore political antagonists.[28]

Haldeman then observed that no matter why Felt was leaking, nothing much could be done about it. With that, Nixon exploded. "Can't *do* anything?" he roared. "*Never!*" Haldeman evenly responded that firing Felt would "do more harm than good." The president's most trusted adviser, John Mitchell, who knew Felt as well as anyone in the administration, strongly believed that if the White House were to "move on him, Christ, he'll go out and unload everything," Haldeman explained. Felt "*knows* everything that's to be known in the FBI," he emphasized.

Nixon's response was a single word: "Shit." But he recognized the soundness of the advice. If he yielded to temptation and "sack[ed] the sonuvabitch" or forced his transfer to a backwater like Butte, Montana, and Felt did respond by talking to the national press, the political repercussions could be enormous.[29]

In essence, the reason for covering up the break-in in the first place now became the reason for not doing anything about Felt. The burglars could not be forsaken because they knew too much about pre-Watergate crimes; similarly, Felt had to be treated gingerly because he also knew too much about the illegal, unethical, and politically controversial actions taken by the administration since 1969. Nixon and Haldeman agreed on one step nonetheless: Pat Gray had to understand that he "*must* not have confidence in Mark Felt any more."[30]

Felt remained very much on the president's mind the next day. Before a campaign swing through Pennsylvania, Nixon met with Haldeman for twenty minutes. Nixon had been expertly schooled in Washington's Byzantine ways, starting with the tortuous Alger Hiss case, which began with Whittaker Chambers's testimony about Hiss's membership in a clandestine Communist cell before the House Committee on Un-American Activities. Now Nixon worried about several things. The information Petersen had conveyed might simply be false. Or it could represent a sinister attempt to frame Felt, in the hope that the White House would react rashly and thereby incite Felt to tell all. Or Petersen's information might be accurate; Haldeman, for one, was sure this was the case. "We found the FBI leak . . . it's at the next to highest level," he noted in his diary."[31]

During a meeting that morning, the president expressed concern over Felt's relationship with John Ehrlichman, the White House liaison to the FBI. Ehrlichman had said that Felt "handled a lot of problems for him," and now Nixon wanted to know just what those problems had been. "Is [John Dean] the fellow who's on top of this?" the president asked his chief of staff, aware that the White House counsel had been handed the thorniest problems to arise since the break-in. Haldeman replied that Dean would be doing everything necessary to follow up on the matter; presumably, whatever they learned about Felt's background would help them divine his motive. They agreed that if Felt proved to be the culprit, he was "working on the basis that he is not known to be doing this and is not going to get caught." The need to "keep Felt from blowing" remained the paramount concern.[32]

That afternoon Nixon went to Camp David to relax over the weekend, in itself striking testimony to his insurmountable leads in the polls. He was not even bothering to campaign, relying instead on voters' revulsion with McGovern. The president had another long talk, this time with both Haldeman and Ehrlichman, about what to do. Assuming the information was accurate, some way had to be found to plug the leaks without letting Felt know he had been found out. As Haldeman wrote in his diary, they had to "tear off any further activities so that it doesn't get any worse." Nixon suggested that perhaps the White House should float a story that the president was "seriously considering" appointing a director other than Pat Gray; if Felt believed a new appointment was imminent and he was a candidate, he might stop leaking, at least for a while, out of fear that he would jeopardize his chances. "That might give some pause," Haldeman agreed. He jotted down specific notes to that end: "Get a story to *Star* or *Post*—Ehrlichman leak . . . that p[resident] seriously considering [Felt] for director. . . . Gray under consideration but p[resident] has high regard for Felt."[33]

Before that plan could be put into effect, Attorney General Kleindienst told Gray about Felt, either on his own initiative or at the White House's behest. "[Mark Felt's] leaking, Pat, and we know it," he told the acting FBI director. Yet Kleindienst refused to reveal the identity of his "unimpeachable source," which served to strengthen Gray's natural instinct to defend a subordinate he considered loyal. Gray thought himself a good judge of character, and "on [Felt's] handsome face" he had detected "none of the telltale signs of jealousy or envy that one might expect of a 30-year career FBI official." Kleindienst persisted, nonetheless, and Gray finally confronted Felt with the allegation. He vehemently denied the charge. "You can transfer me if you don't believe me," Felt said, knowing full well how much Gray relied on him to run the Bureau's day-to-day operations. "Those allegations are not true," he insisted. "You have my word on it."[34]

At about the same time Kleindienst warned Gray, the acting director also received a telephone call from White House special counsel Charles Colson, whom he had known for several years. Colson had one of the best political intelligence–gathering networks of anyone in the White House and was known especially for his good contacts with high-ranking Bureau officials, and also among some journalists. "I have been getting reports," he told Gray on October 23, "that there are leaks in the FBI from the Hoover old guard and from those who are mad at you for politicizing the FBI . . . Sandy Smith is the conduit." Colson did not share the name of his actual source—William Lambert, Smith's former colleague on *Life* magazine's crack investigative unit—nor would it probably have made any difference. Gray replied that he was aware of the problem and trying to get it under control, but otherwise dismissed Colson's warning as he had Kleindienst's.[35]

Then came two leaks mostly unrelated to Watergate, which would have aroused a man with better antennae and a more suspicious nature than Gray. On October 30, *Time* published a story by Sandy Smith alleging that the White House had used the FBI "in an unprecedented way to aid the Nixon campaign." The story claimed that Gray, in response to a September request from Ehrlichman, had ordered all FBI field offices to make suggestions about how the Republicans might address criminal-justice issues during the campaign. (In fact, Gray had been out of town and Felt had sanctioned the directive, although it went out over Gray's signature.) The same article also posed a damaging question: At what level in the White House did ultimate responsibility for the Watergate break-in reside?[36]

Almost simultaneously, Woodward had begun asking the FBI questions about a program, initiated under Hoover, that had routinely collected "biographical data" on major congressional candidates. Before Woodward could actually write it up, Gray managed hastily to disband the program. But the substance and timing of both leaks were clearly calculated to cause Gray problems on Capitol Hill and/or further discourage the president from nominating him. An experienced Washington operator, by this time, would have discerned the pattern and unifying logic behind the leaks that had been bedeviling the acting FBI director since midsummer. Yet Gray still could not.[37]

Kleindienst, in what was probably a calculated decision, chose Felt to convey to Gray the White House's enormous displeasure over the latest *Time* installment. Perhaps the attorney general thought it might rattle Felt a little bit to pass along such a message; if so, it didn't work. Felt coolly relayed its gist: the "president was on the ceiling about *this* leak" [emphasis in the original], and the attorney general believed the leaker "was someone after you [Gray]." Kleindienst also offered, via Felt, some gratuitous advice: Gray should rearrange his schedule if necessary to "be here in Washington, DC between now and election time as much as possible."[38]

Two days later, the attorney general asked to meet with Gray privately after a regular staff meeting. Kleindienst reiterated the president's displeasure over Sandy Smith's latest Watergate/FBI article. Gray, in turn, disclosed that in a quixotic effort to learn Smith's sources, he had met with the *Time* reporter that very morning. Smith, unsurprisingly, had steadfastly refused to disclose from whom he was getting his information. Kleindienst again made the case against Felt, citing an impeccable source. "Pat, you just have to fire Mark Felt," he said. "He is the leaker here." But this time Gray insisted on knowing who Kleindienst's "unimpeachable source" was. "It's Roswell Gilpatric," Kleindienst replied, an answer that must have taken Gray aback. Gilpatric was a Wall Street lawyer prominent in Democratic circles and no friend of the Nixon administration. But he had served in the government and was in a position to know what went on behind the scenes at *Time*; his law firm, Cravath, Swaine & Moore, was the magazine's outside counsel. "[Gilpatric] knows John [Mitchell], and he thinks what Felt's doing is abhorrent," Kleindienst explained. "So when [Gilpatric] learned the source from *Time*'s reporter, he passed it along."[39]

Now that he knew the source of the accusation, Gray once again confronted Felt. But in keeping with a promise he had made to Kleindienst, Gray did not disclose to Felt the source of the allegation. Not that it mattered. Unruffled, Felt again flatly denied leaking. That closed the matter insofar as Gray was concerned. After all, he had Felt's word, and his estimate of Sandy Smith's probity could not be lower. As Gray later wrote in his memoir, "Choosing between the personal word of the number-two man in the FBI, a man sworn to uphold the law, and the frequent unreliability of a reporter, I chose the former without a second thought."[40]

Felt had protected himself by his ingratiating behavior, and by pretending to throw in his lot with the new regime. He was the only one of the old guard who did not seem to mind working with Gray's three young assistants, David Kinley, Daniel "Mack" Armstrong, and Barbara Herwig, none of whom had come up through the FBI's ranks. They had been derisively dubbed the "Mod Squad" by Hoover loyalists, after a then-popular TV show, but Felt pretended to respect them and their boss. He discussed issues with the assistants as if their opinions mattered, a courtesy other executives refused to extend. "We got the feeling that he understood what we were trying to do," one of these aides later said. "We came to see him as a sort of bridge between the old and the new." Felt "appeared to show Gray great loyalty and support," recalled David Kinley.[41]

A man with a normal ego might have been cowed, or even panicked, after having been twice accused. Not Felt. Nor was he deterred by attrition in the upper ranks of the Felt faction. Around the same time Robert Kunkel was exiled to St. Louis, Assistant Director Charlie Bates unexpectedly asked for a transfer to the San Francisco Field Office, where the position as special agent in charge had just opened up. Bates's explanation was that he hated the paperwork and "lack of action" at FBI headquarters, and that he wanted to be the man giving the orders for a change, even though it would mean a demotion in rank and a return to a position he had already held once before. Bates lobbied to retain the rank of assistant director, which was held by the heads of the large field offices in New

York and Los Angeles. When Gray refused, Bates went to San Francisco anyway.[42]

Several weeks later, Charlie Bolz informed Gray that he was leaving the FBI altogether to take a job at the Housing and Urban Development Department. Gray implored him to reconsider but Bolz would not. Although not identified by Paul Daly in 2005 as a leading member of the Felt faction, there is little doubt that if Bolz did not play an active part, he surely was aware of what his immediate boss, Charlie Bates, had been up to. And Bolz's successor as chief of the Accounting and Fraud Section, Richard Long, would, by his own admission to Daly, become a willing participant in the Felt faction after arriving in January.[43]

Whether these departures were actually for the stated reasons cannot be known. But it seems at least plausible that Bates's and Bolz's desire to leave that den of intrigue known as the seat of government within the confines of the Bureau may have had something to do with their participation in or knowledge of the effort to tear Gray down. Not everyone had the stomach for the machinations that Felt reveled in. In scope and frequency, the leaks had gone far beyond the relatively mischievous disclosures of late June. Those who were still working the probe—including case agent Angelo Lano, and the federal prosecutors—were greatly concerned about the cumulative effects of the leaks on either the investigation or upcoming trial of the burglars. If Bates and Bolz had somehow learned about the allegations against Felt, may have figured their careers were just as likely to be jeopardized as rewarded if they remained tethered to him. Or maybe they had simply become embarrassed by the expansion of the scheme and extent of their culpability. Pat Gray may not have been everyone's model of an ideal director, but he had made an impression as a decent fellow.

Felt shoved all these concerns aside, his ambition clouding his judgment. He believed he had successfully parried the charge that he was the leaker, when the reverse was true. He believed his ascension was still vital for the FBI's well-being, as well as his own, and that his plan was still alive. He sincerely thought he was in the running as the FBI's war of succession headed toward its long overdue resolution.

CHAPTER EIGHT

"A Claque of Ambitious Men"

November 1972–January 1973

I now know that many of the high officials in the FBI deeply resented my
appointment as acting director. J. Edgar Hoover clearly had not singled out any one
of these men to be his successor. The result of this egocentric failure on the part of
the late director was to leave a claque of ambitious men straining mightily to hold
the reins of power. . . . I wasn't aware of their animosity at the beginning.
—L. Patrick Gray, In Nixon's Web

Nixon's re-election on November 7 by an overwhelming margin marked an important turning point, second only, perhaps, to the handing down of the indictments on September 15. In the weeks and months to come, Watergate coverage would shift away from the results of the FBI's investigation and toward dramatic events soon to take place in public: the trial of the burglars, followed by the televised investigation by a Senate select committee. In the interim, there was a sharp drop in coverage, to the point where it seemed Watergate might "disappear as an issue." The media were, in effect, reflecting the public's apathy.[1]

At the *Post*, part of the reason for the lull, seemingly, was Woodward's reluctance to contact Deep Throat. On October 25, as part of their continuing emphasis on CRP's secret slush fund, Woodward and Bernstein had written a story that for the first time tied the most powerful man in the White House (apart from the president) to the scandal. They alleged that chief of staff Bob Haldeman controlled disbursements from the fund, which, if true, would put Watergate on the doorstep of the Oval Office. But there was a problem: The story contained an error that gave White House press secretary Ron Ziegler an opening to discredit the entire article, and by extension, the *Post*'s overall Watergate coverage.

The article claimed that former CRP treasurer Hugh Sloan had testified before the grand jury that Haldeman was one of the persons who controlled the purse strings of the committee's slush fund. While the chief of staff *did* have access to the fund, Sloan hadn't actually implicated Haldeman in his grand jury testimony; the prosecutor simply hadn't questioned Sloan about that aspect.

Up to this point, Woodward and Bernstein had had to contend with criticism and aspersions, to be sure. Shortly after the *Post* published what ultimately turned out to be a false allegation against White House aide Ken Clawson, he had confronted his former boss, Howard Simons, in a Washington restaurant, and asked him how he could permit "two young punks" to work on such a prominent national story. "Clawson was hissing in everybody's ear . . . a jerk like Bernstein, and everybody knows he's a jerk, and a snot-nose like Woodward, and everybody knows he's a snot-nose," Simons recalled. It was also being rumored that what Bernstein was really trying to do was avenge his left-wing parents by bringing down Nixon, one of the arch Red-baiters of the 1950s. And there were whispers that Woodward was exploiting contacts he had made with White House aides while a navy liaison officer (which was unwittingly close to the mark!). Nonetheless, the criticisms had never stuck because the *Post* reporting duo had not made an instantly provable mistake in their coverage—until now. Coming just before the election, the error seemed so devastating that Woodward and Bernstein thought they might have to offer to resign. They felt "diminished by the White House attacks and in peril."[2]

Soon they recognized that the error was a technicality (and it was the one and only glaring mistake the *Post* made in the more than fifty stories it ran about Watergate, Bradlee later claimed). The gist of the story was true, and Deep Throat confirmed as much during a 3 a.m. garage meeting on October 28. Bernstein and Woodward then wrote a new article emending their earlier one. The following passage appeared about halfway through it:

> These same [federal] sources, who have provided detailed information on the Watergate investigation, confirmed once more that Haldeman was authorized to make payments from the fund.
>
> One source went so far as to say, "This is a Haldeman operation," and that Haldeman had "insulated" himself, dealing with the fund through an intermediary.[3]

Without Deep Throat's approval, and despite his having told Woodward earlier that he would not be the source on anything having to do with Haldeman, the *Post* duo had quoted Felt. Both sides had bent the ground rules before, but this was a far more serious breach. Woodward later wrote, "I had very bad feelings about quoting Felt so directly. It really was contrary to the rules we had established of deep background. But I was frantic to get a story in the paper correcting our mistake." Fearing that Felt might regard this violation as unforgivable, Woodward did not contact him for weeks. During that time Felt did not signal that he wanted a meeting, either, a fact that probably reinforced Woodward's angst. But it is highly unlikely that Felt intended to cut off the relationship over this breach; it was not in his interest to do so.[4]

During the postelection lull, Bradlee joked he was going to hold Woodward and Bernstein's "heads underwater until [they] come up with a story." Over the first weekend in December, Bernstein and Woodward, with the sanction of their editors, made an ill-considered effort to interview the Watergate grand jurors at their homes. It backfired, almost landing the reporters in jail. When they finally did come up with a significant scoop, Bradlee put it on the front page as if to show that the *Post*, in defiance of the critics and skeptics, was "still in the Watergate business." Published on December 8, the story described how E. Howard Hunt had a special, private telephone when he worked for the White House, and that under a special arrangement the telephone company sent the bill to Kathleen Chenow, the plumbers' secretary. This was one of the most detailed articles about the plumbers' activities yet. A few days later the White House was forced to admit that the plumbers existed. Still, Ziegler maintained (incorrectly) that "it was his understanding" that neither Howard Hunt nor Gordon Liddy had been involved with the secret unit.[5]

If, as Ben Bradlee declared, the *Post* could hardly "get a smell of a story" during the period after the election, the situation wasn't better at *Time* magazine. Not a single Watergate article appeared in its pages in November or December. Yet from Felt's perspective, the postelection void in Watergate coverage was of little concern. What mattered now was whether the preelection leaks had hammered home to Nixon the lesson that Pat Gray simply wouldn't do.[6]

Judging from the overall press coverage, it was less than clear that Felt had succeeded. Notwithstanding all the leaks and, in *Time*, adverse articles, Gray's press had been positive on balance. He had mounted an impressive public relations campaign to win favorable coverage, and the beat reporters from influential newspapers like the *New York Times*, the *Los Angeles Times*, and even the *Post* had treated him well. Gray had been depicted as having brought many positive changes to the Bureau after Hoover's stultifying rule—as if he had opened long-closed windows to fresh air.

On the eve of the election, for example, Sanford J. Ungar, the *Post*'s FBI reporter, wrote an upbeat portrait stating that the chances "are considered very good that Gray will eventually be confirmed if nominated."[7]

But within the confines of the Oval Office, which was the only place that counted, Nixon was in fact dead-set on finding a replacement. Like every senior official in the administration, Gray had been asked to tender his resignation after the election as part of the president's determination to restructure the federal bureaucracy during his second term. And in Gray's case, the president fully intended to accept the offer. In this respect Felt's covert campaign had triumphed. The president believed that Gray wasn't up to the intricacies of the job, and he definitely did not want him exposed to confirmation hearings where Gray would be asked about the FBI's Watergate investigation. Nixon didn't doubt Gray's loyalty, just his effectiveness. He intended to find another post for him, perhaps at the Office of Emergency Preparedness or the Arms Control and Disarmament Agency—any job that didn't require Senate confirmation and where his naïveté would be harmless. But that was only half the story. Because of the leaks, Nixon was adamant about removing the FBI's entire top echelon, beginning but not stopping with Felt. In this larger sense, Felt's scheming had been all for naught—indeed, it had backfired.[8]

By November 12 Nixon had all but settled on an appointee: Jerry Wilson, the chief of police for the District of Columbia since 1969. Aided by a Nixon-ordered budget increase, Wilson, a twenty-year veteran of the force, had rapidly modernized and expanded the Washington police and was credited with a steep drop in the city's crime rate, which had been among the nation's worst. Better yet, Wilson was only forty-four years old. Nixon wanted a young man in the FBI post, someone who could easily stay in the job beyond his term and the next president's, too. He anticipated that the confirmation of a new FBI director would be a lasting legacy of his administration.[9]

Then something unexpected happened: on November 19 Gray was hospitalized for a gastrointestinal problem that periodically flared up because of a ruptured appendix he had suffered during submarine duty in World War II. Though the condition was rarely disabling, this particular episode was serious, requiring emergency surgery and a convalescence that would extend until early January. Nixon did not want to appear callous by replacing Gray while he was flat on his back. In addition, the Senate Judiciary Committee indicated that it wanted to hold confirmation hearings for the FBI appointment after those for the new Justice Department nominees. So what had been considered one of the new term's most important tasks and a no-brainer (at least in the sense of replacing Gray) was suddenly shoved to the back burner.

In late November Richard Kleindienst met with Nixon, Haldeman, and Ehrlichman to go over changes in the Justice Department. The attorney general said that Gray was expected to make a full recovery and that he was in favor of keeping him. The president replied, "We know who leaked over there and it was at the top levels. So they all have to go at that level, not just the one who leaked." Nixon said he was leaning toward Chief Wilson, and this didn't sit well with Kleindienst. "You need a broad-gauge person in that job," he said, "not just a cop." The job required "a lawyer, a philosopher, a student who knows Communism, political forces, [and] dissent. He must be a disciplinarian, tough and fair, and fundamentally loyal to the president." Wilson simply didn't have the depth. "Hoover was a great propagandist, Wilson is not," Kleindienst added. "He has no political references at all. . . . We should try for someone that Teddy Kennedy wouldn't kick out in '76."[10]

Kleindienst also addressed head-on the issue of exposing Gray to confirmation hearings. Any nominee was bound to spark an ideological debate with liberal Democrats about the FBI. And with respect to Watergate, Kleindienst argued, it could only *help* the president to appoint Gray. "The Watergate part would be good to come out in the hearings because it would show that there was a thorough [FBI] investigation and . . . it would be good to have that come out," he asserted. Nixon was not completely persuaded but saw some merit in the argument. When the first round of high-level administration resignations was announced in early December, Gray's name, to the surprise of many observers, was not on the list.[11]

Nearly everyone Nixon subsequently consulted echoed Kleindienst's view: Wilson would be a mistake. Of particular significance was the view of John Connally, the former Texas governor whom the president was grooming as his successor. Connally thought Wilson "lacked depth and scope." He would be sunk in the FBI, unable to cope with the nuances. The director "must be completely the president's man . . . and have the ability to handle the Bureau, which [meant being] a good politician and bureaucrat," Connally observed. The inability of the president and his advisers to settle on a candidate worked in Gray's favor, if only because it strung out the process. Meanwhile, the press was left to speculate. A December 21 article in the *Washington Post* declared that Nixon had firmly decided to appoint Gray; the same day, the *Los Angeles Times* stated with equal certainty that although Gray was not out of the running, Nixon was seriously considering other candidates.[12]

Over Christmas, while Gray was recuperating at his home in Stonington, Connecticut, he began working through a mound of paper that had accumulated during his surgery and hospitalization. Eventually he came across the all-but-forgotten manila envelopes from Howard Hunt's safe that Dean and Ehrlichman had given him in June. Here, he thought, was a good opportunity to dispose of them. He skimmed their contents, noticing what appeared to be some State Department cables about the October 1963 overthrow/assassination of South Vietnamese President Ngo Dinh Diem. These confirmed, in his mind, what Dean and Ehrlichman had told him: the documents had nothing to do with the Watergate break-in. He jammed the papers, along with used holiday wrapping paper, into his backyard incinerator. As far as Gray was concerned, that was the end of the matter.[13]

Several days earlier, on December 22, Earl Silbert, who would be prosecuting the Watergate defendants in January, had asked John Dean, Fred Fielding, and Bruce Kehrli from the White House to come to the Justice Department so that he, along with Henry Petersen, the head of the Criminal Division, could go over the chain of evidence for the items found in Hunt's safe. (Hunt's lawyer had submitted a motion to suppress that evidence.) The group met in a small conference room next to Petersen's office. Dean and Fielding ran through their account of how the safe had been opened and its contents obtained, omitting, of course, the fact that they had "edited" the contents. Silbert seemed satisfied except for one thing: in his motion, Hunt was also claiming that some materials were missing from the government's list. Did Dean know anything about that?[14]

The question was an alarming one for the White House counsel. As soon as he could, he pulled Petersen aside and said, "I've got to talk to you." Not everything from the safe had been turned over directly to the FBI, he explained. "Some of those documents were politically very embarrassing, and we sent them straight to Pat Gray. If there are missing documents, he's got them." Petersen was stunned, even disgusted. "I don't really want to hear it," he said.[15]

Gray had some of the documents, to be sure, but innocuous ones insofar as the prosecution of the Watergate defendants was concerned. Dean was the one who had custody of the notebooks that Hunt now claimed were missing.

In turn, Petersen was not candid with the federal prosecutors working the case. He did not tell Silbert about this extraordinary exchange, even though Silbert, by this time, had gently raised the issue of Dean's too-friendly relationship with Petersen. Silbert had become aware of it during an otherwise unremarkable visit to Petersen's office earlier in December. The assistant attorney general had been chatting frankly about developments in the Watergate case, and after he finished Silbert asked who was at the other end of the telephone. Petersen said John Dean. Silbert was taken aback (and would have been even more mortified had he known that Petersen also shared information from the grand jury proceedings). Silbert had cut himself off from all contact with anyone in the White House that he knew for the duration of the prosecution, except when it concerned official business. He was surprised to find that Petersen had not done the same. "Your talking to Dean . . . is that wise?" he had asked Petersen. "I'm not troubled by it," the assistant AG had responded. "I think Dean is an honest man."[16]

The only step Petersen took in response to Dean's partial admission now was to ask Pat Gray privately about the materials allegedly missing from Hunt's safe when the acting director returned from his convalescence on January 2. Petersen interpreted Gray's negative response as meaning Petersen "had no need to know" and that Dean could be taken at his word. But a few days later Gray approached Dean at a Justice Department luncheon. Forgoing his usual deference, he grabbed Dean's arm and demanded, through clenched teeth, "Why did you mention that file stuff to Petersen?" Dean said he'd had no choice, and Gray exploded. "Goddammit, John. You have got to hang tight on that!" He went on to explain that he couldn't tell Petersen he had gotten the documents because he had destroyed them. Dean said nothing. Fortunately for the White House—or so it seemed at the time—Petersen showed no interest in pursuing the matter, in accordance with his general inclination to overlook what he was assured were purely political facets of the case.[17]

Gray soon turned to what seemed a more pressing matter: a sudden rash of negative articles about his performance. He was still in place, with no word from the White House about whether or not he would be retained. The delay emboldened anti-Gray elements within the Bureau, spearheaded by Felt, to talk more openly to reporters about his supposed failings. The spate of negative coverage was intended to counteract the generally favorable press he had received to that point.[18]

On January 2 the *Washington Star*'s Jeremiah O'Leary came out with a front-page story alleging that Gray had instituted a "purge of old J. Edgar Hoover hands." An even more transparent attack appeared in *Time* on January 8. In "Tattletale Gray," Sandy Smith depicted an increasingly dysfunctional FBI; Gray, he alleged, had been ridding it of "Hooverites" right and left, "yet some agents accuse him of retaining the most hated of Hoover's hard-line policies." Agents were quoted as being offended at having their integrity repeatedly called into question—an accusation straight from Felt's playbook. Furthermore, Smith wrote, Gray's fixation over leaks had "actually slow[ed] down the Watergate investigation."[19]

Well aware of Smith's stellar reputation inside the Bureau, Gray had consistently tried to work with him. Now, once again, he asked Smith to come see him personally so that he could prove the allegations were mistaken. During the meeting, the fabled reporter refused to retract anything that appeared in the article. The Felt faction's allegations carried more weight than Gray's protestations. Gray, his patience exhausted, finally ordered Smith out of his office and told him to never approach the director's office again. He would not be receiving any cooperation so long as Pat Gray was head of the FBI.[20]

A more striking (and accurate) article that month was published by the columnists Rowland Evans and Robert Novak, the latter of whom counted William Sullivan as one of his key FBI sources. Novak had been the first reporter to expose the real tensions that arose between the Nixon administration and Hoover in the year or so before his death. Now he and Evans revealed the continuing intrigue in the Bureau and how it was affecting Gray's tenure. They wrote,

> An undercover campaign by the old-boy FBI network, past and present, against acting Director L. Patrick Gray has fully disclosed to the White House the tainted legacy of J. Edgar Hoover's 40-year reign over the Federal Bureau of Investigation. . . . Whatever happens to Gray, the difficulties he has encountered dramatize an unpleasant fact to the White House: The sudden end of Hoover's long personal tyranny left a political snakepit at the FBI. The Nixon inner circle is determined that the new director, whether Gray or not, must radically clean house.
>
> If Gray is nominated, the old-boy network will slip derogatory information to the Senate Judiciary Committee. Liberal Democratic senators, eager to prove Gray has politicized the FBI serving Mr. Nixon's partisan interests, would be expected to cooperate.[21]

Insightful as it was, the Evans/Novak column did little to change Gray's perception of Felt. That's because it traced the anti-Gray campaign to two other Hoover disciples—Clyde Tolson, long Hoover's right-hand man, and Cartha "Deke" DeLoach, the heir apparent before Sullivan. In fact, the column helped cement the image Felt had been selling all along in a way: that he was on Gray's side, his unwavering ally in combating the die-hard Hoover loyalists still infesting the FBI within and influencing it without. The deception was working so well that Felt fully expected Gray's endorsement once the hapless acting director was himself out of the running.[22]

The one flaw in Felt's plan was that he had been identified as the leaker, yet had deceived himself into believing he had covered his tracks and, more importantly, persuaded everyone of his innocence. He couldn't have been more wrong. Gray had been diminished per Felt's design all right. But in the process Felt had been discovered, and the leaks had underscored to the White House the need for a new FBI director from outside the Bureau.

On January 5, before writing the column, Novak had interviewed John Ehrlichman, the staff member responsible for making the recommendation to the president about the FBI directorship. To get information columnists often offered information. So Novak reported that he was "get[ting] a lot of flack from the [Hoover] old-boys network in the FBI against Gray. They're leaking all over hell—to the press, other people." He asked Ehrlichman, "Can you give me any background if you are concerned at all by this criticism of [Gray]? . . . Jerry O'Leary is kind of a pipeline to the old gang in there." Ehrlichman responded, "Well, not concerned . . . with the merits, so to speak. [But we are] concerned with the *phenomenon*, yes, plenty, because there's a real . . . there are all kinds of symptoms of a breakdown of the integrity of the system there." He added that the eventual nominee would have to tackle the "deterioration of the system" at the FBI, and that the only question about Gray was whether he was tough enough for the job. The president had put the decision aside for the time being because of Gray's illness. But "*whoever* goes in there is going to have to just really undertake a drastic review of the whole setup," Ehrlichman emphasized. Novak came away believing that if Gray was not nominated, the White House would turn to an outsider, and his column with Evans accurately reflected administration thinking.[23]

Nonetheless Felt continued his plotting. After the January flurry of negative articles about Pat Gray, Tom Smith, a Felt ally who worked in the Domestic Intelligence Division, prepared an anonymous nine-page memo, with sixteen pages of press clippings attached, for internal FBI consumption. Titled "New Articles Attacking the Director," it posed a simple question: Who was benefiting from the attacks on Gray? They "seem to . . . be written for the express purpose of causing the president to alter his decision in the matter, [or] . . . to raise questions which might result in a negative attitude during Senate confirmation hearings." That was true enough. But then the memo (which Gray eventually came to believe was Felt's handiwork) went on to state that an analysis of the negative news articles, "coupled with considerable inside information relating to individuals and situations in the Bureau," yielded this answer. "One individual, assisted by a small clique of well-placed followers, feels that he has a lot to gain by discrediting L. Patrick Gray. That individual is William C. Sullivan."[24]

Attributing the negative coverage to Sullivan was both deceptive and clever—just the sort of bureaucratic cunning at which Felt excelled. It also reflected Felt's continuing fixation and mistaken perception that "Crazy Billy" would be his only serious rival once Gray was out of the way.[25]

As the intense competition to succeed Hoover neared a climax, the wheels of justice in the Watergate case began slowly grinding in public.

The long-anticipated trial of the burglars opened on January 8. A week later *New York Times* reporter Seymour Hersh, who had been brought aboard expressly to help the newspaper catch up to the *Post*, broke a front-page story alleging that at least four of the burglars were being paid to keep quiet. The scoop caused a quiet panic at the White House because it drew attention, for the first time, to the cover-up rather than the crime. Fortunately for the administration, the defendants promptly denied receiving "hush money" and the story line soon disappeared. But it was a harbinger of how quickly things might unravel if the focus shifted to the break-in's aftermath rather than the crime itself.[26]

Any chance that the trial itself might reveal the higher-ups behind the break-in was dashed by a spate of guilty pleas, starting with one from E. Howard Hunt on the trial's first day. Four out of five of the burglars caught red-handed quickly followed suit. Not mounting a defense meant the men didn't have to offer an explanation. Had there been a conspiracy involving higher-ups? Judge John Sirica asked Hunt. "To my personal knowledge there was none," he replied. Meanwhile, James McCord and Gordon Liddy chose to stand trial, but they were no more communicative.[27]

The press expressed disbelief at Hunt's professed ignorance, and reporters redoubled the search for those culpable. A week before the trial ended, *Time* posited an answer to Sirica's question. Before Hunt had persuaded them to plead guilty, one or more of the burglars was prepared to testify that the bugging had been approved by John Mitchell and Chuck Colson, the staffer who had suggested that Hunt be hired in the first place. This allegation tracked with what Felt had told Woodward back in October, and it almost certainly originated with Felt again. He was merely recycling widespread speculation about Colson's involvement because of his reputation as the president's political hatchet man.[28]

Nowhere was Time's reporting on Watergate taken more seriously than at the Post. And because of the January 22 article, for the first time in many weeks, Woodward asked to meet with Felt, whom he had not really seen since October 28. (They had met once, very briefly, so that Woodward could give Felt his new address.) If Woodward had any trepidation about trying to reconnect, no matter. The Time scoop made a meeting imperative, and Felt agreed to one. They got together in the parking garage on January 24.[29]

Felt opened the conversation with a friendly greeting. He didn't mention Woodward's October violation of their "deep background" arrangement—and Woodward certainly didn't. Because the trial was obviously a dead end, discussion soon turned to the upcoming Senate investigation. Felt was skeptical about the Senate's ability to crack open responsibility for the break-in. He observed that the select committee would "'have a problem unless they get someone from the inside—without that you come up with lots of money and plans for dirty tricks, but little characterization of the operation.'" When Woodward pressed him for new details that might help him push the envelope in advance of the hearings, Felt declined to provide any genuinely new information. He would only repeat old scuttlebutt, i.e., the Bureau's "'investigative assumption'" that Colson and Mitchell were behind the operation, as the Time article had alleged. He added that the assumption was unproven, and "'if the FBI could not prove it, I don't think the Washington Post can'"—nor, presumably, could the Senate. The most Felt would give Woodward that night was a half-promise that he might consider sharing the FBI's "400+ page report" on Watergate "if the Senate investigation falls apart." Of course, a single Bureau report, 400 pages in length, did not exist.[30]

The meeting amounted to one of Woodward's most frustrating encounters with Deep Throat. "Just once," he later wrote, he "wished Deep Throat would really tell . . . what was up—everything, no questions asked, no tug of wills, a full status report. . . . [But] that night, it was the familiar pattern. He would respond only to new information." When Woodward tried to outline a story that he and Bernstein intended to write about Mitchell and Colson, Felt "didn't seem impressed."[31]

Woodward and Bernstein later characterized Felt's attitude during this meeting as "cavalier." But not only did Felt *seem* cavalier—he didn't really care. He was again playing fast and loose with the facts and manipulating them, as he had begun to do with Woodward at least as early as mid-October. Instead of perceiving the reason for this behavior—it was a reflection of Felt's lack of interest in Watergate per se, except insofar as it could help him advance his agenda—Woodward and Bernstein later wrote that he was still "trying to protect the office [of the presidency], to effect a change in its conduct before all was lost."[32]

The negative results from this encounter led to the most serious rupture between Bernstein and Woodward since they had begun working together. After leaving the garage, Woodward wrote the first draft of a story that used Felt's "investigative assumption" about Mitchell and Colson as its lede, and attributed the information to "reliable sources." Bernstein reworked the story three times. After reading each version, Woodward voiced the same reservation: he didn't think they had enough proof. Bernstein angrily accused Woodward of "playing into the hands of the White House." Maybe the allegations against Mitchell and Colson were unproven, he argued, but so what? According to Deep Throat, that was what those high up in the FBI, including Pat Gray, thought, and on that basis alone the story merited publication. After some heated arguments Woodward prevailed; the story never ran.[33]

The two were lucky it didn't. Colson threatened to file a lawsuit against *Time* because of its article, and eventually the magazine published a letter from him disputing the allegation, along with an editor's note that was all but an explicit retraction. Altogether, the episode put a damper on press coverage for a while, as John Dean happily noted to the president, especially after Evans and Novak also wrote a column highlighting the considerable shortcomings in the *Time* article. Colson, naturally, was Novak's source—though as a condition for giving Novak the story, Colson insisted that Novak write, "Colson declined to talk to us."[34]

The Watergate affair had not even reached its mid-point, but clearly Felt was waning in importance as a *Post* source, the frequency of his contacts with Woodward and the quality of information he was willing to impart in sharp decline.

CHAPTER NINE

The Safe Choice

February 1973

Deep Throat would never deal with [Woodward] falsely.
—All the President's Men

On January 29, 1973, Gordon Liddy and James McCord, the defendants who hadn't pled guilty, were convicted. Federal prosecutors immediately put in motion the legal machinery to compel everyone who had been deemed guilty to testify. Meanwhile, Williams, Connolly and the DNC prepared to resume the civil lawsuit that had been on hold, and the Senate approved, by a vote of 77-0, the formation of a select committee to investigate illegal practices during the 1972 presidential campaign.

This legal and political expansion of Watergate increased exponentially the number of agendas being pursued. Media coverage, and strenuous efforts to manipulate it, grew correspondingly. The FBI's war of succession now became only one of several behind-the-scenes struggles being played out in the media, and perhaps not even the most important one. As more and more people in the Nixon administration and campaign apparatus lawyered up, attorneys engaged in a line of work not taught in law school: influencing, if not trying, their clients' cases in the press. Despite all the turmoil and increasing cacophony, Felt kept his eyes steady on the prize.[1]

On the morning of February 16, after weeks of temporizing, Nixon finally reached a decision about the FBI directorship. The matter had dragged on for so long that Gray was almost certain he would not be nominated. He was almost right. Nixon had been adamant about finding him another much less demanding and sensitive position. "Gray can't cut it [as FBI director]," he told Haldeman on January 8. "He is not able enough [and] lacks the energy." But no one besides the president liked Jerry Wilson as an alternative, so Nixon had continued casting around for a suitable candidate.[2]

For a while he fixed on William D. Ruckelshaus, an Indiana Republican who headed the Environmental Protection Agency. If this idea seemed to come out of nowhere—Ruckelshaus had little stature and no mystique at all—it did have one thing in common with Nixon's interest in Chief Wilson: Ruckelshaus, too, would have been a very young director (he was then forty-one years old) and therefore likely to hold the position for a long time. He topped the list of candidates until early February, when an insurmountable problem surfaced: Ruckelshaus did not want to be the boy wonder who entered the pestilential waters at the FBI's seat of government.[3]

The combination of the weeks of indecision, Ruckelshaus's staunch refusal, and a striking transformation in the political atmosphere finally changed Nixon's mind about Gray. On February 13 the president told his chief of staff that he was "inclin[ed] to go along with Gray at the FBI" provided that Bill Sullivan was put in under him. Perhaps "a known quantity will do what he's told," Nixon observed; besides, "it would look bad to move Gray out at this point." This was the president's way of acknowledging the increasing political potency and momentum the Watergate issue was gaining on Capitol Hill. Despite the November landslide, Nixon's political coattails had proven to be very short. Democrats in the Senate had actually gained two seats, and as a consequence, the administration had not been able to put a damper on what now loomed as one of the biggest Senate investigations in years. If Gray didn't testify about Watergate before the Senate Judiciary Committee, he would surely be hauled before the newly formed select committee anyway. The growing political storm meant that "the only thing worse than nominating Gray would have been not nominating him," as John Dean later observed. If Gray was going to be called to testify about the break-in investigation one way or another, it was better that he face the questioners with his loyalty to the administration intact. Still, the president worried about Gray's political acumen before a Senate committee primed to attack.[4]

Three days later Gray came to the Oval Office for his first meeting with the president since Hoover's funeral. John Ehrlichman was also present. After asking about Gray's health and whether he was up to the physical rigors of the job, Nixon explained the purpose of the meeting. He wanted to know how Gray, if nominated, would handle Watergate during confirmation hearings. Gray made a strong case that he was better equipped than anyone else to answer questions about the FBI's probe. "I think it's a thing we ought to meet head on, on every front," he said, as proud of the investigation as he was ignorant about the president's role in the cover-up. The White House hadn't been pleased by the FBI's diligence the previous summer and fall, but now it was poised to exploit it.[5]

Satisfied by Gray's answer, Nixon turned to a subject that had angered him for months. "You haven't been able to do anything—or have you?—about the leaks coming out of the Bureau," he exclaimed. "The whole story, we've found, is coming out of the Bureau." Then Ehrlichman chimed in, "There's no two ways about it. There is no question about their getting their information right off of the 703s [sic]—or whatever those forms are—the investigation summary forms."[6]

The implication that Gray did not have the FBI fully under control bothered him. For months he'd been listening to Ehrlichman's and Dean's incessant complaints on this score; finally he had a chance to talk to the president about it. Gray did not back down from what he believed—that Felt was not betraying him—but expressions of full confidence in his subordinate gave Nixon no comfort. Gray was undoubtedly loyal, but he was not sufficiently shrewd, suspicious, or ruthless to be, of all things, FBI director. Even after the president reminded him that he knew from Roswell Gilpatric that Felt was the leaker, Gray steadfastly defended Felt.[7]

The conversation meandered. Did he think Petersen's office was putting out the information? Nixon asked. Gray was cautious. As much as he wanted to defend his stewardship, he did not want to falsely accuse others. He did acknowledge that FD-302s were routinely circulated to people outside the FBI—to the U.S. attorneys' office and others in the Justice Department. Soon Nixon returned to the subject of Felt. Sandy Smith "has written stuff that is true, [and] right out of the Bureau," he observed. Still Gray resisted the president's inference. "My recommendation to you now would be to continue Felt," he said, "but what I think I've got to do is . . . come up with an overall plan to submit to you." Nixon wasn't so easily deterred. "The only problem you have with Felt," he said, "is that the lines lead very directly to him, and I can't believe it, but they lead right there." Ehrlichman added, "You know, we've tried to trap [Felt] . . . set traps around to see if we can turn something up." Presumably that meant that some sensitive but erroneous information had been given to Felt alone, to see if he would leak it. But apparently Felt hadn't taken the bait.[8]

Gray parried the allegation against his presumably loyal executive officer with all the firmness he could muster. "I think that the one thing that I should say to you, Mr. President—in fact, I must say it to you—is that those people over there are like little old ladies in tennis shoes, and they've got some of the most vicious vendettas going on. Their gossip mill is churning all the time." The aspersions about Felt, he thought, might have been cast by Hoover loyalists who resented Felt's ostensible support of a director from the outside—a line of thinking that showed how thoroughly Felt had snookered Gray.[9]

What about Bill Sullivan? the president wondered. Would you bring him back? Gray was equally firm on that score, perhaps because of Felt's influence. "I wouldn't bring [Sullivan] back at all," he stated. "I wouldn't touch him at all. His first words, when [I asked him why] he came back to Washington [were] 'for revenge'. . . . The guy is too nervous, [and] he's not articulate at all."[10]

Returning to Felt, Nixon declared,

It would be very, very difficult to have [him] in [the number two] position without having that charge [about leaking] cleared up. And incidentally, let me say this—this is a directive. You should take a lie detector test on him. . . . John [Ehrlichman], you prepare the questions. Has [Felt] talked to *Time* magazine? . . . And he's to do it or he doesn't get the job. That's the way it has to be.[11]

Nixon went on at length about the need for more discipline at the FBI. "I've never known of a leak when Hoover was there," he complained. Gray needed to rule by fear, as Hoover had. When Gray protested that he hadn't exactly been "Mr. Nice Guy" and was trying to put an end to the sycophancy and lying that had become pervasive at the Bureau, Nixon cut him off. "The leaks *are* occurring, and they are from someplace," he declared. "Frankly, I am referring to discipline of the highest sensitivity involving what may be partisan political matters." But if Gray suffered from a grievous lack of deviousness, Nixon had his blind spots, too. The FBI's "sudden" lack of discipline was not sudden at all; the struggle to succeed Hoover had been waged in the media for at least two years. And the leaks, rather than stemming from a lack of fear or discipline, were overwhelmingly a function of that unsettled contest.[12]

Nixon told Gray that it would be a "bloody confirmation" but that if he wanted it, the directorship was his. "[But] from the moment you're nominated, I think you've got to start cracking the whip," Nixon said. "Having in mind, of course, that you don't want to crack any whips that are going to force some bastard to go out and testify against your nomination."[13]

The president then spoke frankly about what he expected from Gray. He wanted a relationship like the one he'd had with Hoover. "Let me tell you," Nixon said, "there were times—and Lyndon Johnson told me this same thing—when I felt that the only person in this goddamned government who was standing with me was Edgar Hoover. He was the only one." Gray would probably have to bend over backwards to prove his neutrality, Nixon acknowledged. "Publicly, you must do that—publicly. But privately what you've got to do is to do like Hoover."[14]

The meeting ended on a light note. Who should be told of the decision to nominate Gray? the president asked. "Well, we haven't told the attorney general yet," Ehrlichman piped up—an observation that evoked hearty laughter from all three men. The attorney general was nominally the director's superior, but no AG had ever been able to control Hoover. "I'd like to get this done by today. We've got to move [on the news] . . . because this nomination's gonna leak. This damn Gray's a leaker!" Nixon said, again to hearty laughter. "Yes, I am, Mr. President," Gray replied, "[and] a Nixon loyalist. You're goddamn right I am."[15]

As Gray left the Oval Office, his elation was undoubtedly, if slightly, tempered by Nixon's directive to either prove Felt's innocence or get rid of him. Gray expected loyalty from his subordinates and gave it in return. He did not relish the day when he would have to carry out these marching orders and did not share them with Felt. As it turned out, he would never have a chance to implement them.

Far sooner than anyone thought possible, Nixon's worst fears about Gray's lack of cunning and political smarts would be realized.

Almost as if he'd overheard the conversation, Felt redoubled his efforts to redirect the White House's anger over leaks away from himself. It didn't matter who was blamed, as long as it wasn't him. A new story by Woodward and Bernstein published a few days after Gray's meeting with Nixon offered a golden opportunity. Like so many earlier articles, it showed the roundabout route a story could take before publication and the subsequent difficulty in tracing exactly where it came from. Then, too, it also illustrated the *Post* reporters' ever-diminishing dependence on Felt.

In mid-January, while Woodward was perusing the witness list for the burglars' trial, he noticed that it included a Los Angeles–based lawyer named Morton B. Jackson. He knew E. Howard Hunt quite well. Hunt had stayed with Jackson after the break-in while he was trying to avoid attention. And although Judge Sirica had instructed Jackson, like the other witnesses, not to discuss his testimony, Woodward got him to talk about some of the things his old friend had disclosed while a guest. The story Woodward and Bernstein wrote, published in February, revealed some of Hunt's earlier escapades for the White House. It also precipitated another leak investigation within the FBI (even though the story had been developed from sources outside the Bureau), thus providing Felt with his chance to redirect blame.[16]

The article was really just a footnote in the larger scheme of all things Watergate. But coming so soon after Nixon's meeting with Gray, it renewed the president's agitation about Felt. The morning it was printed, Nixon told Haldeman, "The point you ought to make about this . . . is that . . . Gray's got to—it seems to me—he's got to get Felt off of this [presumably, the act of leaking or anything remotely connected to Watergate]."[17]

Felt's manipulation of the leak investigation was superb. On February 21, the day the story appeared, he sent a memo ordering an immediate and exhaustive investigation to Robert E. Gebhardt, who had replaced Charlie Bates as assistant director of the General Investigative Division. Felt noted,

> As you know, Woodward and Bernstein have written numerous articles about Watergate. While their stories have contained much fiction and half truths, they have frequently set forth information which they attribute to federal investigators, Department of Justice sources, and FBI sources. . . . On balance and despite the fiction, there is no question but that they have access to sources either in the FBI or in the Department of Justice.[18]

In the course of the probe, Gebhardt discovered that Woodward had contacted Earl Silbert's chief assistant, Donald E. Campbell, while reporting the article. Campbell told Gebhardt that Woodward had merely run the essence of the story by him, and that he had just listened. Felt seized on that admission nonetheless, circled the paragraph describing it, and scrawled in large capital letters, "HERE IS ENTIRE ANSWER." Upon seeing it, Gray—anxious to demonstrate that his defense of Felt was well founded and that the problem lay elsewhere—asked that a memo to this effect be prepared for the attorney general.[19]

Besides continuing to sow uncertainty and confusion about the source of Woodward's articles, Felt now sought to shift his own emphasis from leaks intended to rile the administration, to leaks intended to provoke Senate Democrats. Gray's unexpected nomination was a setback. Yet it was also a contingency he had nonetheless anticipated as possible all along.

As before, Felt turned to Sandy Smith whenever he had especially sensitive information to put out. On February 26—the eve of Gray's confirmation hearings— *Time* published an article that was even more misleading than the previous month's "Tattletale Gray." In "Questions about Gray," Smith depicted him as deeply partisan, blatantly political, and bent on "turning the FBI into an arm of the administration." These exaggerations were coupled with a sensational new disclosure. Back in August, Smith, drawing from information Felt provided, had been the first to connect Hunt and Liddy with the White House's Special Investigations Unit, or plumbers. Now Felt exposed a separate, even darker administration secret: the use of the FBI, from May 1969 to February 1971, to wiretap several White House aides suspected of leaking classified information, along with the newspapermen suspected of receiving it. These so-called "special coverages" had been instituted under the express authority of the president, outside even the FBI's usual procedure for installing wiretaps.[20]

In the end, all this surveillance had been for naught, producing "just gobs and gobs of material [that was only] gossip and bull-shitting," as Nixon later observed. "The tapping was a very, very unproductive thing." Unproductive or not, it was politically explosive, especially in a town where the press largely defined its own prerogatives. The White House would be in an extraordinarily bad position if the information were to be corroborated.[21]

What was flagrantly unfair about this leak was that Gray had nothing to do with these wiretaps—they had ended well before he took over, and he didn't even know about them. But the article claimed that after becoming director Gray had approved the continuation of the wiretaps and that they had persisted for weeks, until a coincidental Supreme Court ruling declared that a court order was needed to initiate electronic surveillance in domestic security cases. This leak underscored again Felt's basic contempt for the media, his willingness to manipulate, if not deceive, Sandy Smith as well as Woodward.[22]

What made Felt's behavior particularly egregious here was that he opened up a perjury trap for Gray. Leaking word of the wiretaps' existence to Sandy Smith made it all but certain that Gray would be asked about them at his confirmation hearings—as indeed he was, on the second day. Gray was in no position to testify truthfully about the wiretaps when the intense questions came, and his innocent denials satisfied no one. Following his unceremonious exit from the FBI, Gray had to endure a serious perjury investigation because of his unwittingly untruthful answers to the Senate.[23]

Smith's article, moreover, was a twofer for Felt. It not only presented a new, unanticipated, and unfair problem for Gray to overcome, but also further reduced whatever slim chance Sullivan had of returning to the Bureau. The information about the wiretaps had been tightly guarded, and only Sullivan knew about them contemporaneously. Regardless of how Gray handled the matter, attention was bound to shift to Sullivan, and Felt obliged by doing what he could to direct unwanted scrutiny to his presumed rival. On February 23 *Time* asked the White House for a response to the story it was about to run about the wiretaps. The press office contacted John Dean, who, in turn, asked Felt two questions: What was the truth, and how such a story could possibly have been leaked? "You really want to know?" Felt said in response to the first question. Dean said yes. Felt then confirmed that the allegations were true, helpfully adding, "Bill Sullivan has all the facts on this." As for the second question, Felt said that he "didn't have any idea."[24]

Although Felt had no way of really knowing, by this point Sullivan was all but out of the running for the directorship, too. Nixon had indicated in his talk with Gray that he hoped Gray would bring Sullivan back as a "reorganization consultant" to help him *really* clean house. Yet no one was seriously thinking about appointing him director should Gray falter. Sullivan had lowered his sights accordingly, while continuing to do his best to ingratiate himself with the administration. As part of the White House's effort to blunt the Senate Watergate hearings, for example, Sullivan would soon offer to testify about politically motivated wiretapping that had occurred during the Kennedy and Johnson administrations. But Felt's leak about the 1969–1971 wiretaps to *Time* meant that as much as the Nixon White House might be tempted to utilize Sullivan, he would have to be kept at arm's length. Gray might be able to sidestep the issue— after all, he had not been involved—but Sullivan could not be allowed to testify, much less return to the FBI.[25]

The *Time* article, naturally, produced another flash of anger within the administration. Ehrlichman ordered that a prompt denial be issued even though he knew the story was accurate. "No one at the White House asked for or ordered any such taps," the statement read. Meanwhile, the *Time* account produced some genuine internal confusion, too. For a few days the White House was left wondering if Sullivan was also leaking now, because it recognized that he was the only FBI official, other than Felt, who knew about the wiretaps. This concern was captured during a twenty-five-minute meeting between Nixon and Dean on February 27, the day after the article appeared.[26]

"Who from the FBI is trying to put out this stuff on us?" Nixon asked. "God, I thought—I wish I knew, Mr. President," Dean replied. "You don't think it's Sullivan?" Nixon replied. No, Dean said. He had confronted Sullivan after Felt indicated that Sullivan "knew all the facts." But when "I said, 'Bill . . . I want to tell you what *Time* magazine said they have,'" Dean recalled, "his reaction was not that of a man who has leaked something." Sullivan sounded genuinely shocked and distraught. He then made, Dean said, an unassailable argument that "he would be one of the last people in the world who would want that story out." Indeed, Sullivan couldn't quite figure out who was responsible, even though Dean had mentioned that "Mark Felt had pointed the finger at him [Sullivan]."[27]

Dean went on to praise Sullivan in Nixon's presence, calling him a "wealth of knowledge" on wiretapping. "The more I . . . sort of generally chat with him about these problems," Dean observed, "the more it comes out he's the man that can also document [what happened]." Sullivan had even expressed a willingness to bear responsibility for the 1969–1971 wiretaps if need be. If this matter ever comes down to the "very short strokes," he had said to Dean, as far as he was concerned "[it] was Hoover and Sullivan. No one else." Taking responsibility for the wiretaps wasn't really a problem, Sullivan believed, because they had been placed for genuine "national security purposes. These people [on the NSC staff] worked with sensitive material on Vietnam that was getting out to reporters."[28]

Dean disagreed with Gray's depiction of Sullivan as bitter and bent on revenge. "[Sullivan] sat back and waited until he could come back in," Dean said. "He didn't try to force or blackmail his way around with knowledge he had." In that sense, Sullivan, despite his well-publicized differences with Hoover, was being loyal to the FBI. But "somebody over there is not," Nixon countered immediately. "Can [Sullivan] help you find out who the hell is not?" Dean explained that Sullivan still wanted to go back to the Bureau, presumably to put his long-held ideas about domestic intelligence-gathering into effect. "Why is it that Gray doesn't want him?" Nixon asked. "I think Mark Felt has poisoned Gray on this issue," Dean said.[29]

The discussion then turned, at last, to Felt. Because Nixon was still undecided about the logic behind Felt's leaks, he had a flicker of doubt. "Do you believe the *Time* magazine lawyer?" he asked Dean. "Is [Felt] capable of this sort of thing?" Dean said not only had he heard about the Sandy Smith link but that Henry Petersen had told him in October about Felt leaking to a publication, which Dean presumed was the *Washington Post*. "Petersen's an old hand over [at the Justice Department], as you know," Dean said. "And bless his soul, he's a valuable man to us. . . . He said that he wouldn't put it past Felt."[30]

"Does Felt know about the Sullivan stuff?" Nixon asked, meaning the 1969–1971 wiretaps. Yes, Dean replied. He reiterated the story about calling Felt on February 23 just before the *Time* story that was about to appear. "He was . . . very cool when I said 'There's a *Time* magazine story running, Mark, that [says] in '69 and so on and so forth.'" Dean said that he had simply asked Felt, "True or false?" Felt had said true, and Dean had then asked, "How do you know that? I've never heard of [the wiretapping] before." Felt replied, "'Well, if you talk to Bill Sullivan, he'll tell you all about it.'" Felt "was just as cool as a cucumber about it," Dean observed.[31]

The president wondered if Felt would support the White House in its stonewalling of the *Time* story. "Is he gonna stand up for the denial?" Nixon asked. Dean replied that Felt had said, "'Well, John, as far as I'm concerned, our phone call is totally off the record. We never had it.'" But, as Nixon shrewdly observed, that cooperation came at a price, meaning "[we] can't blow the whistle on Felt" because it was obvious he knew too much. Haldeman had identified the same problem the previous October, and even though there was no longer a presidential election to worry about, in the interim Watergate had grown into such a political problem that the White House was still hamstrung vis-à-vis Felt. As much as it pained Nixon to give in to Felt again, it would be far more problematic to fire the "son of a bitch." Attorney General Kleindienst had arrived at precisely the same conclusion, Dean said.[32]

The young White House counsel tried to temper the president's obvious frustration. Once Gray was confirmed he could take a lie-detector test, Dean suggested, and then ask everyone in his "immediate shop" to take one, too. Presumably Felt would quietly resign rather than take the test—although the machines could be beaten, so even that plan was not foolproof. For the time being, Nixon advised Dean to "watch [Felt] like a hawk."

"He's too close to Pat Gray now," Dean said.

"Pat Gray is a little naïve," the president replied.[33]

On February 27 Woodward signaled for a rendezvous with Deep Throat. They had not seen each other since the frustrating meeting on January 24, when Felt cavalierly declined to advance *Time*'s allegation about Mitchell and Colson. Woodward and Bernstein wanted a meeting because they were "baffled" and "perplexed" by Gray's nomination. It made no sense ostensibly. The confirmation hearings would inevitably become a lens through which to examine the FBI's Watergate investigation. And from everything Felt had told Woodward about Gray, the reporters could not believe the administration would want that can of worms opened up.[34]

Felt suggested the meeting take place in a Prince George's County tavern rather than the usual spot in the garage. The bar was a working-class dive where they were unlikely to be recognized. When they got together around 9 p.m. Felt seemed very relaxed. He spoke about Nixon's being on the rampage about leaks. The White House "'wants to eat the *Washington Post*,'" he told Woodward, in what might have been an effort to flatter the hungry reporter, since the most damaging disclosure recently had appeared in *Time*. In any event, Felt exuded confidence that the administration's search for the *Post*'s sources would come to naught. He said—falsely—that Nixon thought at least some of the leaks were now coming from the White House, and that Haldeman reportedly suspected Ehrlichman, or someone on Ehrlichman's staff. Yet this subject didn't interest Woodward much because it did nothing to advance the story.[35]

Then Woodward asked about Gray's nomination, saying that it didn't "make any sense." But it made all the sense in the world, Felt replied. He told Woodward—falsely—that an angry Gray had gone to the White House in early February to remind the administration that he had done his job well and limited the FBI's investigation. (According to Nixon's official schedule, there was no such meeting.) "'I'm taking the rap on the Watergate,'" Gray had allegedly said. He then implied, according to Felt, that "all hell could break loose" if he weren't nominated for the directorship to "keep the lid on." Nixon "could have 'thought this was a threat, though Gray is not that sort of guy,'" Felt observed. In any case, the president agreed to send Gray's name up to the Senate at once even though several top aides were against it. So Gray had blackmailed the president? Woodward asked. "I never said that," Felt responded with a laugh.[36]

According to Woodward's notes, Felt also said that "Gray really believes he conducted 'a full court press' on [the] investigation, but he didn't because his sympathies are such a part of his being that he couldn't presume that anyone around the president would directly authorize something illegal." Elsewhere, of course, and months later, Felt would vigorously defend the FBI's Watergate probe as penetrating, detailed, and a thorough investigative effort.[37]

As the two men nursed their Scotches, they also talked about the story in *Time* magazine. Was it true? Woodward asked. Had Gray known about the wiretaps on the White House aides and newsmen? "Affirmative," Felt said—another lie. But information about the wiretaps was so closely held, he added, that Gray could allegedly "deny it under oath because his knowledge was 'out of channels.'" Felt then gave Woodward the names of two of the wire-tapped reporters (none of the names had appeared in Sandy Smith's article). Hedrick Smith and Neil Sheehan of the *New York Times* had been put under surveillance by an "'out-of-channels' vigilante squad of wiretappers" after the newspaper had refused to stop publication of the Pentagon Papers, Felt said—yet another lie. In truth, the wiretapping had ended well before release of the Pentagon Papers, and Neil Sheehan had never been one of the targets.[38]

Felt had come a long way from the cautious leaker who had to have information about E. Howard Hunt's link to the break-in pried out of him. Contemptuous of the media, he seemed indifferent to the possibility of being proven wrong. Writing about the tavern meeting in *All the President's Men*, Woodward said he wondered why Deep Throat was speaking so freely in a public place. Felt seemed to be "flirting with the danger of being discovered," wrote Woodward. He was about to ask Felt why when he realized "it was enough to know that Deep Throat would never deal with [me] falsely."[39]

No piece of information Felt ever shared was so blatantly untrue as the claim that Gray had blackmailed the president into nominating him. It did not appear contemporaneously in the *Post*—the allegation was first leveled in *All the President's Men*—but it was and remains a wonderful demonstration of Felt's true, and very personal, agenda.[40]

Gray Self-Destructs

March–May 1973

The job of the reporter is [to convey] the best obtainable version of the truth . . .
that is what reporting is all about.
—Carl Bernstein

On the morning of the first day of Pat Gray's confirmation hearings, President Nixon asked John Dean how he thought the nominee would fare.

"I think Pat is tough," Dean replied. "He's very comfortable in all of the decisions he has made, and I think he'll be good." But then Dean spoke, almost wistfully, about how different things might have been if Hoover was still alive—and that got the president going again. "The Bureau is leaking like a sieve, and Gray denies it," Nixon complained. "Just says it's not coming from the Bureau. Just who in the hell is it coming from? How in the hell could it be coming from anybody else?" He voiced his fears that should Gray win confirmation, he would insist on keeping Felt on—and "that would worry the hell out of me."[1]

Gray's first day before the Senate Judiciary Committee went smoothly, but from there things went rapidly downhill. Just as he had tried to oblige the White House earlier, now he sought to please the Senate. He proposed to open the entire Watergate investigative file to the committee's chairman, ranking member, and their respective counsels and to make knowledgeable field agents available to answer any questions. Such openness was unheard of and rankled not only the Hooverites in the Bureau but anyone inside the FBI who prized its independence. It was another example of either Gray's refreshing candor or his shocking naïveté.

Back in January, Felt had confidently told Woodward that Gray would "probably not" let the Senate see the FBI's basic reports on Watergate, presumably because they would be too embarrassing. The opposite was true, of course; thus Gray's offer caught his detractors by surprise, but only momentarily. Chief among them was Senator Robert Byrd (D–West

Virginia). Even when Gray's nomination was just a rumor, Byrd had issued a statement vigorously opposing it—it would be a "premature" move, he said—and now he was open about his intention to bottle it up until the separate Watergate hearings were over. Gray was "the bone of contention, the source of division" within the Bureau, Byrd claimed. The FBI had become a "political arm of the administration" under Gray, and its investigation of Watergate "was aimed only at the actual events . . . and avoided any attempt toward tying together the leads concerning where the plot originated." When D. W. Bowers, the FBI's congressional liaison, met with Byrd to find out why he was so dead-set against Gray, the senator replied that Sandy Smith's "Tattletale Gray" article had told him everything he needed to know. Byrd didn't tell Bowers that he was also getting anti-Gray ammunition from contacts inside the Bureau.[2]

Following Byrd's remarks, Gray received a letter from E. Howard Hunt, who was awaiting sentencing. Hunt offered to make the "thoroughness and savagery of the FBI's Watergate investigation" a matter of public record in light of Byrd's allegations.

> From my own experience I am able fully and freely to testify that the Bureau left no grain of sand unturned in its investigation. My late wife and children were interrogated, blackmailed, threatened, and harassed by special agents. . . . My relatives, friends and acquaintances, however remote, were interviewed exhaustively and embarrassingly by FBI personnel across the country. Threats and intimidation were not the least of the investigative tools employed by [agents] under your direction.[3]

For the other senators whose minds were not yet made up, Gray's confirmation hearings were nonetheless the first opportunity they had had to interrogate a member of the administration about Watergate, and they intended to make the most of the occasion. Blissfully unaware of the cover-up, Gray saw no reason to hide anything about the involvement of the White House in the FBI's probe. He would argue that in the absence of information to the contrary, he could not indulge in the presumption that a president of the United States or his legal counsel were engaged in illegal acts. He had assumed regularity and that everyone was acting in accordance with the law.

Up to this point John Dean had scarcely been mentioned in press coverage of Watergate, and nowhere close to the degree of his true involvement. Very early on, in July, his name had surfaced in a *Post* story that stated he was an "informal staff coordinator" of the White House's response to the break-in. Then, during a news conference six weeks later, the president mentioned that Dean had conducted a "complete investigation of all leads which might involve any present members of the White House staff," and had found that "no one . . . presently employed, was involved in this very bizarre incident." That task hardly seemed unusual for the president's counsel, though, and soon Dean's name again slipped below the surface.[4]

By the second day of the hearings, however, Gray had succeeded in making Dean's conduct during the FBI investigation at least as much of an issue as his own. This was a completely unanticipated development. Dean "directed the ugliest possible thoughts at Gray," and "kicked himself" for not having anticipated the problem and protesting the nomination vigorously. Dean, of course, was thinking primarily about his own legal vulnerabilities. But his problems were inextricable from a far larger one. To every degree that he became an issue, the focus shifted from the Watergate crime to the cover-up—and that was an extremely dangerous development for the White House.[5]

Gray intended to keep one big secret from the senators: the papers from Hunt's safe that he had accepted and later destroyed. In a strained telephone conversation with John Ehrlichman on March 6, after it was clear that his relationship with Dean was going to receive minute scrutiny, Gray reminded Ehrlichman that Dean had to "stand awful tight in the saddle and be very careful about what he says, and to be absolutely certain that he knows in his own mind that he delivered everything he had to the FBI." Shortly after the phone call, Ehrlichman told Dean about Gray's hand-wringing, yet neither man espoused any sympathy for his plight. "Well, I think we ought to let him hang there," Ehrlichman said. "Let him twist slowly, slowly in the wind." Dean added, "I was in with the boss this morning and that's exactly where he was coming out. He said, 'I'm not sure that Gray's smart enough to run the Bureau the way he's handling himself.'"[6]

Indeed, Gray's selective candor unhinged the White House so much that Nixon soon decided he did not want him confirmed. "Gray, in my opinion, should not be the head of the FBI," the president said to Dean on March 13. "Not because of any character or other flaws, but because he is going to be too much like Kleindienst. After going through the hell of the hearing, he will not be a good director."[7]

Gray—whom Nixon soon took to deriding as a "big clown"—was in almost daily contact with Dean, asking him how he thought the hearings were progressing or what kind of spin the White House wanted him to put on one aspect or another. Their relationship was as surreal as anything in Washington: Gray thought his testimony was helpful to the administration and himself, but in fact, his admissions and explanations were often ripping the administration's previous statements to shreds. At one point the president asked his chief of staff, who is programming Gray? Haldeman had to remind Nixon that he had told the White House staff not to provide any guidance—to leave it to Attorney General Kleindienst. And Haldeman didn't actually know what the AG was telling Gray. Whatever the guidance was it wasn't working.

The political benefit Nixon had expected to obtain from Gray's nomination—a stout defense of the FBI's thorough Watergate investigation—was not materializing. Indeed, quite the opposite was taking place. The FBI stood falsely but plausibly charged of conducting a toothless investigation; Gray's testimony was putting a "cloud over the institution," as Haldeman wrote in his diary. Whereas Watergate had once looked like a purely political spat between Democrats and Republicans, with one party appearing little better than the other, Gray, almost single-handedly, was transforming it into a battle pitting the forces of law and justice against an administration that seemed to disdain both.[8]

The only group that relished the spectacle of Gray's testimony more than the Democrats did was the press. It was having a field day with his almost daily bombshells.

In the super-heated atmosphere that was beginning to envelop Watergate coverage, many media outlets were quite casual about impugning the FBI's investigation. The worst offender, unsurprisingly, was *Time*. Its March 19 cover story was devoted to the FBI and Gray's nomination and presented the litany of Felt-inspired allegations. "Two-Day Gray" (he had lost a day) had been zealous when it came to protecting the president and his interests but indifferent about the Bureau's integrity and reputation. He had "severely limited the FBI's initial probing" into the Watergate break-in. The article also alleged that when three FBI agents had "insisted on pushing the Watergate investigation" to include the White House, Gray had transferred two of them (at which point the third, rather than be transferred, had retired).[9]

The three executives in question—Charlie Bates, Charlie Bolz, and Robert Kunkel, all members of Felt's faction—were no longer in the positions they had held at the outset of the investigation, of course. Kunkel had been transferred against his will, to St. Louis, but the move had nothing to do with his investigative zeal; rather, it was his presumed inability to stem leaks out of the Washington Field Office that soured his relationship with Gray. Meanwhile, Bates and Bolz had left of their own accord in October and December, respectively, and if their departures could be said to be related to Watergate, it was most likely because they had grown uncomfortable with Felt's campaign to subvert Gray. *Time*'s allegation about Gray's treatment of the three men, in other words, was completely false—but also very plausible, at least superficially.[10]

One sure indicator that Felt was a source of erroneous information in the *Time* story was an anecdote about how Gray's nomination had come about. According to the article,

> as late as last month, [Gray's] appointment was still a matter of sharp controversy within the White House. Some presidential aides, including John Ehrlichman, felt that Gray was vulnerable to attack and had hurt the FBI. . . . The name of [William] Sullivan was again raised by the anti-Gray staffers as a possible permanent FBI chief.
>
> A key intercession was made at this point by presidential counsel [John] Dean. He asked the advice of Gray's No. 2 man at the FBI, veteran agent W. Mark Felt. A longtime foe of Sullivan, Felt said that Sullivan's appointment would throw the Bureau into chaos. Dean accepted that judgment at face value, strongly advised the selection of Gray—and Nixon nominated Gray on February 17. Thus Gray became indebted to Dean as well as to Mitchell.[11]

It was true that Ehrlichman had asked Dean to talk to Felt about Sullivan and Gray as potential nominees. *But Felt had opposed both.* His argument against Sullivan was powerful and persuasive to the White House counsel, his case against Gray much less so. In any event, Dean was only a messenger in this instance and simply reported the gist of the conversation to Ehrlichman. "Gray owed me nothing because I was not involved in the decision," Dean recalled.[12]

By having this misleading account published, Felt achieved two goals. He seriously undermined Gray, and simultaneously, curried his favor. Linking Gray's selection directly to Dean at a time when the White House counsel was becoming increasingly controversial was, of course, not helpful to Gray's chances in the slightest. At the same time, *Time*'s false portrayal of Felt's role—leaving the inference that he supported Gray's nomination—increased the likelihood that when Gray faltered, which seemed more likely by the day, he would suggest that the seemingly loyal Felt be nominated in his place.

Byrd cited the allegations in the *Time* article as the reason for why he was now dedicated to defeating outright, not just stalling, Gray's nomination, "for the good of the FBI." He mentioned Gray's absences from Washington during the Watergate investigation; the doubts that had been raised about the thoroughness, independence, and objectivity of the Bureau's probe; and Gray's "presumption of regularity" on the part of the White House and Dean. And while several other Democratic senators were not yet willing to go that far, they made it clear that without John Dean's testimony before the Judiciary Committee—which the president was refusing to allow, citing "executive privilege"—the Gray nomination was going nowhere.[13]

As Senate opposition to Gray mounted, the White House's disgust and amazement over his behavior also increased, reaching an apex on March 22. That day Gray testified that Dean had "probably" lied to FBI agents when, on June 22, he had claimed not to know whether Hunt still had an office in the White House—three days after he and Fred Fielding had already pawed through the contents of Hunt's office safe while wearing protective gloves. Gray has "screwed us again," Haldeman wrote in his diary.[14]

Gray's staffers had come across this all-but-forgotten inconsistency while reviewing the leak investigation Felt instigated after the *Washington Daily News* scoop. Although the internal report failed to disclose who had leaked information about the contents of Hunt's safe, an attached memo written by case agent Angelo Lano took note of a seeming discrepancy in Dean's statements to the Bureau. It was the only time that Dean had stumbled in his contacts with FBI agents and uttered a palpable falsehood, or so the agents thought. If so, this discovery meant that what started out as a Felt faction leak had inadvertently yielded one of the first real clues about the Augean cover-up of Watergate orchestrated by Dean.[15]

Recognizing that Gray's testimony was instrumental in turning Watergate into an enormous scandal, Nixon phoned Gray the day after his comment about Dean's falsehood, ostensibly to "buck him up." You are taking an unfair beating up there, the president told Gray, but there will come a time when we will be able to retaliate; in any case, there will always be a place for you in my administration. Ever the loyalist, Gray didn't perceive the real reason for the call. With the legal pincers closing, Nixon was trying to establish an alternative narrative. "You will recall, Pat," the president pointedly observed, "that I told you to conduct a thorough and aggressive investigation"—reminding Gray of the exact words he had used the previous July, after Gray's warning to him about his aides' cavalier misuse of the CIA and FBI.[16]

No publication, ironically, found more vindication in Gray's testimony than the *Washington Post*. As Barry Sussman later wrote, "Here was Patrick Gray, for no apparent purpose and certainly no personal gain, exposing all the lies beneath those carefully worded White House statements [from the previous fall]." Each new disclosure by the hapless nominee was cause for celebration at the newspaper, which now appeared completely justified in its devotion to the story. "Gray put the first dent into the whole [thing]," observed managing editor Howard Simons, ". . . Mister Straight Arrow." After one day of particularly damaging testimony, Ben Bradlee raced around the office, pounding his editors on the back and exchanging handshakes while proclaiming that "Pat Gray had rescued the free press." Yet somehow, these revelations did not prompt Woodward and Bernstein to rethink their estimate of Gray, the lies Felt had told about him, or the motive of their *über*-secret source.[17]

Gray's testimony was hardly the only thing chipping away at the administration's cover-up. On March 23, James McCord wrote a letter to Judge Sirica in which he claimed that political pressure had been applied to the Watergate defendants and that CRP witnesses had committed perjury during the trial. Added to this was a troubling behind-the-scenes development: Howard Hunt was asking the White House for complete financial security for his family before he went to prison. He wanted $122,000 (more than $622,000 in 2011 dollars) right away, and on top of what he had already received. Worse, this time he dispensed with circuitous channels and sent his request directly to John Dean. If the money was not forthcoming, Hunt not very subtly threatened to reveal the crimes he had committed as a White House plumber, including breaking into the office of Daniel Ellsberg's psychiatrist.[18]

The White House's intricate but ad hoc containment strategy was collapsing on every front. Not only was direct CRP involvement with the June 17 burglary beginning to emerge in a legal sense, but illegal or politically embarrassing activities before then—the reason for the cover-up in the first place—were in imminent danger of becoming public. Worst of all, the cover-up was unraveling, a development that posed the single greatest legal danger to the administration. As Haldeman noted—with typical understatement—in his diary on March 21, the "only problem for the White House is post-June 17. We did things to hold it down before the election that are right on the border."[19]

Fighting these various battles was possible when they remained discrete struggles. But now the administration was caught in an incredibly complex tangle, if not a vortex. The problem induced vertigo on a White House scale because political concerns often ran counter to the best legal strategy, and vice versa. There was no grand plan that could untie the Gordian knot of politico-legal problems the administration faced. Every day the president and his men vacillated desperately between an "every man for himself" strategy designed to save the White House at all costs, and a "we're all on the same team—no one's going to get flushed" approach. And every day's delay only made matters worse.[20]

On March 24, some ten days after he decided he didn't want Gray confirmed after all, Nixon instructed Ehrlichman to tell the nominee he was through. "We can't get the votes [in the Senate], and . . . even if we did he still wouldn't have [anyone's] confidence . . . he's been irreparably damaged." The White House's disenchantment took just one day to leak out. Nixon then revisited his idea of nominating Jerry Wilson. He also began entertaining the notion of appointing a sitting or former federal judge with prosecutorial experience—someone like William Webster from St. Louis, Lawrence Walsh from New York, or Matthew Byrne from Los Angeles. Even Henry Petersen's name was put forward.[21]

Gray tenaciously held on until on April 5, bowing to the inevitable only when it became obvious he would not get a favorable vote in committee, much less the full Senate. Haldeman delivered the *coup de grâce* that evening. Yet with everything else that was happening, Nixon nonetheless decided to keep Gray in place as acting director for the time being. The issue of a permanent director was put on hold until Watergate quieted down.[22]

That plan, too, went awry. Watergate was a burgeoning crisis and uncontained. Now that Gray had identified Dean as a principal actor, the post–June 17 activities suddenly assumed far more importance than the burglary itself. And while the break-in seemed unlikely to threaten Nixon's presidency, the cover-up easily could. In short order Dean hired a criminal attorney, and together they met with the Watergate prosecutors on April 4. After four days of negotiations, Dean began to reveal what he knew to the flabbergasted federal attorneys, even his initially-limited account provided sufficient grounds for indicting Mitchell, Haldeman, and Ehrlichman immediately on charges of obstructing justice. Eventually, of course, Dean would divulge his knowledge of the plumbers' activities, including the Ellsberg break-in, information about the improper handling of the contents of Hunt's safe. Now everything began to make more sense, although the behavior of the White House was still jaw-dropping at first hearing.

Once Nixon and his top aides realized that Dean was cooperating with prosecutors, they quickly assessed their potential vulnerabilities. One of the crucial issues involved the "special handling" of documents from Hunt's safe. No one in the White House other than Dean actually knew what Gray had done with the papers that had been handed to him. But around 10:45 p.m. on April 15, Ehrlichman, with Nixon and Haldeman in the room, called the acting FBI director to finally ask. Much hinged on whether he could still produce the documents; if he could, it would be relatively easy to fashion a plausible, alternative explanation that did not put the White House in the business of burning evidence. But Gray said he had disposed of the papers, per his instructions—and when Nixon heard this, the blood drained from his face. *The FBI's acting director had destroyed evidence in a criminal case—evidence that had been held inside the White House.* Realizing the implications of what he had just said, Gray offered to deny that the transfer had ever happened. But Ehrlichman cautioned him against trying to hide the truth, given that Dean was now cooperating with prosecutors. Twelve days later, Gray's receipt and disposal of the documents became banner headlines.[23]

The end was mortifying for Gray, who, in the end, had only wanted to be a decent director of the FBI and ably serve a president whom he respected. After initially thinking he might be able to remain in office, Gray learned that senior FBI executives were threatening to resign *en masse* unless he left Bureau headquarters that day for good. The effort to force Gray's instant resignation was spearheaded by Leonard "Bucky" Walters, an executive who was "very close" to Felt. Walters had opposed Gray's nomination and had even started a file of supposedly damaging items that might be useful in torpedoing the confirmation. Until the destruction of the Hunt documents surfaced, however, he didn't believe he had anything sufficiently damning. Now he did. As Walters drove to work in a carpool with William Soyars, Jr., Felt's former top aide who was now assistant director of the newly constituted Computer Systems Division, they hatched a plan. Walters then informed Mark Felt: the idea was to organize all eleven assistant directors to resign simultaneously if Gray didn't leave immediately. Felt was completely in favor of the scheme, and Walters, as he was leaving, paused at the door to Felt's office, waiting for him to say, "I'll join in." But he didn't.[24]

Walters had lined up all the assistant directors behind his plan and asked Felt, Do you want me to tell Gray or do you want to tell him? Felt said he would deliver the ultimatum. After receiving it, Gray asked to be given a moment to talk to the president. When he later met with the assistant directors, Gray explained that he was leaving because he could not think of a way to rationalize what he had done; and if he tried to stay any longer, there would be an "insurrection and mutiny" against his leadership. As soon as the disgraced acting director left headquarters, Felt ordered that all documents and materials in Gray's two safes be moved to his own office.[25]

To complete the humiliation, Gray now became a target of investigation, and not just because he had destroyed the Hunt documents. His Watergate files were sequestered, and both the FBI and a federal grand jury began looking into whether he had played a role in the conspiracy to obstruct the investigation, including whether he had tried to help the White House pin responsibility for the break-in on the CIA. Out of either sheer habit or spite, Felt would subtly misrepresent Gray's position during the Bureau's internal inquiry. Felt would falsely claim that *he* had urged Gray to contact the president directly after the attempted obstruction, and that Gray "indicated that he did not think communication with the president was a proper course to pursue."[26]

Gray departed the seat of government without ever having recognized Felt's deceit and covert subversion of his year-long directorship. He had never truly understood the milieu he was in, or exercised the caution that a suspicious commander in enemy bureaucratic waters should exhibit. Indeed, as Gray departed, he said he had recommended "that Felt be designated director, but I don't know whether those White House people will pay any attention to what I say." This positive recommendation squared with an evaluation he had just written about Felt for a public service award:

> It has been continually necessary for me to rely on his advice and counsel in difficult and unusual matters; and my admiration for him personally, as well as my confidence in him professionally, has constantly grown. . . .
>
> He has supervised all phases and facets of FBI endeavors, and his performance has been truly brilliant. He is one of the most talented, tireless, and dedicated public servants whom it has been my privilege to know, to observe, and to admire. . . .
>
> His future potential can be limited only by what he will be asked to do.[27]

On the evening of April 26, the night before Gray left headquarters in disgrace, Felt had called Woodward at the newsroom—a breach of his normal procedure, but he was too excited to worry about such things now. "You've heard the Gray story?" he asked. "Well, it's true." Woodward later wrote that he "could hear a certain joy in Felt's voice," although he would never figure out why Deep Throat sounded triumphant. So Felt undoubtedly believed he was on the cusp of reaching his long-sought goal. With all the pressure, controversy, and questions swirling around, not only about Watergate and the White House, but about the FBI's basic integrity, *surely* Nixon would realize that appointing a reliable Bureau professional was the only way to avoid more bungling.[28]

Nixon, too, had recognized that Gray would have to resign instantly once the document-destruction story was about to break. "He's a needless casualty in doing a dumb thing," the president told Henry Petersen, who had been meeting regularly with Nixon to discuss the Justice Department's expanded investigation. "Who would be the best—who is the second man over there?" Nixon asked, forgetting in the heat of the moment that it was his *bête noire*. "Mark Felt's the second man at the Bureau," Petersen responded. "Let me say one thing, Mr. President. You know, I don't give a damn whether I get that job or not . . . next to the presidency of the United States, it may be the toughest job in America. . . . [But] I don't want to see anybody from the inside take that job." Petersen was being somewhat coy, but with reason. He probably did not know whether Nixon was aware of the part he played in unmasking Felt the previous fall, and this was no time to get into particulars. Nixon hardly needed convincing. The FBI's "got to be cleaned out," he replied.[29]

The president had no time to waste in finding a replacement. Under the law, Felt, as the number two official, automatically became the acting FBI director after Gray left. And that was wholly unacceptable.[30]

Bereft of easy options, Nixon harked back to an earlier preference: William Ruckelshaus. As he explained to Kleindienst the next day, "I just talked to Bill Ruckelshaus [who] is a Mr. Clean, and I want a fellow in there that is not part of the old guard and that is not part of that infighting in there." Nixon hoped that this time around Ruckelshaus just might accept the permanent post, given the crisis the FBI (and the presidency) was now in. But the most he was willing to do was to become the acting director for a few weeks until Nixon could find a suitable candidate. "Temporary isn't the answer," Nixon said when Ehrlichman delivered the disappointing news. "We've just got to lay it to Ruckelshaus that he's got to take the job on a permanent basis." The president immediately arranged to meet with him on the afternoon of April 27. But not even forty-two minutes of presidential jaw-boning could persuade Ruckelshaus to relent and take a job he didn't want. But at least Nixon had someone other than Felt in place.[31]

Felt's account of his thoughts during April 26–27 is quite revealing, though inadvertently so. The exactness of his recollection about his short time in charge speaks volumes, as do his false humility and exaggerated pride. He had at last succeeded in attaining the directorship, even if it was only due to a legal technicality.

> Certainly I would have wanted the appointment. But uppermost in my thoughts was the state of mind at the FBI. . . . Could we keep the Bureau on course? The FBI had always been a closely knit and dedicated organization. Now it was confronted by another major change and the possibility that a new outsider would be brought in. I kept thinking, "if only the president sees the light and appoints a new director from the ranks this time."
>
> Several of the top officials were well-qualified. My own chances should have been good since I was next in line as associate director and had been running the Bureau while Gray was learning the ropes and delivering speeches. When one of the wire services reported that I was to be named director, I thought the problem had been solved—and my secretary spent a busy half-hour assembling photos and biographical data.
>
> Then, as suddenly as it had started, the rumor subsided. I was left again to sit at my desk wondering—but not for long. At 2:50 p.m., the president announced, without consultation with anyone at the Bureau, that he was appointing William B. [sic] Ruckelshaus to succeed Pat Gray. . . .
>
> I was and am proud of my FBI record and of the fact that I am the only insider ever to have climbed to the top of the FBI pyramid, if only for two hours and fifty minutes.[32]

Felt learned of Ruckelshaus's surprise appointment when a reporter called to ask about it; caught off guard, he answered, "I don't know anything about him." And although his 1979 memoir gives the impression that he immediately became resigned to the situation, that was hardly the case.[33]

When Nixon met with Ruckelshaus, he was advised to watch out for Felt. "Yes, the president mentioned [Felt's leaking] to me when he asked me to become the director of the FBI," Ruckelshaus explained in a 2007 interview. Specifically, the president described the damaging leaks to *Time* magazine. Nixon did not order Ruckelshaus to remove Felt; he merely issued a warning, which Ruckelshaus took under advisement, not knowing yet whether the information was true. "I suspended belief," Ruckelshaus said. "I simply chronicled that's what the president believes, or at least that's what he told me."[34]

When Ruckelshaus walked into his office for the first time on April 30—a day Felt later described as "blue Monday"—the first thing he found was a telegram on his desk. Addressed to the president and signed by more than seventy-one FBI officials, from Felt on down to the agents in charge of most of the field offices, the petition objected to the caretaker appointment and asserted that the FBI sorely needed a director who was a career professional. Felt hastened to explain to Ruckelshaus that it wasn't "personal"; it was just that "we really think somebody from the FBI should be appointed." Later that afternoon Ruckelshaus learned that the telegram had been leaked to the press. "I subsequently found out that Felt was the drafter of the letter," Ruckelshaus said.[35]

Although Ruckelshaus repeatedly stated that he had no interest in staying on permanently, Felt did not believe this was true, given his own hunger for the post. Once Ruckelshaus got his hands on the levers of FBI power, Felt thought, he would surely change his mind. The veneer of deception that Felt had maintained under Pat Gray was harder to sustain this time. Ruckelshaus found himself thinking that Felt was trying *too* hard to ingratiate himself. Felt's actual disdain for Ruckelshaus is manifest in his 1979 memoir. Felt wrote "that I was a stooge for the White House and he was trying to overcome all that," Ruckelshaus recalled. "That was just pure fabrication. I mean, you [can] call me a stooge or not, that's a judgment. But his version of the facts was not right." (Felt alleged that Ruckelshaus was a "security guard sent to see that the FBI did nothing which would displease Mr. Nixon.")[36]

As he had done when Gray was director, Felt looked for something to leak, in order to prove that Ruckelshaus, too, could not control the FBI— although this action would be completely gratuitous since Ruckelshaus had no intention of staying on. There was precious little left to leak about Watergate after the domino-like resignations of Haldeman, Ehrlichman, and Kleindienst, and Dean's dismissal on April 30. But Felt did know something about Vice President Spiro T. Agnew that might disturb the political order if it appeared in print.

In early May—shortly after the *Post* won a Pulitzer for its 1972 Watergate coverage—Felt told Woodward that the FBI's files contained an unverified allegation about Agnew, namely, that he had accepted a bribe while serving as vice president. Agnew had allegedly taken $2,500 in cash from a contractor in Baltimore County, the sprawling suburban area where Agnew got his political start. A federal grand jury was investigating construction kickbacks there, Felt explained, and he predicted that the vice president would eventually become a target.[37]

Woodward and another *Post* reporter then spent a day in Baltimore trying to interview a disgruntled contractor who reportedly knew about the kickback, but they were not able to corroborate the information. With Watergate exploding daily, Woodward could not spend any more time chasing the story, so he reluctantly passed it along to Richard Cohen, the *Post* reporter whose beat was Maryland politics. Woodward described it as coming from "his most trusted source," a government official code-named Deep Throat. Cohen found the story almost preposterous: a sitting vice president taking penny-ante bribes from a contractor? Nonetheless he knew that during the recent legislative session in Annapolis, rumors had abounded that Agnew was under some kind of investigation.[38]

Two weeks later Cohen and a colleague, Bill Richards, wrote a front-page story about a secret federal grand jury probe of kickbacks in Baltimore County. They had not been able to corroborate Deep Throat's information; indeed, they reported that "widespread rumors to the contrary," Agnew was *not* a target of the investigation and not likely to become one. He had ceased being the Baltimore County chief executive in 1966, so the statute of limitations had run out on any bribes received while he was a local official.[39]

Thus, Felt's leak went for naught, if his intention was to incite the White House against Ruckelshaus (though ultimately the information about Agnew, of course, turned out to be true). In any event, the White House had much more serious problems to worry about. Even if the Cohen/Richards story had been able to corroborate Felt's leak, no one in the administration would probably have paid much attention to the source of the information per se, though Agnew would surely have been furious. Yet Nixon and his advisers considered Agnew a political lightweight and paid him little heed, although he was simultaneously considered some of the best insurance the president had against impeachment. Perhaps Felt even realized that, and reasoned that this condideration would be why the leak would work to Ruckelshaus's disadvantage. Still, the effort to sabotage Ruckelshaus was superfluous. True to his word, he stepped down from the directorship in early June.[40]

But by that time Felt would be gone, too, a victim of his longtime nemesis, Bill Sullivan.

The events that precipitated Felt's departure began with a Woodward and Bernstein article on May 3. Citing "two highly placed sources in the executive branch," it claimed that wiretaps supervised by Howard Hunt and Gordon Liddy had been placed on two unnamed *New York Times* reporters after publication of the Pentagon Papers. Felt had given Woodward this information, along with the names of the two reporters, supposedly Hedrick Smith and Neil Sheehan, during their tavern meeting in late February. But Woodward and Bernstein had not been able to do anything with the information for weeks, as they needed time to obtain confirmation and more details.[41]

The information Felt had given Woodward was grossly inaccurate, and the May 3 article reflected those inaccuracies. While the FBI *had* wiretapped two *Times* reporters, Hedrick Smith and William Beecher (*not* Sheehan), during 1969–1971, the taps had had nothing whatsoever to do with the Pentagon Papers. And neither Hunt nor Liddy had been involved—as Felt well knew.[42]

The second "highly placed source" who provided general corroboration had been Donald E. Santarelli, an associate deputy attorney general during Nixon's first term, and a rising Republican star in legal circles. Santarelli was articulate and analytical, and he and Woodward had become social friends well before Watergate became a news story. And while Santarelli had nothing to do with Watergate either before or after the break-in, he knew all the key actors in Justice and the FBI, many in the White House, including John Dean, and several in the CRP, among them, Gordon Liddy. Indeed, because he thought so little of Dean, Santarelli had lobbied John Mitchell, Bob Haldeman, and John Ehrlichman hard, but unsuccessfully, to prevent Dean's appointment as White House counsel in 1970. Now Santarelli believed the White House was reaping a political whirlwind because it had put Dean in such a sensitive post.[43]

Because Santarelli and Woodward were friends—and also because Santarelli was known for being outspoken, informed, and frank—"Bob would call me regularly," Santarelli later recalled. Although Woodward would ask him questions related to Watergate that were often beyond the scope of his direct knowledge, Santarelli would try his best to answer them, with the understanding that he was providing the information on background. Such was the case with respect to the NSC wiretaps. During a March 24 interview with Woodward, Santarelli roughly corroborated Felt's February account. The word "roughly" is key: information about the 1969–1971 wiretaps was closely held, and Santarelli had never been briefed officially or directly about the surveillance. "I just picked [information about the NSC taps] up," he said later. "I was never briefed on them." Santarelli accurately relayed that one of the *Times* reporters wiretapped (Beecher, though no name was used) had broken stories on arms control talks with Moscow, but he did not confirm that either Liddy or Hunt had been involved. Santarelli also conveyed several inaccuracies, too, saying, for instance, that the project had begun in 1971 and that the wiretaps had been "[former assistant attorney general Robert] Mardian's idea." Altogether, there were enough inconsistencies between Felt's and Santarelli's accounts that Woodward worried about having a hopelessly confused story. Nonetheless, he and Bernstein went ahead with the article on the grounds that they could claim, if just barely, that Felt's account had been corroborated.[44]

With a small bomb going off nearly every day since the start of the Gray hearings in late February, Woodward and Bernstein were not able to put the finishing touches on their wiretap article until early May. Despite this delay, and even though the story was riddled with errors when it did appear, the article still represented something of an advance on Sandy Smith's February 26 account.[45]

In it the *Post* conveyed for the first time a central truth about Watergate: that the cover-up stemmed not just from CRP's involvement in the break-in, but from apprehension that earlier "White House horrors" would come out, too. A paragraph buried halfway through the article described these fears, quoting Felt directly; that part of the "deep background" agreement was, by now, more honored in the breach than in the observance. The piece said, "According to one source [Felt] . . . the June 17, 1972 arrest at the Watergate set those people 'off the edge' with worry that the Watergate break-in would lead to discovery of the earlier wiretapping by the Nixon administration."[46]

Notwithstanding the muddled nature of the Woodward and Bernstein account—or perhaps because of it—Ruckelshaus was spurred into action. A factor that contributed to Ruckelshaus's desire to get to the bottom of the wiretapping was the ongoing federal trial in Los Angeles of Daniel Ellsberg, who had leaked the Pentagon Papers. Judge Matthew Byrne, after reading about the alleged White House wiretaps on newsmen, expressed concern that the case against Ellsberg might be irrevocably tainted by government misconduct. So Ruckelshaus promised to get at the truth, once and for all. He might be only a caretaker director, but he was still determined to do what he could to restore order to the FBI during his time on the job, whether it was measured in days, weeks, or months. He ordered an urgent investigation into the allegations, telling skeptical subordinates that he wanted the truth. "I want to be kept constantly advised of progress on this matter," he wrote in a memo to Felt. A select squad of agents was immediately assembled for the task.[47]

As the FBI executive responsible for the initial leak to *Time* magazine in February, Felt had reason to be worried about such an investigation. Even though the focus was supposedly on the wiretaps themselves—who had ordered them, who was put under surveillance, when, and why, and what had happened to all the paperwork—the source of the initial leak to the news media was a natural avenue of inquiry as well. (And in fact, when agents eventually interviewed John Mitchell, the former attorney general would flatly tell them, while refusing to divulge his source, that "Mark Felt . . . was responsible for these [wiretap] leaks.") Yet, besides expressing skepticism about such a probe to Ruckelshaus, there was not much Felt could do about it except cross his fingers and hope that the question of who leaked the information in the first place would never come to the fore. The investigation would be daunting, which was a big factor in Felt's favor. The relevant records had been removed from the FBI premises—an unheard-of action—and were mistakenly believed to have been destroyed.[48]

Then, in the midst of the Ruckelshaus-instigated internal probe, an article about the 1969–1971 wiretaps by John M. Crewdson appeared in the *New York Times* on May 11. Crewdson's account was accurate and authoritative—which was not surprising, considering that his source was William Sullivan. No one knew more than Sullivan about the wiretaps.

When precisely Sullivan realized he had an opportunity to turn the tables on Mark Felt, utilizing the very same secret that Felt had wielded against him, is unknowable. It had taken Sullivan a while to recognize that the original leak to *Time* magazine had come from inside the FBI, and therefore, must have been crafted by his internal adversaries to eradicate his chances of ever re-achieving a position of power inside the Bureau. But for Sullivan—the executive who had been in charge of the FBI's COINTELPRO operations against homegrown radicals and the American Communist Party—a man whose favorite quotation was "Oh, what a tangled web we weave, When first we practice to deceive!"—framing Mark Felt could not have been much of a stretch, or overly complicated. He knew that Felt had become aware of the tightly held secret because just before Sullivan left the FBI, they had a confrontation over the missing files. All that Sullivan needed to do was devise some ruse whereby his disclosure would be solidly attributed to Felt.[49]

Crewdson's article reignited the administration's anger over leaks, but it also arrived at a moment when a distracted president was suddenly facing a new and even more serious threat. The previous summer's abortive effort to invoke CIA equities was now beginning to surface. During an hour-long meeting between Nixon and his new chief of staff, Alexander Haig, on May 11, the conversation careened back and forth between how to handle the allegation that the White House had sought to impede the FBI's investigation, and the implications from Crewdson's piece. Before the meeting both Haig and Elliot Richardson, the attorney general–designate, had tried to determine Crewdson's unnamed source. And just as Sullivan had hoped and planned, the administration presumed it was Mark Felt.[50]

> *Haig:* First, there's a suspicion that Felt leaked. The fact that—
> *Nixon:* I know about that. Felt's supposed to be the leaker.
> *Haig:* Bad guy. Now, last night he gave the whole thing, the results of the Ruckelshaus investigation [into the wiretaps] to the *New York Times.*
> *Nixon:* Felt did?
> *Haig:* Yeah. Now he's got to go. But we've got to be careful as to when to cut his nuts off. . . . He's bad.[51]

Nixon went off on a tangent before returning to the subject of Felt's latest alleged leak. At last Felt's motive all along was laid bare, courtesy of his archrival.

> *Nixon:* Do we know that Felt leaked this to the *Times*?
> *Haig:* Well, according to Elliot [Richardson], they're sure. And, as a matter of fact, I talked to Bill Sullivan yesterday, and what Felt is doing is trying to kill Bill Sullivan so he can be director of the FBI and not Bill Sullivan. These guys are just unbelievable. . . . That place [the FBI] is riddled and rotten.[52]

Later in the conversation Nixon came back to the subject of the leak, as if he just could not believe Felt was at it again.

> *Nixon:* And Felt leaked this to the *Times?*
> *Haig:* That's the report Elliot has, and Sullivan told me that's what's going on.

Nixon: Oh, he used to leak to *Time* magazine. He's a bad guy, you see.

Haig: Very bad; he's got to go. . . .

Nixon: What's [Sullivan] think [Felt's] up to?

Haig: [Sullivan] thinks he's trying to—

Nixon: Be head of the Bureau—

Haig: Be head of the Bureau and block anybody else. I don't know whether to believe these guys, except I have great confidence in Sullivan. For years he's been really the best man in the Bureau.

Nixon: But Hoover didn't like him. Hoover fired him.

Haig: True, because he kept pressing Hoover to do the things that had to be done, the reforms.[53]

Sullivan had obviously succeeded in convincing the White House that Felt was responsible for the Crewdson story. Still, the main target was Ruckelshaus; he, more than anyone else, had to be persuaded. The acting director was likely to respond harshly to the unauthorized disclosure of new and important details about the wiretaps, at a time when he was racing to get the Bureau out in front of the story. And indeed, Ruckelshaus was furious about being undercut when he was working overtime to reestablish a modicum of credibility for the Bureau. He had not taken the Felt-instigated petition personally, but he wasn't going to allow this kind of behavior to occur with impunity.[54]

Nixon's secret Oval Office recordings add one last wrinkle to Sullivan's sting: the White House knew in advance that Ruckelshaus would be moving against Felt. Shortly after noon, Haig and the president had another meeting that again touched on Crewdson's article.

Haig: There have been leaks of this information before the [wiretap] investigation [ordered by Ruckelshaus] was completed and among those was this man who's being discharged.

Nixon: Felt.

Haig: Fire his ass. . . .

Nixon: Blame it on Felt. . . .

Haig: Sir, he's going to do it [leak] whether we fire him or we keep him, and if we fire him and discredit him, everything he says from there on is going to be—

Nixon: [Does Ruckelshaus] want him fired?

Haig: Yes. Now I haven't talked to him, but I got that indirectly.[55]

Crewdson's article appeared on a Friday, and Felt was out of the office until Monday, so Ruckelshaus could not act immediately. Over the weekend, at Camp David, Nixon began second-guessing the decision to get rid of Felt, worried that it might attract undue attention. Given the super-heated political atmosphere, Nixon feared that Felt might not be discredited, as would normally occur, but instead might be hailed in the press as a martyr who was fired for trying to blow the whistle on government misconduct. He decided to give his new chief of staff a little tutorial on Felt over the telephone.

> *Nixon:* I think the thing to do is to wait until we get the new man, and then the new man is told—
> *Haig:* I agree.
> *Nixon:* —to *clean* house. In the meantime, Felt—everybody's to know that he's a god-damn traitor, and just watch him damn carefully.
> *Haig:* That's right.
> *Nixon:* And—*he* has to go, of course. Because it's now obvious, you see. We have these reports . . . an interesting thing. I have these reports, Al. I got 'em directly, you know, that [said] that he was leaking to *Time* magazine, from their attorney. This was, oh, months ago. And before I sent Pat Gray's name up, I said, "Pat, I want you to check these leaks." He said, "Oh, they couldn't be from the Bureau." I said, "Yes, they *are*." I said, "Some are." And I said, "We have a *very* good authority that they're from Felt." [Gray said] "Oh, it couldn't be from Felt." I said, "Dammit, they may be—you oughta give him a lie-detector test." You know—verify. "Oh, I can't do that," he says. But he says, "I *vouch* for Felt." I also raised it with [then Attorney General] Kleindienst. *Kleindienst* vouched for Felt, which shows how clever *Felt* is.
> *Haig:* Yeah.
> *Nixon:* But my point is, that this is three [or] four months ago, Al, that we were on to the sonuvabitch. And, you know, and we had a lead, and it shows you how important it is that you and I gotta be sure that [when] we get leads like this in the future, we don't disregard them.
> *Haig:* That's right. That's right.
> *Nixon:* Isn't that interesting?
> *Haig:* That's stunning.[56]

If Nixon intended to issue a new marching order that would have Ruckelshaus act cautiously, it failed to reach the interim director in time. Instead, Ruckelshaus girded himself for what he knew would be a tense meeting with Felt on May 14.

Felt's memoir makes mention of several unpleasant encounters between the two men. "My decision to retire undoubtedly pleased [Ruckelshaus]," Felt wrote, as "he regarded me as a thorn in his side because I frequently disagreed with what he wanted to do." Yet somehow Felt doesn't describe the one clash that really mattered. His forced retirement is written with aplomb, although the experience clearly shook him to the core at the time.[57]

By sheer coincidence, Woodward asked Felt for a meeting on May 16, the day after Felt's "retirement," which had not yet been announced publicly. Bernstein and Woodward were preparing an important article that was, in essence, going to be a bookend to their "centerpiece" story of the previous October. In a banner story on the front page of the *Washington Post*, on the eve of the Senate Watergate hearings, the reporters were going to allege that the Nixon administration had carried out an "elaborate, continuous campaign of illegal and quasi-legal undercover operations" since 1969. Some of the information, including use of the term "vigilante squad," had come directly from Felt (who would be cited as a "highly placed source in the executive branch"). Still, Woodward had dozens of questions he wanted to ask the night the article went to press.[58]

Shattering events, including the departures of Haldeman, Ehrlichman, Kleindienst, and Dean, had occurred since Woodward's last clandestine meeting with Felt. The flood had come, just as Deep Throat had once predicted it would, and it had swept away the president's closest aides— and this was before the Senate's Watergate hearings had even begun. Naturally, Woodward "figured his friend would be in a good mood." After all, weren't they on the same side?[59]

But when Woodward arrived at the garage, shortly before midnight, he found Felt pacing nervously. His lower jaw "seemed to quiver" as he spoke, and he raced through what little he had to say. "It was clear that a transformation had come over [him]," Woodward later wrote. During Felt's near-monologue, he raced through a series of statements that were a by-now familiar admixture of facts, falsehoods, and exaggerations, save that Woodward still took everything he heard as gospel. For the first time—but nearly a year after the fact, and as the information was coming out elsewhere—Deep Throat alluded to the early effort to use the CIA to obstruct aspects of the FBI probe. "CIA people [Helms and Walters] can testify that Haldeman and Ehrlichman said that the president orders you to carry this out, meaning the Watergate cover-up," Felt revealed.[60]

Anyone who has ever read or watched *All the President's Men* will recall what happened next. Woodward returned to his apartment, told Bernstein to come over, and began typing out what Felt had told him. He dared not say it out loud, for fear his apartment was bugged. Felt's most outlandish claim was that "everyone's life is in danger" and that "electronic surveillance is going on," conducted by the CIA. Although it was 2 a.m., the two reporters raced over to Ben Bradlee's home, waking him so that he could read Deep Throat's latest advisory. They talked until four in the morning.[61]

A few hours later, Bradlee called a meeting of the entire Watergate team—himself, Howard Simons, Harry Rosenfeld, Barry Sussman, Woodward, and Bernstein—along with the national editor, Richard Harwood, to discuss the previous night's events. Harwood, who had been the most prominent internal skeptic at the outset of the *Post*'s Watergate coverage, thought Woodward and Bernstein "had finally gone around the bend and [were] nearing the edge of fantasy." They were engaging in "a kind of paranoid delusion of persecution."[62]

Years later, Woodward would admit that his report was "a little overly emotional." Yet given what we now understand about the true circumstances of Felt's departure, and what probably was his state of mind that evening, it is clear that Woodward was in fact accurately conveying Deep Throat's own paranoia after the sudden collapse of his scheme. He had been outdone by his old nemesis, who had proven even more cunning than he. No wonder Felt's hurried monologue on the night of May 16 included inventions far wilder than anything he had previously fed Woodward. A year of painstakingly weaving a web of deceit, denial, and self-deception had taken its toll. Felt was probably on the verge of a nervous breakdown.[63]

Hoover's top echelon of hard-bitten men always prided themselves on their ability to deceive those outside the FBI, if not one another; the word *con* was one of the most frequently used words in their vocabulary. And Crazy Billy had pulled off one of the shrewdest cons ever. He had gotten his revenge. Dispatching Felt meant that none of Hoover's loyal disciples (in other words, Sullivan's enemies) would ever get the top job.[64]

Felt's only solace, perhaps, was that his arch nemesis had also been denied. The same month Felt left the FBI after thirty-one years of service, Sullivan retired from his Justice Department post, having recognized, finally, he could never return to the FBI.[65]

CHAPTER ELEVEN

The Making of Deep Throat

1973–1981

Folks may be getting fuzzy about the Watergate details, but at least they remember the movie: a couple of nosy journalists and an informer, wasn't it?
—*Wilfrid Sheed*, Essays in Disguise

In the few weeks in the Bureau that remained to him, Felt managed to regain his equilibrium while putting out self-serving accounts of the long year since J. Edgar Hoover's death. He told one favored reporter, Jeremiah O'Leary of the *Washington Star,* that he had been "uncomfortable" during the entire interregnum. "[Felt] and others were appalled by the damage to Bureau morale during the tenure of the naïve and inexperienced Gray," O'Leary wrote on May 27, some two weeks after the confrontation with Ruckelshaus and five days after the official announcement of Felt's "retirement." This story marked the first time that Felt was open in public about his true attitude toward Gray all along.[1]

Woodward and Bernstein, naturally, worried that they might be handicapped by Deep Throat's departure from the FBI. They needn't have. By now their reputations were firmly fixed, and they had little trouble finding sources as Watergate passed into a new phase. As one contemporaneous account observed, "Almost everyone . . . wants to open a line of communication with them, to plant his version of what has been going on, to try to find out how much the young reporters know." The lengthening list of Watergate defendants became sources, as their lawyers maneuvered for favorable treatment. Federal prosecutors became much more talkative about their efforts, and willing to expose what the White House had done to stymie their case. Even staffers at the White House, including Leonard Garment, a counsel, and David Gergen, a speechwriter, eventually became willing sources.[2]

And by the spring of 1973, Woodward and Bernstein were no longer solely devoted to daily journalism. The previous fall they had signed a $55,000 contract (nearly $300,000 in 2011 dollars) with Simon & Schuster to write a conventional political narrative about the scandal, one that would go well beyond their cautious stories in the *Post*. They were not making good progress, however, on what was supposed to be a "short, quick" book due at the end of 1973. Trying to fashion a self-contained narrative when the story was mushrooming and changing weekly was daunting; how could they write a book when there was no end in sight? It got to the point where the book's tentative title—*A Point in Time*—seemed self-mocking. Frustration set in, and by early spring, the thought was percolating that "maybe [the book] isn't such a good idea" and the advance ought to be returned.[3]

Then Woodward had a serendipitous conversation with actor Robert Redford, who, having long disliked Richard Nixon, had taken a keen interest in the *Post*'s coverage. Redford had starred in *The Candidate*—a well-received 1972 film about modern politics—and wanted to make a movie about Woodward and Bernstein's perseverance when many veteran reporters cynically regarded Watergate as "business as usual in the nation's capital." He was drawn to the odd-couple quality evident in the Woodward/Bernstein relationship, and it struck him immediately as grist for a potential film. "I remember thinking, 'This is very interesting, a study in opposing characters and how they work together,'" Redford would recall when the film was released.[4]

He first tried to contact Woodward shortly after the 1972 election, but they did not actually meet until April 1973, when Redford came to Washington for a screening of *The Candidate*. Bernstein didn't attend, but the actor started talking to Woodward about the Watergate book. After Woodward described the problem he and Bernstein were confronted with, Redford responded with a valuable tip: borrow his conception. Instead of writing a book about *what* they discovered, Redford advised, readers were more likely to be interested in *how* they discovered it. That was what intrigued him, and he wanted to produce a film that was a re-enactment of their actual reporting. Eventually Redford bought the option to make the movie for $450,000 (more than $2 million in 2011 dollars). But that Hollywood windfall for Bernstein and Woodward paled next to the value of the actor's advice.[5]

At first Bernstein thought the suggestion a poor one. Recasting the book in this way essentially meant starting over, and he believed readers would react negatively to such an egocentric narrative. Nor did Simon & Schuster think well of the idea initially, although Woodward and Bernstein's editor, Alice Mayhew, was open to reading a few chapters utilizing this approach—anything to get the book done. There was some reason to think it just might appeal to a wide audience. By early 1973, as the journalism awards for the previous summer and fall's work began to mount, there was increasing interest in how Woodward and Bernstein had managed to outpace more experienced reporters. Initially, Ben Bradlee had prohibited them from talking about their Watergate coverage, but given the ceaseless requests, in January he began to relent. One of the first people allowed to interview them on the record was the journalist Timothy Crouse, who was writing a book about media coverage of the 1972 election.[6]

In addition to putting themselves in the center of the narrative, recasting the book à la Redford meant Woodward and Bernstein would have to write about their sources: how they got them, what the sources knew, what the sources told them, and when; otherwise there was no story. Gradually they saw how such a narrative could be constructed, and if there was one thing they were most proud of, it was their sources. As Woodward had told Crouse over dinner at the exclusive Hay-Adams Hotel, "people seem to have a conception of our sources as the classic, Jack Anderson leaker-who-mails-documents-in-the-night. But our sources weren't like that." None of them—whether in the FBI, Justice Department, or CRP—was a leak, Bernstein and Woodward insisted. Rather, they were responsible people "with no ax to grind," who wanted only to help make their Watergate coverage accurate.[7]

There was one catch, though. Telling the story was not going to be a problem when the sources had already been identified or quoted in the *Post*. But how were they to treat all those who had spoken on background and with the assurance that their identity would remain secret? Above all, how would they handle Deep Throat?

Woodward and Bernstein methodically went back to their sources and asked if they were willing to be identified for the purposes of the book. Several quickly agreed, in some cases with stipulations. Hugh Sloan, the former CRP treasurer, had no compunction about being fully identified. His unwitting involvement in criminal behavior mortified him; insofar as he was concerned, the book, along with his upcoming testimony before the Senate Watergate Committee, represented opportunities to clear his name. Other CRP sources, including Judy Hoback and Penny Gleason, agreed to have their cooperation and position generally described so long as they were not actually named.[8]

Sources who had been inside the White House or government, and anticipated going back in, such as John Sears, were less willing to drop their cloak of anonymity, but no one was more adamant than Felt. When

Woodward first broached the idea, Deep Throat "went bananas" over the notion that Woodward would even think about identifying him. The ground rules from August still applied. His role as a source was not to be acknowledged; no specific information was to be attributed to him; nothing he had said could be quoted.[9]

This was a huge obstacle. None of the other government sources who refused to be identified were really critical to the story. But if Bernstein and Woodward couldn't discuss Felt's role, how could they possibly tell the story of Woodward's first real scoop? Or of the *Post*'s long run of exclusives, especially the October 10 centerpiece article? Some specific events and stories could be elided, yet not his role altogether. If Felt were left out of the account, moreover, the book as a whole would be false, and known by several people to be so. It was not as if the secret were held only by Felt and Woodward. Bernstein had been informed of Deep Throat's identity, the ground rules notwithstanding; in addition, and to varying degrees, Deep Throat's existence and his role in the coverage were common knowledge among several other reporters, along with the *Post* editors who had worked on Watergate. It was Howard Simons, of course, who had irreverently dubbed Woodward's valued source. There was the possibility that someone in the know might speak up and point out the omission if Deep Throat were left out of the book—not to mention how difficult and misleading it would be to write it that way.

Even before Felt left the Bureau in May, Woodward and Bernstein had begun making discrete disclosures that amounted to, in effect, trial balloons, to test whether Felt might be amenable to dispensing with his anonymity. The first such balloon was floated in a *New York* magazine story, "How the *Washington Post* Gave Nixon Hell," written by Aaron Latham. Published in early May, before Felt's confrontation with Ruckelshaus, the piece did not identify Felt or describe the instrumental role he had played. But it did reveal his existence, as it opened with a detailed description of Woodward's nocturnal meetings in a dark garage with "a man [who] would appear out of the shadows . . . a wary informant." Felt would know instantly that this was him, and that it meant he was almost certainly going to appear in any forthcoming book.[10]

Shortly after the article appeared, Felt's departure from the Bureau was announced. Woodward and Bernstein apparently thought this development might surely lead Felt to relent. They sent up another, even more revealing trial balloon, as if to signal Deep Throat that it might not be bad to be in the public eye now that his government service was over; in the political environment that was emerging, his role might be celebrated if only it were known.

The venue was an article by Laurence Stern, the *Post*'s most distinguished and intellectual reporter. Stern had virtually free rein at the newspaper and moved effortlessly between the biggest stories, both national and international. In the late spring of 1973, he shrewdly decided to write an article that juxtaposed the first year of Watergate with what had been one of the most traumatic years ever at the FBI. The seed for the piece was probably planted in May, when Stern wrote a series of articles on one of the scandal's hottest elements, e.g., the administration's effort to falsely invoke CIA equities. Interviewing Agency director Richard Helms, who strongly suspected that the most telling leaks had emanated from the Hoover-less Bureau, no doubt piqued Stern's interest.[11]

Stern's article appeared on June 17, the first anniversary of the break-in. He wrote that the scandal had "brought egg to [the FBI's] face and demoralization to its ranks." Pat Gray was only the obvious victim; the Bureau as a whole stood accused of "leaking like a sieve, relaxing surveillance of domestic subversives, and turning its back on the rest of the intelligence community." Bereft of Hoover, whom Stern aptly described as the "Compleat Bureaucratic Infighter," the FBI faced more questions and uncertainty about its future than at any time since 1924, when Hoover, then just twenty-nine, took over an agency steeped in scandal, political intrigue, and illegal activities.[12]

Stern then retraced the stunning estrangement that had developed between the FBI and the Nixon administration. He observed that the past year had witnessed a "form of guerrilla warfare against the administration from within the ranks of the FBI," the primary evidence being that the FBI "may have been instrumental in getting the initial Watergate revelations into public print." To support this point, Stern quoted numerous sources: an anonymous "highly placed FBI executive"; the acting FBI director, William Ruckelshaus; and former White House liaison John Ehrlichman, who had just finished testifying before the Senate Watergate committee.

The most intriguing corroboration of Stern's thesis, however, came from a journalist identified only as a "Watergate reportorial specialist." According to Stern,

> Reporters who covered the case acknowledge the role of [FBI] agents in opening up the initial peepholes in the cover-up façade some administration officials were trying to erect.

"It wasn't a matter of getting rancorous leaks dumped in your lap," said one Watergate reportorial specialist. "You'd have to go to them and say, what about this or what about that? They'd respond, 'Yes, that's right.' I can think of one guy in the Bureau without whom we wouldn't have gotten anywhere."[13]

This was, of course, a reference to Felt. The "Watergate reportorial specialist" was either Woodward or Bernstein, the only two *Post* reporters at the time who knew for certain where Deep Throat had worked.[14]

Stern then went on to quote Felt, whom he may have spoken with at Woodward's or Bernstein's suggestion. Stern did not cite Felt by name, identifying him instead as a "recently retired senior official with more than a quarter century in the Bureau." But there is no doubt about whom Stern was quoting. "When Gray first arrived we all wanted him to succeed," the "recently retired senior official" told Stern. "Then we became aware of those . . . frequent absences from Washington. That's when he got the nickname 'Two-Day Gray.'" The identical criticism and nickname appeared a few years later in Felt's memoir.[15]

Woodward and Bernstein launched their third and final balloon later in the summer in the *Columbia Journalism Review*. This magazine article, written by James McCartney, a national correspondent for the Knight Newspaper chain, included the most detailed account to date about how the October 10 centerpiece story had come about, although Deep Throat's role was entirely left out. However, the article did make numerous references to "FBI agents" who, like Woodward and Bernstein, were "trying to puzzle out Watergate." And it quoted Woodward as saying that "FBI investigators were speaking out because they were upset, because there was a cover-up going on." The primary "FBI investigator" who leaked to Woodward, of course, was Felt.[16]

These trial balloons did nothing to sway Deep Throat, assuming he even read them, and Felt's only remaining hope was that moral suasion would persuade Woodward to keep their agreement in full force. If Felt were exposed, anyone loyal to the FBI or Justice Department would find his conduct abhorrent, regardless of the rationale offered. He would be forever ostracized by his peers and the only community he had and was comfortable in, the tightly knit fraternity of former FBI executives and agents. Then, too, exposure would inexorably lead to questions about why he had leaked, and the answers would not be satisfactory ones. Indeed, here and there in the press, the Woodward and Bernstein explanation for why "FBI investigators" leaked was under challenge. In mid-August 1973, for example, John Crewdson wrote a story for the *New York Times* that contained, buried deep within it, the following observation:

> Almost from the inception of . . . Watergate . . . Federal law enforcement agencies, especially the FBI, have been accused of being the source of leaks to the press of confidential investigative information about the case. . . .
>
> In some cases, sources have said, leaks from Bureau agents were intended to prevent the nomination of Mr. Gray as the FBI's permanent director, by signaling the White House that he did not have the respect of many agents and could not control them, and that if he were nominated the Bureau would "leak like a sieve."[17]

Felt surely understood that his actions could never withstand scrutiny; he was not, after all, a whistle-blower or hero, and his leaks had been first and foremost calculated and timed to be self-serving.

Woodward's fullest explanation for his decision to break the agreement with Felt was published in *The Secret Man*. The stories in the *Post* had made "numerous references in print to FBI files," Woodward noted. How was that going to be explained? Felt, moreover, had been quoted several times, albeit anonymously, in violation of their deep background agreement, and yet he had never objected. "I . . . thought it gave me some leeway," Woodward wrote. It "never really crossed my mind to leave out the details of Deep Throat's role. It was important."[18]

Another explanation for why Woodward found his way to breaching the understanding may be traced to the nature of their relationship, as analyzed by an expert "profiler." In 2002, Roger L. Depue, the former chief of the FBI's Behaviorial Sciences Unit, studied the depiction of Deep Throat in *All the President's Men* for NBC's *Dateline* program. Depue concluded from the way Woodward wrote about Felt that he had very mixed feelings toward the man. One of the giveaways, to Depue, was the assignment of Felt's code name. True, the moniker had been chosen by Howard Simons, Depue recalled in a recent interview, but "it was kind of a demeaning name and [Woodward] let it stand." That alone indicated some "psychological distancing" between Woodward and his invaluable source. "I detected that not only was Felt an angry man," Depue said, "but that Woodward didn't particularly like him. It seemed like more of a utilitarian relationship. . . . There wasn't much mutual respect there."[19]

During the time between the decision to recast the book and its publication, Woodward met once more with Felt. This was in November 1973, a month before a strong first draft of the book was finished, and in the midst of the titanic struggle over Nixon's secret tape recordings, the existence of which had been revealed dramatically during the Senate Watergate hearings.

Felt had long since recovered from the collapse of his scheme and resigned himself to reality. The same could not be said of his wife, Audrey, who had not just shared but nursed his ambition. Before Hoover's death in 1972, she had been literally measuring the drapes in the director's office. Always an intense person, she was overtly bitter about the entitlement denied her husband—and her, considering the sacrifices she had made to further his career. (She had moved their family seventeen times and was often a single parent because of the devotion Mark had to show Hoover.) That fall the new permanent FBI director, Clarence M. Kelley, who had succeeded Ruckelshaus in early July, was told about a phone call from Mrs. Felt to a person identified only as a "good friend of the FBI's." She had launched into a "tirade" over the telephone, alleging that her husband actually ran the FBI for years and was responsible for many of the things Hoover had gotten credit for. Mark had been treated badly, she complained, and the only reason he had retired was because he had not been named director.[20]

When Woodward asked for a meeting in November on the off chance that Felt knew something about the Nixon tapes, none of the resentment or bitterness that was a daily reality in Felt's home was manifest. When Deep Throat arrived at the garage, he was as urbane and cool as ever. Did Felt know anything about the tapes that might propel the *Post* to the front of the pack again? Felt did have a kernel of startling information that was not yet public. One of the tapes showed signs of deliberate erasure, he told Woodward, who incorporated this information into a story published on November 8. The article quoted Felt as saying that reported problems with the tapes "are of a suspicious nature" and "could lead someone to include [*sic*] that the tapes have been tampered with." Felt was identified only as one of "five [White House] sources."[21]

It was Deep Throat's "last great leak," and the only one that could be described as having been done out of sheer bitterness at the Nixon White House. Thirteen days later the president's lawyers informed Judge John Sirica about the gap. The 18½-minute erasure had obliterated what was said between Nixon and Haldeman during a pivotal meeting three days after the break-in. Ironically, the November 8 article would later be the main reason why many Deep Throat sleuths, including Nixon himself, ruled Felt out. He did not, and never had, fit the description of a "White House source" in conventional journalese.[22]

The quotation of Felt concerning the erasure was another infraction of the deep background arrangement, but a miniscule one compared to the disclosures contained in *All the President's Men*, which would be published seven months later. In the spring of 1974 the public became privy to Deep Throat's existence, his instrumentality, much of what he had told Woodward (in renderings derived from the reporter's typewritten notes), and when. The book, in other words, peeled away nearly every condition Felt had set in August 1972. It tied Felt to specific revelations and precise articles, though it did not reiterate the stark, specific admission published the previous year in Laurence Stern's article. Lastly, the book drew a misleading portrait of why Deep Throat leaked.

Of course, a great deal was also left out. Some of Felt's remarks had been such dead-giveaways—such as a reference to "'reports . . . on Gray's desk'"—that they never made it into the book. As the manuscript had progressed through various drafts, moreover, it had been steadily scrubbed to remove references to Deep Throat whenever possible. On one page of an early draft, for example, someone scribbled this marginal notation: "Bob, too close on ID of Throat here?" The referenced passage read, "He was perhaps the only person in the government in a position to possibly understand the whole scheme and not be a potential conspirator himself." Other deleted phrases referred to the fact that Woodward and Felt were "fast friends," and that Felt was an "older person." Still, virtually the only fig leaves left for Felt to hide behind were his risqué code name (which he undoubtedly learned about for the first time when the book was published, along with the rest of the reading public) and the name of the "executive branch" agency he worked for.[23]

All the President's Men was also notable for its unfair portrait of Pat Gray, although this aspect went largely unremarked at the time. His photo was included on the book jacket, along with those of Haldeman, Ehrlichman, Dean, and Mitchell, as if he were just another one of the president's men. Even more egregious, the book put forward Felt's allegation, as if it were true, that Gray had effectively blackmailed Nixon into nominating him for the directorship. This charge had never been printed in the pages of the *Washington Post*, though it would seem to have been newsworthy if true. The bottom of the book page containing the allegation included a footnoted rebuttal from Gray's attorney, to the effect that the charge was "outrageously false." But this disclaimer seemed more designed to avoid legal liability than to cast any doubt on the assertion. Instead of rethinking Gray's role, in light of everything that had gone on, Woodward and Bernstein simply replicated Felt's caricature of him, alongside misleading characterizations of the FBI's investigation.[24]

Because of *All the President's Men*, the ongoing Watergate saga (Nixon's resignation was still several months away) evolved into yet a third phase: how the crime and cover-up were supposedly cracked. The timing of the book, as media critic W. Joseph Campbell later observed, was one factor in placing "Woodward and Bernstein at the center of Watergate in popular consciousness," thus making the "heroic-journalist myth the dominant popular narrative of the Watergate scandal."[25]

While lots of books would be written about Watergate, none would prove quite as enduring as *All the President's Men*. A key element in keeping it at the forefront of public consciousness was that Bernstein and Woodward had also created an engrossing and ongoing mystery, almost inadvertently. Two months prior to the book's publication, and before excerpts of it appeared in *Playboy* (which paid $30,000, or $125,000 in 2011 dollars, for the right to publish two installments), the Associated Press carried a long story on the revelations in *All the President's Men*. The disclosure of clandestine meetings between Woodward and "a member of the executive branch . . . dubbed Deep Throat" took up a third of the article, for he supposedly epitomized "the very notion of the confidential source." The *Post* reporters professed genuine surprise at all the attention being lavished on Deep Throat. "When we wrote the book, we didn't think his role would achieve such mythical dimensions," Bernstein later observed.[26]

Despite the authors' best efforts at misdirection, details in *All the President's Men*, together with snippets from Nixon's tape recordings released in April 1974 as part of the impeachment process, immediately made Mark Felt the prime suspect. *The Washingtonian* magazine was the first to write about the capital's new favorite parlor game. Relying on the insights of Frank Waldrop, a longtime newspaper editor who was a razor-sharp observer of the Washington scene, and "absolutely wired [in] to the FBI," the magazine singled out Felt as the most plausible suspect the same month the book was published.

> The best gossip in town these days is the Deep Throat guessing game. . . . Like a good detective, let's ignore all of Woodward and Bernstein's red herrings and look at motive and opportunity and method. . . . Who had access to all the material? Who had the resources to set up a system to leak it?

The FBI, that's who. Read the February 28 and March 13 presidential transcripts and then try someone like Mark Felt on for size. A Hoover loyalist and number-two man to Pat Gray, he had every reason and resource for leaking the Watergate story and destroying Nixon. Why would someone like Felt pick Woodward and Bernstein? Why not? Why pick someone like Jeremiah O'Leary of the [*Washington*] *Star* who has been getting FBI leaks for years? Why not pick the last two reporters who would ever be suspected of being FBI conduits?[27]

The only real flaw with this line of thinking (which would also color all future efforts to discern Deep Throat's identity) was its presumption that the end result—the dismantling of the Nixon administration—had been intended from the start.

In public, Felt responded to this article and others with an air of nonchalance. He even affected bemusement, although friends who kept giving him "knowing winks" were annoying. He told John Limpert, the writer of *The Washingtonian* article, "I can tell you that it was not I and it is not I." To a *Wall Street Journal* reporter he said, "I don't disagree with the reasoning, but I do disagree with the conclusion. Because I'm just not that kind of person." If someone had managed to recall Laurence Stern's article from June 1973, it is difficult to believe that Felt's denials would have ever carried much weight, however.[28]

When Limpert wrote a follow-up article conveying Felt's denial, he also tried to dig up more information that would either exculpate the former FBI executive or definitively finger him. A "former Justice Department official" provided "very solid supporting" information, Limpert wrote.

What about [Felt's] motive? In the June issue, we speculated that the old Hoover people at the FBI might have wanted to leak Watergate material to hurt FBI Director Gray and President Nixon, who were bent on tearing down the Hoover organization. Asked about this, a former top Justice Department official said: "Maybe it was revenge. But I think it was ambition, too. I can see Mark Felt as Deep Throat. He had all the information, and he badly wanted to be the director. He had enough contact with the press that he might have tried to use his Watergate information to hurt Gray and to curry favor with an important newspaper like the *Post*. In fact, *you ought to look into why Felt left the FBI so quietly in June of 1973* [emphasis added]. Leaks may have had something to do with it."[29]

Limpert did not follow up on this very good tip. But one journalist who did, in a way, was Edward Jay Epstein, writing for *Commentary* magazine. Epstein did not specifically investigate Felt's abrupt departure. But he talked to unnamed "prosecutors" at the Justice Department. They told him they believed the "mysterious source" was probably "Mark W. Felt" [*sic*], because one statement Bernstein and Woodward attributed to Deep Throat "could only have been made by Felt." According to these prosecutors, inside the Bureau "there was a veritable revolt against the directorship of L. Patrick Gray, because he was too liberal." Thus, the purpose of the FBI leaks was not to expose Watergate or drive President Nixon from office, but simply "to demonstrate to the president that Gray could not control the FBI. . . . The intention was to get rid of Gray." Epstein's reporting and analysis was marred only by his own speculation, to wit, "I personally suspect that . . . 'Deep Throat' is a composite character."[30]

All the speculation generated by *All the President's Men* did have one possible silver lining for Felt. The publicity about Deep Throat, he thought, was likely to boost demand for him on the lecture circuit. Free to speak for the first time in more than thirty years, he was spending most of his time now seeking speaking engagements, in the belief that Americans were anxious to hear from the one official who had "more knowledge about the FBI than anybody in the world." He started out with grand plans of touring college campuses all over the country "to clear up some of the misconceptions the public, especially students, have about the FBI." Staying in the public eye would also build an audience for a memoir he intended to write.[31]

But this had proved to be a miscalculation, too—and, in a sense, part and parcel of Felt's self-deception. In the year or so before *All the President's Men* appeared, all he could manage was a few dates in small venues, before sparse crowds. No matter how dramatic he tried to be, his assertions never got beyond the local newspaper, if that. Which is not to say he didn't try to garner more attention.

Speaking before an audience of twelve persons at Rutgers University in October 1973, for example, Felt said he could have been director of the FBI if only "he had played the game." He'd quit the Bureau because "there was too much interference from the White House" after the death of Hoover. Appearing before a small group of Oberlin College students the same month, Felt asserted that while he was Hoover's number three man, the longtime director always backed his policy decisions. "But after Hoover died, I kept getting overruled by L. Patrick Gray and William D.

Ruckelshaus. They were both team players with the president, but they have since realized that they should have taken more independent positions." On occasion, too, Felt did speak honestly, telling a University of New Haven audience early in 1974 that "there was no cover-up inside the FBI" with regard to the Watergate scandal.[32]

When *All the President's Men* appeared, it did nothing to improve Felt's fortunes on the lecture circuit. The only real stars now were Bernstein and Woodward, unless Felt was willing to come forward as Deep Throat. Few people were interested in the observations of a still mostly unknown FBI executive, even if he did rise to the number two post (and the number one job for nearly three hours). In a harbinger of the lack of interest that would greet his memoir, Felt's engagements remained in second-rate venues, in front of tiny audiences.

Felt tried his best to be provocative. Speaking at American University in September 1975, he said he was "shamed" when Nixon appointed Gray in May 1972, adding, "I'm glad he did not get to be director." At times he advocated a sweeping reorganization of the government, one that would establish the FBI as an independent agency responsible to Congress rather than the executive branch. He also devoted a portion of every speech in an attempt to counteract the burgeoning myth that Bernstein and Woodward had uncovered Watergate—a myth propagated by the book itself and the bravado that accompanied it (e.g., "two young *Washington Post* reporters whose brilliant investigative journalism smashed the Watergate scandal wide open"). He criticized the reporters' portrayal of the FBI and suggested the Bureau deserved some of the acclaim being heaped upon the *Post* for uncovering the scandal. But changing that widespread misperception—fostered in the first place by Felt—was an uphill struggle.[33]

Felt's critique foreshadowed the FBI's own analysis of *All the President's Men*. Armed with the details from the book, the FBI finally realized it had been less an issue of leaked "302s" and more a matter of Bernstein and Woodward replicating its interviews:

A comparison of the chronology of our investigation with the events cited in *All the President's Men* will show we were substantially and constantly ahead of the *Washington Post* investigative reporters. In essence, they were interviewing the same people we had interviewed but subsequent to our interviews and often after the interviewee had testified before the grand jury. The difference, which contributes greatly to the false image, is that the *Washington Post* blatantly published whatever they learned (or thought they learned) while we reported our findings to the U.S. attorney and the Department [of Justice] solely for prosecutive consideration.[34]

Another feature common in Felt's speeches was his effort to confound seekers of Woodward and Bernstein's fabled secret source by dispensing a little more disinformation. He was one of the first prominent voices to suggest that Deep Throat was not a single individual but "a literary thing they [Bernstein and Woodward] dreamed up for their book. I think [he] must have been a composite." It was a brilliant ruse, Woodward thought, precisely because it was both false and so very plausible.[35]

All the President's Men, besides coming harrowingly close to exposing Felt, also played a role in instigating a leak investigation of the former executive by the FBI. Unlike the pseudo-leak hunts Felt had presided over, this one nearly resulted in his indictment.

The complicated chain of events began with yet another John Crewdson story in the *New York Times.* On July 9, 1973, the newspaper published the first of his two-part series on Donald Segretti. Felt had been gone for about three weeks by this time, and it was the first day on the job for the new permanent director, Clarence Kelley. He found it a not particularly auspicious way to begin, since the series was obviously based on a hemorrhage of information "gathered by government investigators," i.e., the FBI.[36]

Two weeks later, Archibald Cox, the special Watergate prosecutor, asked to see Kelley in person because, he said, he had developed some alarming information. Two of his prosecutors had recently interrogated Segretti, and he told them that when Crewdson interviewed him in mid-June in Beverly Hills, California, the *Times* reporter had brought with him a foot-high stack of photocopied FBI documents. Crewdson had explained that he wanted to impress Segretti with the data he had accumulated so that the Republican trickster would "open up." The *Times* reporter alluded to acquiring the documents in Washington, from "someone in Justice" who wanted it known that the FBI had conducted a "thorough investigation."[37]

The earlier Watergate leak-hunts had come to naught because tracing, much less prosecuting, leaks transmitted orally was almost impossible. Proving that government documents had been given to someone not entitled to receive them, however, was a much more promising avenue.

Kelley immediately ordered O. T. Jacobson, head of the Inspection Division, to begin an internal probe. In addition, something that Ruckelshaus had said to Kelley in passing, while handing over the keys to the director's office, suddenly took on added significance. The interim director had mentioned having plugged a leak within the Bureau during his short stint; now Kelley wanted to know more.

The next day, Ruckelshaus told his successor about the confrontation with Felt over Crewdson's May 11 article. Ruckelshaus also shared, for apparently the first time, the private warning that President Nixon had sounded in April: that Felt had leaked to *Time* and was not to be trusted. This was good enough for Kelley to make the FBI's former number two executive the "prime suspect" in a new and much more vigorous leak investigation.[38]

The irony here was that once again Felt was innocent of this particular leak. Ruckelshaus was the executive who had actually authorized the release of documents to Crewdson, probably through his special assistant Jack Conmy, who was in frequent contact with the *Times* reporter. The document dump was the kind of sanctioned leak that Hoover had pioneered, and was done for purely institutional reasons. Ruckelshaus wanted a true account of Segretti's activities to be published so that it was known the Bureau had conducted a thorough investigation; it was part of his efforts to rebuild the FBI's reputation without delay. But he wasn't about to admit that to Kelley now, even if the leak had been for a good reason. It would be much too embarrassing to admit that a stack of raw FBI reports had been simply handed over to a *New York Times* reporter.[39]

Over the next few months the investigation proceeded in a desultory manner. O. T. Jacobson, having been made aware that Crewdson—or more accurately, a man posing as Crewdson—had supposedly disclosed Felt's role once before, actually began the inquiry by requesting Ruckelshaus/Conmy to ask Crewdson if he would be willing to disclose his source for a second time! Naturally, the *Times* reporter declined that peculiar request. A subsequent plea from Kelley to *Times* publisher Arthur Ochs Sulzberger was also rebuffed. Having exhausted these obvious but unlikely avenues, Jacobson then ordered the Inspection Division to undertake a systematic review of all of Crewdson's articles, hoping to find a pattern that would pinpoint his source in the FBI. Crewdson had joined the *Times*'s Washington bureau the day after the Watergate break-in and began writing articles under his own byline in early 1973. An article-by-article analysis revealed that he had undeniably had access to internal documents, the last of which appeared to be dated May 30, 1973. The only conclusion that could be drawn, however—and it was a tentative one—was that Crewdson's source was perhaps no longer with the FBI—a finding that corresponded with the status of the prime suspect, Felt.[40]

By this time, April 1974, as news about the upcoming revelations in *All the President's Men* began to spread, there was already a "strong belief" in the Bureau's higher echelons that Felt had engaged in unauthorized leaks. The considerable prepublication publicity, aided by serialization of the book in *Playboy*, only added to Kelley's determination to punish this kind of behavior. No matter how one regarded *All the President's Men*—and no one inside the FBI, including Gray's detractors, believed its treatment of the Bureau was remotely fair—some of its disclosures had obviously come from within. And the best way of demonstrating a commitment to preventing leaks was to make an example of someone, regardless of their former rank, who had provably engaged in this egregious behavior.[41]

On April 4, Jacobson and Kelley met with Leon Jaworski, Archibald Cox's successor as the Watergate special prosecutor, to discuss a possible criminal prosecution with respect to the Segretti documents. Jacobson laid out the results from his ten-month investigation, noting that the Inspection Division had not been able to produce anything tangible linking Felt to the unauthorized distribution of the records. Jaworski revealed that some White House tape recordings, which only his office was privy to, corroborated suspicions about Felt, i.e., the president himself was overheard accusing the former number two executive of leaking. Jacobson and Jaworski agreed that the next logical step was to confront Felt.[42]

On June 13, almost two years to the day since the break-in, and just a few days short of the official publication date of *All the President's Men*, two agents from the Washington Field Office showed up at Felt's Virginia home at 10:15 a.m. All three men then drove to a nearby Holiday Inn by prearrangement. The agents didn't want to conduct the interview with Audrey Felt present, and bringing Felt into FBI headquarters, or conducting the interview at a field office, it was thought, would be much too embarrassing. Felt, with his impressive mane of white hair, was instantly recognizable to many employees.

Felt almost didn't get into the car when he saw that one of the two agents was Angelo Lano, the Watergate case agent. Lano was especially eager to find the culprit who had caused him and his Watergate squad so much grief. "I'm not getting in the car with him," Felt yelled when he saw Lano sitting in the front passenger seat. But the agents said they were prepared to tell Kelley that Felt had been uncooperative and refused to be interviewed. After a moment's hesitation, he got in.[43]

The interview began on an adversarial note, as the agents advised Felt of his legal rights. He made no effort to hide his disgust over the interrogation. The session lasted almost three hours and Felt was at his wiliest, striving to give the impression of honesty even as he dissembled. He did not deny outright that he had had contacts with the media—specifically mentioning Bob Woodward of the *Washington Post* and Sandy Smith from *Time* magazine—probably because he realized his former secretaries were likely to be interviewed. He cagily observed that Smith had a lot of friends in the FBI and was still obtaining "inside stories from someone." As for Felt's own contacts, he had had a policy of telling reporters who were shopping for information "nothing."[44]

There had been only one exception to this policy, he said, and it occurred in May 1973, when John Crewdson called to ask him about the White House–initiated wiretaps from 1969 to 1971. Fearing the *Times* reporter would publish a false story harmful to the Bureau's image, Felt claimed that he had tried to straighten out the obvious falsehoods fed to Crewdson by William Sullivan. Felt asserted that Ruckelshaus was well aware that Sullivan was the original source for the May article; Ruckelshaus "personally told him he knew Sullivan did it." The incident, he also averred, had nothing to do with his sudden retirement. By then he was "disillusioned and disenchanted" because, he said, "I knew I wasn't going to be the director." Lastly, Felt denied up, down, and sideways the allegation that he had ever furnished FBI documents to any reporter, much less John Crewdson.[45]

It was a bravura performance—so much so that Lano later wondered if Felt, relying on his network of contacts, had been informed of all the questions in advance. Prior to the interview, Lano had been told to submit his questions for vetting by the legal department. The Watergate case agent also suspected Felt was surreptitiously taping the session. The number two executive brought with him a leather satchel that he conspicuously kept open for the duration of the session.[46]

If Felt was forearmed because he was forewarned, it was also the case that at least half of his denials were true. Indeed, he ended with a flourish, notwithstanding his initial protest that the entire exercise was insulting and degrading. He did not think the agents would ever identify the person or person(s) who leaked, but if there was anything he could do to help the investigators, why, he would be happy to oblige. By the way, he added gratuitously, "he was not the individual known as Deep Throat" despite what some newspapers and magazines were suggesting.[47]

That same day, a separate team of agents simultaneously interviewed

Felt's secretaries, one of whom was Carol Tschudy, a Bureau employee for seventeen years. Tschudy was questioned specifically about her former boss's relationship with Crewdson, particularly any visits he may have made to the office. None of her recollections corroborated the allegation that Felt had made documents available to the *Times* reporter. But she did mention *another* reporter that Felt had been in frequent contact with: Bob Woodward of the *Washington Post*. "There were several telephone conversations between Woodward and Mr. Felt and I am unable to recall at this time how many calls transpired; however, the frequency of Woodward's calls seemed to depend upon various developments in the Watergate case," Tschudy said.[48]

Three days later, FBI agents based in New England interviewed William Sullivan at his New Hampshire home. Had he known that Felt was the prime suspect, Sullivan might have tried to implicate his former archrival. But since he had no way of knowing whom the Bureau really suspected and had his own vulnerability vis-à-vis Crewdson, Sullivan simply played dumb. He obligingly told the agents that after his retirement in October 1971, the *Times* reporter had contacted him telephonically on four or five occasions. He got the impression that Crewdson "had a good contact in the Bureau" and had "seen information in FBI files." But no, Sullivan said, he had not at any time furnished information or documents to the *Times* reporter.[49]

Felt, meanwhile, went on the offensive, raging against both the false and true accusations in a personal letter to Kelley. As it happened Felt knew the new director quite well; in 1960, when Felt was the special agent in charge of the Kansas City Field Office, Kelley headed up the Memphis Field Office and they had worked together on several cases. Then, in 1961 Felt has been instrumental in helping Kelley become Kansas City's police chief when he decided to retire from the FBI. Felt's letter to his old colleague was blistering:

> To be treated as a prime suspect in a sordid example of crass disloyalty to the FBI is a humiliating and degrading experience. . . .
>
> My contacts with the press have been limited. On only one occasion did I ever "leak" information and that was years ago and on instructions from the Bureau. I have never given Bureau documents to unauthorized persons!
>
> For me to be suspected of stealing a miscellany of Bureau documents for release to a member of the news media is ridiculous.

Incidentally, I am not "Deep Throat" either, as speculated about by a reporter for *The Washingtonian*.[50]

Kelley sought to assure Felt that he was not "being singled out . . . without any basis whatsoever," and that the interview had no significance "other than . . . to round out this investigation." He also sympathized with Felt's concern over the speculation in the wake of Bernstein and Woodward's book, which had just been published. "I am sure that some of the recent news articles concerning 'Deep Throat' are very disturbing to you," he wrote.[51]

Amidst this exchange of letters, *All the President's Men* was receiving rave reviews, and bookstores could barely manage to keep in stock the fastest-selling nonfiction hardback book in the history of American publishing. (The paperback rights would be auctioned eventually for a then-record $1,050,000 or $5.4 million in 2011 dollars.) Curiously, no reviewers raised questions about the breach of Woodward's "deep background" agreement with Deep Throat, namely that it had been observed, more or less, while reporting for the *Washington Post* but violated when writing for Simon & Schuster. The fascination, if not fixation, over Deep Throat obscured the unilateral abrogation of the agreement; instead Woodward and Bernstein were hailed for their fidelity and near-fanatic devotion to protecting their sources' identities. Of the many Watergate legends that would take hold, perhaps this was the oddest. Yes, Woodward and Bernstein were religious about not confirming that Mark Felt was Deep Throat. But they had had no problem exposing just about everything else about him.[52]

As the book shot to the top of the national best-seller lists, Woodward called Felt. He was "dying to know" what Deep Throat thought about *All the President's Men*. When he heard the familiar voice, Felt banged the receiver down, leaving Woodward listening to a dial tone. For days afterwards, the reporter was haunted, imagining the worst. He feared that Felt might do anything from take his own life, to "the higher likelihood that he would go public and denounce me as a betrayer and scum who had exploited our accidental friendship." The barrier that had always existed between them went from being a "protective shield" to a "cement wall." Felt had ample reason to be furious, but what Woodward did not know, apparently, was that his former source was also living under a cloud because of the FBI's unprecedented investigation—a probe driven, at least in part, by the book that was now garnering near-universal acclaim and a considerable fortune for the *Post* duo.[53]

Yet, rather than achieve greater clarity with each successive interview, the FBI's leak hunt was getting hopelessly bogged down. A major reason was that the investigating agents were operating on a reasonable but incorrect assumption. They had presumed that the same FBI source was responsible for both the wiretap (May '73) and Segretti (July '73) leaks to Crewdson. And while both had been attributed to Felt, he was responsible for neither. The agents were further stymied by seemingly irreconcilable accounts, in particular, the variance between the Felt and Ruckelshaus versions of their confrontation.

Agents made several efforts to make sense of everything, primarily through re-interviews of Ruckelshaus. Both times the former interim director expressed strong opposition to continuation of the probe. In exchange for Felt's resignation, Ruckelshaus said, he had "an unspoken understanding" with the former executive that no further punitive action would be taken. Of course, for Ruckelshaus, it was not only a matter of keeping his word. The possibility that Felt might face criminal prosecution for providing FBI documents to Crewdson—something Ruckelshaus knew he hadn't done—was worrisome. He energetically argued that "further administrative or criminal action against Felt would serve no useful purpose, and in fact, would possibly bring discredit to the Bureau. . . . [Felt] had sacrificed a great deal when he offered to retire" since he still had aspirations of becoming director.[54]

Just as the investigation was petering out, word of the internal leak-hunt began to trickle out in the media: first in a *New York Times* article, and then, two months later, in the *Los Angeles Times*. The second account, by Ronald J. Ostrow, was actually the more detailed. The FBI was investigating Felt—and only Felt—in what was described as a "highly unusual" action. According to the article,

> Felt offered his own theory on how he became suspected of leaking information to [Crewdson].
> He attributed it to reports, the most prominent of which was published in the June issue of *The Washingtonian*, that he could have been "Deep Throat." . . . Felt said he thought FBI agents had interviewed him . . . "because of all this 'Deep Throat' business. . . . Because of the 'Deep Throat' allegation, they said, 'Well, it must have been Felt who gave Crewdson all the papers.'"
> "But I did not leak any information to Woodward or Bernstein. I'm not 'Deep Throat.' I did not leak any information to Crewdson.

I did not give him any documents. And I think the whole thing is ridiculous and insulting."[55]

Altogether, Ostrow's article came close to cracking open the FBI's war of succession and all that had gone with it. The article revealed that in the fall of 1972, then–attorney general Kleindienst had told Pat Gray "point-blank to fire [Felt]" because he was the source of Watergate-related leaks to the media. Ostrow also presented a much more accurate account of Felt's abrupt departure than had ever appeared before, alluding to a "confrontation" that had occurred between Ruckelshaus and Felt. Although Ruckelshaus declined to give details, Felt was quoted as saying, "I made up my mind to retire because of a lot of circumstances. And it had absolutely nothing to do with Crewdson or with Ruckelshaus." Finally, Ostrow observed that the investigation of Felt "sheds some light on the intense power struggle in the FBI in the months after Mr. Hoover's death." In this insight Ostrow stood virtually alone: Because of Watergate, a national election, and events in Vietnam and the Middle East, there had been too much news to print in 1972–1973, and almost nothing had been written about the no-holds-barred war of succession. Certainly, the coverage had not come close to garnering a level of attention remotely commensurate with its import or impact.[56]

Sanford Ungar, who covered the Justice and FBI beats for the *Washington Post*, was the other reporter who came closest to breaking the story in the mid-1970s, when it presumably would have counted the most. In the fall of 1973 he took a leave of absence from the *Post* to write a book about the Bureau both during and after Hoover's reign. Though not an authorized history, it received official sanction and cooperation. Published in late 1975, Ungar's 682-page *FBI* provided the most extensive treatment yet of the internecine struggle to succeed Hoover. Ungar portrayed Pat Gray's brief reign fairly and, with Ruckelshaus's apparent cooperation, described the confrontation with Felt over the Crewdson story. The book was both a triumph of tireless reporting and an example of its limits. Without access to documentation—only a few of the presidential recordings were then available—the author was at the mercy of his FBI sources, none of whom would admit to the Machiavellian traps and maneuvers that had occurred at the Bureau's highest reaches. Ungar addressed the issue of Deep Throat in a footnote: "Inevitably speculation centered on Mark Felt, among others. Felt denies it; the author is inclined to believe him."[57]

_____

In April 1976, a taut film version of *All the President's Men* was released, and a best-seller became a Hollywood blockbuster, the first political movie to gross large profits since *Mr. Smith Goes to Washington* in 1939. Nominated for eight and the winner of four Academy Awards, the film exalted and romanticized the press—a "paean to investigative journalism," the historian William E. Leuchtenburg called it—and claimed verisimilitude to actual events. In fact, it simplified the story even more than the book had. The film virtually ignored or denigrated the critical roles two *Post* editors—Howard Simons and Barry Sussman—played in pursuit of the story, and in piecing together the Watergate puzzle. And the movie made it appear as if the FBI, federal prosecutors, and the grand jury were ciphers that had played no important role in exposing the scandal. Its visual hyperrealism, coupled with the fact that the country had just lived through the period, helped affix a fable in the national psyche, a story that would persist long after the details about what Nixon had or had not done faded away. As the sociologist Michael Schudson wrote in *Watergate in American Memory*,

> At its broadest, the myth . . . asserts that two young *Washington Post* reporters brought down the president of the United States. This is a myth of David and Goliath, of powerless individuals overturning an institution of overwhelming might. It is high noon in Washington, with two white-hatted young reporters at one end of the street and the black-hatted president at the other, protected by his minions. And the good guys win. The press, truth its only weapon, saves the day.[58]

The director, Alan Pakula, even managed to convey a sense of building tension and near-paranoia in the film, although the end was known to every politically-sentient American. Hal Holbrook's menacing portrayal of Felt (he was always in the shadows, half-hidden), and his memorable admonition to "follow the money" (a phrase invented by screenwriter William Goldman, and something Felt apparently never said) dramatized Woodward's secret source as a romantic truth-teller. Extreme close-ups transformed typewriters and teletypes into powerful tools of truth. Largely depicted in darkness, Washington appeared secretive and oppressive, a scary place of massive buildings that towered over human beings. In contrast, the glaring whiteness of the *Post*'s newsroom implied honesty and openness. The movie's point of highest tension was the scene in Woodward's apartment on the morning of May 17, just after his meeting with

Felt (who had just "retired," although that was missing from the movie as it had been from the book). Woodward turns up the stereo and types out a message to Bernstein: they might be under surveillance, according to Deep Throat, and their lives endangered.[59]

Though it liberally mixed fiction with fact, the documentary-like style of the film made Deep Throat an indelible icon. That Felt had been given a "sexy moniker" didn't hurt, either. As with all myths, what really powered it was not the veneer of truth, but the fact that people wanted to believe it was true.[60]

Around the same time the film was released, Woodward and Bernstein's second book, *The Final Days*, was published. This happy conjunction created a tsunami of publicity, but not all of it was good. Ben Bradlee's constant refrain to Woodward was "keep your head down," but the book and movie had turned the *Post* duo into celebrities. Increasingly they were making news as much as reporting it. They had obviously benefited from the symbolic elevation of Deep Throat; however, the frenzied speculation about his identity, including the allegation that he did not really exist, even as a composite character, was not working in their favor. The doubts became underscored with publication of *The Final Days*. Reviewers of the second Woodward and Bernstein book criticized the authors for their overuse of anonymous sources and for "getting inside the heads" of people (most prominently Richard Nixon) whom they had not interviewed. Their novelistic style had worked well in *All the President's Men*, but that book had been about them. As biographer Alicia C. Shepard wrote, "many journalists pilloried Woodward and Bernstein for their 'Trust me. I know this stuff is true' attitude."[61]

Amid growing concerns that the *Post*'s credibility was also at stake, in the spring of 1976 Ben Bradlee finally did what he had desisted from doing in October 1972: he asked Woodward for Deep Throat's name, thereby becoming the only person other than the two reporters to know.[62]

Woodward, who had grown weary of answering the same incessant question, simultaneously took a new tack with respect to Deep Throat's identity. He unveiled it during a terse April 1976 interview in *Time* magazine. Woodward prefaced his remarks by noting that he didn't think "reporters trying to identify other reporters' sources was the noblest kind of journalism," and then described the new condition under which he would finally reveal Deep Throat's name.

> When we wrote *All the President's Men*, [Deep Throat] declined to be named. . . . He has [*sic*] a career in government. He thinks that while

he might be a hero to some, he would be a rat or a snitcher in some eyes.

Some day he'll come forth. If he were to die, I would feel obliged to reveal his identity. Some day he'll write a really fascinating book. Carl and I would like to work on it with him.[63]

This promise to identify Deep Throat after his death put a damper on the conjecture, though it still didn't free Woodward entirely from having to repeat endlessly what became a new rote answer. Once again, this revision to the deep background agreement had been done unilaterally, though in the future it would often be couched as if it were a mutually agreed-upon decision.

Four months later, Felt appeared on a Sunday news program, CBS's *Face the Nation*. One of the panelists was Ronald J. Ostrow from the *Los Angeles Times*, and the FBI beat reporter used one of his allotted questions to ask Felt about a subject of "persistent speculation." Felt replied, "No, I am not Deep Throat. . . . And the only thing I can say is that I wouldn't be ashamed to be, because I think whoever [it was] helped the country, no question about it."[64]

If Woodward was going to reveal his identity at some date unknown, then the least Felt could do was contribute to making the mantle a heroic one. By that time, perhaps, none of his former peers or colleagues from the FBI would be around to contradict the myth about Deep Throat's design.

Among all the efforts to pierce the mystery over the next few decades, the one mounted by *Time* magazine stands out as the most ironic.

As Hays Gorey prepared to interview Woodward in April 1976, the ten-year *Time* veteran became fixated on trying to expose Deep Throat's identity. Off and on for the next several years, and with varying degrees of intensity, Gorey, and another *Time* correspondent named John F. Stacks, would pore over the accumulated evidence and speculation, confident that armed with their knowledge of how Washington and journalism worked, they could crack the secret. Gorey was said to know "Washington politics and Watergate as well as his own children," as he had been one of the correspondents assigned to cover Watergate when the story burgeoned far beyond Sandy Smith. On an emotional level, Gorey believed Woodward when the *Post* reporter insisted Deep Throat was a single individual; intellectually, he had trouble buying the proposition.[65]

At one point Gorey worked with a crack private investigator, and he and Stacks also occasionally compared notes with other interested parties. In 1982, for example, John Dean briefed Gorey on his own considerable body of detective work, which Dean had undertaken after initially thinking that Deep Throat was a literary device and fictional composite, and then, for a time, concluding that it was White House speechwriter David Gergen. Dean was interested in the question because he thought Deep Throat's "motives and actions might show the connections among various institutions of government." He had even developed two sources inside the *Post* who were willing to help him, and referred to them by the single, tongue-in-cheek code-name "Deep Thought." They told Dean that Deep Throat had been someone in the FBI, "close to Pat Gray." Dean was skeptical of this answer, even though he knew from being Nixon's counsel that Mark Felt had been identified as a leaker. But this solution seemed too obvious. Instead, Dean thought Deep Throat had to be someone inside the White House, primarily because he had known about the tape erasure.[66]

Sandy Smith also worked with Stacks and Gorey on *Time*'s on-again, off-again investigation. In the early '80s, Smith and Stacks had a hunch (along with Dean) that Alexander Haig was Deep Throat, and they all worked hard to prove it. But it turned out that Haig had not been in Washington on a key date: October 9, 1972, when Deep Throat provided Woodward with the information that resulted in the *Post*'s "centerpiece" story. Moreover, when Haig was confronted with their finding that he was Woodward's secret source, his denial was so energetic it was persuasive.

It never occurred to Gorey, Stacks, or Smith that the reason their magazine ran such a close second to the *Post* in its coverage, and was even ahead of the newspaper on some vital angles, was because its most important source and the *Post*'s were one and the same person (or faction).

The unquestionable wisdom behind Felt's dogged unwillingness to come forward was underscored in 1979. On April 10, after much internal debate, Jimmy Carter's Justice Department indicted W. Mark Felt, L. Patrick Gray III, and Edward S. Miller, the former chief of the Domestic Intelligence Division, for reviving the FBI practice of "black-bag jobs" after J. Edgar Hoover's death in May 1972. The targets of these warrantless and surreptitious entries had been the homes of New York and New Jersey relatives and friends of Weather Underground fugitives, all of whom stood accused of terrorist bombings and other felonies. Felt and Miller openly admitted authorizing at least some of the illegal break-ins, while

Gray denied sanctioning the practice. It turned out that it had been carried out without his knowledge, and ultimately he was not even tried.

The moral and financial support offered up by the fraternity of former FBI agents and executives—backing that would never have been forthcoming had his identity as Deep Throat been known—proved instrumental to Felt's ability to get through the trial. Mounting a defense would have easily bankrupted him, apart from having to bear the ignominy of being the highest-ranking FBI executive ever indicted. The day Felt appeared at the arraignment, a sea of more than 700 current and former agents (a number he inflated to 1,200 in his memoir) surrounded him in the plaza outside the federal courthouse in Washington. More than 200 agents from New York alone had taken a day's leave, boarding buses at 4:30 a.m., to demonstrate their solidarity. After the first hearing, the agents promptly began passing the hat to finance the defense.[67]

The ordeal lasted two and a half years, and in the middle of it Felt decided to publish his memoirs. Ralph de Toledano, who obviously shared his views on politics and national security, agreed to be his ghostwriter. A well-known journalist and one of the founding editors of *National Review*, de Toledano had first achieved renown in 1950 with a best-selling book about the Alger Hiss case. Richard Nixon had been one of his chief sources, and the two men had remained staunch political allies afterwards. De Toledano was initially cautious, not wanting to assist the man who many had fingered as Deep Throat. But Felt personally "swore" that he was not, and that he "had never leaked information to the Woodward-Bernstein team or anyone else."[68]

The first draft of Felt's book read like Oliver Wendell Holmes's *The Autocrat of the Breakfast-Table:* one-sided and haughty. De Toledano was a good wordsmith, however, and the end result, *The FBI Pyramid: From the Inside*, was a brisk read and stout defense of the postwar Bureau under Hoover. In addition to offering up Felt's boilerplate disclaimer about being Deep Throat, the memoir included a supposedly "blow-by-blow" account of the "palace intrigue" engaged in by that notorious back-stabber, Bill Sullivan. He, according to Felt, had been the root cause of all the problems afflicting the FBI. The memoir went into great detail about that "feisty little man's" forced retirement, but said nothing about Felt's own forced departure. Felt claimed that his sole purpose in staying on after Hoover's death was "to help" the neophyte Pat Gray. "I certainly did not stay on out of any hope that I might become director if Gray failed," Felt wrote.[69]

For the discerning reader, the false humility in the memoir could not help but be inadvertently revealing. Felt could not desist from highlighting certain facts. "Now that I have carefully reviewed the White House tapes," he wrote, "I know that there was never a possibility that Nixon would appoint anyone from the professional staff to head the FBI." (The Nixon-Haldeman tape from August 1, 1972, had not been released in full when Felt wrote that sentence, so he was spared the revelation that his scheme had actually worked and that only his own impatience prevented it from coming to fruition.) Nor could Felt resist telegraphing his true views and/or projecting his motives onto others. One blatant example of this occurred during his account of why Kleindienst accused him in the fall of 1972 of leaking. The accusation "startled" him and came as an "unpleasant surprise," he wrote; his contact with Kleindienst had been frequent and friendly, and he couldn't fathom why the attorney general would think such a thing. But later, when Felt realized that the allegation actually emanated from the White House, the logic behind it became "obvious."[70]

> I was supposed to be jealous of Gray for having received the appointment as acting director instead of myself. They felt that my high position in the FBI gave me access to all the Watergate information and that I was releasing it to Woodward and Bernstein in an effort *to discredit Gray so that he would be removed and I would have another chance at the job.* [emphasis added][71]

Still, *The FBI Pyramid* was a bust when published in 1979. Felt's ongoing prosecution had raised his public profile but it didn't translate into sales. The *Washington Post* called the book an "unremarkable autobiography. . . . We learn little about the FBI that we do not already know . . . [while Felt] seeks to perpetuate a view of Hoover and the FBI that is no longer seriously peddled even on the backs of cereal boxes."[72]

Meanwhile, the trial of Felt and his co-defendant Miller was postponed repeatedly because of disputes over access to classified materials. In pretrial motions, their lawyers indicated they intended to argue that both men acted on higher authority in approving the break-ins; that black-bag jobs had been a routine FBI investigative tactic for decades; and that they were legal because of alleged ties between the Weather Underground and hostile foreign powers. Government lawyers countered that these arguments represented an attempt at "graymail," that is, an effort to entangle the case in documents that the government would be unwilling to declassify, until at some point the prosecution has to be dropped. There was an attempt at a plea bargain, but Felt and Miller were only willing to plead guilty to a misdemeanor, which the government found unacceptable.

When the trial finally commenced in September 1980, Felt and Miller were able to draw from a healthy legal defense fund that totaled $1.2 million (more than $3 million in 2011 dollars). Dozens of high-level government officials, including several former attorneys general, testified over the next eight weeks. No appearance was more stunning, however, than that of Richard Nixon. Although Felt's leaks had infuriated and damaged him, Nixon was willing to brush that aside in order to achieve a larger historical purpose. Felt's legal position coincided with his own: a sitting president could lawfully order the Bureau to conduct surreptitious entries. In other words, what was otherwise illegal became lawful if and when a president ordered it. Putting forward this view was an attempt to justify, in a court of law, the break-in into the office of Ellsberg's psychiatrist, and so merited, from Nixon's perspective, a court appearance.[73]

Nixon did not appear as a witness for the defense, though, except in intent. Felt's lawyers had come to believe that an appearance by the disgraced president would have a negative impact on a jury drawn from the liberal enclave of Washington, D.C., so they decided against calling him. Instead, the government summoned Nixon to the witness stand, and precisely because of his presumed effect on the jury. In forty-six minutes of testimony, the former president—interrupted by shouts of "liar," "thief," and "war criminal" from courtroom spectators—defended the illicit behavior authorized by Felt and Miller, though he denied giving them an express order. His testimony played out exactly as the prosecution had hoped, helping sway the jury to convict Felt and Miller.[74]

On November 6, 1980, three days after the American electorate overwhelmingly rejected Jimmy Carter's bid for a second term, Felt and Miller were found guilty on all counts after just eight hours of deliberation. Felt wore the conviction as a badge of honor. The day the verdict was announced, hundreds of sympathetic agents again crowded into the plaza in front of the court, demonstrating against what they regarded as a wrong-headed prosecution. Unspoken but clearly on everyone's mind was the promise that the conviction would soon be overturned, given Ronald Reagan's landslide victory. He had pledged, on the campaign trail, to reward, rather than indict, government officials like Felt and Miller who ostensibly kept Americans safe from domestic terrorists. Reagan's election all but guaranteed a pardon.

Later that month Woodward contacted Deep Throat for the first time in several years. Felt was facing up to ten years in prison (though no one expected him to get that much), a possible $10,000 fine, and certain disbarment; in addition, his wife, Audrey, was ill. Woodward had fantasized periodically about persuading Felt to let him tell the story about their relationship in a book. But Felt was unyielding despite his predicament. The answer was "no," and he reminded Woodward not to do anything else "to further exploit [their] relationship."[75]

Reagan's pardon was not long in coming. Before a formal request was even submitted, and weeks before the inauguration, he ordered incoming White House counselor Edwin Meese to gather material on the case. After a slight delay because of the attempt on his life, Reagan granted a full and complete pardon on April 15, without bothering to conduct the standard consultation with the chief prosecutor. In letters to Felt and Miller, Reagan apologized for taking so long, saying he couldn't "push [the] bureaucracy into a higher speed." In gratitude, Felt sent the president a copy of his memoir, autographed, *"To Ronald Reagan, a great president!! With appreciation, respect, and much admiration!"* For his part, Nixon sent Felt an inscribed copy of *The Real War,* his latest book. The inscription inside read, *"To Mark Felt. With appreciation for his years of service to the nation. Richard Nixon."*[76]

Epilogue

1982–2011

When the legend becomes fact, print the legend.
—John Ford's The Man Who Shot Liberty Valance

Over the next two decades the search for Deep Throat became a journalistic, if not national, obsession and thriving cottage industry. The "parlor game that would not die" kept Bernstein and Woodward in the public eye, of course, far longer than they otherwise would have been. It also had the effect, with every passing year, of elevating Deep Throat's role as a source and cementing the myth about the *Post* reporters' own roles in uncovering Watergate. All this was made possible by a largely compliant media, which sought reflected glory by perpetuating the heroic-journalist construct.[1]

One of the most interesting yet overlooked dissents, given his role in Watergate coverage, came from none other than Sandy Smith. The reporter who broke, in retrospect, as many significant stories about Watergate as anyone in the press, felt strongly about the matter.

> There's a myth that the press did all this, uncovered all the crimes. . . . It's bunk. The press didn't do it. People forget that the government was investigating all the time. In my material there was less than two percent that was truly original investigation. There was an investigation being carried out here. It may have been blocked, bent, botched, or whatever, but it was proceeding. The government investigators found the stuff and gave us something to expose.[2]

Nonetheless, the epic narrative of journalists saving the day proved much more powerful and durable.

From time to time, Woodward divulged meaningful clues about Deep Throat's identity, such as in 1997, when he said that Deep Throat had already been publicly named and had denied the allegation. Around the same time, Woodward told Leonard Garment that Deep Throat's role and persona had changed radically since Watergate, and was now so discordant with his former behavior that he "would never come forward to identify himself." On another occasion, Woodward predicted in 2000 that curious people will not be surprised. "You'll say, 'Ah, okay, now I see, it makes sense.'"[3]

But for the most part, the extent of Woodward's involvement was to fend off efforts to end the guessing game, even if it meant lying, on the grounds that he had to keep his word. In 1981, his *Post* colleague, columnist Richard Cohen, declared his intention to identify Felt as Deep Throat. Cohen cited, among other things, the tip about Spiro Agnew that Woodward had passed along from Deep Throat in the spring of 1973; Cohen had noticed the initials "M.F." written across the top of Woodward's notes at the time. Yet Woodward denied that he had identified the source as Deep Throat and insisted that the initials stood not for "Mark Felt" but for "my friend." Eventually Cohen desisted after being persuaded by Woodward that he was only trying to keep Cohen from writing something "monumentally stupid." In a somewhat similar vein, during a 1989 interview in *Playboy*, Woodward said Deep Throat had not been part of the "intelligence community." But the FBI has always been responsible for domestic counterintelligence operations, and a member of the intelligence community ever since that term became part of Washington parlance.[4]

There was invariably a flurry of activity around major anniversaries. During these occasions, observers would always express puzzlement over why an ostensible national hero was so reluctant to come forward and claim his just reward. As the journalist Richard Reeves once put it, "if there is a Deep Throat he's worth $10 million on the hoof and he should have been promoting his book by now on the *Today* show." ABC anchorman Ted Koppel, during a *Nightline* show marking the tenth anniversary of the break-in, noted that Deep Throat's silence gave credence to those who said Woodward and Bernstein either "made it all up" or that the secret source was actually a composite. "We have been absolutely scrupulous in describing the events involving that person," Bernstein replied. "We're not clever enough to make it up."[5]

Still, Deep Throat's modesty and self-effacement seemed downright "un-American," as Fred Emery suggested. Emery had been the chief correspondent for the *Times* of London during Watergate, and was the author of a well-regarded history of the scandal. He had witnessed nearly everyone involved cash in: the burglars, judge, convicted White House staffers, senators (and their counsels), members of Nixon's Cabinet, special prosecutors, and, of course, journalists. Why was Deep Throat intent on staying in the shadows?[6]

On the twentieth anniversary of the break-in, James Mann wrote one of the more insightful articles about the mystery. Published in *The Atlantic*, his essay attempted to identify Deep Throat by analyzing institutional motives and bureaucratic politics. Mann also had the unquestioned benefit of having worked with Woodward on several Watergate-related stories for the *Post,* prior to taking a leave of absence from the newspaper in September 1972, just as things were heating up. Mann wrote that Woodward, during the summer and early fall, spoke to him repeatedly of "'my source at the FBI,' or, alternatively, of 'my friend at the FBI'—each time making it plain that this was a special, and unusually well-placed, source." Mann concluded, after taking Felt's memoir at face value, that Deep Throat had to have been a high-ranking official at the FBI, most likely Felt but perhaps Charlie Bates or Robert Kunkel. He had acted to protect the integrity of the Bureau's investigation from a White House seeking to "gain political control" over the FBI following Hoover's death. Mann did allow that there may have been "personal motivations at work," yet barely mentioned the fierce war of succession.[7]

Woodward and Bernstein declined to comment publicly on Mann's thesis. But Woodward called him directly to complain, arguing that discussions within the newsroom should be protected, and in any case, it was "not for [Mann] to decide to reveal alleged details about my source." He also denied that he had ever spoken as freely as Mann was now claiming. "Any reporter who's ever had a good source knows how important and vital sources are to the news business," he told Howard Kurtz, the *Post's* media reporter, who wrote an article that questioned Mann's ethics. "My feelings about it are almost ecclesiastical." In response, Mann discounted the notion that he had violated a confidence by quoting private conversations with Woodward. "I don't see what possible harm there could be to a source after 20 years," he said. "I think this is a matter of history. The motivations of the person who became known as Deep Throat are a matter of history."[8]

One reason for believing that Woodward spoke as freely about his special friend as Mann claimed comes, interestingly enough, from the FBI's Behavioral Sciences Unit. Their research and experience over the years have shown that at the initial stage of a new enterprise, behavior invariably tends to be more open and careless. Over time there is a greater need to disguise and protect that behavior—or in Woodward's case, his source. As the stakes grew higher outside and inside the *Post* newsroom, Woodward began to tighten up, if only to prevent the story from being taken away from him and Bernstein and assigned to more experienced senior reporters. The ultimate expression of this increasing secrecy, of course, was Woodward's strong preference not to disclose Felt's identity in 1972 to Sussman, Simons, or Bradlee—a position that these editors respected at the time, although Bradlee himself later questioned it. Still later, there would be an overwhelming tendency on Woodward's part to deny that any clues had ever been let out of the bag to anyone.[9]

Woodward also used the occasion of the twentieth anniversary to reiterate his pledge to reveal Deep Throat's identity after his death. "I've never had anyone ask me to extend anonymity past their death," he said—neglecting to mention that he had not offered Felt that option. Contingency plans had even been put in place should Woodward and Bernstein both predecease Deep Throat. The mere mention of such elaborate-sounding arrangements fostered the false impression that Felt was a willing partner to the plan.[10]

The spring of 1992 also marked the broadcast of a two-hour special on Watergate by CBS News, reported by Walter Pincus in conjunction with the Washington Post Company's television stations. This effort was the first journalistic analysis that utilized primary documents, including thousands of pages of recently released papers from the FBI's Watergate file and the Watergate special prosecutor's office. The CBS special posited that Pat Gray was Deep Throat (which Nixon, among many others, found impossible to believe). This gross error was, in a sense, balanced by a major journalistic admission against interest. The documents demonstrated beyond a doubt that the Bureau had been far ahead of the press in investigating Watergate.[11]

The primary documents also proved that several of Felt's statements to Woodward had been false and/or misleading. Perhaps that was why Woodward, during an interview by CBS's Mike Wallace, acknowledged for the first time that Deep Throat occasionally imparted bad information: "Sometimes [Deep Throat] was wrong," he disclosed, without going into any details. Woodward may have had in mind, among other things, Felt's allegation that Gray had marched over to the White House and blackmailed the president into nominating him. Wallace did not follow up what should have been seen as a striking disclosure, and the myth of Deep Throat's unerring accuracy went undisturbed. Thus, in Ben Bradlee's memoir, published three years later, he could still aver that "the information and the guidance [Deep Throat gave] Woodward were never wrong, never."[12]

In 1999, the *Hartford Courant* published a front-page story reporting that Carl Bernstein's son, Jacob, had let the secret of Deep Throat's identity slip out while attending an exclusive summer camp. When queried, Bernstein engaged in the same kind of dissembling responses Woodward had perfected over the years. "I hate to ruin your story . . . ," he laughingly told the *Courant* reporter, David Daley. "Is Mark Felt still alive?" But Daley was not so easily discouraged, and went to the trouble of locating and contacting Felt, who now lived in California with his daughter, Joan. He had moved there in 1991 after a devastating personal tragedy. In July 1984, three years after the Reagan pardon, his wife, Audrey, committed suicide using Felt's service revolver. She had never truly recovered from the disappointment of having all their sacrifices come to naught, not to mention the bitterness engendered by the "unjust persecution" of Mark.[13]

When David Daley reached Felt, he was far removed from the Washington scene and had constructed a new life as a doting but strict grandfather. Nonetheless, the old instincts immediately kicked in when Daley put the question to him. "No, it's not me," Felt said during the brief telephone interview. Along with the denial Felt shrewdly offered a kernel of truth, a correction to the long-held, but erroneous presumption that Deep Throat always intended to bring the Nixon White House down. "I would have done better," he added. "I would have been more effective. Deep Throat didn't exactly bring the White House crashing down, did he?"[14]

In the years before the mystery ended, the most persistent and energetic promoter of Felt-as-Deep-Throat was *Slate* columnist Timothy Noah. Over a six-year period beginning in 1999, he wrote a series of columns that revisited the issue whenever a new wrinkle or rumor appeared. On one such occasion, in August 1999, he interviewed Felt at length about Mann's article; read him excerpts of Nixon's October 19, 1972, conversation with Haldeman—the one in which they first discussed the revelation that Felt was leaking—and brought up tensions within and without the FBI. It was perhaps the most informed questioning of Felt that had ever been attempted.[15]

> *Noah:* Let's just say you *were* Deep Throat. Would that really be so terrible?
>
> *Felt:* It *would* be terrible. This would completely undermine the reputation that you might have as a loyal, logical employee of the FBI. It just wouldn't fit at all.
>
> *Noah:* But a lot of people think Deep Throat is a hero for getting the truth out about Nixon and Watergate.

Felt: That's not my view at all. It would be contrary to my responsibility as a loyal employee of the FBI to leak information. . . .

Noah: Did you want the top job [at the FBI?]

Felt: I certainly wouldn't have objected [to it].

Noah: Were you disappointed when you didn't get it?

Felt: I can't say that I was.

Noah: Didn't the White House interfere with the FBI investigation of Watergate?

Felt: I don't have any recollection of any specifics like that.[16]

In 2002, the thirtieth anniversary, another former *Post* reporter, Ronald Kessler, weighed in on the subject. His suggestion did not rest on any new analysis of the evidence, but rather on simple reporting. In a new history of the FBI, Kessler wrote that many of the agents who had been involved in the Watergate investigation had come to the conclusion that Felt was Deep Throat. Adding credence to their belief was the fact that in February 2000, Woodward, after delivering a lecture at UC Davis, had shown up unexpectedly at the Santa Rosa, California home of Joan Felt. Kessler learned that Mark Felt had treated Woodward like an old friend; the meeting was more like a celebration than an interview. (Woodward would later write about this visit, too, saying that he had dropped by in the hopes of getting answers to questions that had been nagging at him for almost thirty years. But Felt was incapable of providing them because he was already suffering from dementia. Despite his friendly demeanor he appeared to remember nothing about their relationship or even his 1980 conviction.) When Kessler eventually talked directly to Felt about Woodward's visit, Felt didn't remember it at all, confusing Woodward with a government attorney. "I was definitely not Deep Throat," he told Kessler.[17]

"Modern journalism's greatest unsolved mystery" came to an abrupt end in May 2005, when *Vanity Fair* published Felt's admission, penned by John D. O'Connor, a lawyer and family friend. The dénouement was bound to be anticlimactic, given that Felt had been on the short list of candidates, if not the number one suspect, since 1974. But no one had ever imagined Woodward and Bernstein would be soundly beaten on the story.[18]

Joan Felt had become suspicious after Woodward's 2000 visit. When she later observed that her father seemed to have unusually clear although nonspecific memories of him, Woodward responded, "He has good reason to remember me." In the spring of 2002, Felt finally acknowledged to his family that he was Deep Throat, and they began trying to persuade Woodward to cooperate on a joint project. John O'Connor, a San Francisco litigator, represented the Felts' interests pro bono. During the delicate negotiations, Woodward sometimes began the discussion with a caveat: "Just because I'm talking to you, I'm not admitting that he is who you think he is." Woodward's frequently expressed concern was that Felt was being pressured and did not necessarily understand what he was being asked to do. All the while Woodward left O'Connor, and Mark Felt, Jr., who also participated in the discussions, with the distinct impression that there was a long-standing agreement between him and Felt, Sr., about the timing of the disclosure, and that Woodward's greatest concern was honoring it.[19]

Twice Woodward scheduled visits to Santa Rosa, presumably to satisfy himself that Felt wanted to come forward of his own volition, and that he was in a clear mental state, fully cognizant of what he would be doing. Both visits were canceled. Meanwhile, with Felt obviously in decline, Woodward wrote the book that would fulfill his actual promise to the public. He completed a confidential first draft by late May 2002 and began contemplating the sale of book, serial, and film rights.[20]

The Felt family believed they deserved part of what was anticipated to be a huge financial windfall, although they later claimed they weren't doing it for the money primarily, only to give Felt his due. Since Woodward and the Felts could not agree on terms, O'Connor began exploring alternatives. An early attempt by O'Connor to interest *People* magazine fizzled. A freelance writer, Jess Walter, was brought in, but Felt was so addled by age that four hours of interviews produced nothing usable; Walter found it "riddling" to talk to him. One day he would acknowledge being Deep Throat, the next day he would strenuously deny it. In 2003 (the year Woodward and Bernstein sold their Watergate papers to the University of Texas for $5 million), O'Connor contacted Graydon Carter, the editor of *Vanity Fair*, about breaking the secret there; eventually the magazine agreed to publish an account of the story that had eluded "squads of ace reporters for 30 years." The next month the Felt family sold the film rights to Tom Hanks's production company as part of a package deal worth an estimated $1 million.[21]

Woodward and Bernstein initially tried to respond to the *Vanity Fair* article as if it were just another Deep Throat identification that could be quashed. Their response, posted on the internet at 12:15 p.m. on May

31 by *Editor & Publisher* magazine, was smoothly noncommittal. Woodward argued that his agreement with Deep Throat was still in force—and included a reiteration of their pledge to only identify their secret source upon his death. The *Post* followed suit with a brisk "no comment." But then, during an intense meeting at the paper, executive editor Leonard Downie overrode Woodward's objections and declared the obvious: "Bob, it's over." He had read Woodward's manuscript in March, after deciding that the paper, not just the reporter, had to be prepared for Deep Throat's demise. Now he was unwilling to be party to a nondenial denial. At 5:29 p.m. the newspaper confirmed on its website that Felt was Deep Throat. "We've kept that secret because we keep our word," said Woodward, almost defiantly. He and Bernstein then began "their victory lap of the news cycle," as Graydon Carter later described the nostalgia-tinged, wall-to-wall coverage. It could easily have been mistaken as a "last hurrah" for the mainstream media establishment, what David Halberstam once labeled "the powers that be."[22]

A few discordant notes were sounded. As *Washington Post* columnist Ruth Marcus perceptively observed on June 5, "I am glad, I suppose, to finally know the secret of Deep Throat. I am less confident that Mark Felt wanted me to know." The Felt family insisted that he was "very present and cogent and capable of making decisions." But they kept the press at arm's length, prompting Marcus to suggest that they had maneuvered Felt into the revelation:

> To comprehend how thoroughly Felt believed that it wouldn't fit for him to be both Mark Felt and Deep Throat, consider how insistently he kept his secret hidden from his own family. The more you read of *Vanity Fair*'s account of the outing, the sorrier you feel for a failing old man prodded and even tricked by his relatives into telling all—to get "closure," as his daughter put it, perhaps finally to profit from what the family, if not Felt, viewed as his heroism.[23]

It was natural for the Felt family to present him in the best possible light, the supposed conscience of the FBI and a "great American hero who went well above the call of duty, at much risk to himself, to save his country from a horrible injustice." (And the slightly reworked Felt memoir, which appeared in 2006, followed precisely these lines.) What was more interesting was the extent to which this slant was a shared interest with Woodward, Bernstein, the *Washington Post*, and the media at large. Some dissent was voiced on both the left and the right. The former were unwilling to accept that anyone who had been J. Edgar Hoover's number three man could ever be a hero. Meanwhile, a prominent spokesman for the latter, former Nixon speechwriter Pat Buchanan, declared that Felt was an "FBI hack who . . . ratt[ed] out [Nixon] for passing him over as director." Yet, by and large, the media coverage was overwhelmingly favorable. Felt was depicted as a "reluctant" or "quaint" folk hero, someone who leaked "as a matter of conscience." And even if there was an element of pique in his motive, his leaks, made at "considerable personal risk," were a "gift to the Republic."[24]

Pat Gray was one of the few FBI contemporaries of Felt still able to comment, and utter a dissent with some authority. The news came as a "tremendous surprise to me," Gray told ABC newsman George Stephanopoulos. Gray said he now realized "[Felt] was a really formidable character and, as it turned out, a formidable foe," primarily because he was such "a skilled liar."

> He told me time and again he was not Deep Throat. . . . He was under suspicion by everyone but his immediate boss, because I was working with the man on a daily basis, and he presented to me a picture of an honorable individual doing his job. I was not going to subject him to the degradation of a lie-detector case. . . .
>
> I could not have been more shocked and more disappointed in a man whom I had trusted. And I felt totally at a loss as to understand why he did not come to me and tell me what his problems were.
>
> I think he was treacherous only to me, the man who trusted him. That's all. That's a deep inner hurt.[25]

Gray also said he believed Felt was guided by "a revenge motive and a desire to get rid of me." He was maneuvering for the top job and had to show the interim appointee was not up to the task.[26]

Another interesting set of reactions came from the Society of Former Special Agents of the FBI, in existence since 1937. Myth and fable had become so embedded in the Deep Throat saga that not even Bureau insiders could separate truth from self-serving fictions.[27]

Felt's disclosure had stunned Jack McDermott, the special agent in charge of the Washington Field Office from October 1972 onwards; he had long thought Deep Throat was a composite meant to fuzz up the identities of several discrete sources. But McDermott was even more shocked by the number of former agents and executives, most of whom had no first-hand knowledge of the case, who now gave Felt a free ride, and in some cases, actually endorsed his behavior. The common thread in these comments was the supposed need "to expose information which otherwise would have been suppressed." Rather than go public with his criticism, McDermott wrote a short essay for *the Grapevine*, the society's monthly publication for and about members. He believed a direct explanation, "within the family" so to speak, was called for.[28]

To his astonishment, *the Grapevine* refused to publish his three-page analysis, "Concerning Watergate and the Role of W. Mark Felt," or any other contributions he cared to make on the topic. An editor's note explained that the magazine "will not publish any letters or articles about this matter. . . . *the Grapevine* does not deal with controversial subjects or print negative material about members of the FBI family." McDermott thought the refusal to take a stand was spineless. "It's embarrassing to some degree for the Bureau to be exposed as having had such people as Felt and Sullivan," he observed. But if the society that represented former agents was unwilling to express "shock, dismay and disgust at Felt's perfidy," McDermott said, the public could hardly be expected to see through Felt's "heroic" conduct.[29]

The sole redeeming gesture, from McDermott's point of view, occurred when Felt applied for reinstatement to the society. Felt had apparently let his membership lapse years earlier, and presumably the society was going to be a prime audience for the reworked memoir that John O'Connor was now writing. Society by-laws required every applicant to be sponsored by two members in good standing, and only one name was attached to Felt's application. As word got out that Felt was applying for reinstatement, approximately 500 negative telephone calls, e-mails, and letters arrived in protest, all of which said, in effect, that Felt's application should be denied because he had violated the Bureau's integrity. An application with the requisite number of sponsors was never resubmitted.[30]

The book about Deep Throat that Woodward had been writing was published on July 6, little more than a month after the *Vanity Fair* article appeared. *The Secret Man* was notable for Woodward's hand-wringing over his fraught relationship with Felt, along with his description of the chill that descended between them after publication of *All the President's Men*. As in all his books, Woodward laid out the story in detail but shied away from explaining what it all meant; he still could not make up his mind about such basic questions as Felt's motivation. He did admit to having used Mark Felt, which had been largely unspoken but evident since 1974. Reading the book, the Felt family was stunned to learn that there was not, and never had been, a deal between Woodward and Mark Felt save for the original "deep background" agreement, which had been observed mainly in the breach. One of the few reviewers to remark on Woodward's exploitation of Felt was *Slate*'s Tim Noah. He did not fault Woodward outright for betraying Felt in order to produce a more readable and accurate narrative in 1974. But he did suggest there was an element of "unconscious sadism" in committing the infraction while constantly seeking Felt's approbation.[31]

Although Woodward wrote that he wanted *The Secret Man* to be the "full story . . . with nothing held back," like *All the President's Men*, it was also notable for what it did not disclose. There was nothing about the fact that Felt, in all likelihood, had not acted alone. Nor did Woodward squarely address the issue of the false and misleading information that Felt had supplied him, although he had to have been aware of that since at least 1992, when he examined the FBI's Watergate files, and probably much earlier.[32]

Perhaps the most glaring omission concerned the truth about why Felt had abruptly left the FBI in 1973. Elements of the story had been public knowledge since the mid-1970s, when Woodward's former colleague at the *Post*, Sanford Ungar, published his 682-page history of the Bureau. Woodward had also known, sometime after it was revealed in the late 1990s, that in mid-October 1972 Haldeman singled out Felt as the primary culprit for the leaks that were bedeviling the White House. Why hadn't Felt been summarily fired *then* was a logical question to research, especially since Pat Gray and William Ruckelshaus were still around to answer it.[33]

In fact, Ruckelshaus had taken it upon himself to bring this information to Woodward's attention after the *Vanity Fair* article. On June 21, 2005, the former acting FBI director called Woodward because he presumed Woodward would be coming out with a book, and he thought Woodward deserved to have the "full picture" about Felt now that he had come forward as Deep Throat. Ruckelshaus proceeded to tell Woodward the entire story of his confrontation with Felt, beginning with Crewdson's May 1973 scoop about the national security wiretaps; the subsequent telephone call from a man who identified himself as "Crewdson"; and what Ruckelshaus had taken to be Felt's dishonesty in the matter. Woodward listened carefully before responding. "It's too late to put it in my book," he said, because it had already been sent off to Simon & Schuster. But "this is an important fact; I'll make sure that it gets out," he assured Ruckelshaus. Still, nothing about the true circumstances of Felt's departure appeared under Woodward's byline in the *Post*, or in the paperback edition of *The Secret Man* when it came out a year later. And Woodward has continued (as recently as December 2010) to leave the impression that Felt's departure from the FBI was nothing out of the ordinary.[34]

When asked in October 2011 about his knowledge of Felt's resignation, Woodward acknowledged talking to Ruckelshaus about it, but said he thought the conversation occurred "after *The Secret Man* came out." He continued, "I talked to Ruckelshaus because he was *claiming* he had fired Felt." What Ruckelshaus actually said, however, seemed "somewhat contradictory" to the assertion that he had fired Deep Throat. If Felt left a resignation letter on Ruckelshaus's desk rather than risk an internal investigation, Woodward observed, "then that's not a firing."[35]

That distinction is certainly valid. Nonetheless, the episode remains central to understanding Felt and its elision is curious—what might be called an instance of offering up a partial truth to deflect the raw truth. Such omissions were instrumental to the flattering, if fuzzy and unsatisfying, portrait of Deep Throat that Woodward drew in *The Secret Man*. Inclusion of any one of the missing pieces might have prompted a discerning reader to think, Hey, wait a minute . . . this doesn't make sense! But continuing to elide them allowed Felt to remain largely unchanged from the enigmatic icon Deep Throat had become, even though anonymity no longer shrouded him from close inspection. Felt's motive was left as impenetrable as ever. Every explanation was offered up except the most plausible one, as the reporter lauded for his ability to plumb the innermost workings of the White House, Supreme Court, Pentagon, and CIA turned a blind eye to the ferocious politics of succession at the FBI. Deep Throat had once spoken of the White House's "switchblade mentality," but where that culture really thrived was at the Bureau's uppermost echelons.[36]

Joan Didion, in a 1996 review of several of Woodward's best-selling books, wrote perhaps the best description of his selective interest in his sources, which actually runs like a thread throughout Woodward's body of work:

> Every reporter, in the development of a story, depends on and coddles, or protects, his or her sources. Only when the protection of the source gets in the way of telling the story does the reporter face a professional, even a moral, choice: he can blow the source . . . or he can roll over, [and] shape the story to continue serving the source. The necessity for making this choice between the source and the story

seems not to have come up in the course of writing Mr. Woodward's books, for good reason: since he proceeds from a position in which the very impulse to sort through the evidence and reach a conclusion is seen as suspect, something to be avoided in the higher interest of fairness, he has been able, consistently and conveniently, to define the story as that which the source tells him.[37]

In November 2008, Bernstein and Woodward traveled to Santa Rosa to say hello and goodbye. Felt was in home hospice care and not expected to live much longer. The three men visited for some two hours, an event the reporters likened to a "family reunion," though it was the first time Bernstein and Felt had ever actually met. The press took the farewell trip as further evidence of Woodward's "scrupulousness" about protecting his sources, and Felt's death, just before Christmas, served primarily as an occasion to reaffirm the heroic interpretation. Both Bernstein and Woodward spoke at the service the following month and conveyed Ben Bradlee's respects.

"There is an unknown source and an unknown force behind every great story in history," Woodward quoted Bradlee as saying. "[Felt] was that source and that force in the Nixon administration." Discarding even the more nuanced explanation adopted for *The Secret Man*, Woodward hyperbolically asserted that Felt "was confronted with . . . nothing less than a war—organized, well-practiced, and well-funded by President Richard Nixon—a war aimed at the system of justice. Mark's great decision in all of this was his refusal to be silenced. . . . He was a truth teller."[38]

In June 2005, just after Felt came forward, Ben Bradlee made a typically brisk remark about Deep Throat's motive. Speaking on the Sunday talk show *Face the Nation*, Bradlee observed that good reporters understand that "when some source talks to them, they do it for their own reasons." It is therefore incumbent on a reporter, he said, to "discover those reasons, look at them, filter them out, and decide up or down" before using the source. Unfortunately, he then added, "I think one of [Felt's] motives [was] that he wanted to be head of the FBI. That's one of the purest, noblest motives that I've run into in 30 years. What's the matter with that?"[39]

If the second half of what Bradlee said is discarded, what is left is a trenchant statement about the importance of divining a source's motives. Around the same time, Harry M. Rosenfeld, the *Post*'s metro editor during Watergate, made the same observation even more succinctly: "Editors and reporters have the responsibility of assessing motives when they weigh the reliability of the informant."[40]

If the *Post's* reporters or editors had sized up Felt correctly in the summer of 1972, it still would have been perfectly proper for Woodward and Bernstein to use whatever information and guidance he was willing to provide. As Tim Noah has pointed out, "If the free flow of vital information about our government depended on the purity of heart of all concerned, we would know very little. Happily, we are as likely to learn what we need to know through the pursuit of cheap advantage." Still, a recognition that Felt was seeking personal advancement first and foremost would have led to heightened scrutiny of his claims and a better version of the obtainable truth.

Forty years later, the damage wrought by continuing to misinterpret or misrepresent Mark Felt is no longer to an individual (Pat Gray), an institution (the FBI), or the legal process. Rather, it is to history, to public understanding of Watergate and the Nixon presidency, and to the story of how the break-in brought a president down. For decades, the romance of Watergate was that a bold, free press uncovered the scandal when the justice system was not working, leading to the resignation of a president with too little regard for the law. To their credit, Woodward, Bernstein, and others associated with the *Post's* coverage, have often tried to put forward a more nuanced view, one that acknowledges the roles played by other institutions, e.g., John Sirica's courtroom, Sam Ervin's select committee, and for that matter, the secret Nixon tapes. Nonetheless, they still claim an exalted role for the press and that cliché is imprinted on the public memory.

An accurate rendering of Felt's motive forces a long-overdue revision, if only because it reminds us who the real whistle-blowers were. CRP employees like Judith Hoback, Hugh Sloan, and Penny Gleason took genuine risks, and gained nothing but their self-respect, by telling FBI agents or federal prosecutors the truth. Moreover, the real reason behind Felt's disclosures underscores, yet again, that the Nixon administration did not truly succeed in obstructing the FBI investigation. Rather, the dissonance between what the *Post* reported and the initial paucity of legal results had political and legal repercussions, and most importantly, opened a dangerous credibility gap for the White House. This gap is what gave great momentum to the arguably politicized investigations that proved to be the president's undoing, exacerbated by his persistent inability and/or unwillingness to level with the country—not to mention the secret tape recordings.

It is also true, though, that the criminal justice system was far from being finished with the case in January 1973. Earl Silbert, the chief prosecutor, has said that the sum total of *Washington Post* coverage in the summer and fall of 1972 added "virtually nothing" to the government's understanding of the case. This was (and remains) a far cry from the public's perception. And although most Americans were indifferent to having the media run ahead of the wheels of justice in the Watergate case, the lawyers for John Mitchell, Bob Haldeman, and John Ehrlichman, the three main defendants in the 1974 cover-up trial, were justifiably concerned and rightly, though unsuccessfully, sought a change in venue.

When their convictions, among others, were appealed, one federal appellate judge wholeheartedly agreed that the defendants had been denied a basic constitutional right—the right to a fair trial by an untainted jury. Judge George E. MacKinnon, a Nixon appointee, was known for his fierce independence and frequent dissents from the majority (although he had a good track record in eventually being upheld by the Supreme Court). And in October 1976, MacKinnon, in a biting opinion, argued that the cover-up trial should have been held in a jurisdiction outside of Washington, the scene of singularly heavy coverage. "If ever in the history of our country there was a criminal case which by law had to be transferred to another place for trial because of prejudicial pretrial publicity *alone*, this is that case," MacKinnon concluded, after noting that "the pretrial publicity in this case [was] unequivocally unique in American history . . . swelling in an ever increasing crescendo. . . . [It] worked as an indivisible whole, casting 'All the President's Men' as criminals." The same rule of law that the defendants were charged with betraying, in other words, should not be manipulated or ignored to obtain convictions. In hindsight, MacKinnon seems more right than his five colleagues on the appeals panel, who "mincingly alluded" to the issue (in the judge's words) while affirming the guilt of Messrs. Mitchell, Haldeman, and Ehrlichman.[41]

The failure to move the cover-up trial out of Washington, to be sure, was an error committed by the legal system and not the media's responsibility. Still, it is not desirable to have a case tried in the media, no matter how flagrant the crime. The American system of justice has consciously been designed not to work that way, (i.e., the tight secrecy over grand jury proceedings), and for ample reason. There are too many instances when justice has been denied because of unfair, inflammatory, or inaccurate media coverage. The press, in the end, is not one of the three branches of government, as MacKinnon noted.[42]

Felt's success at manipulating the media is a cautionary tale, and one that remains a potent lesson even now, forty years later. While he clearly contributed to Richard Nixon's undoing, that was not his original intent. More broadly, Felt's machinations make the history of Watergate, and how the scandal brought Nixon down, considerably messier and less of a fairy tale.

But it is what it is.

Acknowledgments

Like many interesting projects, this one didn't start out the way it ended up.

I was never a Watergate buff, even though I worked for George McGovern's campaign in Los Angeles as a twenty-one-year-old. I believed there was much more to the break-in, of course, and kept a McGovern bumper sticker on my car for months after the November 1972 landslide as a small act of political defiance. And naturally, during the summer of 1973, I was glued to the television as a parade of administration witnesses appeared before Sam Ervin's Senate select committee.

But afterwards, I read none of the copious Watergate literature, and aside from a passing interest in the identity of Deep Throat, paid little attention to the story. Although I was part of the generation that flocked to journalism schools in the wake of *All the President's Men*, my role model was less Bob Woodward or Carl Bernstein and more I. F. Stone, who could not get published in the *Washington Post*.

In 2007, a short article in the *Post* attracted my attention: it described the $5 million sale of Woodward and Bernstein's Watergate-related papers to the Ransom Center at the University of Texas. I was looking for subjects to write about for a website I had just started, *Washington Decoded* (www.washingtondecoded.com), and having done research in archives for years, I thought any newly opened papers were likely to contain at least a few new insights into an old crisis.

Soon afterwards, I hooked up with William Gaines, a Pulitzer Prize–winning reporter who had become a journalism professor. He had attracted national attention prior to 2005 for using successive classes to try to ferret out the identity of Deep Throat. Though he and his students ultimately guessed wrong, I found Gaines's perspective unique—that of a working journalist rather than historian, yet one who believed in the importance of the documentary trail. His knowledge of the subject was unparalleled. Moreover, he was willing to share it and brainstorm.

We collaborated on a May 2007 website article, "Deep Throat 3.0," which attempted to shed new light on the nature of the relationship between W. Mark Felt and the *Post*'s coverage. Subsequently, I wrote two more articles: "The Secret That Wasn't: Deep Throat Exposed in 1973" (September 2008) and "Richard Nixon's Own Deep Throat" (November 2009), the latter of which was also published in *The Washingtonian* in an abridged version. The more time I spent catching up with the Watergate literature, the more fascinated I became with the journalistic angle to the story. It became apparent that the press had not applied any of its well-honed skepticism to the pat story about Deep Throat. The coverage of W. Mark Felt's death in 2008 underscored my sense that the treatment had been self-congratulatory, if not self-adulatory, rather than thoughtful.

Several people enabled me to develop a new perspective on Mark Felt. Ed Gray's book with his father, L. Patrick Gray III, caused me to rethink my vague recollection that the acting FBI director was just another of the president's men. Daniel Armstrong, one of Gray's top aides during his short tenure, was a patient guide to that tumultuous year. James Mann helped me understand the inner workings of the *Post*, and Harry M. Rosenfeld was open to talking about the paper's Watergate coverage anew. Barry Sussman, Richard M. Cohen, and Carl Bernstein responded to specific questions. I also benefited from talking with reporters at other publications, especially Ronald J. Ostrow of the *Los Angeles Times*, Stephan Lesher, formerly with *Newsweek*, and from *Time* magazine, John F. Stacks and John M. Wilhelm. John M. Crewdson, formerly of the *New York Times*, was helpful when it mattered most. Bob Woodward was generous with his time despite his skepticism about anyone being able to decipher "a secret man." I did not have as many questions for Woodward as I might have, because his 2005 memoir about his relationship with Mark Felt was better than any interview could be.

Cartha "Deke" DeLoach, Ray Wannall, William D. Ruckelshaus, and John J. McDermott were pivotal in helping me comprehend the mysteries of FBI culture in the early 1970s. My patient guide to Watergate itself from the Bureau's perspective was Angelo J. Lano, the case agent, and I am greatly in his debt. All three of the original federal prosecutors, Earl J. Silbert, Donald Campbell, and Seymour Glanzer, were also willing to share their recollections of the event. Silbert, the chief prosecutor, was especially accommodating. Donald E. Santarelli also provided an invaluable perspective, that of someone who knew and was a keen observer of many of the Washington actors. Meanwhile, Mark Felt could not have a better advocate than John D. O'Connor.

While interviews, memoirs, and the secondary literature have been important to this book, without access to contemporaneous FBI documents it would not have been possible to write this story. The Bureau's main file on Watergate has been open to the public since the early 1990s, but I also benefited enormously from the main files on W. Mark Felt, L. Patrick Gray, William C. Sullivan, and, most importantly, documents generated during the Watergate Inspection Division Investigation. I am indebted to the FBI's Freedom of Information Office for prompt release of these papers, which fill up a five-drawer file cabinet.

The Nixon tape recordings are a unique and irreplaceable source of information. Without them, one would not know that the White House first learned in mid-October 1972 that Mark Felt was leaking to the media, or how that information came to the president's attention. Transcribing the tapes and cataloguing the information was arduous and time-consuming, and this book could not have been done without the exceptional work of Lauren Wilson and Laura Choi Stuart, both former editorial assistants at *Washington Decoded*. Abigail Stewart, another former assistant, performed the all-important function of fact-checking.

The papers of the Watergate Special Prosecution Force at the National Archives in College Park, Maryland, also proved to be vital. For guiding me to and through this collection I am indebted to David Paynter, James Mathis, and John W. Dean.

The collection of Woodward and Bernstein papers at the Harry Ransom Center in Austin, Texas, originally piqued my interest in Watergate. I was prepared to spend weeks examining these papers carefully and submitted a detailed proposal for a grant to defray the costs involved. That application was turned down, however, so I was unable to research the collection first-hand. Stephen Mielke, a Ransom Center archivist, helped me overcome this deficit by patiently answering all the questions that occurred to me from a review of the finding aid, and after reading documents obtained through the mail or via a researcher. Richard Workman and Arcadia Falcone of the Ransom Center were also of assistance, and I thank Frederic A. Maxwell for being my proxy.

I also drew from oral histories compiled by the Society of Former Agents of the FBI and the Richard M. Nixon Library. Susan Rosenfeld, formerly the FBI's historian, made me aware of the former, and Sandra Robinette, the administrator of the Society's oral history project, made all the relevant transcripts available promptly. Meanwhile, Ryan Pettigrew supplied the oral histories as they became available from the Nixon Library, and the Periodical Reading Room staff at the Library of Congress helped me retrieve many obscure articles.

Michael Briggs and Fred M. Woodward at the University Press of Kansas were quick to recognize the merits of another look at a well-worn subject. I am grateful to them for a prompt decision to go ahead, and to the editorial and production staff, especially Larisa Martin, for her patience and help in turning the manuscript into a book. Copy editor Martha Whitt caught innumerable errors and exhibited a devotion to the project that was out of the ordinary. It has already been a pleasure brainstorming with Susan Schott over how to market the book. We'll soon see how it turns out. The manuscript was vetted for the University Press of Kansas by John W. Dean and Keith W. Olson, both of whom made constructive suggestions that I incorporated almost without exception. I had discussed many of the issues and personalities involved with Dean before he read the manuscript, and he understood what I was aiming to accomplish. It is not often that a participant in a great scandal becomes a thoughtful student of it, and he was an invaluable sounding board.

For general encouragement or assistance along the way, I would like to thank John Batchelor, William Burr, David Coleman, Ken DeCell, Chip Fleischer, John Fox, Garrett Graff, Ken Hughes, Stanley I. Kutler, Steve Lagerfeld, John Limpert, Richard A. Moss, Cullen Murphy, Luke A. Nichter, Tim Noah, Jeffery Paine, Tom Powers, Bob Shuster, Virginia Vaught, and Wayne Weber. My agent, Elaine Markson, thought the project worthy enough to find a home for it despite other obligations.

Three people, above all, deserve my deepest gratitude, because they spent more time reading the manuscript and getting it into shape than anyone else. Amy Meeker made the narrative taut, and if it's a page-turner, she deserves the credit. Jay Peterzell, a former *Time* magazine correspondent in Washington, read the manuscript carefully and made sure that the book's argument comported with the evidence at every point. Finally, Irwin F. Gellman, who is writing a multivolume biography of Richard Nixon, put his vast knowledge of all things Nixon at my disposal.

I have yet to hear of a book that doesn't have any errors. The ones in here are my own.

Max Holland
December 2011

Notes

ABBREVIATIONS USED IN NOTES AND BIBLIOGRAPHY

ATU: Albany (NY) Times Union
BG: Boston Globe
CT: Chicago Tribune
CIA: Central Intelligence Agency
COINTELPRO: FBI contraction for counterintelligence program
FBI: Federal Bureau of Investigation
FOIA: Freedom of Information Act
HEP: Henry E. Petersen Main File, FBI
HRC: Harry Ransom Center, University of Texas at Austin
JECL: Jimmy E. Carter Library
LAT: Los Angeles Times
LPG: L. Patrick Gray III Main File, FBI
NARA: National Archives and Records Administration
NYT: New York Times
RMNL: Richard M. Nixon Library
RWRL: Ronald W. Reagan Library
SAC: Special agent in charge
SCPCA: Senate Select Committee on Presidential Campaign Activities
SIU: Special Investigations Unit (the "plumbers")
SMOF: Staff Member & Office Files
SOCXFBI: Society of Former Special Agents of the FBI
WBWP: Woodward and Bernstein Watergate Papers
WCS: William C. Sullivan Main File, FBI
WDN: Washington Daily News
WFO: Washington Field Office, FBI
WG: Watergate Main File, FBI
WHCF: White House Central Files
WHSF: White House Special Files
WIDI: Watergate Inspection Division Investigation, FBI
WMF: W. Mark Felt Main File, FBI
WP: Washington Post
WS: Washington Star
WSJ: Wall Street Journal
WSPF: Watergate Special Prosecution Force

1 Carl Bernstein and Bob Woodward, *All the President's Men* (New York: Simon & Schuster, 1974), 243; Gary Arnold, "Meticulous . . . and Incomplete," *WP*, 4 April 1976, 107.

2 Bob Woodward, *The Secret Man: The Story of Watergate's Deep Throat* (New York: Simon & Schuster, 2005), 104–105, 215.

Before Woodward embraced it, the most persuasive analysis of the institutional motive was journalist James Mann's 1992 article in *The Atlantic*, in which he famously concluded that the fabled secret source was most likely Mark Felt. Not privy to Deep Throat's identity, Mann worked backwards, basing his analysis on the details provided in *All the President's Men;* a Washington reporter's familiarity with how the U.S. government worked; and his own involvement in the *Post*'s early coverage of Watergate, which included working on some stories with Woodward. James Mann, "Deep Throat: An Institutional Analysis," *Atlantic*, May 1992, 106–112.

For a slightly more cynical take on the "turf" explanation, see Jack Shafer, "Why Did Deep Throat Leak?" http://www.slate.com/id/2120148/, 2 June 2005.

3 After *Playboy* published excerpts of *All the President's Men* in its April 1974 issue, Felt immediately became a prime suspect because he had been passed over for the directorship. The first publication to nominate Felt as Woodward's secret source was *The Washingtonian* magazine; see John Limpert, "Deep Throat: If It Isn't Tricia It Must Be . . . ," *Washingtonian,* June 1974, 17; see also David Corn, "Deep Throat: More Hero Than Not," http://www.thenation.com/blog/156174/deep-throat-more-hero-not, 1 June 2005.

4 "Higher Authority," *The Nation*, 2 May 1981, 516; Athan G. Theoharis, ed., with Tony Poveda, Susan Rosenfeld, and Richard Gid Powers, *The FBI: A Comprehensive Reference Guide* (Phoenix, AZ: Oryx Press, 1999), 130–131.

Some observers may see a distinction between surreptitious entries carried out by private groups for the purposes of political espionage and ones designed by the FBI to gather information in counterterrorism cases. But federal prosecutors and courts did not.

5 W. Mark Felt, *The FBI Pyramid: From the Inside* (New York: G. P. Putnam's Sons, 1979), 258. Three days after the break-in, acting Director Pat Gray ordered that FBI field offices conduct, under the personal supervision of the agents-in-charge, an "absolute, thorough, immediate [and] imaginative investigation." Later, an internal FBI investigation mounted after Gray's departure reported that "investigating agents, supervisory personnel and Bureau officials connected with the Watergate case were quizzed on two occasions to determine if they felt there were any leads they were not permitted to pursue. In all instances the answer was 'no.'" Earl J. Silbert, the lead prosecutor of the Watergate burglars, has also stated that "the FBI did a terrific job investigating the case," apart from the improper aspects of the relationship between acting director Gray and John Dean. L. Patrick Gray III with Ed Gray, *In Nixon's Web: A Year in the Crosshairs of Watergate* (New York: Times Books, 2008), 63; OPE Analysis, "FBI Watergate Investigation," 5 July 1974, 45–46, WG, FBI FOIA; Leon Friedman and William F. Levantrosser, eds., *Watergate and Afterward: The Legacy of Richard M. Nixon* (Westport, CT: Greenwood Press, 1992), 47.

The White House received several courtesies that would not normally have been extended to any other government entity or private organization. Most notably, White

House aides were allowed to pack up the contents of Hunt's office and safe, rather than having FBI agents come in and collect the materials. Sanford J. Ungar, "FBI Hindered at First," *WP*, 12 October 1972, A1.

6 Woodward, *Secret Man*, 104; Memo, Legal Counsel to Acting Director, "Confirmation: Disclosure of FD-302," 1 March 1973, LPG, FBI FOIA.

7 Bob Woodward Oral History, 14 December 2010, RMNL.

Edward Jay Epstein was the first to point out that the press, including the *Washington Post*, did not truly reveal the story of the initial break-in and subsequent cover-up. Rather, it reported the results from ongoing investigations being conducted by the FBI, federal prosecutors, and a grand jury in the summer/fall of 1972. Earl Silbert, the chief Watergate prosecutor; John Dean, in his memoirs; and Professor Stanley I. Kutler, in his Watergate history, have all concurred with Epstein's point. Edward Jay Epstein, "Did the Press Uncover Watergate?" *Commentary*, July 1974, 22; Earl Silbert Oral History, 17 September 2008, RMNL; John W. Dean, *Lost Honor* (Los Angeles: Stratford Press, 1982), 83–84; Stanley I. Kutler, *The Wars of Watergate: The Last Crisis of Richard Nixon* (New York: Alfred A. Knopf, 1990), 190; see also Memo, Long to Gebhardt, "James W. McCord Jr., et al.," 25 March 1975, WG, FBI FOIA.

According to Woodward, a few years after the burglars' trial Judge Sirica told him that he had read closely the stories in the *Post*, and the inability of the federal prosecutors to bring a case that squared up with what had been reported was a major source of his consternation. Woodward, *Secret Man*, 92–93; John W. Dean, "Why the Revelation of the Identity of Deep Throat Has Only Created Another Mystery," http://writ.news.findlaw.com/dean/20050603.html, 3 June 2005.

8 Leonard Garment, *Crazy Rhythm: My Journey from Brooklyn, Jazz, and Wall Street to Nixon's White House, Watergate, and Beyond* (New York: Times Books, 1997), 249.

Felt had been among a dozen top FBI officials who sent letters to Senator McGovern (D–South Dakota), denouncing him for suggesting that Hoover was getting senile and that a congressional investigation of the Bureau was long overdue. McGovern had received an anonymous letter from some FBI agents, who argued that the Bureau spent an inordinate amount of time polishing Hoover's image. Jack Nelson, "Hoover's Top 12 Men Denounce McGovern," *LAT*, 9 March 1971, 4. Theoharis, *FBI*, 125.

9 Woodward Oral History, 14 December 2010; http://bobwoodward.com/question-answer; author interview with Bob Woodward, 12 October 2011.

10 Christopher Hitchens, "The Insider," *NYT Book Review*, 24 July 2005, F8.

11 Limpert, "If It Isn't Tricia," 17.

CHAPTER 1. A FORCED DEPARTURE: MAY 1973

1 Bob Woodward, *The Secret Man* (New York: Simon & Schuster, 2005), 102–103, 107; AP, "FBI's No. 2 Man to Retire June 22," *WP*, 22 May 1973, A9; W. Mark Felt, *The FBI Pyramid: From the Inside* (New York: G. P. Putnam's Sons, 1979), 303–304.

2 Laurence Stern, "Bureau Hurt by Watergate," *WP*, 17 June 1973, A1.

Stern's article even quoted Felt (albeit anonymously) about the problems facing the FBI.

3 The reporter who broke the story of the confrontation leading to Felt's retirement was Ronald J. Ostrow writing in the *Los Angeles Times* in November 1974. Subsequently, a

more or less accurate rendition of Felt's forced resignation was published in Sanford J. Ungar's 1976 history of the FBI. See Ronald J. Ostrow, "FBI Investigating Its Former No. 2 Official," *LAT*, 17 November 1974, A1; Sanford J. Ungar, *FBI* (Boston: Little, Brown, 1976), 556–557. In June 2005, the *Washington Post* itself published an account based on Ungar's version; nonetheless Woodward reiterated the cover story about Felt's retirement in *The Secret Man*. See Michael Dobbs, "Watergate and the Two Lives of Mark Felt: Roles as FBI Official, 'Deep Throat' Clashed," *WP*, 20 June 2005, A1.

4 John M. Crewdson, "'69 Phone Taps Reported on Newsmen at 3 Papers," *NYT*, 11 May 1973, 18; (Sandy Smith) "Questions about Gray," *Time*, 5 March 1973 (published February 26), 14–15; Felt, *FBI Pyramid*, 143.

When the full details became known, it turned out that a total of seventeen persons were wiretapped during the two years: four reporters and thirteen government employees. Athan G. Theoharis, ed., with Tony Poveda, Susan Rosenfeld, and Richard Gid Powers, *The FBI: A Comprehensive Reference Guide* (Phoenix, AZ: Oryx Press, 1999), 76–77; U.S. Congress, Senate, Select Committee to Study Government Operations with Respect to Intelligence Activities, *Final Report*, 94th Cong., 2nd sess., vol. 3 (Washington, DC: Government Printing Office, 1976), 321–327.

5 FD-302, "Jack L. Conmy," 19 August 1974, WIDI, FBI FOIA; Robert H. Phelps, *God and the Editor: My Search for Meaning at the* New York Times (Syracuse, NY: Syracuse University Press, 2009), 191.

6 Author interviews with William D. Ruckelshaus, 12 June 2007 and 8 December 2010; William D. Ruckelshaus Oral History, 12 April 2007, RMNL, 7.

7 Ruckelshaus interviews, 12 June 2007 and 8 December 2010; Ruckelshaus Oral History, 12 April 2007, 7.

8 Memo, Jacobson to Callahan, "Watergate—Alleged Leak to *New York Times*," 20 June 1974, WMF, FBI FOIA; Ungar, *FBI*, 557.

Ironically, in a matter of a few weeks, Ruckelshaus would authorize leaking to Crewdson a briefcase-full of FBI documents about Donald Segretti. But this was a "good" leak insofar as the FBI was concerned (or at least standard operating procedure), i.e., it was officially sanctioned by the then-director to get the true story of Segretti's controversial activities publicly known, along with the thoroughness of the FBI's investigation into his activities. See *Leak*, chapter 11, 164–165.

9 FD-302, "William D. Ruckelshaus," 27 August 1974, WIDI, FBI FOIA; FD-302, "Jack L. Conmy," 19 August 1974, WIDI, FBI FOIA; Memo, Bassett to Callahan, "Watergate—Alleged Leak to *New York Times*," 5 September 1974, WIDI, FBI FOIA.

10 Ruckelshaus interview, 12 June 2007; FD-281a, "Receipt for Government Property: Key to the Director's Suite," 14 May 1973, WMF, FBI FOIA; FD-302s, "William D. Ruckelshaus," 18 July 1974 and 27 August 1974, WIDI, FBI FOIA.

11 Ruckelshaus interview, 12 June 2007; AP, "FBI's No. 2 Man to Retire June 22"A9; Jeremiah O'Leary, "Veteran Agent May Head FBI," *WS*, 27 May 1973, A1.

"It is my earnest hope that the standards of thoroughness, fairness, and impartiality that became the hallmark of the FBI during J. Edgar Hoover's forty-eight years as director will continue to be maintained, and the FBI will remain a career service staffed at all levels by law enforcement professionals," Felt wrote on May 16. Ruckelshaus responded on May 17, "Your contributions have certainly added luster to this organization's reputation, and I want to express my appreciation for the capable and diligent manner in which you have discharged your duties. You have established a record of which you can indeed be proud." Ungar, *FBI*, 557.

In a 2005 interview with the *Post*'s Michael Dobbs, Ruckelshaus described the resignation in this way: The evidence that Felt was leaking was "'certainly strong enough to convince me. I told [Felt] that I was very angry with him and suggested that he sleep on it overnight, and decide what he wanted to do.' Felt resigned from the FBI the next day." Dobbs, "Watergate and the Two Lives of Mark Felt," A1.

In a 2009 speech, Ruckelshaus reiterated the reason for Felt's resignation. "The [FBI] deputy director, Mark Felt, of 'Deep Throat' fame, who was actively lobbying for the job as director, subsequently resigned when confronted by me for leaking classified information to the *New York Times*—an unforgivable sin for an FBI agent." William Ruckelshaus, "Remembering Watergate," 3 October 2009, speech before the National Association of Former U.S. Attorneys, 7.

12 Author interview with John M. Crewdson, 5 June 2008.

13 Memo, "*New York Times* and *Washington Post* Articles Concerning Alleged Wiretaps on Newsmen," 26 February 1973, WCS, FBI FOIA; Felt, *FBI Pyramid*, 140.

   According to John Dean, who studied who knew, the information was known only to Richard Nixon, Henry Kissinger, John Ehrlichman, John Mitchell, Robert Mardian, William Sullivan, Mark Felt, and Alexander Haig. John W. Dean, *Lost Honor* (Los Angeles: Stratford Press, 1982), 347.

14 E-mail to author from John M. Crewdson, 20 June 2008; e-mail to author from John M. Crewdson, 25 June 2008; e-mail to author from Ed Gray, 11 May 2010; "William C. Sullivan, Ex-FBI, 65, Is Killed in Hunting Accident," *NYT*, 10 November 1977, 94; J. Y. Smith, "William C. Sullivan, Once High FBI Aide, Killed by Hunter," *WP*, 10 November 1977, C8; Paul V. Daly Oral History, 10 February 2005, SOCXFBI, 35.

15 Kutler wrote, "A special thank-you to the anonymous source who, in 1973 or 1974, referred to Watergate as the 'War of the FBI Succession.'" Stanley I. Kutler, *The Wars of Watergate: The Last Crisis of Richard Nixon* (New York: Alfred A. Knopf, 1990), xii.

16 Thomas E. Bishop Oral History, 3 February 2004, SOCXFBI, 151; Leonard M. "Bucky" Walters Oral History, 4 March 2003, SOCXFBI, 8.

17 Edward Jay Epstein, writing in July 1974, cited federal prosecutors as theorizing that Deep Throat leaked "to demonstrate to the president that Gray could not control the FBI. . . . In other words, [his] intention was to get rid of Gray." The theory was correct, although the real goal was not simply Gray's ouster but the elevation of Felt to the exclusion of anyone else. Edward Jay Epstein, "Did the Press Uncover Watergate?" *Commentary*, July 1974, 24.

18 John J. McDermott, "Concerning Watergate and the Role of W. Mark Felt," prepared after 1 June 2005, courtesy of the author.

19 Letter, John J. McDermott to Craig Detlo, 1 November 2006, courtesy of the author.

CHAPTER 2. THE "WAR OF THE FBI SUCCESSION": 1969–1972

1 In February 1973, just before the confirmation hearings for Pat Gray, John Dean offered a wishful perspective. He told the president, "While it might have been a lot of blue chips to the late director, I think we would have been a lot better off during this

whole Watergate thing if he'd been alive, because he knew how to handle that Bureau." But it would have been more in keeping with Hoover's past behavior for him to march into the Oval Office. Author transcript, tape recording, Nixon and Dean, Conversation no. 865-14, 28 February 1973, RMNL.

2 Moss transcript, tape recording, Nixon and Gray, Conversation 719-12, 4 May 1972, RMNL; John Ehrlichman, *Witness to Power: The Nixon Years* (New York: Simon & Schuster, 1982), 156–157; Irwin F. Gellman, *The Contender: Richard Nixon, The Congress Years, 1946–1952* (New York: Free Press, 1999), 236–243.

As a result of the Hiss case, Nixon told Pat Gray, Hoover "knew that he could trust me, [and] I knew I could trust him." Author transcript, tape recording, Nixon, Ehrlichman, and Gray, Conversation 858-3, 16 February 1973, RMNL.

3 Athan G. Theoharis, ed., with Tony Poveda, Susan Rosenfeld, and Richard Gid Powers, *The FBI: A Comprehensive Reference Guide* (Phoenix, AZ: Oryx Press, 1999), 153.

4 H. R. Haldeman, *The Haldeman Diaries: Inside the Nixon White House*, CD-ROM (Los Angeles: Sony Imagesoft, 1994), 8 September 1970; author transcript, tape recording, Nixon, Haldeman, and Ehrlichman, conversation no. 247-4, 13 April 1971, RMNL; Sanford J. Ungar, *FBI* (Boston: Atlantic Monthly Press, 1976), 255–256; H. R. Haldeman Oral History, 12 April 1988, RMNL, 175–176; U.S. Congress, Senate, Select Committee to Study Governmental Operations with Respect to Intelligence Activities (hereafter Church Committee), *Final Report*, 94th Cong., 2nd sess., vol. 3 (Washington, DC: Government Printing Office, 1976), 924.

5 Ungar, *FBI*, 472–473; Church Committee, *Final Report*, vol. 3, 924–982; Memo, Huston to Haldeman, "Domestic Intelligence," 5 August 1970, LPG, FBI FOIA.

The Huston plan threatened to encroach on the FBI's turf and prerogatives from Hoover's vantage point. And in point of fact, the White House was completely unaware of the extent of the FBI's vigorous counterintelligence programs (COINTELPROS), designed to disrupt, confuse, and ultimately vitiate domestic groups deemed subversive. Ultimately the FBI acknowledged six COINTELPRO targets: the U.S. Communist Party (1956–1971); Puerto Ricans seeking independence (1960–1971); the Socialist Workers Party (1961–1971); white hate groups, including the KKK (1964–1971); black militant groups, such as the Black Panthers (1967–1971); and the so-called New Left (1968–1971). All COINTELPROS were terminated in April 1971 following a break-in at the FBI resident office in Media, Pennsylvania. Church Committee, *Final Report*, vol. 3, 3–77; Theoharis, *FBI*, 125–127; Ungar, *FBI*, 477–478; Paul V. Daly Oral History, 10 February 2005, SOCXFBI, 11.

6 Theoharis, *FBI*, 125–127; Haldeman, *Diaries* CD-ROM, 4 February 1971.

7 Lou Harris, "Poll Splits Evenly on Hoover Quitting," *WP*, 6 May 1971, A22; Bruce Oudes, ed., *From: The President: Richard Nixon's Secret Files* (New York: Harper & Row, 1989), 255–256; Ungar, *FBI*, 494.

8 I. F. Stone, *In a Time of Torment* (New York: Random House, 1967), 330; Haldeman, *Diaries* CD-ROM, 20 September 1971.

At one time or another, Mitchell, Haldeman, Ehrlichman, and Buchanan all expressed the thought that Hoover's time had passed. Buchanan put it most colorfully in February 1971, when he wrote that Hoover ought to retire while his reputation was still largely unsullied. Otherwise he would "wind up his career a dead lion—chewed up by the jackals of the Left." Oudes, ed., *From: The President*, 217–218, 323; Haldeman Oral History, 12 April 1988, RMNL, 177.

9 Ehrlichman, *Witness to Power*, 168; Haldeman, *Diaries* CD-ROM, 1 November 1971; Moss transcript, tape recording, Nixon and Gray, Conversation 719-12, 4 May 1972, RMNL; Oudes, ed., *From: The President*, 345; Haldeman Oral History, 12 April 1988, RMNL, 176.

10 Graham J. Desvernine Oral History, 4 October 2006, SOCXFBI, 39.

11 WSPF transcript, tape recording, Nixon and Colson, Conversation 394-21, 8 January 1973, RMNL; author transcript, tape recording, Nixon, Ehrlichman, and Gray, Conversation 858-3, 15 February 1973, RMNL; tape recording, President Nixon and John Dean, 28 February 1973, Conversation 865-14, RMNL; Ungar, *FBI*, 291.

According to Felt, the South Vietnamese embassy in Washington was put under electronic surveillance, but not any Republican politicians. Richard G. High, "GOP Campaign Bug Claim Denied by Ex-FBI Aide," *Twin Falls (ID) Times News*, 9 May 1974, 1. On the so-called Chennault affair in general, see James Rosen, *The Strong Man: John Mitchell and the Secrets of Watergate* (New York: Doubleday, 2008), 52–54, 59–62.

12 Cartha D. "Deke" DeLoach, *Hoover's FBI: The Inside Story by Hoover's Trusted Lieutenant* (Washington, DC: Regnery, 1995), 416; Robert J. Donovan, "FBI Change Indicates Hoover Plans to Stay," *LAT*, 6 June 1970, A1; author interview with Donald E. Santarelli, 2 June 2011.

13 Edward S. Miller Oral History, 28 May 2008, SOCXFBI, 111.

14 Sullivan oversaw the laboratory, domestic intelligence, and investigative divisions, while Mohr was head of the identification, training, administrative, files and communication, and crime records divisions. Ungar, *FBI*, 296, 305.

15 Letter, Sullivan to Hoover, "Personal," 5 April 1971, WCS, FBI FOIA; Richard Connolly, "Hoover Erratic in Last Years, Former Aide Says," *BG*, 17 May 1973, A1; Theoharis, *FBI*, 355–356.

16 Theoharis, *FBI*, 354; Ken W. Clawson, "Top FBI Official Forced Out in Policy Feud with Hoover," *WP*, 2 October 1971, A1; W. Mark Felt, *The FBI Pyramid: From the Inside* (New York: G. P. Putnam's Sons, 1979), 142; Miller Oral History, 23 May 2008, 91.

The Sullivan firing almost precipitated the dismissal of Hoover, but again, Nixon could not bring himself to do it. Rowland Evans and Robert Novak, "Deterioration of the FBI," *WP*, 11 October 1971, A19; L. Patrick Gray III with Ed Gray, *In Nixon's Web: A Year in the Crosshairs of Watergate* (New York: Times Books, 2008), 9, 11; Robert M. Smith, "Nixon Names Aide as Chief of FBI until Elections," *NYT*, 4 May 1972, 1; Ray Wannall, *The Real J. Edgar Hoover: For the Record* (Paducah, KY: Turner Publishing, 2000), 121, 143.

17 William C. Sullivan with Bill Brown, *The Bureau: My Thirty Years in Hoover's FBI* (New York: W. W. Norton, 1979), 248.

18 Author interview with John J. McDermott, 11 November 2010; Mark Memmott, "'Deep Throat' Wasn't Only Watergate Source," *USA Today*, 9 June 2005, A5; Robert M. Smith, "FBI Man's Promotion Raises Question for Hoover Successor," *NYT*, 21 August 1971, 8.

19 Santarelli interview, 2 June 2011.

20 Miller Oral History, 28 May 2008, 109; Associated Press, "Tapes Show a Besieged Nixon Saw Enemies All Over," http://www.usatoday.com/news/washington/2008-12-03-nixon-disclosures_N.htm, 3 December 2008.

21 Ungar, *FBI*, 273.

22 DeLoach, *Hoover's FBI*, 415–416.

23 Felt, *FBI Pyramid*, 208.

24 Haldeman handwritten Notes, Folder 1, SMOF, April–15 May 1972, Box 45, WHSF, RMNL.

25 Ungar, *FBI*, 278–279; Handwritten Notes, Haldeman Notes, Folder 1 April–15 May 1972, Box 45, White House Special Files, RMNL; typed summary, "Meeting with Ackerman and Martin," 8 January 1975, Calls and Meetings with President [Nixon], 1971–1973, Folder 1, Box 65, Charles W. Colson Papers.

26 (Sandy Smith), "The Fight over the Future of the FBI," *Time*, 26 March 1973 (published March 19), 19; Haldeman, *Diaries* CD-ROM, 2 May 1972; Haldeman handwritten Notes, Folder 1, SMOF, WHSF, April–15 May 1972, Box 45, RMNL; Gray, *In Nixon's Web*, 10.

27 Author interview with Richard D. Rogge, 28 May 2008; Paul P. Magallanes Oral History, 25 August 2005, SOCXFBI, 4; John W. Dean, *Blind Ambition: The End of the Story* (Palm Springs, CA: Polimedia Publishers, 2009), 584–585; Joan Hoff, *Nixon Reconsidered* (New York: Basic Books, 1994), 321; W. Mark Felt and John O'Connor, *A G-Man's Life: The FBI, Being "Deep Throat," and the Struggle for Honor in Washington* (New York: PublicAffairs, 2006), 288, 291.

A former agent recalled, "We would probably not have pissed on [Felt] if he was on fire." One of Felt's most controversial inspection tours occurred in September 1970, when he was responsible for the summary removal of the San Francisco SAC, Harry Morgan, for participating in a satirical skit sponsored by the local press club. Author interview with Robert P. Campbell, 28 November 2011; Dick Alexander, "An FBI 'Reign of Terror' with 'Deep Throat' to Blame," http://www.scrippsnews.com/node/35902, 1 September 2008.

28 Sanford J. Ungar, "Kleindienst Aide Calls Media Biased," *WP*, 29 April 1972, A3; Ungar, *FBI*, 507.

29 Ungar, *FBI*, 498–506; Gray, *In Nixon's Web*, 10; Editorial, "Politics and the FBI," *NYT*, 6 May 1972, 34; typed summary, "Meeting with Ackerman and Martin," 8 January 1975, Calls and Meetings with President [Nixon], 1971–1973, Folder 1, Box 65, Charles W. Colson Papers.

A Naval Academy graduate and submarine commander during World War II and the Korean War, Gray had first met Nixon at a cocktail party in the late 1940s. He immediately hit it off with the young California congressman who had exposed Alger Hiss. The two men stayed in touch, and Gray abandoned a promising naval career to join Nixon's personal staff for the 1960 campaign. Afterwards, he joined a law firm in Connecticut, having studied law while in the navy. Although Gray did not play as active a role in the 1968 campaign, he was nonetheless awarded some plum posts in the administration, including a stint at the Justice Department as head of the civil division. On the day he was appointed acting director, Gray was actually awaiting Senate confirmation of his nomination to be deputy attorney general.

30 U.S. Congress, Senate, Committee on the Judiciary, *Hearings, Louis Patrick Gray III*, 93rd Cong., 1st sess. (Washington, DC: Government Printing Office, 1973), 136; Ungar, *FBI*, 507; Felt, *FBI Pyramid*, 165–174.

31 Santarelli interview, 2 June 2011.

32 Smith, "Nixon Names Aide," 1; Ungar, *FBI*, 276, 497.

According to columnist Novak, Nixon "fully intended to make [Gray's interim appointment] permanent." Rowland Evans and Robert Novak, "J. Edgar Hoover's Legacy: A Political Snakepit at the FBI," *WP*, 10 January 1973, A23.

33 Homer A. Boynton Oral History, 2 March 2006, SOCXFBI, 8.

34 Ungar, *FBI*, 278; Leonard M. "Bucky" Walters Oral History, 4 March 2003, SOCXFBI, 6.

35 Laurence Stern, "Helms Becomes Latest Victim of Watergate," *WP*, 16 May 1973, A10; Felt, *FBI Pyramid*, 294.

CHAPTER 3. FELT'S PRIVATE COINTELPRO: JUNE 1972

1 Sanford J. Ungar, *FBI* (Boston: Atlantic Monthly Press, 1976), 514.

2 Ungar, *FBI*, 496; W. Mark Felt, *The FBI Pyramid: From the Inside* (New York: G. P. Putnam's Sons, 1979), 190; author transcript, tape recording, Nixon and Gray, conversation 719-2," 4 May 1972, RMNL; Robert M. Smith, "Gray Discusses Agency," *NYT*, 5 May 1972, 1; Richard G. High, "GOP Campaign Bug Claim Denied by Ex-FBI Aide," *Twin Falls (ID) Times News*, 9 May 1974, 1.

3 FD-302, "Mrs. Marge Neenan," 9 December 1974, LPG, FBI FOIA; Ungar, *FBI*, 513; Robert M. Smith, "Gray Plans Wide Change in FBI Policy and Style," *NYT*, 12 May 1972, 1.

4 Clark R. Mollenhoff, a syndicated columnist for the Cowles newspaper chain, was the most persistent about pointing out Gray's conflict of interest. Clark R. Mollenhoff, *Game Plan for Disaster: An Ombudsman's Report on the Nixon Years* (New York: W. W. Norton, 1976), 267.

5 Indeed, on June 21, during John Dean's very first meeting with Gray after the break-in, the White House counsel stressed the need to avoid leaks. L. Patrick Gray III with Ed Gray, *In Nixon's Web: A Year in the Crosshairs of Watergate* (New York: Times Books, 2008), 63.

6 Ungar, *FBI*, 284–285; Thomas E. Bishop Oral History, 3 February 2004, SOCXFBI, 105; John Limpert, "If It Isn't Tricia It Must Be . . . ," *Washingtonian*, June 1974, 17.

Leaking information to "certifiably reliable" reporters and columnists was a central component in all the FBI's COINTELPRO and also used as part of its orchestrated effort to discredit Martin Luther King, Jr. Athan J. Theoharis, "Deep Throat: Was What He Did Unprecedented?" http://hnn.us/node/12299, 6 June 2005.

Pat Gray, during his brief tenure, even learned which journalists were close to which FBI officials: Sandy Smith was favored by Mark Felt and Charlie Bates, while Robert Novak got much of his information from William Sullivan. Gray, *In Nixon's Web*, 125.

7 Felt, *FBI Pyramid*, 101, 132, 146.

Evans and Novak were among the first to expose the genuine strains in the Nixon administration's relations with Hoover. That set their columns apart from the slew of articles about the impending end of Hoover's tenure. The administration's "expression of total confidence in Hoover is mainly eyewash," wrote Evans and Novak in June 1971. "The truth is that both President Nixon and [Attorney General John] Mitchell are deeply concerned by the prospect of Hoover, now 76, as permanent lifelong director." An October column was even harsher, calling the "deterioration of the FBI" one of Washington's most carefully hidden scandals. In Novak's 2007 memoir, he described Sullivan as "the best source I ever had inside the FBI" and confirmed that Sullivan was the source for the remarkable columns critical of Hoover. Rowland Evans and Robert Novak, "Boss of FBI Knows Who's Boss," *WP*, 2 June 1971, A19; Rowland Evans and Robert Novak, "Deterioration of the FBI," *WP*, 11 October 1971, A19; Robert D. Novak, *The Prince of Darkness: 50 Years Reporting in Washington* (New York: Crown Forum, 2007), 208–210.

8 Bob Woodward Oral History, 14 December 2008, RMNL.

9 Leonard Downie, Jr., *The New Muckrakers: An Inside Look at America's Investigative Reporters* (Washington, DC: New Republic Books, 1976), 2; Felt, *FBI Pyramid*, 215–217; James McCartney, "The *Washington Post* and Watergate: How Two Davids Slew Goliath," *Columbia Journalism Review*, July/August 1973, 10.

In *The Secret Man*, Woodward wrote that his May 18 article on the Wallace shooting was a "front page story," but it actually appeared on page A17 of the final edition. He did coauthor, with Jim Mann, a front-page story on Bremer's travels the day before. In any case, before the Wallace shooting, most of Woodward's stories appeared in the newspaper's "B" or "C" sections, although he did happen to have a front-page story in the *Post* on the day of the break-in. Bob Woodward, *The Secret Man: The Story of Watergate's Deep Throat* (New York: Simon & Schuster, 2005), 49–50; Bob Woodward and Jim Mann, "Suspect Followed Wallace for Weeks," *WP*, 17 May 1972, A1; Bob Woodward, "Bremer's Car Called Motel on Wheels," *WP*, 18 May 1972, A17; Bob Woodward, "U.S. Official Pushed Sale of Insurance," *WP*, 17 June 1972, A1.

Nixon wanted to depict Bremer as a pro-McGovern radical, even though he was generally apolitical and basically a nihilist. The president discussed with Charles Colson the possibility of planting left-wing tracts in Bremer's apartment, and Colson was in frequent contact with Mark Felt the night of the attempted assassination. The Associated Press, interestingly, distributed a story that evening (citing a source close to the investigation) that alleged scraps of paper in Bremer's apartment "showed he allied himself with 'left-wing causes.'" Bob Woodward and Carl Bernstein, "Hunt Says Colson Ordered Break-in at Bremer Home," *WP*, 21 June 1973, A1; George Lardner, Jr., "25 Years after Break-in, Nixon's Words Endure," *WP*, 17 June 1997, A1; Luke A. Nichter, "Caught on Tape: The White House Reaction to the Shooting of Alabama Governor and Democratic Presidential Candidate George Wallace," http://hnn.us/articles/45104.html, 3 December 2007; James W. Clarke, *American Assassins: The Darker Side of Politics* (Princeton, NJ: Princeton University Press, 1982), 182–188; E. Howard Hunt with Greg Aunapu, *American Spy: My Secret History in the CIA, Watergate, and Beyond* (Hoboken, NJ: John Wiley & Sons, 2007), 207; Charles Colson Oral History, 17 August 2007, RMNL, 42–43; Jonathan Aitken, *Charles W. Colson: A Life Redeemed* (New York: Doubleday, 2005), 173–174.

10 Woodward, *Secret Man*, 50; Memo, Felt to Hoover, 19 November 1971, WMF, FBI FOIA.

11 H. R. Haldeman, *The Haldeman Diaries: Inside the Nixon White House* (New York: G. P. Putnam's Sons, 1994), 471; Karlyn Barker and Walter Pincus, "Watergate Revisited: 20 Years after the Break-in, the Story Continues to Unfold," *WP*, 14 June 1992, A1.

Besides McCord, who had retired from the Agency in 1970, the other four burglars (three of whom were Cuban Americans) had been CIA contacts in the Miami area, and one of them, Eugenio Rolando Martinez, was still on a $100-a-month retainer as an informant, identifying Cuban refugees who might be of interest to the Agency.

All four had also participated in the CIA-supported attempted invasion of Cuba in 1961. Richard Helms with William Hood, *A Look over My Shoulder: A Life in the Central Intelligence Agency* (New York: Random House, 2003), 6; Robert M. Hathaway and Russell Jack Smith, *Richard Helms as Director of Central Intelligence, 1966–1973* (Washington, DC: CIA Center for the Study of Intelligence, 1993), 188; U.S. Congress, House of Representatives, Special Subcommittee on Intelligence of the Committee on Armed Services, *Report, Inquiry into the Alleged Involvement of the Central Intelligence Agency in the Watergate and Ellsberg Matters,* 93rd Cong., 1st sess. (Washington, DC: Government Printing Office, 1973), 12; U.S. Congress, Senate, Committee on Foreign Relations, *Hearings, Nomination of Richard Helms to Be Ambassador to Iran and CIA International and Domestic Activities,* 93rd Cong., 1st sess., 1974 (Washington, DC: Government Printing Office, 1974), 24.

12 Helms and Hood, *Look over My Shoulder,* 12.

13 Author interview with Angelo J. Lano, 4 November 2010; Bob Woodward and E. J. Bachinski, "White House Consultant Tied to Bugging Figure," *WP,* 20 June 1972, A1; Woodward Oral History, 14 December 2010, RMNL.

14 Gray handwritten notes, "TCF R[ichard] G[.] K[leindienst]," 19 June 1972, LPG, FBI FOIA.

15 Carl Bernstein and Bob Woodward, *All the President's Men* (New York: Simon & Schuster, 1974), 23; Woodward, *Secret Man,* 57–58; Woodward and Bachinski, "White House Consultant Tied to Bugging Figure," A1.

16 "[Howard] Simons interview," circa 1973, 8, Series I, 8.2, WBWP, HRC; Memo, Bates to Bolz, "James W. McCord Jr., et al.," 22 June 1972, WG, FBI FOIA; Woodward and Bachinski, "White House Consultant Tied to Bugging Figure," A1; WSPF, transcript, tape recording, Nixon and Colson, conversation no. 342-27, 20 June 1972, RMNL; Bob Woodward and Scott Armstrong, "White House Tapes Contradict [Nixon's] Previous Claim," *WP,* 1 May 1977, A1; John W. Dean, *Blind Ambition: The End of the Story* (Palm Springs, CA: Polimedia Publishers, 2009), 139–141; Aitken, *Charles W. Colson,* 167–170.

Henry Petersen, head of the Justice Department's Criminal Division, was erroneously told that Felt's very first leak to Woodward probably came from a police sergeant in on the raid. Memo, Bates to Felt, "James W. McCord Jr., et al.," 20 June 1972, WG, FBI FOIA; Dean, *Blind Ambition,* 105, 108, 125; John Ehrlichman, *Witness to Power: The Nixon Years* (New York: Simon & Schuster, 1982), 348.

17 Ehrlichman, *Witness to Power,* 347–348; Dean, *Blind Ambition,* 108.

Felt could not have been motivated by the White House's attempt to cover up any involvement. It was not until the morning of June 20—the day that Woodward's Hunt story appeared—that the president first discussed the need to keep "a lid on" the FBI's investigation, lest an unfettered investigation reveal a host of questionable activities. What would eventually become known as the infamous, 18½-minute gap on the secret Nixon tapes occurred during one of the June 20 meetings. Stanley I. Kutler, *Abuse of Power: The New Nixon Tapes* (New York: Free Press, 1997), 47.

18 Dean, *Blind Ambition,* 141–142.

19 W. Mark Felt and John O'Connor, *A G-Man's Life: The FBI, Being "Deep Throat," and the Struggle for Honor in Washington* (New York: PublicAffairs, 2006), 198.

20 Curtis Prendergast with Geoffrey Colvin, *The World of Time Inc.: The Intimate History of a Changing Enterprise 1960–1980* (New York: Atheneum, 1986), 353; "Covering the

Mob," *Time*, 20 April 1959 (published April 13), 53–54; "A Letter from the Publisher," *Time*, 12 July 1971, 2; Russell Working, "Investigative Reporter Exposed Workings of the Mob," *CT*, 12 December 2005, 2:6; Jason Felch and Marlena Telvick, "Unsung Hero," http://www.ajr.org/article.asp?id=369929, June/July 2004; Ungar, *FBI*, 285; author interview with Frank McCulloch, 12 September 2011.

The other members of McCulloch's dream team were William G. Lambert, Russell Sackett, and Denny Walsh, all prize-winning investigative journalists who, like Smith, had developed excellent sources in the FBI and Justice Department. Lambert, who had won a Pulitzer Prize for exposing labor racketeering in the Northwest, also was guaranteed special handling of his files (and his expense accounts) to mask his sources. Sackett, notably, would go on to score an important Watergate scoop about E. Howard Hunt while working for *Newsday* in 1973. Prendergast, *World of Time Inc.*, 52; Downie, *New Muckrakers*, 241–242; Russell Sackett and Martin Schram, "A Watergate, ITT Link," *Newsday*, 8 February 1973, 3.

21 Prendergast, *World of Time Inc.*, 353; author interview with John L. Wilhelm, 24 June 2011; Downie, *New Muckrakers*, 242.

22 Roger Cohen, "Killed Book Is Haunting Time Warner," *NYT*, 16 April 1990, D1; Graham J. Desvernine Oral History, 8–9 March 2007, SOCXFBI, 11–12.

Indeed, one criticism of Smith that would eventually be leveled was that he was *too* close to the FBI—he would later be identified as one of the reporters who regularly received COINTELPRO leaks. But while "he was close to the FBI, he was not a patsy," maintained Seymour Hersh, an up-and-coming investigative reporter in the 1970s who regarded Smith as his mentor. Chip Berlet, "FBI COINTELPRO Media Operations: The Corporate Press," http://www.publiceye.org/liberty/Feds/media/fbi-media-corporate .html, 2008; Working, "Investigative Reporter," 2:6.

Eventually, almost every member of *Time*'s nineteen-man Washington bureau would be involved in covering the first year of Watergate, including correspondents David Beckwith, Stanley Cloud, Simmons Fentress, Dean Fischer, Hays Gorey, and Neil MacNeil, while newly-arrived Washington news editor John Stacks coordinated the various assignments. But as the bureau's acknowledged "investigative expert," Sandy Smith always maintained the leading role in reporting on Watergate and the federal law enforcement agencies. "A Letter from the Publisher," *Time*, 6 August 1973 (published July 30), 2.

23 Memo, Bates to Bolz, "James W. McCord Jr., et al.," 22 June 1972, WG, FBI FOIA; Gray, *In Nixon's Web*, 68, 72–73.

Gray was originally apprised in the morning of the "24 to 48 hour" rumor by John Dean. Coincidentally, Gray and Mitchell had both been staying at the same hotel in Newport Beach, California, the day after the arrests.

24 Memo, Bates to Bolz, 22 June 1972, "James W. McCord Jr., et al.," WG, FBI FOIA.

25 Moss transcript of conversation no. 719-12, prepared by Rick Moss, 4 May 1972, RMNL; Gray handwritten notes, "TCT Sandy Smith," 23 June 1972, LPG, FBI FOIA.

26 Paul P. Magallanes Oral History, 25 August 2005, SOCXFBI, 13–14.

27 Lano interview, 4 November 2010; John W. Mindermann Oral History, 7 March 2007, SOCXFBI, 13–17; Magallanes Oral History, 25 August 2005, 12–14.

28 Lano interview, 4 November 2010; Mindermann Oral History, 7 March 2007, 16; Magallanes Oral History, 25 August 2005, 14.

29 Mindermann Oral History, 7 March 2007, 17.

The Inspection Division interviewed twenty-nine WFO employees; seven General Investigative Division employees; six Laboratory Division employees; and three Identification Division employees, all with "negative results." OPE Analysis, "FBI Watergate Investigation," 5 July 1974, 47, WG, FBI FOIA.

30 Gray, *In Nixon's Web*, 75–76; Memo, Bates to Bolz, "James W. McCord Jr., et al.," 22 June 1972, WG, FBI FOIA; Memo, Gallagher to Gebhardt, "James W. McCord Jr., et al.," 27 December 1972, WG, FBI FOIA; Memo, "Watergate—Events at Initial Stage of Case," 7 June 1973, WG, FBI FOIA; (Sandy Smith), "The Bugs at the Watergate," *Time*, 3 July 1972 (published June 26), 10–11. Like many magazines, *Time* purposely dated its issues a week late, so a story that appeared in the July 3 issue actually hit newsstands on June 26.

Many years later, Hays Gorey, *Time's* chief congressional correspondent, would observe, "Sandy Smith and I . . . worked together for a long period covering Watergate, and there was never a story Sandy dug up that did not hold up." That was almost true, especially if one did not count the stories he reported that did not make it into the magazine. Cohen, "Killed Book Is Haunting Time Warner," D1.

Although not in *Time*, Smith's initial allegations, interestingly enough, appeared almost verbatim in the *National Observer*, an influential weekly newspaper owned by Dow Jones & Company, publisher of the *Wall Street Journal*. See Nina Totenberg, "Politics and the FBI Chief," *National Observer*, 8 July 1972, 14. When queried, Totenberg did not recall any sources for the information in her article. E-mail to author from Nina Totenberg, 6 October 2011.

31 Prendergast, *World of Time Inc.*, 353.

32 (Smith), "Bugs at the Watergate," 10–11; Felt, *FBI Pyramid*, 248; Felt and O'Connor, *A G-Man's Life*, 198.

Gray would later come to suspect Bates—a "Hoover sycophant," according to Robert Novak—as being "one of the falsehood peddlers," and with some justification. Bates wrote a clever memo describing his own contact with Sandy Smith on Saturday, June 24. Bates said Smith claimed his source was "probably a member of [Democratic Party chairman] Larry O'Brien's staff." Yet O'Brien had personally told Gray that he believed the FBI investigation was being conducted with complete professionalism. Gray, *In Nixon's Web*, 74, 76; Rowland Evans and Robert Novak, "Deterioration of the FBI," *WP*, A19; Memo, Bates to Bolz, "James W. McCord Jr., et al.," 22 June 1972, WG, FBI FOIA.

33 U.S. Congress, Senate, Committee on the Judiciary, *Hearings, Louis Patrick Gray III*, 93rd Cong., 1st sess. (Washington, DC: Government Printing Office, 1973), 357.

34 At this stage, the president was not yet certain the most damaging leaks were coming from the FBI; he thought a staffer in the administration, specifically, someone in Colson's office, might be responsible. Actually, Nixon wasn't that far off. A secretary who worked for one of Colson's assistants, and knew Hunt slightly, did provide information to Bernstein for a later story. WSPF, transcript, conversation no. 342-27, 20 June 1972, RMNL; Woodward and Armstrong, "White House Tapes Contradict [Nixon's] Previous Claim," A1; Bernstein and Woodward, *All the President's Men*, 30–31.

35 Ehrlichman, *Witness to Power*, 352; SCPCA, *Hearings, Watergate and Related Activities*, 93rd Cong., 1st sess., vol. 9 (Washington, DC: Government Printing Office, 1973), 3467.

36 SCPCA, *Hearings, Watergate and Related Activities*, vol. 3, 948–949; vol. 9, 3467; H.

R. Haldeman, *The Haldeman Diaries: Inside the Nixon White House* CD-ROM (Los Angeles: Sony Imagesoft, 1994), 26 March 1973.

One folder contained two cables fabricated by Hunt (in place of the ones allegedly missing) that directly implicated President Kennedy in the 1963 assassination of South Vietnamese President Ngo Dinh Diem; the other folder allegedly was a dossier on Massachusetts Senator Edward M. Kennedy's escapades. Both projects had been overseen by Charles Colson. SCPCA, *Final Report*, 93rd Cong., 2nd sess. (Washington, DC: Government Printing Office, 1974), 125–127; Laurence Stern, "Suspect Cable Tied US to Diem Death," *WP*, 28 April 1973, A14; Woodward, *Secret Man*, 96; Dean, *Blind Ambition*, 133–134; Hunt, *American Spy*, 192–193. Dean retained in his possession two Hermes spiral-bound notebooks (which contained Hunt's sensitive operational notations), an address book, and, according to Hunt, documents pertaining to the CRP's intelligence-gathering operation. Dean would use his office shredder to destroy these Watergate-related items in late January. SCPCA, *Final Report*, 36; Dean, *Blind Ambition*, 219; Hunt, *American Spy*, 261.

37 Dean, *Blind Ambition*, 142.

38 Gray, *In Nixon's Web*, 82; Ehrlichman, *Witness to Power*, 352; SCPCA, *Hearings, Watergate and Related Activities*, vol. 3, 948–949; vol. 6, 2614; vol. 9, 3467.

39 Gray, *In Nixon's Web*, 82; Homer A. Boynton Oral History, 2 March 2006, SOCXFBI, 6–7.

40 Gray, *In Nixon's Web*, 82; Dean, *Blind Ambition*, 122.

41 In his memoir, Felt mistakenly stated the scoop first appeared in the *Washington Post*. The *Post* did a story, of course, but it was based wholly upon the statement of a Justice Department spokesman *responding* to the scoop in the *Washington Daily News*. Felt, *FBI Pyramid*, 259; Bob Woodward and Jim Mann, "Jury Probes Lawyer in 'Bug' Case," *WP*, 1 July 1972, A1.

42 Memo, Ponder to Felt, "*Washington Daily News* Story . . . June 30, 1972," 30 June 1972, WG, FBI FOIA; Letterhead Memo, "Article Appearing in 6/30/72 City Edition of the *Washington Daily News*," 30 June 1972, WG, FBI FOIA; author interview with Patrick Collins, 9 September 2009.

The FBI did not actually open Hunt's safe; instead, John Dean arranged to hand over what he alleged were its total contents on June 26. See OPE Analysis, "FBI Watergate Investigation," 5 July 1974, 21, WG, FBI FOIA; Patrick Collins, "Gun, Bug, Map of Democratic HQ Found in Desk of White House Aide," *WDN*, 30 June 1972, 1, 3.

43 Gray handwritten notes, "TCF W[.] M[ark] F[elt]," 30 June 1972, WG, FBI FOIA.

After interviewing 45 agents privy to the information, the Inspection Staff reported that all the agents denied being acquainted with Collins or anyone else at the *Daily News*, and "they had no knowledge of how the information could have come into the possession of the newspaper." Memo, Ponder to Felt, "*Washington Daily News* Story . . . June 30, 1972," 30 June 1972, WG, FBI FOIA.

44 Gray handwritten notes, "TCF J[ohn] W[.] D[ean]," 30 June 1972, WG, FBI FOIA; SCPCA, *Hearings, Watergate and Related Activities*, vol. 9, 3456; Kutler, *Abuse of Power*, 78; U.S. Congress, House of Representatives, Special Subcommittee on Intelligence of the Committee on Armed Services, *Hearings, Inquiry into the Alleged Involvement of the Central Intelligence Agency in the Watergate and Ellsberg Matters*, 94th Cong., 1st sess. (Washington, DC: Government Printing Office, 1975), 221.

45 John H. Kauffmann, a prominent member of the three families that jointly owned the *Star*, supported Nixon financially. While Collins continued on the Watergate beat

when he joined the *Star* from the defunct *Daily News*, he never had another scoop akin to his June 30 story, with one exception. His *Star* story on August 31 was first to place both E. Howard Hunt and G. Gordon Liddy in the vicinity of the break-in on June 17 (scooping the *Post* by one day), at a time when the White House was trying to suggest that the criminal behavior went no higher than Hunt and Liddy. Overall, however, the *Star*'s coverage of Watergate was almost grudging, or worse. It published one story that transparently propagated the administration line, i.e., that "right-wing Cubans" financed and conducted the Watergate break-in because they feared the leading Democratic candidates were pro-Castro. And the *Star* frequently did not bother to write stories that followed up the *Post*'s scoops, or if it did, the stories featured the White House's nondenial denials. Sally Quinn, "Like a Dance at the Club," *WP*, 27 September 1972, B3; Collins interview, 9 September 2009; "Democrats Bugged 'For a Long Time,'" *WS*, 7 July 1972, A1; Joseph Volz and Patrick Collins, "Liddy, Hunt Reported Near Site of Break-in," *WS*, 31 August 1972, A1; Bob Woodward and Carl Bernstein, "Liddy and Hunt Reportedly Fled during Bugging Raid," *WP*, 1 September 1972, A1; Bernstein and Woodward, *All the President's Men*, 79, 91.

46 Robert Smith had taken a shine to Gray, writing three front-page stories, all highly favorable, about the new acting director and his plans for the FBI. See, for example, Smith, "Gray Plans Wide Change in FBI Policy and Style." Given this coverage, Smith was unlikely to play leaked stories the way Felt intended them to appear; he might even disclose the source of the leaks to Gray. Robert H. Phelps, *God and the Editor: My Search for Meaning at the* New York Times (Syracuse, NY: Syracuse University Press, 2009), 176; Gray, *In Nixon's Web*, 42.

Reporters at the *Los Angeles Times* (Robert L. Jackson, Jack Nelson, Ronald J. Ostrow), *Newsweek* (Nicholas Horrock), and *Newsday* (Anthony Marro, Russell Sackett, Martin J. Schram) would also break significant stories during the first six months of the scandal.

47 During May, his first month as director, Gray was in his office 13 days out of 20 weekdays; in June, 15 out of 22; in July, 12 out of 21; in August, 12 out of 23; in September, 9 out of 21; and in October, 9 out of 22. He almost never worked on Saturdays. Felt, *FBI, Pyramid*, 221; calendar, May 1972–February 1973, LPG, FBI FOIA; Leonard M. "Bucky" Walters Oral History, SOCXFBI, 6, 7.

48 Gray, *In Nixon's Web*, 65; Paul V. Daly Oral History, 10 February 2005, SOCXFBI, 28.

49 Author interview with Angelo J. Lano, 1 November 2010; Collins interview, 9 September 2009.

Collins would not divulge much about the leak except to confirm that it did not come from Felt directly. He did, however, vaguely recall seeing the FBI's "302" on the safe's contents.

50 According to Woodward, Felt "never explained" how he managed to keep an eye on the balcony or circle page 20. Woodward Oral History, 14 December 2010; see also Bernstein and Woodward, *All the President's Men*, 72; Woodward, *Secret Man*, 65–67; FD-302, "David D. Kinley," 22 November 1974, LPG, FBI FOIA.

51 One of those aides, Wason G. Campbell, retired from the Bureau in 1974 as an assistant director. He was suffering from Alzheimer's when Felt came forward, and died in 2007. He died in March 2007. His wife, Mary, when contacted in 2005, said that whenever the subject of Deep Throat came up her husband never indicated he knew Felt was the leaker. "I am sure that Wason never knew it," she said. "He's not that good

an actor. Mark was able to keep this a secret from his assistant." David Corn and Jeff Goldberg, "How Mark Felt Fooled the FBI," *The Nation*, 4 July 2005, 19–23.

52 It seems significant that Long only took up his new job at FBI headquarters in January 1973. That meant he had no first-hand knowledge of what transpired the previous summer and fall, when most of the Watergate leaks occurred. The bottom line, however, is that of the nine top FBI officials most involved in the Watergate investigation (Gray, Felt, Bates, Gebhardt, Bolz, Long, Kunkel, McDermott, Nuzum, and Lano), at least five participated in or knew about the leaks (Felt, Bates, Bolz, Long, and Kunkel). Yet when interviewed for the CBS News twentieth anniversary program on Watergate, Bates said, "I don't believe Deep Throat was an FBI official or an FBI agent." Memo, Gebhardt to Felt, "James W. McCord Jr., et al.," 20 February 1973, WG, FBI FOIA; CBS News, transcript, "Watergate: The Secret Story," 17 June 1992, 9; Brendan Lyons, "Deep Throat's Tale Revealed," *ATU*, 5 June 2005, A1; Brendan Lyons, "Account Adds Intrigue to Deep Throat Story," *ATU*, 7 June 2005, A1; Murray Waas, "FBI Cleared W. Mark Felt of Watergate Leaks," *Village Voice*, http://www.villagevoice.com/2005-06-07/news/fbi-cleared-w-mark-felt-of-watergate-leaks/, 7 June 2005; Rex Smith, "When Big News Is Met with Shrugs," *ATU*, 11 June 2005, A7; Dan Eggen, "At FBI, Reflections on Felt and Loyalty," *WP*, 2 June 2005, A21; Daly Oral History, 10 February 2005, 28–29; "FBI Promotes Dallas Agent," *Dallas Morning News*, 19 January 1973, 12.

　　In 1978, Daly was helping to retrieve FBI documents about surreptitious entries at the homes of friends and relatives of Weather Underground members, and Richard Long headed a special FBI task force formed to assist the Justice Department's prosecution of Mark Felt, among others. In the course of working together, the two men discussed problems that might arise should Felt take the witness stand in his own defense. Long then disclosed to Daly that Felt was Deep Throat, and that others in the FBI had been simultaneously and consciously involved. Memo, Director to Attorney General, "Safeguarding of National Security Information and Material," 9 May 1978, LPG, FBI FOIA; and Memo, Skolnik to McDermott, "United States v. Gray, et al.," 19 December 1978, LPG, FBI FOIA.

53 Lyons, "Deep Throat's Tale Revealed," A1.

　　When Paul V. Daly was re-interviewed by the author, he retreated somewhat from the account published in the *Times Union*. In 2011, he said that Richard E. Long was part of a team that briefed Felt, and thus became aware that Felt was leaking like a sieve to the *Washington Post*. But Long was not conniving in the scheme, nor was Kunkel likely to have been a party to leaking, according to Daly. Brendan Lyons, the *Times Union* reporter who broke the story, nonetheless stands by his original 2005 account, and Daly made no attempt to request a correction or clarification then despite ample opportunity. Author interview with Paul V. Daly, 25 May 2011; author interview with Harry M. Rosenfeld, 31 May 2011; author interview with Brendan Lyons, 31 May 2011; e-mail to author from Brendan Lyons, 2 June 2011.

54 Bates died in February 1999 at the age of seventy-nine in Redwood City, California; Kunkel died in March 1991 at the age of sixty-six in Fairfax, Virginia. "Charles W. Bates—Led Patty Hearst Probe," *San Francisco Chronicle*, 26 February 1999, A25; "Robert G. Kunkel, FBI and Bank Official," *WP*, 3 April 1999, D4.

55 Rudolph Unger, "Marlin Johnson Will Leave FBI on June 15," *CT*, 24 April 1970, A15; "New FBI Chief Here Tells of His Aims," *CT*, 20 October 1971, D6.

56 Daly oral history, 10 February 2005, 28–29.

1 John W. Mindermann Oral History, 7 March 2007, SOCXFBI, 13.

2 Leonard Garment, among others, has argued that the effort to implicate the CIA, as revealed in the so-called "smoking gun" tape from June 23, was perhaps not as legally damning, harmful, or different from other evidence already released. Yet Garment also notes, correctly, that by that time the White House was so demoralized and the president himself so enfeebled that even Nixon's "oldest and staunchest political comrades were now saying, 'Enough.'" Leonard Garment, *Crazy Rhythm: My Journey from Brooklyn, Jazz, and Wall Street to Nixon's White House, Watergate, and Beyond* (New York: Times Books, 1997), 281, 294–295.

3 L. Patrick Gray with Ed Gray, *In Nixon's Web: A Year in the Crosshairs of Watergate* (New York: Times Books, 2008), 80; Richard Helms with William Hood, *A Look over My Shoulder: A Life in the Central Intelligence Agency* (New York: Random House, 2003), 7; Laurence Stern, "FBI Leaks Feared by Helms," *WP*, 8 November 1973, A10; William Chapman, "Break-in Probe and FBI, CIA," WP, 12 July 1974, A16.

   Helms was particularly exercised by five stories written by *New York Times* reporter Tad Szulc in late June 1972. His consistent theme was that the parties culpable for the break-in were the same people responsible for the Agency's Bay of Pigs operation in 1961, that is, CIA officers and anti-Castro Cubans. See Tad Szulc, "Democratic Raid Tied to Realtor," *NYT*, 19 June 1972, 1; Tad Szulc, "Ex-GOP Aide Linked to Political Raid," *NYT*, 20 June 1972, 1; Tad Szulc, "Ex-GOP Aide Rebuffs FBI Queries on Break-in," *NYT*, 21 June 1972, 1; Tad Szulc, "Cuban Veterans Group Linked to Raid on Democratic Offices," 23 June 1972, 1; Tad Szulc, "From the Folks Who Brought You the Bay of Pigs," *NYT*, 25 June 1972, E2.

4 OPE Analysis, "FBI Watergate Investigation," 5 July 1974, 25, 57–58, WG, FBI FOIA; Memo, Bolz to Bates, "James W. McCord Jr., et al.," 26 June 1972, WG, FBI FOIA; U.S. Congress, House of Representatives, Committee on the Judiciary, *Report, Impeachment of Richard M. Nixon, President of the United States*, 93rd Cong., 2nd sess. (Washington, DC: Government Printing Office, 1974), 48; U.S. Congress, House of Representatives, Special Subcommittee on Intelligence of the Committee on Armed Services, *Report, Inquiry into the Alleged Involvement of the Central Intelligence Agency in the Watergate and Ellsberg Matters*, 93rd Cong., 1st sess. (Washington, DC: Government Printing Office, 1973), 16; Stanley I. Kutler, *Abuse of Power: The New Nixon Tapes* (New York: Free Press, 1997), 67–69; Helms, *Look over My Shoulder*, 9–10; E. Howard Hunt with Greg Aunapu, *American Spy: My Secret History in the CIA, Watergate, and Beyond* (Hoboken, NJ: John Wiley & Sons, 2007), 202, 228.

   Nixon's grudge against the CIA went back to the 1960 election, when he believed the Agency took a position on the so-called "missile gap" that favored the Democrats. Robert M. Hathaway and Russell Jack Smith, *Richard Helms as Director of Central Intelligence, 1966–1973* (Washington, DC: CIA Center for the Study of Intelligence, 1993), 209.

5 Author interview with John W. Dean, 18 May 2011; Kutler, *Abuse of Power*, 67.

6 Helms, *Look over My Shoulder*, 10–11; Special Subcommittee on Intelligence, *Report, Inquiry into the Alleged Involvement of the Central Intelligence Agency*, 4; Kutler, *Abuse of Power*, 67.

7 U.S. Congress, House of Representatives, Special Subcommittee on Intelligence of

the Committee on Armed Services, *Hearings, Inquiry into the Alleged Involvement of the Central Intelligence Agency in the Watergate and Ellsberg Matters*, 94th Cong., 1st sess. (Washington, DC: Government Printing Office, 1975), 205; Helms, *Look over My Shoulder*, 9; Gray, *In Nixon's Web*, 66.

During their first conversation on June 17, Helms even tried to give Gray a lead: "You might want to look in the relationship of John Ehrlichman . . . with McCord and Hunt," the CIA director suggested. Helms knew Ehrlichman had asked the CIA to provide some assistance on "security matters" to Hunt in July 1971, when he joined the White House as a consultant after publication of the Pentagon Papers. Helms, *Look over My Shoulder*, 5; Hathaway and Smith, *Richard Helms*, 188.

8 Hunt had been supplied with alias identification gear, disguises, and some technical materials (a tape recorder and clandestine camera) soon after joining the White House staff as a consultant in mid-1971. The assistance was abruptly cut off in late August after the Agency became concerned about the propriety of Hunt's requests. Special Subcommittee on Intelligence, *Report, Inquiry into the Alleged Involvement of the Central Intelligence Agency*, 3, 8.

9 Special Subcommittee on Intelligence, *Hearings, Inquiry into the Alleged Involvement of the Central Intelligence Agency*, 107–108. Walters wrote that Haldeman indicated "it was the president's wish" that the CIA's deputy director go see Gray. During his House testimony in May 1973, however, Walters said the phrase was not actually uttered by Haldeman; only that the thought was implicit. Ibid., 109.

10 Helms, *Look over My Shoulder*, 10; Hathaway and Smith, *Richard Helms*, 191; Special Subcommittee on Intelligence, *Report, Inquiry into the Alleged Involvement of the Central Intelligence Agency*, 15–17.

In Nixon's earlier talk with Haldeman, the president may have been referring obliquely to persistent rumors that the CIA had been involved in attempts to assassinate Fidel Castro. This activity was among the Agency's darkest secrets at the time, and Nixon's somewhat clumsy allusion may have been intended as a signal to Helms. See Max Holland, *The Kennedy Assassination Tapes: The White House Conversations of Lyndon B. Johnson Regarding the Assassination, the Warren Commission, and the Aftermath* (New York: Alfred A. Knopf, 2004), 389–410; Terry F. Lenzner Oral History, 5 December 2008, RMNL.

11 The early effort by the White House to involve the CIA would have lasting consequences. The Agency, secretive and recalcitrant to begin with, became downright uncooperative in response to legitimate queries from the federal prosecutors trying the case. Leon Friedman and William F. Levantrosser, eds., *Watergate and Afterward: The Legacy of Richard M. Nixon* (Westport, CT: Greenwood Press, 1992), 49.

12 Kutler, *Abuse of Power*, 70; Hathaway and Smith, *Richard Helms*, 190–191.

13 Hathaway and Smith, *Richard Helms*, 191; Vernon A. Walters, *Silent Missions* (Garden City, NY: Doubleday, 1978), 588.

14 Special Subcommittee on Intelligence, *Hearings, Inquiry into the Alleged Involvement of the Central Intelligence Agency*, 108–109; Helms, *Look over My Shoulder*, 9, 12; Special Subcommittee on Intelligence, *Report, Inquiry into the Alleged Involvement of the CIA*, 15–16; Mindermann Oral History, 11.

15 Kutler, *Abuse of Power*, 71; Hathaway and Smith, *Richard Helms*, 192.

16 Helms, *Look over My Shoulder*, 13.

17 Special Subcommittee on Intelligence, *Hearings, Inquiry into the Alleged Involvement of the Central Intelligence Agency*, 97–98.

18 Ibid., 46, 97–98.

19 Ronald Kessler, "Experts Heap Scorn on Bungled 'Bug' Caper," *WP*, 19 June 1972, A7; Special Subcommittee on Intelligence, *Hearings, Inquiry into the Alleged Involvement of the Central Intelligence Agency*, 110–111.

20 Special Subcommittee on Intelligence, *Hearings, Inquiry into the Alleged Involvement of the Central Intelligence Agency*, 206–208, 210, 217.

21 Gray handwritten notes, "Friday: 12:52 PM from Meter," 30 June 1972, WG, FBI FOIA.

  Petersen insisted to Gray that the Justice Department had to have in writing all claims regarding the involvement of CIA equities. Transcript, "Conference between Special Prosecutor Archibald Cox, Assistant James Vorenberg, and Assistant Attorney General Henry Petersen," 29 May 1973, Box 81, WSPF, NARA, 5.

22 Special Subcommittee on Intelligence, Hearings, *Inquiry into the Alleged Involvement of the Central Intelligence Agency*, 218, 220; Gray, *In Nixon's Web*, 77.

23 Helms, *Look over My Shoulder*, 9; Gray, *In Nixon's Web*, 80; Special Subcommittee on Intelligence, *Hearings, Inquiry into the Alleged Involvement of the Central Intelligence Agency*, 219–220; U.S. House of Representatives, Committee on the Judiciary, Report, *Impeachment of Richard M. Nixon President of the United States*, 93rd Cong., 2nd sess. (Washington, DC: Government Printing Office, 1974), 50.

24 Teletype, SAC, WFO to Acting Director, "James W. McCord Jr., et al.," 29 June 1972, provided to author by Angelo J. Lano; e-mail to author from Angelo Lano, 31 August 2010; Gray handwritten notes, "TCF W[.] M[ark] F[elt]," 30 June 1972, WG, FBI FOIA; author interview of Angelo J. Lano, 18 March 2011; Special Subcommittee on Intelligence, *Hearings, Inquiry into the Alleged Involvement of the Central Intelligence Agency*, 221.

  According to Lano's teletype, delays were also encountered in interviewing former Attorney General John Mitchell; White House aide David Young; and Kathleen Chenow, Young's former secretary. These aspects did not involve CIA equities. Teletype, SAC, WFO to Acting Director, "James W. McCord Jr., et al.," 29 June 1972, provided to author by Angelo J. Lano.

25 E-mail to author from Angelo J. Lano, 31 August 2010.

26 Commission on CIA Activities within the United States, *Report to the President* (Washington, DC: Government Printing Office, 1975), 199–203.

27 Special Subcommittee on Intelligence, *Hearings, Inquiry into the Alleged Involvement of the Central Intelligence Agency*, 111–112.

28 Ibid.; Gray, *In Nixon's Web*, 87–89.

29 Kutler, *Abuse of Power*, 78; SCPCA, *Hearings, Watergate and Related Activities*, 93rd Cong., 1st sess., vol. 9 (Washington, DC: Government Printing Office, 1973), 3457; H. R. Haldeman, *The Haldeman Diaries: Inside the Nixon White House* CD-ROM (Los Angeles: Sony Imagesoft, 1994), 6 July 1972.

30 SCPCA, *Hearings, Watergate and Related Activities*, vol. 9, 3462; Clark R. Mollenhoff, *Game Plan for Disaster: An Ombudsman's Report on the Nixon Years* (New York: W. W. Norton, 1976), 267; Gray, *In Nixon's Web*, 90.

31 Gray, *In Nixon's Web*, 65, 76, 80, 84, 87.

It should be noted that the Watergate special prosecutor's indictments against Haldeman, Mitchell, and Ehrlichman did not include the charge that they attempted to obstruct justice by misrepresenting to the FBI the CIA's interests in the Watergate case. The special prosecutor decided that it might not be able to prove the charge beyond a reasonable doubt in court, owing to the "aroma" of CIA involvement initially. In addition, there was a problem of spillover: if a jury was left unconvinced about this matter, it might seriously damage other aspects of the prosecution's case. Thus, charges stemming from the effort to invoke the delimitation agreement were never brought against any potential defendants. Nonetheless, this obstruction became an enormous political issue—the veritable straw that broke Nixon's back—because of the way the president mishandled Watergate, as John Dean points out. See Memo, Rient to BenVeniste, "White House Interference with FBI Watergate Investigation," 16 January 1974, Investigative Memoranda, January 1974, Box 1, Watergate Task Force, WSPF, RG 460, NARA; e-mail to author from John Dean, 18 May 2011.

32 "Listing of Contacts with the Central Intelligence Agency in Connection with the Investigation of the Watergate Incident," undated, WG, FBI FOIA; Gray, *In Nixon's Web*, 84; Bob Woodward Oral History, 14 December 2010, RMNL; see OPE Analysis, "FBI Watergate Investigation, 5 July 1974, 41–46, WG, FBI FOIA; Laurence Stern, "CIA Spurned Nixon Aides on Cover-up," *WP*, 15 May 1973, A1; Carl Bernstein and Bob Woodward, *All the President's Men* (New York: Simon & Schuster, 1974), 318; James McCartney, "The *Washington Post* and Watergate: How Two Davids Slew Goliath," *Columbia Journalism Review*, July/August 1973, 22.

When asked if he ever queried Felt about the "smoking gun" tape, Woodward answered, "Not really, no." Woodward Oral History, 14 December 2010.

Felt's account of this episode in his memoir is typically tendentious and self-serving. He wrote that by July 5, the obstruction to the FBI investigation had gotten to such a point that he, Kunkel, and Bates requested an urgent meeting with Gray to discuss the matter. "'Look,' I [Felt] told Gray, 'the reputation of the FBI is at stake. As acting director, this is even more important to you than to us. In the future, you are going to have to convince skeptical U.S. Senators that we did a good job on this case. We can't delay . . . any longer!'" Facing an alleged "near mutiny," Gray promptly bowed to the executives' "ultimatum." W. Mark Felt, *The FBI Pyramid: From the Inside* (New York: G. P. Putnam's Sons, 1979), 255.

33 W. Joseph Campbell, *Getting It Wrong: Ten of the Greatest Misreported Stories in American Journalism* (Berkeley, CA: University of California Press, 2010), 123; Sussman cited in Alicia C. Shepard, *Woodward and Bernstein: Life in the Shadow of Watergate* (Hoboken, NJ: John Wiley & Sons, 2007), 55.

34 Kutler, *Abuse of Power*, 103.

35 Garment, *Crazy Rhythm*, 295; author interview with Daniel M. Armstrong, 18 June 2008.

36 Dean raised the matter of access to FBI information with Richard Kleindienst, Henry Petersen, Robert Mardian, and John Ehrlichman before raising it with Gray himself. It was an indicator of how much had changed since Hoover's demise, since none of these opinions would have mattered then. On August 29, the president publicly declared during a news conference that Dean was "conducting an investigation," thus affirming Gray's understanding of the counsel's role. John W. Dean, *Blind Ambition: The End of the Story* (Palm Springs, CA: Polimedia Publishers, 2009), 113, 143, 151; Gray, *In Nixon's Web*, 82–83.

Gray's general willingness to do the White House's bidding was also in evidence in August, when, at Ehrlichman's request, he provided the White House with the Bureau's file on Henry Kimelman, the finance chair of the McGovern campaign. In 1969, the Justice Department had opened an investigation into some Interior Department rulings involving the Virgin Islands, where Kimelman was a major landowner. But nothing untoward had been found. Telephone conversation, Ehrlichman and Gray, 10 August 1972, dictabelt #457, Box 28, Ehrlichman, SMOF, WHSF, RMNL; Spencer Rich, "U.S. Probing Udall Ruling for Airport," *WP*, 19 September 1969, A1; Bob Woodward and Carl Bernstein, "White House Had Agencies Spy on Political Rivals," *WP*, 10 August 1973, A1.

37 Tad Szulc, "Expensive Line-up of Legal Talent Enters Case of Raid on Democratic Office," *NYT*, 10 July 1972, 14; Robert H. Phelps, *God and the Editor: My Search for Meaning at the* New York Times (Syracuse, NY: Syracuse University Press, 2009), 166–169; Szulc, "Democratic Raid Tied to Realtor," 1; Szulc, "Ex-GOP Aide Linked to Political Raid," 1; Szulc, "Ex-GOP Aide Rebuffs FBI Queries on Break-in," 1; Szulc, "Cuban Veterans Group Linked to Raid on Democratic Offices," 1; Szulc, "From the Folks Who Brought You the Bay of Pigs," *NYT*, E2. In mid-August, syndicated columnist James J. Kilpatrick would also help advance the explanation that the break-in was the brainstorm of Cuban exiles. James J. Kilpatrick, "The Watergate Caper: Does the Key Lie in Havana?" *LAT*, 20 August 1972, H7.

38 Phelps, *God and the Editor*, 169; Barry Sussman, *The Great Cover-up: Nixon and the Scandal of Watergate* (Arlington, VA: Seven Locks Press, 1992), 71–72; "[Howard] Simons interview," circa 1973, 3, Series I, 8.2, WBWP, HRC; McCartney, "The *Washington Post* and Watergate," 12–13.

In Alicia Shepard's book, she pegs the formal pairing of Woodward and Bernstein to articles by Walter Rugaber that appeared in the *Times* on 25 and 27 July 1972. However, in Barry Sussman's book he is quite specific that managing editor Howard Simons called him into his office on July 10 to express frustration over the lack of progress on the Watergate story. Shepard, *Woodward and Bernstein*, 35; Sussman, *Great Cover-up*, 71–72.

39 J. Anthony Lukas, *Nightmare: The Underside of the Nixon Years* (New York: Viking Press, 1976), 297.

40 Leonard Downie, Jr., *The New Muckrakers: An Inside Look at America's Investigative Reporters* (Washington, DC: New Republic Books, 1976), 3, 28; Shepard, *Woodward and Bernstein*, 10, 36.

41 Downie, *New Muckrakers*, 5, 32; Shepard, *Woodward and Bernstein*, 37.

Bernstein had asked Bishop off the record—"strictly off the record"—if the FBI was investigating Washington as a candidate for the mayoral position, which at the time was an appointed office. Bishop replied, "Off the record—yes." The next day a front-page story appeared in the *Post* that revealed the FBI was completing a special investigation of Washington. Bishop called up Bernstein and said he was going to cut off the reporter in the future. "You can't cut off the press on your whim!" Bernstein protested. "It's not on a whim," Bishop said. "You broke your oath." Thomas E. Bishop Oral History, 3 February 2004, SOCXFBI, 108; "Walter Washington Seen as Top Choice for D.C. 'Mayor,'" *WP*, 24 August 1967, A1.

42 Downie, *New Muckrakers*, 38; Shepard, *Woodward and Bernstein*, 16; 31, 35, 38, 40.

43 Downie, *New Muckrakers*, 5; Shepard, *Woodward and Bernstein*, 29.

1 Carl Bernstein and Bob Woodward, "Bug Suspect Got Campaign Funds," *WP*, 1 August 1972, A1; James McCartney, "The *Washington Post* and Watergate: How Two Davids Slew Goliath," *Columbia Journalism Review*, July/August 1973, 13–14; Robert H. Phelps, *God and the Editor: My Search for Meaning at the* New York Times (Syracuse, NY: Syracuse University Press, 2009), 172; Bob Woodward, *The Secret Man: The Story of Watergate's Deep Throat* (New York: Simon & Schuster, 2005), 58; James M. Perry, "Watergate Case Study," in Tom Rosenstiel and Amy S. Mitchell, *Thinking Clearly: Cases in Journalistic Decision-Making* (New York: Columbia University Press, 2003), 153; Bob Woodward Oral History, 14 December 2010, RMNL.

The White House also noticed the *Post* story. It was a topic of conversation between the president and his chief of staff that morning, and they expressed the belief that the leak came from somewhere in the Justice Department—the same source of the leak that plagued them three to four weeks ago, Haldeman said, in what was probably a reference to the *Washington Daily News* scoop. He assured the president that the earlier leak had been plugged and that this new story was from another Justice Department source. "We got people in there that are *against* us," said Haldeman. "They're *trying* to keep it all bottled up. They've done, I must say—considering the explosive nature of what's there—they've done a pretty good job." Author transcript, tape recording, Nixon and Haldeman, conversation no. 758-11, 1 August 1972, RMNL.

2 Carl Bernstein and Bob Woodward, *All the President's Men* (New York: Simon & Schuster, 1974), 72–73; Woodward, *Secret Man*, 61.

Although Woodward's by-line was carried on several Watergate-related stories in late June, July, and early August, he never directly linked Felt with any of them in either *All the President's Men* or *The Secret Man*, save for the June 20 story about Hunt's involvement.

3 Memo, "Watergate—Events at Initial Stage of Case," 7 June 1973, WG, FBI FOIA; John W. Mindermann Oral History, 7 March 2007, SOCXFBI, 23; Memo, Bolz to Bates, "James W. McCord Jr., et al.," 21 July 1972, WG, FBI FOIA.

4 Rowland Evans and Robert Novak, "Key to Success of New Political Aide Is Total Access to President Nixon," *WP*, 15 May 1969, A19; Robert B. Semple, "Nixon's Inner Circle Meets," *NYT Magazine*, 3 August 1969; Leonard Garment, *In Search of Deep Throat: The Greatest Political Mystery of Our Time* (New York: Basic Books, 2000), 41, 58–59.

5 Garment, *In Search of Deep Throat*, 60; Carl Bernstein, "Employer of 2 Tied to Bugging Raised Money for Nixon," *WP*, 22 June 1972, A9.

While Sears was nowhere mentioned in the article, he was the original source of the information according to an early draft of *All the President's Men*. Draft manuscript, "All the President's Men," undated, 33–35, Watergate Collection, HRC.

6 Bernstein and Woodward, *All the President's Men*, 27–28.

7 John W. Dean, *Blind Ambition: The End of the Story* (Palm Springs, CA: Polimedia Publishers, 2009), 154; Ronald J. Ostrow and Robert L. Jackson, "Probe Ties GOP Funds to Attempt at Bugging," *LAT*, 4 August 1972, A5; Joseph Volz and Patrick Collins, "Liddy, Hunt Reported Near Site of Break-in," *WS*, 31 August 1972, A1.

8 Woodward, *Secret Man*, 61; author interview with Bob Woodward, 12 October 2011.

9 Bernstein and Woodward, *All the President's Men*, 72–73.

10 Woodward, *Secret Man*, 65–66.

11 Curt Gentry, *J. Edgar Hoover: The Man and the Secrets* (New York: W. W. Norton, 1991), 624–626; Michael Dobbs, "Watergate and the Two Lives of Mark Felt," *WP*, 20 June 2005, A1.

12 Stanley I. Kutler, *Abuse of Power: The New Nixon Tapes* (New York: Free Press, 1997), 109–111.

13 Author transcript, conversation no. 758-11, 1 August 1972, RMNL.

14 Phelps, *God and the Editor*, 186; Perry, "Watergate Case Study," 156.

15 Letter, Felt to Gray, "Dear Boss," 20 September 1972, WMF, FBI FOIA.

16 Woodward, *Secret Man*, 9–11.

17 David Corn and Jeff Goldberg, "How Mark Felt Fooled the FBI," *The Nation,* 4 July 2005, 19–23.

   One such wild goose chase occurred on September 11. That day Felt ordered agents in Miami to interview every FBI man who had been in contact with Richard Gerstein, the Dade County prosecutor and a Democrat, on the grounds that Gerstein was the original source of information that had appeared in the *Post*. But Woodward and Bernstein were clearly in direct contact with Gerstein's office, so there was little reason to believe FBI agents in Miami were culpable. In any case, such a probe was hardly going to lead back to Felt or even FBI headquarters. Memo, Felt to Bates, "James W. McCord Jr., et al.," 11 September 1972, WG, FBI FOIA.

18 W. Mark Felt, *The FBI Pyramid: From the Inside* (New York: G. P. Putnam's Sons, 1979), 249.

19 Phelps, *God and the Editor*, 182; H. R. Haldeman, *The Haldeman Diaries: Inside the Nixon White House* CD-ROM (Los Angeles: Sony Imagesoft, 1994), 11 July 1972.

20 Dean, *Blind Ambition*, 148; Louis Harris, "Bugging, Fund Charges Leave Public Apathetic," *WP*, 19 October 1972, A29.

21 Memo, Mohr to Tolson, "William C. Sullivan," 29 November 1971, WCS, FOIA FBI; typed summary, "Meeting with Ackerman and Martin," 8 January 1975, Calls and Meetings with President [Nixon], Folder 1, Box 65, Charles W. Colson Papers; Jack Nelson, "Ex-FBI Man Hits 'Fossil' Bureaucracy," *LAT*, 10 January 1972, A9.

22 Ronald J. Ostrow, "Man Forced by Hoover to Retire May Get Post," *LAT*, 12 July 1972, A5.

23 Sanford J. Ungar, *FBI* (Boston: Atlantic Monthly Press, 1976), 312.

24 Ray Wannall, *The Real J. Edgar Hoover: For the Record* (Paducah, KY: Turner Publishing Company, 2000), 111; Ungar, *FBI*, 312–313; Felt, *FBI Pyramid*, 147–148.

25 Gray handwritten notes, "Bill Sullivan," 6 July 1972, LPG, FBI FOIA.

26 Transcript, Felt Testimony, 23 October 1980, LPG, FBI FOIA.

27 Leon Friedman and William F. Levantrosser, eds., *Watergate and Afterward: The Legacy of Richard M. Nixon* (Westport, CT: Greenwood Press, 1992), 88.

28 Apart from the wiretaps, Kissinger also lobbied the president to do something about the hemorrhage of state secrets contained in the Pentagon Papers, even though it dealt with policymaking prior to the Nixon administration. Long after Watergate had played out, *Washington Post* managing editor Howard Simons observed that he harbored the "delicious thought" from time to time that "a temper tantrum by Henry Kissinger resulted in Watergate. That it, indeed, started a chain of events that led to the resignation of Mr. Nixon." Friedman and Levantrosser, *Watergate and Afterward*, 184.

29 Kutler, *Abuse of Power,* 468, 471.

Nixon, as Garry Wills was the first to observe, saw the undoing of Ellsberg as a reprise of his earlier undoing of Alger Hiss. The president also considered the wiretaps "totally justifiable . . . because they involve[d] national security." Author transcript, tape recording, Nixon, Haldeman, and Ehrlichman, conversation no. 247-4, 13 April 1971, RMNL; Garry Wills, "The Hiss Connection through Nixon's Life," *NYT Magazine,* 25 August 1974, 8; U.S. Congress, House of Representatives, Special Subcommittee on Intelligence of the Committee on Armed Services, Report, *Inquiry into the Alleged Involvement of the Central Intelligence Agency in the Watergate and Ellsberg Matters,* 93rd Cong., 1st sess. (Washington, DC: Government Printing Office, 1973), 8.

30 James Rosen, *The Strong Man: John Mitchell and the Secrets of Watergate* (New York: Doubleday, 2008), 311; H. R. Haldeman Oral History, 13 April 1988, RMNL, 100–101; Kutler, *Abuse of Power,* 72–73; Earl Silbert Oral History, 17 September 2008, RMNL; Egil "Bud" Krogh, with Matthew Krogh, *Integrity: Good People, Bad Choices, and Life Lessons from the White House* (New York: PublicAffairs, 2007), 121–123.

31 Before leaving the Bureau, Sullivan had transferred the special files to Assistant Attorney General Robert C. Mardian; Sullivan claimed he did so to prevent Hoover from using them to blackmail the White House. Memo, Miller to Rosen, "Sensitive Coverage Placed at Request of the White House," 20 October 1971, WCS, FBI FOIA; Memo, Felt to Tolson, "William C. Sullivan, Sensitive Files," 2 November 1971, WCS, FBI FOIA; FD-302, "Edward S. Miller," 12 May 1973, WCS, FBI FOIA; Felt, *FBI Pyramid,* 140, 155–157; Bernstein and Woodward, *All the President's Men,* 270; Paul V. Daly Oral History, 10 February 2005, SOCXFBI, 24; Wannall, *J. Edgar Hoover,* 114.

If nominated, of course, Felt might be questioned about these same issues. But the difference between him and Sullivan was that the latter had directly participated in the 1969–1971 wiretaps, and Felt's knowledge was after the fact.

32 In December 1972, Bernstein and Woodward would break a significant story about the plumbers, identifying, for the first time, all four of them (David Young, Egil Krogh, Gordon Liddy, and Howard Hunt). But the story was based entirely on an interview with the plumbers' former secretary, Kathleen Chenow, whose name was obtained from a legal document. Carl Bernstein and Bob Woodward, "Bug Case Figures Used Covert Executive Phone," *WP,* 8 December 1972, A1; Bernstein and Woodward, *All the President's Men,* 214–218.

Felt finally confirmed the accuracy of Smith's account to Woodward in early March 1973 when asked about it. But earlier, in January, he refused to say much about the SIU: he "would not be towed [by Woodward] on a fishing expedition about the plumbers." Bernstein and Woodward, *All the President's Men,* 243, 270.

33 General Investigative Division, "Summary," 25 July 1972, WG, FBI FOIA; Judith Bender and Anthony Marro, "Nixon Committee Aide Fired; Balked at FBI Bugging Inquiry," *Newsday,* 22 July 1972, 3; Robert F. Keeler, Newsday: *A Candid History of the Respectable Tabloid* (New York: Arbor House, 1990), 507.

34 Curtis Prendergast with Geoffrey Colvin, *The World of Time Inc.: The Intimate History of a Changing Enterprise, 1960–1980* (New York: Atheneum, 1986), 351. (Sandy Smith), "Watergate, Contd.," *Time,* 14 August 1972 (published August 7), 21–22; (Sandy Smith), "The Watergate Issue," *Time,* 28 August 1972 (published August 21), 20.

Although Smith's article was the first to use the term "plumbers," a *New York Times* article published months before the Watergate break-in was actually the first to reveal an organized White House effort, following disclosure of the Pentagon Papers, to investigate and prevent leaks to reporters. The *Times* article reported the effort was headed up by Egil Krogh from Ehrlichman's staff and David Young from the National Security Council, although it was "not known specifically what Mr. Krogh and Mr. Young have done in the five months since the security assignment was added to their duties." Krogh and Young, of course, were two of the four White House plumbers, the other two being Liddy and Hunt. Robert M. Smith, "White House Took Steps to Stop Leaks Months before Anderson Disclosures," *NYT*, 9 January 1972, 18.

35 Bernstein and Woodward, *All the President's Men*, 207.

During the summer, the White House responded with a "no comment" when asked if the plumbers existed. Then, in December, after the election, and after Bernstein and Woodward had written an article disclosing that Young, Krogh, Liddy, and Hunt had comprised the unit, press secretary Ron Ziegler acknowledged the plumbers' existence and role. Yet he continued to deny the involvement of Liddy and Hunt in the SIU or that it had any connection with Watergate. Bernstein and Woodward, *All the President's Men*, 207; Carl Bernstein and Bob Woodward, "Bug Case Figures Used Covert Executive Phone," *WP*, 8 December 1972, A1; "Nixon Had 2 Aides Fight News Leaks," *NYT*, 13 December 1972, 19; Wannall, *J. Edgar Hoover*, 133.

36 E-mail to author from John Stacks, 17 May 2011; "No Denial," *NYT*, 19 October 1972, 46; Bernstein and Woodward, *All the President's Men*, 159; Prendergast, *World of Time*, 352–353.

37 Barry Sussman, *The Great Cover-up: Nixon and the Scandal of Watergate* (Arlington, VA: Seven Locks Press, 1992), 125.

Woodward, when asked if he ever wondered whether Felt was also Sandy Smith's source, replied that he did have his suspicions. "Anything was possible," he said. Decades earlier, Woodward had admiringly told David Halberstam that Sandy Smith "really has a lock on the FBI." Woodward interview, 12 October 2011; Woodward cited in Alicia C. Shepard, *Woodward and Bernstein: Life in the Shadow of Watergate* (Hoboken, NJ: John Wiley & Sons, 2007), 58.

38 In line with Sussman's observation, *All the President's Men* contained numerous references to *Time*'s Watergate-related articles:

- "*Time*'s [October 23] story was better than the *Post*'s [October 15 article] in some respects. Though it was based on anonymous government sources . . . it had several additional details."
- "Woodward, his Sunday shot to hell by *Time* magazine—not for the first or last time, he was sure. . . ."
- "Although *Time* had developed information as damaging as the *Washington Post*'s, [only] the paper had been selected as [White House press secretary Ron Ziegler's] target."
- "Woodward and Bernstein were aware that *Time*'s access to FBI files was unquestioned."

In the first example, a Felt-sourced story appeared first in the *Post*, immediately followed by an even better account in *Time*, which had also been sourced by Felt. Ironically, the *Post* then ran *another* story citing the *Time* article as corroboration. Bernstein and Woodward, *All the President's Men*, 159, 161; Carl Bernstein and Bob

Woodward, "Key Nixon Aide Named as 'Sabotage' Contact," *WP*, 15 October 1972, A1; (Sandy Smith), "More Fumes from the Watergate Affair," *Time*, 23 October 1972 (published October 16), 23; Woodward and Bernstein, "Lawyer for Nixon Said to Have Used GOP's Spy Fund," *WP*, 16 October 1972, A1.

CHAPTER 6. RETRACING THE BUREAU'S STEPS: AUGUST–OCTOBER 1972

1 Barry Sussman, "Watergate, 25 Years Later: Myths and Collusion," http://watergate.info/sussman/25th.shtml, June 1997.

In his article on the twentieth anniversary of the break-in, Sussman also took issue with the importance of Deep Throat as a source, saying that "an anonymous bit player, a minor contributor, has become a giant." He "barely figured" in the *Post*'s coverage, although he "was nice to have around." Sussman was correct in that Felt was only one source among dozens. But others involved in the coverage, such as former *Post* reporter James Mann, recall that Woodward contemporaneously regarded Felt as a "special, and unusually well-placed, source." James Mann, "Deep Throat: An Institutional Analysis," *Atlantic*, May 1992, 110.

2 James McCartney, writing in the *Columbia Journalism Review* in 1973, identified these key stories: the connection between the burglars and the White House; the tracing of Nixon campaign funds to the burglars; the "laundering" of campaign money through Mexico; the involvement of John Mitchell, Dwight Chapin, and H. R. Haldeman in Watergate; and the Nixon campaign's use of political espionage and sabotage against the Democrats. Felt was a source of varying importance in nearly every one of these stories. James McCartney, "The *Washington Post* and Watergate: How Two Davids Slew Goliath," *Columbia Journalism Review*, July/August 1973, 8–9.

3 Howard Bray, *The Pillars of the Post: The Making of a News Empire in Washington* (New York: W. W. Norton, 1980), 124.

4 Bob Woodward, "O'Brien Sues GOP Campaign," *WP*, 21 June 1972, A1. The reason for O'Brien's confidence, apparently, was that he had been in contact on June 19 with John Cassidento, the lawyer for Alfred C. Baldwin III, who was acting as a lookout during the break-in. See Walter Pincus, "A Watergate Mystery: Was There a Second 'Deep Throat'?" *WP*, 28 June 1992, C3.

5 Joseph A. Califano, Jr., *Inside: A Public and Private Life* (New York: PublicAffairs, 2004), 268–272, #283; Evan Thomas, *The Man to See: Edward Bennett Williams, Ultimate Insider; Legendary Trial Lawyer* (New York: Simon & Schuster, 1991), 269–274, 283.

Edward Bennet Williams was also friends with Ben Bradlee, as was Califano.

6 Robert Pack, *Edward Bennett Williams for the Defense* (New York: Harper & Row, 1983), 4–5; Lou Cannon, "Dole Lays Dirty Politics to McGovern," *WP*, 26 October 1972, A7; Carl Bernstein and Bob Woodward, *All the President's Men* (New York: Simon & Schuster, 1974), 181–182.

Eventually, it would even be alleged that Williams was Woodward's Deep Throat. Thomas, *Man to See*, 274–275.

7 Ibid., 275.

Bradlee reiterated this statement for a 1992 *Post* article by Walter Pincus, who speculated (correctly) that there was another Deep Throat–like character during Watergate, namely Williams. Pincus, "Watergate Mystery," C3.

8 The purpose of the June 17 reentry was to fix the bug on the telephone of Larry O'Brien's secretary; it had been initially installed on May 28. Barry Sussman, *The Great Cover-up: Nixon and the Scandal of Watergate* (Arlington, VA: Seven Locks Press, 1992), 6–7.

9 Califano, *Inside*, 272; author interview with J. Alan Galbraith, 26 October 2009. Bill Kovach, "O'Brien Asserts Bugging of Offices Preceded Raid," *NYT*, 16 August 1972, 20; Bob Woodward and Carl Bernstein, "13 Face Quiz in 'Bugging' Case," *WP*, 16 August 1972, A8; Carl Bernstein and Bob Woodward, "More Phone Taps, Charged," *WP*, 8 September 1972, A1.

10 Carl Bernstein and Bob Woodward, "Bugging 'Participant' Gives Details," *WP*, 11 September 1972, A1; author interview with J. Alan Galbraith, 6 October 2009; Mann, "Deep Throat," 110.

   Bernstein first got an inkling of Woodward's special friend in the summer of 1972, before he was even dubbed Deep Throat. Woodward described him as an old friend from his navy days who now worked in the Justice Department; subsequently, Woodward specified that he worked in an office adjacent to the acting director. Sometime in the fall, Bernstein told Woodward he needed to know who Deep Throat was and Woodward shared the secret in full. Bob Woodward, *The Secret Man: The Story of Watergate's Deep Throat* (New York: Simon & Schuster, 2005), 226–227; author interview with Harry M. Rosenfeld, 20 October 2011; e-mails to author from Leonard Downie, Jr. and Barry Sussman, 21 October 2011.

11 Bernstein and Woodward, "Bugging 'Participant' Gives Details," A1; Bernstein and Woodward, *All the President's Men*, 65, 108–109.

   Presumably because Galbraith's role as a source violated the supposedly impermeable wall at the newspaper, Bernstein and Woodward later obscured how they got the story. In *All the President's Men* they passively wrote that "The reporters had learned of [Baldwin] while making some routine checks." The book also minimized the importance of this scoop (while reprising much lesser stories in great detail), i.e., it stated that "A few days earlier, the *Post* had reported that there was another participant in the bugging whose identity had not been disclosed; and that he had been granted immunity from prosecution and was talking." When asked specifically in 2009 how they got the September 11 story, Bernstein and Woodward said, "neither of us has a clear recollection of where the first information . . . came from." E-mail to author from Carl Bernstein, 28 October 2009. The Woodward and Bernstein Watergate Papers (WBWP) that are currently open to research at the Harry Ransom Center do not shed any light on the Baldwin scoop; if there are any relevant files, they are still closed.

12 Memo, "Conversation with John Cassidento," 12 September 1972, Earl Silbert Chron Files, Box 51, WSPF, NARA; H. R. Haldeman, *The Haldeman Diaries: Inside the Nixon White House* CD-ROM (Los Angeles: Sony Imagesoft, 1994), 11 September 1972.

13 A profane, outspoken ex-Marine known for his ability to get to the bottom of deceptions by those in power, Harwood had been one of Bradlee's key hires during his effort to purge the *Post* of its perceived liberal bias and transform it into one of the nation's leading newspapers. Harwood despised using the paper to promote causes of any kind, and referred to the pre-Bradlee *Post* as a "schlock newspaper," much too accepting of liberal nostrums. Harwood—who was not privy to the existence of

Woodward's secret source—played the role of Cassandra as the paper's commitment to the Watergate story deepened. He argued that the "Woodstein" articles, with their wholesale use of anonymous sources, could end up making the *Post* look ridiculous. Chalmers M. Roberts, *The* Washington Post: *The First 100 Years* (Boston: Houghton Mifflin, 1977), 380, 433; Leonard Downie, Jr., *The New Muckrakers: An Inside Look at America's Investigative Reporters* (Washington, DC: New Republic Books, 1976), 30.

14 Thomas, *Man to See*, 275; Ben Bradlee, *A Good Life: Newspapering and Other Adventures* (New York: Simon & Schuster, 1995), 359; Alicia C. Shepard, *Woodward and Bernstein: Life in the Shadow of Watergate* (Hoboken, NJ: John Wiley & Sons, 2007), 41; Bray, *Pillars of the Post*, 132.

Bradlee was not hard to persuade either, as there was nothing he liked more than a story that was going to make a difference. At one point, according to national editor Ben Bagdikian, he said, "I want every fucking cocktail party in Georgetown talking about this [Watergate]." Cited in Michael Schudson, *Watergate in American Memory: How We Remember, Forget, and Reconstruct the Past* (New York: Basic Books, 1992), 107.

On September 12, 1972, U.S. District Court Judge Charles Richey temporarily halted the taking of depositions in the DNC civil suit, and on September 21, he issued a permanent ban until after the criminal trial. Lawrence Meyer, "Trial of Watergate Suit before Nov. 7 Held 'Impossible,'" *WP*, 22 September 1972, A1.

15 Thomas, *Man to See*, 19; Galbraith interview, 6 October 2009.

Early in 1973, Williams also played a role in getting Sam Dash to hire Terry F. Lenzner as an investigator for the Senate Watergate Committee. Terry Lenzner Oral History, 4 December 2008, RMNL.

16 Jack Nelson and Ronald J. Ostrow, "Bugging Witness Tells Inside Story on Incident at Watergate," *LAT*, 5 October 1972, A1; Alfred C. Baldwin III, "An Insider's Account of the Watergate Bugging," *LAT*, 5 October 1972, C7; Nelson cited in Shepard, *Woodward and Bernstein*, 57.

17 Author interview with Angelo J. Lano, 4 November 2010; Fred Emery, "So Who Was Deep Throat?" *Guardian*, 20 April 1994, T2; author interview of Bob Woodward, 12 October 2011.

18 Memo, Bolz to Bates, "James W. McCord Jr., et al.," 11 September 1972, WG, FBI FOIA; Memo, Felt to Bates, "James W. McCord Jr., et al.," 11 September 1972, WG, FBI FOIA.

19 John W. Dean, *Blind Ambition: The End of the Story* (Palm Springs, CA: Polimedia Publishers, 2009), 159, 228; John W. Dean, *Lost Honor* (Los Angeles: Stratford Press, 1982), 185.

20 By the time the indictments were handed down, a total of 333 agents had worked on the case at one time or another; 51 separate field offices had been involved; agents had spent 15,000 man-hours on the case (not including clerical time); more than 1,600 persons had been interviewed, and 130 separate reports, totaling 3,500 pages, had been submitted to the federal prosecutors. Memo, Bolz to Bates, "James W. McCord Jr., et al.," 12 September 1972, WG, FBI FOIA; Memo, Bolz to Bates, "James W. McCord Jr., et al.," 13 September 1972, WG, FBI FOIA; Memo, Bolz to Bates, "James W. McCord Jr., et al.," 3 November 1972, WG, FBI FOIA.

21 Bernstein and Woodward, *All the President's Men*, 70; L. Patrick Gray III with Ed Gray,

In Nixon's Web: A Year in the Crosshairs of Watergate (New York: Times Books, 2008), 123–124; Karlyn Barker and Walter Pincus, "Watergate Revisited: 20 Years after the Break-in, the Story Continues to Unfold," *WP*, 14 June 1992, A1.

The prosecutors had deep qualms about acting in a manner that revealed they knew an election was coming up. Nonetheless they offered McCord a great deal—the chance to plead to only one count of conspiracy—if he came forward immediately and disclosed everything he knew. But nothing came of the offer.

22 Bernstein and Woodward, *All the President's Men*, 69–70, 101.

23 According to *All the President's Men*, "in mid-August, [Bernstein and Woodward] began visiting CRP people at their homes in the evening." But in *The Secret Man*, Woodward wrote that he and Bernstein were already engaged in this task when he met Felt in early August. Perhaps Felt assisted Woodward by sharing with him how the FBI had managed to make progress despite the CRP's stonewalling, either by steering a frustrated Woodward to the CRP employees who had already talked candidly to the FBI, or giving him the idea of working through the entire roster while pointing out who was likely to be receptive to the reporters' questions. Apart from the Baldwin interview, the CRP, of course, was precisely where the FBI had made the most progress. Bernstein and Woodward, *All the President's Men*, 58; Woodward, *Secret Man*, 67.

24 Walt Harrington, *American Profiles: Somebodies and Nobodies Who Matter* (Columbia, MO: University of Missouri Press, 1992), 32; Edward Walsh, "Woman Follows Dad's Steps," *WP*, 11 August 1972, C4.

25 Memo, Bolz to Bates, "James W. McCord Jr., et al.," 3 July 1972, WG, FBI FOIA.

26 Memo, "Penny Gleason . . . Pertinent Results," 1 July 1972, WG, FBI FOIA; Paul P. Magallanes Oral History, 25 August 2005, SOCXFBI, 10–11; John W. Mindermann Oral History, 7 March 2007, SOCXFBI, 7–8.

27 Mindermann Oral History, 7 March 2007, 24.

28 Magallanes Oral History, 25 August 2005, 7–8; Mindermann Oral History, 7 March 2007, 24; Memo, Long to Gebhardt, "James W. McCord Jr., et al.," 15 June 1973, WG, FBI FOIA; undated list, "Committee to Reelect the President Personnel," LPG, FBI FOIA.

29 Gray handwritten notes, "TCT J[ohn] W[.] D[ean]," 19 September 1972, WG, FBI FOIA.

30 Bernstein and Woodward were deliberately vague on why they believed Hoback, among other CRP employees, had gone back to the FBI or prosecutors to give more information. Felt may have confirmed that some witnesses were cooperating with, rather than stonewalling, the federal investigation. Bernstein and Woodward, *All the President's Men*, 58, 63–64.

31 Woodward, *Secret Man*, 6.

32 Carl Bernstein and Bob Woodward, "Spy Funds Linked to GOP Aides," *WP*, 17 September 1972, A1; Bernstein and Woodward, *All the President's Men*, 73, 76; Woodward, *Secret Man*, 69; Mann, "Deep Throat," 110.

No direct meetings are specified in *All the President's Men* or *The Secret Man* in the roughly six weeks after the August meeting in Felt's home. Woodward hints that there was at least one meeting during that period, via a vague reference to "their last meeting" prior to the September 17 telephone call. Yet if there were no meetings, that would mean that after the elaborate signaling system had been set up, Woodward had no communication with Felt until the reporter telephoned on September 16. Bernstein and Woodward, *All the President's Men*, 76.

33 Bernstein and Woodward, "Spy Funds Linked to GOP Aides," A1; see also Carl Bernstein and Bob Woodward, "2 Linked to Secret GOP Fund," *WP*, 18 September 1972, A1.

Both articles contained anonymous quotes that were Hoback's words. Magallanes Oral History, 25 August 2005, 12; Mindermann Oral History, 7 March 2007, 9, 12; see also Bernstein and Woodward, *All the President's Men*, 86–87.

34 H. R. Haldeman, *The Haldeman Diaries: Inside the Nixon White House* (New York: G. P. Putnam's Sons, 1994), 505.

35 Bernstein and Woodward, *All the President's Men*, 75.

36 Bernstein and Woodward, "2 Linked to Secret GOP Fund," A1.

37 Draft manuscript, "All the President's Men," undated, 150, Watergate Collection, HRC; Bernstein and Woodward, *All the President's Men*, 74–75.

38 After the September 17 and 18 articles appeared, Pat Gray would personally call Robert Kunkel, the Washington Field Office's special agent in charge, and order him to make sure that the *Post* was not getting leaks from the rank-and-file agents working the investigation. Bernstein and Woodward, *All the President's Men*, 86–87.

39 Bernstein and Woodward, *All the President's Men*, 76; draft manuscript, "All the President's Men," 157–158, Watergate Collection, HRC; Woodward, *Secret Man*, 71.

40 Ronald J. Ostrow, "Ex-FBI Agent Said to Be Data Source in Watergate Case," *LAT*, 17 September 1972, A1; "Ex-FBI Agent Named as Bugging Case Witness," *NYT*, 17 September 1972, 39; Bernstein and Woodward, "Spy Funds Linked to GOP Aides," A1; Memo, "Conversation with Robert Mirto and Alfred Baldwin," 27 September 1972, Earl Silbert Chron Files, Box 52, WSPF, NARA; Nelson and Ostrow, "Bugging Witness Tells Inside Story on Incident at Watergate," A1; Baldwin, "An Insider's Account of the Watergate Bugging," C7; Bernstein and Woodward, *All the President's Men*, 109–110, 225; Shepard, *Woodward and Bernstein*, 55–57; David Halberstam, *The Powers That Be* (New York: Alfred A. Knopf, 1979), 637–641.

41 Draft manuscript, "All the President's Men," undated, 109A, Series II, 43.1, WBWP, HRC; Carl Bernstein and Bob Woodward, "Bug Memos Sent to Nixon Aides," *WP*, 6 October 1972, A1; Bob Woodward and Carl Bernstein, "$100,000 Gift to Nixon Campaign Is Traced to Texas Corporation," *WP*, 6 October 1972, A1; Shepard, *Woodward and Bernstein*, 57.

42 Bernstein and Woodward, "Bug Memos Sent to Nixon Aides," A1.

43 Bernstein and Woodward, *All the President's Men*, 111.

44 Draft manuscript, "All the President's Men," 4–5, WBWP, HRC.

45 Ibid., 5.

46 Ibid., 8.

"Woodward had not taken notes and asked Deep Throat to review the steps again so he [Woodward] could get them straight." According to Woodward he managed to live with this stricture by sitting down immediately after every meeting and typing up everything he could remember that Felt had said. Ibid.; Amy Argetsinger and Roxanne Roberts, "Watergate Papers: Who Leaked What When?" *WP*, 10 April 2007, C3.

47 Draft manuscript, "All the President's Men," 6–7, WBWP, HRC.

48 Ibid., 8; E. Howard Hunt with Greg Aunapu, *American Spy: My Secret History in the CIA, Watergate, and Beyond* (Hoboken, NJ: John Wiley & Sons, 2007), 228.

Probably because the article all but proved that Deep Throat was in the FBI, this entire episode was elided from *All the President's Men,* although it was included in an early draft. There was no discussion about how the October 6 article came about—indeed, the article itself was deleted from the published book—even though it represented, in the words of the authors, "the first detailed example of the Stans fund[-]raising operation." Media critic McCartney, after analyzing the complete run of Woodward and Bernstein's Watergate coverage, would term the October 6 story one of the seven "watershed articles" written by them between August and October. Yet insofar as they revealed anything about the money-laundering angle at all in *All the President's Men,* Woodward and Bernstein referred only to their earlier story published on August 27. McCartney, "The *Washington Post* and Watergate," 14.

49 William Safire, *Safire's Political Dictionary* (New York: Oxford University Press, 2008), 257; Thomas, *Man to See,* 275; Shepard, *Woodward and Bernstein,* 105; Stanley I. Kutler, *The Wars of Watergate: The Last Crisis of Richard Nixon* (New York: Alfred A. Knopf, 1990), 226; Robert H. Phelps, *God and the Editor: My Search for Meaning at the* New York Times (Syracuse, NY: Syracuse University Press, 2009), 196.

Another accounting showed that the *Post* ran 201 staff-written stories about Watergate from June to December 1972, while the *New York Times* and *Los Angeles Times* published (respectively) ninety-nine and forty-five staff-written stories during the same period. Louis W. Liebovich, *Richard Nixon, Watergate, and the Press: A Historical Perspective* (Westport, CT: Praeger, 2003), 67.

50 Downie, *New Muckrakers,* 40; Roberts, Washington Post: *The First 100 Years,* 433.

51 Downie, *New Muckrakers,* 40; Richard Reeves, "Lots of Footwork, No Footnotes," *NYT Book Review,* 18 April 1976, 174.

52 Shepard, *Woodward and Bernstein,* 104–105; Mark McGuire, "Revelation Troubles Watergate Veteran," *ATU,* 1 June 2005, A5.

53 Sussman, *Great Cover-up,* 102–103; author interview with Barry Sussman, 19 October 2011; author interview with Harry M. Rosenfeld, 20 October 2011.

CHAPTER 7. RICHARD NIXON'S OWN "DEEP THROAT": OCTOBER 1972

1 L. Patrick Gray III with Ed Gray, *In Nixon's Web: A Year in the Crosshairs of Watergate* (New York: Times Books, 2008), 118–119; Ronald J. Ostrow, "Gray Outs Head of Capital FBI Office," *LAT,* 30 September 1972, A1; Sanford J. Ungar, "D.C. Chief of FBI Punished," *WP,* 30 September 1972, A1; "Mr. Gray's Active Broom," *WP,* 9 October 1972, A22; author interview with Daniel M. Armstrong, 18 June 2008.

2 Leonard M. "Bucky" Walters Oral History, 4 March 2003, SOCXFBI, 6; author interview with John J. McDermott, 11 November 2010.

3 Memo, Bolz to Bates, "James W. McCord Jr., et al.," 12 October 1972, WG, FBI FOIA.

4 "Sen. Muskie Insults Franco-Americans," *Manchester Union Leader,* 24 February 1972, 1; Carl Bernstein and Bob Woodward, *All the President's Men* (New York: Simon & Schuster, 1974), 113–114, 127.

5 Bernstein and Woodward, *All the President's Men,* 130–135.

6 Typewritten notes, "Interview with X," 9 October [1972], Series I, 75.18, WBWP, HRC; Memo, General Investigative Division, "Bugging of Democratic National Headquarters," 7 October 1972, WG, FBI FOIA; Memo, Bolz to Bates, "James W. McCord Jr.,

et al.," 10 October 1972, WG, FBI FOIA. See note 10 below for an explanation of why double quotation marks are used when citing the typewritten notes.

After the *Post*'s first story on Segretti appeared, Felt would promptly confirm for a *Newsweek* reporter, Stephan Lesher, what he refused to discuss with Woodward, i.e., Segretti's connection to the White House. Mark Memmott, "'Deep Throat' Wasn't Only Watergate Source," *USA Today*, 9 June 2005, A5; author interview with Stephan Lesher, 5 June 2008; "The Story of a GOP Trickster," *Newsweek*, 30 October 1972, 30, 35–36.

7 Typewritten notes, "Interview with X," 9 October [1972], Series I, 75.18, WBWP, HRC; Bernstein and Woodward, *All the President's Men*, 131–132, 135.

8 John W. Dean, *Blind Ambition: The End of the Story* (Palm Springs, CA: Polimedia Publishers, 2009), 170–171; John W. Dean, *Lost Honor* (Los Angeles: Stratford Press, 1982), 82; Dwight Chapin Interview, 2 April 2007, RMNL, 58–61; Carl Bernstein and Bob Woodward, "FBI Finds Nixon Aides Sabotaged Democrats," *WP*, 10 October 1972, A1; Bernstein and Woodward, *All the President's Men*, 135; Seymour M. Hersh, "Teams of Agents," *NYT*, 3 May 1973, 1; Robert H. Phelps, *God and the Editor: My Search for Meaning at the* New York Times (Syracuse, NY: Syracuse University Press, 2009), 173–174; "Witness Summary: Donald Segretti," undated, *US v. Chapin*, WSPF, NARA; Memo, Bolz to Bates, "James W. McCord Jr., et al.," 18 October 1972, WG, FBI FOIA; John W. Dean, "Why the Revelation of the Identity of Deep Throat Has Only Created Another Mystery," http://writ.news.findlaw.com/dean/20050603.html, 3 June 2005.

John Crewdson wrote the most detailed examination of Segretti's varied exploits ten months later, based on the FBI's investigation. Almost a year later, journalist Edward Jay Epstein was the first to point out that the Segretti affair was "a detour, if not a false trail." John M. Crewdson, "Sabotaging the GOP's Rivals: Story of a $100,000 Operation," *NYT*, 9 July 1973, 1; John M. Crewdson, "Sabotage by Segretti: Network of Amateurs," *NYT*, 10 July 1973, 1; Edward Jay Epstein, "Did the Press Uncover Watergate?" *Commentary*, July 1974, 24.

The final reports of the Senate Watergate Committee and Watergate Special Prosecution Force both developed perspectives on Segretti and his network of provocateurs that were in sharp contrast to the *Post*'s account. Most of the serious legal problems stemmed from an attempt to cover up the activities rather than the activities themselves. In any case, the temper of the times and party rule changes instituted by the Democrats themselves had far more to do with the selection of the eventual nominee, George McGovern, than any scheme hatched by the Nixon White House or campaign. See SCPCA, *Final Report*, 93rd Cong., 2nd sess. (Washington, DC: Government Printing Office, 1974), 158–187, and WSPF, *Report* (Washington, DC: Government Printing Office, 1974), 55–57.

9 Mark Feldstein, *Poisoning the Press: Richard Nixon, Jack Anderson, and the Rise of Washington's Scandal Culture* (New York: Farrar, Straus and Giroux, 2010), 302.

10 Bernstein and Woodward, *All the President's Men*, 134; typewritten notes, "Interview with X," 9 October [1972], Series I, 75.18, WBWP, HRC.

There are marked differences between the accounts of Woodward's conversations with Felt as presented in *All the President's Men*, written about a year after the meetings occurred, and what Woodward noted down in his more contemporaneous typewritten notes, three instances of which are extant in Woodward's papers. Much of what Deep Throat said was excised, partly to protect Felt's identity presumably. But in addition, phrases that are not enclosed in quotation marks in the notes are presented within quotation marks in the book, lending the impression that Felt spoke those exact words. Many sentences are also moved around and the progression of Felt's remarks rearranged. Occasionally the meaning of what he said is substantially changed. For example, the October 9 typewritten notes read, "Hunt op[eration] not really to check leaks to news media but to give them out" (not enclosed in quotation marks). In the book, however, this sentence is rendered (with quotation marks) as follows: "That [Hunt] operation was not only to check leaks to the papers but often to manufacture items for the press."

Most notably, as the foregoing example suggests, the account in the book also contains words, phrases, and sometimes whole sentences that are not present in the typewritten notes at all. The typewritten notes, for example, do not reflect *any* exchange or discussion about the Canuck letter. Yet the book states, "It [the Canuck letter] was a White House operation—done inside the gates surrounding the White House and the Executive Office Building," quoting Felt, as if he had uttered these exact words.

When asked about these discrepancies, Woodward said that during the course of writing *All the President's Men*, "I may have had a distinct recollection that something was in quotes . . . and so I may have put quotes in it." Regarding the book passages that do not appear in the typewritten notes at all, he responded, "It's just like when you testify under oath in a courtroom. You may have some notes, and you may say, 'the notes say this, but I recall *that* in addition.'" Author interview with Bob Woodward, 12 October 2011.

11 Both the Senate Watergate Committee and the Watergate Special Prosecution Force, after extensive investigations, could not determine for sure who sent the Canuck letter—except that it was not Ken Clawson, and it was not provably a "White House operation." When the matter was discussed by President Nixon and his top aides on October 10 and 12, they evinced no familiarity with the letter—indeed, it had to be explained to them. Haldeman also noted in one conversation, without a hint of irony, that Clawson had convincingly refuted the allegation. SCPCA, *Final Report*, 207; WSPF. *Report* (Washington, DC: Government Printing Office, 1975), 55–57; author transcript, tape recording, Nixon, Haldeman, Ziegler, and Colson, conversation no. 795-1, 10 October 1972, RMNL; author transcript, tape recording, Nixon and Haldeman, conversation no. 796-4, 12 October 1972, RMNL. See also Dean, *Lost Honor*, 334–335; Mark Felt and John O'Connor, *A G-Man's Life: The FBI, Being "Deep Throat," and the Struggle for Honor in Washington* (New York: PublicAffairs, 2006), 222; and note 18 below.

12 Bernstein and Woodward, *All the President's Men*, 131.

When queried about the bad information Felt repeatedly imparted, Woodward said he could only respond to specific examples, case-by-case. Felt's May 16, 1973 assertion—that Mitchell (and others) had contributed "their own personal funds" to the cover-up, and that because Mitchell "couldn't meet his quota" they "cut Mitchell loose"—was raised as one example. Woodward agreed that no evidence for this allegation ever emerged in any of the Watergate investigations. "But [Felt] may have had reason to believe that, and that it might have been true, and it simply is plausible," Woodward said. Bernstein and Woodward, *All the President's Men*, 318; Woodward interview, 12 October 2011.

13 Bernstein and Woodward, *All the President's Men*, 311. Felt may have began imparting

misleading information to Woodward before the October 9, 1972 meeting, but at this writing notes from earlier conversations have not been made available in Woodward's papers.

14 Bernstein and Woodward, "FBI Finds Nixon Aides Sabotaged Democrats," A1.

Woodward recalled in 2010 that the wording "massive campaign of political spying and sabotage" was Bernstein's phraseology. Bob Woodward Oral History, 14 December 2010, RMNL.

15 Memo, Bolz to Bates, "James W. McCord Jr., et al.," 12 October 1972, WG, FBI FOIA; Memo, Bolz to Bates, "James W. McCord Jr., et al.," 18 October 1972, WG, FBI FOIA; Memo, Gebhardt to Baker, "Confirmation," 15 March 1973, WG, FBI FOIA.

16 Bernstein and Woodward, "FBI Finds Nixon Aides Sabotaged Democrats," A1; Barry Sussman, *The Great Cover-up: Nixon and the Scandal of Watergate* (Arlington, VA: Seven Locks Press, 1992), 105; Bob Woodward, *The Secret Man: The Story of Watergate's Deep Throat* (New York: Simon & Schuster, 2005), 79; Phelps, *God and the Editor*, 176; James McCartney, "The *Washington Post* and Watergate: How Two Davids Slew Goliath," *Columbia Journalism Review*, July/August 1973, 16; Alicia C. Shepard, *Woodward and Bernstein: Life in the Shadow of Watergate* (Hoboken, NJ: John Wiley & Sons, 2007), 41–42; Woodward Oral History, 14 December 2010.

17 Bernstein and Woodward, *All the President's Men*, 145–146; Ben Bradlee, *A Good Life: Newspapering and Other Adventures* (New York: Simon & Schuster, 1995), 365; Shepard, *Woodward and Bernstein*, 41–42.

18 Gray handwritten notes, "TCT W[.] M[ark] F[elt]," 11 October 1972, WG, FBI FOIA; Memo, Bolz to Bates, "James W. McCord Jr., et al.," 10 October 1972, WG, FBI FOIA; Memo, Dalbey to Felt, "James W. McCord Jr., et al.," 12 October 1972, WG, FBI FOIA; Memo, Bolz to Bates, "James W. McCord Jr., et al.," 12 October 1972, WG, FBI FOIA; Bernstein and Woodward, "FBI Finds Nixon Aides Sabotaged Democrats," A1.

The Watergate special prosecutor later found that neither Clawson nor anyone else working for Nixon was remotely responsible for the letter. "'Canuck Letter' Said Destroyed," *WP*, 29 July 1973, A10; Arthur C. Egan, Jr., "Note Denied," *Manchester Union Leader*, 11 October 1972, 1; William Loeb, "The Misleaders," *Manchester Union Leader*, 13 October 1972, 1; William Loeb, "Canuck Letter vs. Watergate," *Manchester Union Leader*, 28 July 1973, 1; Memo, Davis to Files, "'Canuck Letter' Investigation—Marilyn Berger," 9 January 1974, Dirty Tricks Task Force, Box 14, WSPF, NARA.

19 Gray, *In Nixon's Web*, 128; Memo, Bolz to Bates, "James W. McCord Jr., et al.," 19 October 1972, WG, FBI FOIA.

20 SCPCA, *Final Report*, 184–187; "White House: No Comment," *WP*, 11 October 1972, A13; Dean, *Blind Ambition*, 165, 171; Bob Woodward and Bernstein, "Lawyer for Nixon Said to Have Used GOP's Spy Fund," *WP*, 16 October 1972, A1; Author transcript, conversation no. 795-1, 10 October 1972, RMNL.

21 (Sandy Smith), "More Fumes from the Watergate Affair," *Time*, 23 October 1972 (published October 16), 23; Memo, Bolz to Bates, "James W. McCord Jr., et al.," 10 October 1972, WG, FBI FOIA; Woodward and Bernstein, "Lawyer for Nixon Said to Have Used GOP's Spy Fund," A1.

22 (Sandy Smith), "Denials and Still More Questions," *Time*, 30 October 1972 (published October 23), 18–19; Gray, *In Nixon's Web*, 129.

23 Bradlee, *Good Life*, 342; Benjamin C. Bradlee, "Watergate: The Biggest Story and the

Most Intense Moment of Our Lives," *WP*, 14 June 1992, C1; Woodward Oral History, 14 December 2010, RMNL.

24 Author transcript, tape recording, Nixon and Haldeman, conversation no. 370-9, 19 October 1972, RMNL; Stanley I. Kutler, *Abuse of Power: The New Nixon Tapes* (New York: Free Press, 1997), 170–172; author transcript, conversation no. 795-1, 10 October 1972, RMNL; author transcript, tape recording, Nixon and Haldeman, conversation no. 797-3, 13 October 1972, RMNL; author transcript, tape recording, Nixon and Colson, conversation no. 797-11, 13 October 1972, RMNL.

When he first became aware of this conversation, Woodward said he was "bowled over by how certain" Haldeman and Nixon seemed to be about the allegation against Felt. Woodward interview, 12 October 2011.

25 Teletype, Washington Field [Office] to Acting Director, "Interception of Communication," 17 June 1972, WG, FBI FOIA; Transcript, "Conference between Special Prosecutor Archibald Cox, Assistant James Vorenberg, and Assistant Attorney General Henry Petersen," 29 May 1973, Box 81, WSPF, NARA, 19-21; Memo, "Re Henry Petersen Interview," 6 June 1973, Box 81, WSPF, NARA.

The special presecutor would later investigate Petersen for his actions, but no charges were brought. Petersen always maintained that he had done nothing wrong, either ethically or legally. After criticism waned, he resigned from the Justice Department in November 1974. See John M. Crewdson, "Petersen Called Conduit for Data," *NYT*, 26 June 1973, 1.

As Walter Pincus pointed out in a 1973 article in *The New Republic*, there was some precedent for keeping the White House informed about an ongoing investigation that was politically sensitive. During the Johnson administration, while the FBI was investigating Robert G. "Bobby" Baker, Herbert J. Miller, Jr., then head of the Justice Department's Criminal Division, prepared a weekly summary for the White House based on FBI reports. Walter Pincus, "Misusing the FBI," *New Republic*, 24 February 1973, 18.

26 Petersen learned the information from a source who has never been identified except as a lawyer who worked at the publication. According to John Dean, the lawyer might not have intended or expected Petersen to inform the White House and likely believed the information would go no further than the Justice Department.

When Petersen shared this information with Dean, the White House counsel "presumed" Petersen was referring to the *Washington Post*. During the ensuing conversation between Haldeman and the president, Haldeman refers to the source as a former FBI or Justice Department man who works at the publication and somehow learned that Felt was the source for the stories appearing in that publication. While many students of Watergate, including Bob Woodward and this author, instinctively made the same presumption that Dean made in 1972—that the publication in question was the *Post*—it is not absolutely clear that that was the case. In the same month Petersen imparted his information to Dean, John Mitchell learned, reportedly from Wall Street lawyer Roswell Gilpatric (who never worked for the FBI or Justice Department), that Felt was leaking to *Time* magazine. In several subsequent taped conversations, President Nixon refers to this ostensibly second transmission belt of information (*Time* magazine to Gilpatric to Mitchell) and no other as the basis for his belief that Felt was leaking. The bottom line is that even now, it is unclear whether two different lawyers, affiliated respectively with the *Washington Post* and *Time* magazine, both disclosed separately, and almost simultaneously, that Felt was leaking to their publications, or whether only one did. What is not in dispute is that on October 19, 1972 President Nixon unequivocally learned that Felt was the suspected leaker the White House had been worried—and complaining—about for months. Kutler, *Abuse of Power*, 111; Dean, *Blind Ambition*, 129, 245, 315, 584; Woodward, *Secret Man*, 87; author transcript, conversation no. 370-9, October 19, 1972, RMNL; Max Holland, "Richard Nixon's Own Deep Throat," http://www.washingtondecoded.com/site/2009/11/richard-nixons-own-deep-throat.html, 3 November 2009; author interview with John W. Dean, 20 November 2010; e-mail to author from John Dean, 14 June 2011; Michael Dobbs, "Watergate and the Two Lives of Mark Felt," *WP*, 20 June 2005, A1.

27 Kutler, *Abuse of Power*, 108; H. R. Haldeman, *The Haldeman Diaries: Inside the Nixon White House* (New York: G. P. Putnam's Sons, 1994), 514; H. R. Haldeman, *The Haldeman Diaries: Inside the Nixon White House* CD-ROM (Los Angeles: Sony Imagesoft, 1994), 10 October 1972; author transcript, tape recording, Nixon and Dean, conversation no. 865-14, 28 February 1973, RMNL; Holland, "Richard Nixon's Own Deep Throat"; Memo, Higby to Haldeman, 25 September 1972, H. R. Haldeman, Box 102, SMOF, WHSF, RMNL; AP, "Nixon Medical File Reportedly Rifled in 1972 Campaign," *LAT*, 4 May 1973, A1.

28 Author transcript, conversation no. 370-9, 19 October 1972, RMNL; see also Kutler, *Abuse of Power*, 170–172; Gray, *In Nixon's Web*, 129–131.

29 Author transcript, conversation no. 370-9, 19 October 1972, RMNL.

30 Ibid.

31 Garry Wills, "The Hiss Connection through Nixon's Life," *NYT Magazine*, 25 August 1974, 8; Haldeman handwritten notes, "10/20–11/17/1972," Oct-Nov-Dec 1972, Box 46, SMOF, WHSF, RMNL; Haldeman, *Diaries* CD-ROM, 20 October 1972.

32 Kutler, *Abuse of Power*, 172; Haldeman, *Diaries* CD-ROM, 20 October 1972; Haldeman handwritten notes, "10/20–11/17/1972," Oct-Nov-Dec 1972, Box 46, SMOF, WHSF, RMNL.

33 Robert D. Novak, *The Prince of Darkness: 50 Years Reporting in Washington* (New York: Crown Forum, 2007), 232; Haldeman, *Diaries* CD-ROM, 21 October 1972; Haldeman handwritten notes, "10/20–11/17/1972," Oct-Nov-Dec 1972, Box 46, SMOF, WHSF, RMNL.

34 Gray, *In Nixon's Web*, 45, 129.

Gray "was almost totally dependent upon Felt to handle the day-to-day routine matters that a new man could not learn overnight." Sanford J. Ungar, *FBI* (Boston: Atlantic Monthly Press, 1976), 513. According to John Dean, Gray "typically said he would have to check with Felt and get back to me" when they were discussing FBI business. Dean, "Why the Revelation of the Identity of Deep Throat Has Only Created Another Mystery."

35 Typed summary, "Meeting with Ackerman and Martin," 8 January 1975, Calls and Meetings with President [Nixon], 1971–1973, Folder 1, Box 65, Charles W. Colson Papers; Gray, *In Nixon's Web*, 131; e-mail to author from Charles W. Colson, 7 June 2011.

Lambert was the journalist whom Chuck Colson had contacted in September 1971 when he was trying to get someone interested in E. Howard Hunt's forged cables about the Diem assassination. SCPCA, *Final Report*, 126–127.

36 (Sandy Smith), "Political Orders," *Time*, 6 November 1972 (published October 30), 48, 50; Gray, *In Nixon's Web*, 112–114, 141; "FBI Ends Compilation of Data on Those in Congressional Races," *NYT*, 28 October 1972, 1.

37 Woodward contacted the Bureau seeking information about the program on October 24. Gray, *In Nixon's Web*, 134–136; Gray handwritten notes, "TCF W[.] M[ark] Felt," 25 October 1972, WG, FBI FOIA.

38 Gray handwritten notes, "TCF W[.] M[ark] F[elt]," 30 October 1972, WG, FBI FOIA.

39 (Sandy Smith), "How High?" *Time*, 6 November 1972 (published October 30), 50; Gray, *In Nixon's Web*, 133.

On the surface, Gilpatric was just about the unlikeliest source imaginable. He had served as Deputy Secretary of Defense during the Kennedy administration, and publicly opposed Nixon's policies on Vietnam and ballistic missile defense in the early '70s. But Gilpatric's service in the government had apparently instilled in him a strong aversion to leaks, and presumably prompted him to compromise the identity of Smith's best source. Gilpatric probably learned the name from John F. Dowd, the longtime chief editorial counsel for *Time*, who was a former Cravath lawyer. "John F. Dowd Dead; Ex-*Time* Aide was 60," *NYT*, 17 February 1977, 42; Holland, "Nixon's Own Deep Throat."

According to FBI agent Paul V. Daly, Clare Boothe Luce, the sixty-nine-year-old widow of Time Inc. founder Henry Luce and a prominent conservative journalist in her own right, also "called John Mitchell up and told him that Mark Felt was leaking stuff." This is not implausible, as Mrs. Luce had an enormous sense of editorial entitlement and may have elicited the information from Dowd. She never wavered in her support of Nixon, publicly lambasting *Time* in April 1974 for its "obsessional and below-the-belt" reporting on Watergate, and "editorial overinvestment in the destruction of the president." Myra McPherson, "On Journalistic Advocacy and Presidential Efficacy," *WP*, 4 May 1973, B1; Letters, "The Press and Nixon," *Time*, 8 April 1974, 5, 7; Paul V. Daly Oral History, 10 February 2005, SOCXFBI, 29.

40 Gray, *In Nixon's Web*, 124; W. Mark Felt, *The FBI Pyramid: From the Inside* (New York: G. P. Putnam's Sons, 1979), 226.

41 Unidentified aide quoted in Ungar, *FBI*, 514; Edward S. Miller Oral History, 28 May 2008, SOCXFBI, 181; Felt, *FBI Pyramid*, 215; e-mail to author from David Kinley, 27 May 2011.

Gray's three young assistants all sensed the resentment his appointment as acting director engendered, but were unable to persuade their boss that it was "us against them." Gray, *In Nixon's Web*, 51.

42 U.S. Congress, Senate, Committee on the Judiciary, *Hearings, Louis Patrick Gray III*, 93rd Cong., 1st sess. (Washington, DC: Government Printing Office, 1973), 123–124, 207; Gray, *In Nixon's Web*, 119, 194; Jack Anderson, "Gray Throws FBI into a Tizzy," *WP*, 22 December 1972, D15.

Bates would receive national attention in 1974 when he supervised the FBI investigation into the kidnapping of Patty Hearst.

43 Gray, *In Nixon's Web*, 194; Brendan Lyons, "Deep Throat's Tale Revealed," *ATU*, 5 June 2005, A1.

1 Bob Woodward, *The Secret Man: The Story of Watergate's Deep Throat* (New York: Simon & Schuster, 2005), 12; James McCartney, "The *Washington Post* and Watergate: How Two Davids Slew Goliath," *Columbia Journalism Review*, July/August 1973, 21; Louis Harris, "Bugging, Fund Charges Leave Public Apathetic," *WP*, 19 October 1972, A29.

Notwithstanding the lull in coverage, the administration was keen on paying back the *Post* for its coverage the previous fall. *Post* reporters were frozen out while reporters from the *Washington Star* received exclusives, and challenges were made to the lucrative TV licenses in Jacksonville and Miami owned by the *Post's* holding company. The possibility of bringing even more financial pressure to bear on the *Post* was the subject of a January 1973 memo by Charles Colson, who was soon to leave the White House. Charles W. Colson, "Memorandum for the File," 15 January 1973, P Memos 1973, Box 230, SMOF, WHSF, RMNL.

2 Carl Bernstein and Bob Woodward, "Testimony Ties Top Nixon Aide to Secret Fund," *WP*, 25 October 1972, A1; Carl Bernstein and Bob Woodward, *All the President's Men* (New York: Simon & Schuster, 1974), 186; Bob Woodward Oral History, 14 December 2010, RMNL; Alicia C. Shepard, *Woodward and Bernstein: Life in the Shadow of Watergate* (Hoboken, NJ: John Wiley and Sons, 2007), 43, 218; Leonard Downie, Jr., *The New Muckrakers: An Inside Look at America's Investigative Reporters* (Washington, DC: New Republic Books, 1976), 13, 39–40.

The article also alleged, erroneously, that the FBI had questioned Haldeman about disbursements from the fund; the Bureau, in fact, had not talked to Haldeman. Gray handwritten notes, "TCF W[.] M[ark] F[elt]," 25 October 1972, WG, FBI FOIA.

The "business with [Bernstein's] parents' background" only came to the attention of the *Post* editors belatedly. Well before that, however, they were aware that Bernstein did not like Nixon. Shortly after the break-in, Bernstein wrote a five-page memo entitled the "Chotiner Theory," which suggested that the president's longtime political tactician, Murray Chotiner, was the brains behind the Watergate break-in. Shepard, *Woodward and Bernstein*, 34, 218.

3 Bernstein and Woodward, *All the President's Men*, 193; Carl Bernstein and Bob Woodward, "Magazine Says Nixon Aide Admits Disruption Effort," *WP*, 30 October 1972, A1; Ben Bradlee Oral History, 14 December 2010, RMNL; Benjamin C. Bradlee, "Watergate: The Biggest Story and the Most Intense Moment of Our Lives," *WP*, 14 June 1992, C1; Ben Bradlee, *A Good Life: Newspapering and Other Adventures* (New York: Simon & Schuster), 339; Downie, *New Muckrakers*, 37.

4 Bernstein and Woodward, *All the President's Men*, 173; Woodward, *Secret Man*, 92.

For an independent definition of "deep background," see Howard Kurtz, "'Game Change': Howard Kurtz on Background Sourcing Issues," *WP*, 18 January 2010, C1.

5 Carl Bernstein and Bob Woodward, "Bug Case Figures Used Covert Executive Phone," *WP*, 8 December 1972, A1; "Nixon Had 2 Aides Fight News Leaks," *NYT*, 13 December 1972, 19; Carl Bernstein and Bob Woodward, "Executive Phone Used to Hunt 'Leaks,'" *WP*, 13 December 1972, A10; Bernstein and Woodward, *All the President's Men*, 220; Woodward Oral History, 14 December 2010.

6 James M. Perry, "Watergate Case Study," in Tom Rosenstiel and Amy S. Mitchell,

Thinking Clearly: Cases in Journalistic Decision-Making (New York: Columbia University Press, 2003), 168.

7 Clark R. Mollenhoff, *Game Plan for Disaster: An Ombudsman's Report on the Nixon Years* (New York: W. W. Norton, 1976), 267–268; Sanford J. Ungar, "After 6 Months as Chief, FBI's Gray Eyes Past, Present, Future," *WP*, 6 November 1972, A2.

8 H. R. Haldeman, *The Haldeman Diaries: Inside the Nixon White House* CD-ROM (Los Angeles: Sony Imagesoft, 1994), 22 and 28 November 1972.

9 Ibid., 12 November 1972.

10 Ibid., 27 November 1972.

11 Ibid.; Stanley I. Kutler, *Abuse of Power: The New Nixon Tapes* (New York: Free Press, 1997), 178.

12 Haldeman, *Diaries* CD-ROM, 28 November 1972; Sanford J. Ungar, "Nixon to Name Gray Regular FBI Chief," *WP*, 21 December 1972, A1; Ronald J. Ostrow, "Gray's Replacement at FBI Reportedly Studied by Nixon," *LAT*, 21 December 1972, A1.

13 L. Patrick Gray III with Ed Gray, *In Nixon's Web: A Year in the Crosshairs of Watergate* (New York: Times Books, 2008), 138–139.

14 Memo, "Summary of Petersen Interview," 11 July 1974, Box 81, WSPF, RG460, NARA, 5–6.

15 John W. Dean, *Blind Ambition: The End of the Story* (Palm Springs, CA: Polimedia Publishers, 2009), 203–204.

16 Earl Silbert Oral History, 17 September 2008, RMNL; author interview with Earl J. Silbert, 29 April 2011.

One piece of grand jury information that Petersen learned from Silbert and passed on to Dean involved Magruder's testimony. "It's really close," Silbert reported to Petersen, meaning that Magruder's explanation, which stopped the conspiracy at the Hunt/Liddy level, had appeared just barely believable. Petersen then told Dean that Magruder had gotten through the grand jury "by the skin of his teeth." Silbert interview, 29 April 2011; SCPCA, *Hearings, Presidential Campaign Activities of 1972*, vol. 3, 93rd Cong., 1st sess. (Washington, DC: Government Printing Office, 1973), 952.

17 Memo, "Summary of Petersen Interview," 11 July 1974, Box 81, WSPF, NARA, 5–6; Dean, *Blind Ambition*, 204; Gray, *In Nixon's Web*, 215–216.

Shortly after this encounter, Dean destroyed the notebooks that had been in Hunt's safe and then in his possession since June. Gray would continue to deny until late April that he ever took possession from Dean of documents from Hunt's safe. SCPCA, *Final Report*, 93rd Cong., 2nd sess. (Washington, DC: Government Printing Office, 1974), 36; Memo, "John Ehrlichman," undated, Box 81, WSPF, NARA, 5–6.

18 See, for example, Walter Pincus, "Misusing the FBI," *New Republic*, 24 February 1973, 17–18.

19 Jeremiah O'Leary, "8 More Hoover Men Transferred," *WS*, 2 January 1973, A4; (Sandy Smith), "'Tattletale Gray,'" *Time*, 15 January 1973 (published January 8), 20; W. Mark Felt, *The FBI Pyramid: From the Inside* (New York: G. P. Putnam's Sons, 1979), 248–249; Memo, Gallagher to Gebhardt, "James W. McCord Jr., et al.," 27 December 1972, WG, FBI FOIA.

The December 27 memo describes a conversation Smith had with Charlie Bolz, in which Smith said he was writing an article about Gray's tenure as acting director. Smith asked Bolz about Gray's alleged meeting with Mitchell on the West Coast right after the break-in and raised again the supposed restriction on checking Charles Colson's long-distance calls.

20 Gray, *In Nixon's Web*, 146.

21 Rowland Evans and Robert Novak, "J. Edgar Hoover's Legacy: A Political Snakepit at the FBI," *WP*, 10 January 1973, A23.

22 W. Mark Felt and John O'Connor, *A G-Man's Life: The FBI, Being "Deep Throat," and the Struggle for Honor in Washington* (New York: PublicAffairs, 2006) 223.

23 Telephone conversation, Ehrlichman and Novak, 5 January 1973, dictabelt #465, Box 28, Ehrlichman, SMOF, WHSF, RMNL; Gray, *In Nixon's Web*, 142–143.

24 Gray, *In Nixon's Web*, 146–147.

25 Sanford J. Ungar, *FBI* (Boston: Atlantic Monthly Press, 1976), 555–556.

26 Dean, *Blind Ambition*, 218–219.

27 "Starting on Watergate," *Time*, 22 January 1973 (published January 15), 19; Carl Bernstein and Bob Woodward, "Still Secret: Who Hired Spies and Why?" *WP*, 31 January 1973, A1.

Initially, the White House helped the defendants by making secret payments totaling $229,000 ($1.1 million in 2011 dollars) for their subsistence and lawyers' fees. By October, as the profile of the case mounted, the emphasis turned to one of trying to keep the defendants silent by promising support to their dependants until such time as executive clemency could be extended. U.S. Congress, House of Representatives, Special Subcommittee on Intelligence of the Committee on Armed Services, *Report, Inquiry into the Alleged Involvement of the Central Intelligence Agency in the Watergate and Ellsberg Matters*, 93rd Cong., 1st sess. (Washington, DC: Government Printing Office, 1973), 12.

A friend of Hunt's, Los Angeles lawyer Morton B. Jackson, who had let Hunt stay at his home when he was wanted by the FBI for questioning, told Woodward around this time that "Howard wants to become the Alger Hiss of the Right." Bernstein and Woodward, *All the President's Men*, 238.

According to McCord, pressure had been brought on the defendants as late as December to blame the operation on the CIA; but since he would not go along with the false claim against the Agency he had worked for from 1951 to 1970, the effort failed. James W. McCord, Jr., "Pressure on the Defendants to Blame the Watergate Operation on CIA," 4 May 1973, WG, FBI FOIA.

28 (David Beckwith), "The Spy in the Cold," *Time*, 29 January 1973 (published January 22), 17, 20; typewritten notes, "Interview with X," 9 October [1972], Series I, 75.18, WBWP, HRC.

Much of the January 29 article in *Time* was based on an exclusive interview of Hunt by correspondent David Beckwith—but, as it turned out, *not* the central allegation regarding Mitchell's and Colson's alleged involvement. *Time*'s editorial process was undoubtedly responsible for this disconnect. At the time, correspondents sent in a long dispatch, called a file, which was often written as a story but sometimes just consisted of unexpurgated information from their reporting notebooks. A writer in New York would turn this file into a story, sometimes mixing in information from files submitted by other *Time* correspondents. This unusual editorial process insured that all copy exhibited *Time*'s inimitable, breezy style. But the published story rarely resembled the original file, and errors frequently crept in, since style and the magazine's editorial slant trumped fact gathering. Or as Smith himself put it succinctly, he did not write the stories, he merely furnished the information to New York where it was written.

When Colson threatened to file a libel suit, Beckwith, in a sworn affidavit, stated that Hunt did not give him the information and he had not alleged as much to his editors. Thus, a reasonable inference is that it came from Felt via Sandy Smith, *Time*'s principal reporter on Watergate, and was inserted into Beckwith's account by a writer in New York. (Beckwith), "Spy in the Cold," 17, 20; Rowland Evans and Robert Novak, "Charles Colson vs. *Time*: A Reminder for the Press," *WP*, 28 January 1973, B7; Letters, "Words about Watergate," *Time*, 5 February 1973 (published January 29), 9; Curtis Prendergast with Geoffrey Colvin, *The World of Time, Inc.: The Intimate History of a Changing Enterprise, 1960–1980* (New York: Atheneum, 1986), 353; Memo, Bates to Bolz, "James W. McCord Jr., et al.," 22 June 1972, WG, FBI FOIA; Charles Colson Oral Histories, 15 June 1988 and 17 August 2007, RMNL.

29 Bernstein and Woodward, *All the President's Men*, 242–243.

30 Ibid., 243–245; typewritten notes, "Interview with My Friend," 24 January [1973], Series I, 75.18, WBWP, HRC; Woodward, *Secret Man*, 93. As before, double quotes are used to differentiate between what is and what is not enclosed in quotes in Woodward's contemporaneous typewritten notes.

Colson's role with respect to Watergate writ large was primarily exhortative, i.e., encouraging Nixon's worst instincts, together with a penchant for taking the president's demands literally, which Haldeman and Ehrlichman did not always do. But Colson's involvement was minor in terms of criminal behavior, although he did unwittingly supply the funds for the plumbers' burglary of the office of Daniel Ellsberg's psychiatrist. See Jonathan Aitken, *Charles W. Colson: A Life Redeemed* (New York: Doubleday, 2005), 147–171.

31 Bernstein and Woodward, *All the President's Men*, 243; typewritten notes, "Interview with My Friend," 24 January [1973], Series I, 75.18, WBWP, HRC.

32 Bernstein and Woodward, *All the President's Men*, 243, 245.

As John Dean pointed out in 2005, what Felt provided Woodward on January 24 was information again that turned out not to be true, although it actually may have been the "investigative assumption" of the FBI's top minds. John W. Dean, "Why the Revelation of the Identity of Deep Throat Has Only Created Another Mystery," http://writ.news.findlaw.com/dean/20050603.html, 3 June 2005.

33 Bernstein and Woodward, *All the President's Men*, 246.

34 Evans and Novak, "Charles Colson vs. *Time*," B7; Letters, "Words about Watergate," 9; author transcript, tape recording, Nixon and Dean, conversation no. 865-14, 28 February 1973, RMNL; Robert D. Novak, *The Prince of Darkness: 50 Years Reporting in Washington* (New York: Crown Forum, 2007), 234–235.

CHAPTER 9. THE SAFE CHOICE: FEBRUARY 1973

1 John W. Dean, *Blind Ambition: The End of the Story* (Palm Springs, CA: Polimedia Publishers, 2009), 358. On the leaks that would plague the Senate Watergate Committee, see, for example, Spencer Rich, "Leaks Stir Storm on Hill," *WP*, 22 June 1973, A1.

2 H. R. Haldeman, *The Haldeman Diaries: Inside the Nixon White House* CD-ROM (Los Angeles: Sony Imagesoft, 1994), 8 January 1973.

3 Ibid., 8 January 1973, 7 February 1973; Robert D. Novak, *The Prince of Darkness: 50 Years Reporting in Washington* (New York: Crown Forum, 2007), 238; Stanley I. Kutler, *Abuse of Power: The New Nixon Tapes* (New York: Free Press, 1997), 209.

4 Haldeman, *Diaries* CD-ROM, 13 February 1973; Dean, *Blind Ambition*, 221. See also WSPF transcript, tape recording, Nixon and Erlichman, conversation no. 856-4, 14 February 1973, RMNL.

5 Author transcript, tape recording, Nixon, Ehrlichman, and Gray, conversation no. 858-3, 16 February 1973, RMNL.

6 L. Patrick Gray III with Ed Gray, *In Nixon's Web: A Year in the Crosshairs of Watergate* (New York: Times Books, 2008), 158–160; author transcript, conversation no. 858-3, 16 February 1973, RMNL.

7 Gray, *In Nixon's Web*, 160; author transcript, conversation no. 858-3, 16 February 1973, RMNL.

    "Be a good conspirator," Nixon told Gray, when he first appointed him. "You've got to be totally ruthless. You've got to appear to be a nice guy, but you've got to be steely, and tough. That, believe me, is the way to run the Bureau." Moss transcript, tape recording, Nixon and Gray, conversation no. 719-12, 4 May 1972, RMNL.

8 Gray, *In Nixon's Web*, 160–163; author transcript, conversation no. 858-3, 16 February 1973, RMNL.

9 Gray, *In Nixon's Web*, 164; author transcript, conversation no. 858-3, 16 February 1973, RMNL.

10 Author transcript, conversation no. 858-3, 16 February 1973, RMNL.

11 Gray, *In Nixon's Web*, 165.

12 Author transcript, conversation no. 858-3, 16 February 1973, RMNL.

13 Gray, *In Nixon's Web*, 174.

14 Author transcript, conversation no. 858-3, 16 February 1973, RMNL.

    In the recording, Nixon recounted some specific examples of sensitive or derogatory information Hoover had shared; these have been excised.

15 Ibid.

16 Carl Bernstein and Bob Woodward, *All the President's Men* (New York: Simon & Schuster, 1974), 237–238, 251–252, 254–256; Bob Woodward and Carl Bernstein, "Hunt Linked to Dita Beard Challenge," *WP*, 21 February 1973, A1.

    An earlier article in *Newsday* actually broke the news about one of Hunt's earlier escapades, i.e., a trip he took to Colorado, but had not explained why he went there. Russell Sackett and Martin Schram, "A Watergate, ITT Link," *Newsday*, 8 February 1973, 3. On the leak investigation, see Bob Woodward, *The Secret Man: The Story of Watergate's Deep Throat* (New York: Simon & Schuster, 2005), 7–12.

17 Author transcript, tape recording, Nixon and Haldeman, conversation no. 859-38, 21 February 1973, RMNL.

18 Memo, Felt to Gebhardt, "Watergate," 21 February 1973, WG, FBI FOIA.

19 Ibid.; Memo, Acting Director to Attorney General, "James W. McCord Jr., et al.," 23 February 1973, WG, FBI FOIA.

20 Memo, Glanzer to Silbert, "National Security 'Taps,'" 7 May 1973, Box 51, Earl Silbert Chron File, WSPF, NARA.

21 Author transcript, tape recording, Nixon and Dean, conversation no. 865-14, 28 February 1973, RMNL.

22 (Sandy Smith), "Questions about Gray," *Time*, 5 March 1973 (published February 26), 14–15; "A Flat-Out Lie," *Time*, 9 July 1973 (published July 2), 38–39; W. Mark Felt, *The FBI Pyramid: From the Inside* (New York: G. P. Putnam's Sons, 1979), 278; author transcript, tape recording, Nixon, Haldeman, and Ehrlichman, conversation no. 247-4, 13

April 1971, RMNL; Memo, Jacobson to Walters, "Sensitive Coverage Placed at Request of the White House," 12 May 1973, WCS, FBI FOIA.

All the wiretaps instituted in 1969 had ended by early 1971. And while there were several domestic wiretaps ongoing when Gray became acting director, only one had anything to do with classified information. Three were on the Black Panther Party; a fourth was on the sister of a Weathermen fugitive; and a fifth was on the Communist Party headquarters in New York. Only the sixth, concerned with a navy ensign suspected of leaking to syndicated columnist Jack Anderson, involved the transmission of classified information. The Anderson surveillance was instituted in December 1971 and all wiretaps in connection with it (including one on Anderson) were discontinued by June 1972. Memo, "*New York Times* and *Washington Post* Articles Concerning Alleged Wiretaps on Newsmen," 26 February 1973, LPG, FBI FOIA.

23 Letter, Daniel Armstrong to author, 18 May 2010; Transcript, Nixon Grand Jury Testimony, NARA, 287–288, 296.

24 SCPCA, *Hearings, Watergate and Related Activities*, 93rd Cong., 1st sess., vol. 3 (Washington, DC: Government Printing Office, 1973), 920, 1069; John W. Dean, *Lost Honor* (Los Angeles: Stratford Press, 1982), 67–75.

Felt's revised memoir frankly states that "Felt leaked details of the Kissinger wiretaps on newsmen and policymakers to *Time* magazine, all but guaranteeing that Gray would be asked about the taps at his hearings. Gray had nothing to do with the operation, but Sullivan played a central role and was bound to see his chances for taking the FBI's top spot crushed in the glare of publicity." Mark Felt and John O'Connor, *A G-Man's Life: The FBI, Being "Deep Throat," and the Struggle for Honor in Washington* (New York: PublicAffairs, 2006), 223.

25 Haldeman, *Diaries* CD-ROM, 13 March 1973; Sanford J. Ungar, *FBI* (Boston: Atlantic Monthly Press, 1976), 312; William C. Sullivan with Bill Brown, *The Bureau: My Thirty Years in Hoover's FBI* (New York: W. W. Norton, 1979), 227; Dean, *Lost Honor*, 68.

Felt warned Gray, however, that there would be a "mutiny" if Sullivan were reinstated in any capacity at the Bureau. Gray, *In Nixon's Web*, 164.

26 Curtis Prendergast with Geoffrey Colvin, *The World of Time, Inc.: The Intimate History of a Changing Enterprise, 1960–1980* (New York: Atheneum, 1986), 353; (Smith), "Questions about Gray," 14–15; Haldeman, *Diaries* CD-ROM, 25 February 1973; SCP-CA, *Hearings, Watergate and Related Activities*, vol. 3, 920–921, 1070; author transcript, conversation no. 865-14, 28 February 1973, RMNL.

27 Author transcript, tape recording, Nixon and Dean, conversation no. 864-4, 27 February 1973, RMNL; author transcript, tape recording, Nixon, Dean, and Haldeman, conversation no. 878-14, 13 March 1973, RMNL; Dean, *Lost Honor*, 68; SCPCA, *Hearings, Watergate and Related Activities*, vol. 3, 920–921, 1069.

Nixon also discussed the leak to *Time* under oath in 1975; see Transcript, Nixon Grand Jury Testimony, NARA, 289–290.

28 Author transcript, conversation no. 864-4, 27 February 1973, RMNL; author transcript, conversation no. 878-14, 13 March 1973, RMNL.

29 Author transcript, conversation no. 864-4, 27 February 1973, RMNL; author transcript, conversation no. 878-14, 13 March 1973, RMNL.

As a result of this meeting, Sullivan agreed to provide Dean with a secret "Eyes Only" memorandum about controversial activities undertaken by the FBI at the behest of President Johnson. Sullivan expressed a willingness to testify that the Nixon administration's abuses were no worse than those of previous administrations. Later, Sullivan vehemently denied there was a quid pro quo, that is, that in exchange for his testimony the administration would reinstate him in the Bureau. Letter, Sullivan to Dean, "Eyes Only Mr. John Dean" with enclosure, undated, WCS, FBI FOIA; Richard J. Connolly, "FBI Ex-Official Charges Dean Lied," *WP*, 19 May 1974, F10.

30 Author transcript, conversation no. 864-4, 27 February 1973, RMNL.

In Haldeman's original telling, he had only told the president that a "guy at Justice told John Dean." Author transcript, tape recording, Nixon and Haldeman, conversation no. 370-9, 19 October 1972, RMNL.

31 Ibid.

32 Author transcript, conversation no. 864-4, 27 February 1973, RMNL.

Dean said he had recently talked about the matter to Kleindienst, and the attorney general warned him that because of what Felt knew, if he "gets way out of joint we are in serious trouble." Ibid.

33 Ibid.

34 Although the notes are dated March 5, in *All the President's Men* the meeting was described as having taken place "shortly before the [Gray] hearings" were to begin, which was February 28. The notes also reflect information published in *Time* on February 26, making February 27 the most likely date for the rendezvous. Bernstein and Woodward, *All the President's Men*, 267–268; typewritten notes, "Interview w[ith] X," 5 March [1973], Series I, 75.18, WBWP, HRC; Woodward, *Secret Man*, 12.

35 As before, double quotes are used to differentiate between what is and what is not enclosed in quotes in Woodward's contemporaneous typewritten notes. Typewritten notes, "Interview w[ith] X," 5 March [1973], Series I, 75.18, WBWP, HRC; Bernstein and Woodward, *All the President's Men*, 268.

The Nixon campaign had filed a civil lawsuit in January against several media organizations, including *Time* and the *Washington Post*, seeking disclosure of their sources as one of its chief objectives.

36 Typewritten notes, "Interview w[ith] X," 5 March [1973], Series I, 75.18, WBWP, HRC; Bernstein and Woodward, *All the President's Men*, 270; Woodward, *Secret Man*, 13; President Richard Nixon Daily Diary, February 1973, RMNL; Memo, "Watergate—Events at Initial Stage of Case," 7 June 1973, WG, FBI FOIA. See also Felt, *FBI Pyramid*, 278.

Felt did not include the blackmail allegation in his own memoir.

37 Typewritten notes, "Interview w[ith] X," 5 March [1973], Series I, 75.18, WBWP, HRC.

38 Bernstein and Woodward, *All the President's Men*, 270; typewritten notes, "Interview w[ith] X," 5 March [1973], Series I, 75.18, WBWP, HRC.

Regular FBI agents had maintained the tap on Hedrick Smith, and the surveillance, which began in June 1969, ended before release of the Pentagon Papers. The allegations are so jumbled that either Felt was purposely conflating the activities of the White House plumbers with the earlier 1969–1971 wiretaps, or Woodward misunderstood him when reconstructing the conversation. See also Seymour M. Hersh, *The Price of Power: Kissinger in the Nixon White House* (New York: Summit Books, 1983), 93.

39 Bernstein and Woodward, *All the President's Men*, 271.

40 Ibid., 270.

In *All the President's Men*, Bernstein and Woodward included this disclaimer from Gray's lawyer in a footnote: "The suggestion that Gray had pressured or blackmailed the president was 'outrageously false.'" When queried in October 2011 about Felt's disputed allegation, Woodward again acknowledged that in January 1974 it was "heatedly denied" by Gray's lawyer, Stephen Sachs. But, Woodward continued, "I remember at one [later] point reading a tape where . . . Ehrlichman [was] reporting to the president about Pat Gray essentially being quite exercised, to say the least, and it being *interpreted*—given what Pay Gray knew—as a threat. I remember seeing that later on and saying, 'Ah, that may have been what he [Felt] was talking about.'" Ibid., and author interview with Bob Woodward, 12 October 2011.

CHAPTER 10. GRAY SELF-DESTRUCTS: MARCH–MAY 1973

1 Author transcript, tape recording, Nixon and Dean, conversation no. 865-14, 28 February 1973, RMNL.

   This conversation illustrates yet again that the White House had not fully grasped by February what Felt was trying to accomplish. Nixon said he wasn't worried about Felt "at the present time"; his concern was for the future. Yet if Gray were to be installed as the permanent director, presumably Felt would have either resigned outright or accepted his fate and stopped leaking. Dean shared Nixon's misperception, stating that "things can only get more complex over there [the FBI] as we move along." In fact, they probably would have stabilized, and WSPF transcript, tape recording, Nixon and Colson, conversation no. 854-17, 13 February 1973, RMNL. Ibid.

2 Typewritten notes, "Interview with My Friend," 24 January [1973], Series I, 75.18, WBWP, HRC. "Gray Reported Chosen to Head FBI as Permanent Director," *NYT*, 17 February 1973, 21; Robert C. Byrd, "Political Partisanship Should Have No Place in the FBI," *Congressional Record*, 19 February 1973, 4349–4350; UPI, "Byrd Opposed to Gray as FBI Director," *WP*, 17 February 1973, 3; UPI, "Mansfield Says He Is 'Inclined' to Back Gray," *WP*, 20 February 1973, A3; Sanford J. Ungar, *FBI* (Boston: Atlantic Monthly Press, 1976), 534.

   Gray extended a similar offer (a specially prepared summary of all the FBI's investigative reports) to the Senate select committee investigating Watergate.

3 Letter, Hunt to Gray, "Dear Mr. Gray," 17 February 1973, WG, FBI FOIA.

4 John W. Dean, *Blind Ambition: The End of the Story* (Palm Springs, CA: Polimedia Publishers, 2009), 142. Carl Bernstein and Bob Woodward, "'Bug' Case Figure Faces Quiz," *WP*, 8 July 1972, A1; *The Public Papers of the Presidents of the United States, Richard Nixon, 1972* (Washington, DC: Government Printing Office, 1974), 828.

   It had also been reported early on—alarmingly from the administration's perspective—that Howard Hunt wanted Dean to assist him in finding a lawyer. But this mention, too, was forgotten. Tad Szulc, "Figure in Raid on Democrats Is Reported to Have Asked a Friend to Seek White House Assistance," *NYT*, 7 July 1972, 32.

5 Dean, *Blind Ambition*, 221. For the president's contemporaneous reactions to the Gray confirmation hearings, see Stanley I. Kutler, *Abuse of Power: The New Nixon Tapes* (New York: Free Press, 1997), 213–217, 219–225, 226–228, 232–233, 259, 288–290.

6 SCPCA, *Hearings, Watergate and Related Activities*, 93rd Cong., 1st sess., vol. 7 (Washington, DC: Government Printing Office, 1973), 2951; Ungar, *FBI*, 536, 543; Stanley I. Kutler, *The Wars of Watergate: The Last Crisis of Richard Nixon* (New York: Alfred A. Knopf, 1990), 266–271.

7 Author transcript, tape recording, Nixon, Dean, and Haldeman, conversation no. 878-14, 13 March 1973, RMNL.

8 H. R. Haldeman, *The Haldeman Diaries: Inside the Nixon White House* CD-ROM (Los Angeles: Sony Imagesoft, 1994), 24 March 1973.

9 (Sandy Smith), "The Fight over the Future of the FBI," *Time*, 26 March 1973 (published March 19), 17–20, 25–26, 28.

10 L. Patrick Gray III with Ed Gray, *In Nixon's Web: A Year in the Crosshairs of Watergate* (New York: Times Books, 2008), 118–119; Memo, O'Connor to Jacobson, "Watergate: Analysis of Possible Involvement of L. Patrick Gray," 26 June 1973, WG, FBI FOIA.

11 (Smith), "The Fight over the Future of the FBI," 19.

12 E-mail to author from John Dean, 15 July 2010.

13 Memo, Bowers to Kinley, "Confirmation," 21 March 1973, LPG, FBI FOIA; Memo, Bowers to Kinley, "Confirmation," 23 March 1973, LPG, FBI FOIA.

14 Haldeman, *Diaries* CD-ROM, 22 March 1973.

On June 22, FBI agents understood Dean as saying that he wasn't aware that Howard Hunt still had an office in Room 308 of the Executive Office Building. On June 27, however, Dean's assistant, Fred Fielding, disclosed that on June 20 he and Dean had reviewed the contents of two cartons containing Hunt's personal effects, which had been removed from Room 308 on June 19. The seeming inconsistency between these two statements was noted at the time, but the Bureau was far from realizing that John Dean was also the desk officer for the cover-up. Letterhead Memo, "Article Appearing in 6/30/72 City Edition of the *Washington Daily News*," 30 June 1972, WG, FBI FOIA; Memo, Gebhardt to Baker, "Confirmation," 7 March 1973, WG, FBI FOIA.

In his Senate testimony, and later in *Blind Ambition*, Dean stated that a careful parsing of the FBI agents' June 22 question to him shows that he didn't lie but was simply misunderstood. Thus, Senator Byrd managed to get Pat Gray to call Dean a liar over what was really a misunderstanding. Dean, *Blind Ambition*, 259, 266; e-mail to author from John Dean, 2 June 2011.

15 Author interview with Angelo J. Lano, 4 November 2010; Letterhead Memo, "Article Appearing in 6/30/72 City Edition of the *Washington Daily News*," 30 June 1972, WG, FBI FOIA; Gray handwritten notes, "Cha[rles] Nuzum Came In . . . ," 27 March 1973, WG, FBI FOIA.

16 Gray, *In Nixon's Web*, 231–232.

17 Barry Sussman, *The Great Cover-up: Nixon and the Scandal of Watergate* (Arlington, VA: Seven Locks Press, 1992), 159; "[Howard] Simons interview," circa 1973, 48, Series I, 8.2, WBWP, HRC; Carl Bernstein and Bob Woodward, *All the President's Men* (New York: Simon & Schuster, 1974), 274.

18 Dean, *Blind Ambition*, 232, 239.

19 Haldeman, *Diaries* CD-ROM, 24 March 1973.

20 Ibid., 2 April 1973.

21 Rowland Evans and Robert Novak, "They've Given Up on Mr. Gray," *WP*, 25 March 1973, C7; Haldeman, *Diaries* CD-ROM, 24 and 31 March 1973.

22 Memo, Bowers to Kinley, "Confirmation," 5 April 1973, LPG, FBI FOIA; Haldeman, *Diaries* CD-ROM, 26 March and 5 April 1973.

23 Haldeman, *Diaries* CD-ROM, 15 and 26 April 1973; Kutler, *Abuse of Power*, 318–319.

24 Ronald Kessler, *The Secrets of the FBI* (New York: Crown, 2011), 54; Leonard M. "Bucky" Walters Oral History, 4 March 2003, SOCXFBI, 8–9.

25 Ronald Kessler, *Bureau: The Secret History of the FBI* (New York: St. Martin's Press, 2002), 181; FD-302, "Mrs. Marge Neenan," 9 December 1974, LPG, FBI FOIA; Walters Oral History, 4 March 2003, 8.

26 Memo, Felt to Walters, "Watergate," 22 May 1973, WG, FBI FOIA; Gray, *In Nixon's Web*, 90, 184–185; Memo, "Watergate—Events at Initial Stage of Case," 7 June 1973, WG, FBI FOIA.

27 W. Mark Felt, *The FBI Pyramid: From the Inside* (New York: G. P. Putnam's Sons, 1979), 293; Letter, Gray to Rockefeller Public Service Awards, Princeton University, "Felt Nomination," 17 April 1973, WMF, FBI FOIA.

28 Bob Woodward, *The Secret Man: The Story of Watergate's Deep Throat* (New York: Simon & Schuster, 2005), 97; Bernstein and Woodward, *All the President's Men*, 288.

29 Kutler, *Abuse of Power*, 345; John M. Crewdson, "Nixon Withdraws Gray Nomination as FBI Director," *NYT*, 6 April 1973, 1; Ronald J. Ostrow, "Nixon Sounded Him Out about Heading FBI, Petersen Testifies," *LAT*, 31 May 1974, A1.

30 Haldeman, *Diaries* CD-ROM, 26 April 1973.

31 Kutler, *Abuse of Power*, 347; Haldeman, *Diaries* CD-ROM, 26 and 27 April 1973; President Richard Nixon Daily Diary, 27 April 1973, RMNL; William Ruckelshaus Oral History, 12 April 2007, RMNL, 4–5.

32 Felt, *FBI Pyramid*, 293–295.

33 Warren Weaver, "Morale of FBI Sagged before Gray Resignation," *NYT*, 28 April 1973, 14.

34 Author interview with William D. Ruckelshaus, 12 June 2007; Ruckelshaus Oral History, 12 April 2007, 6.

35 Felt, *FBI Pyramid*, 296; Ungar, *FBI*, 545; "FBI Officials Urge President to Appoint Insider as Director," *NYT*, 1 May 1973, 32; Ruckelshaus interview, 12 June 2007; Ruckelshaus Oral History, 12 April 2007, 5.

According to Ungar, every special agent in charge signed the letter except Wallace Estill, head of the Knoxville, Tennessee Field Office. He was a longtime supporter of Sullivan, and "suspected the telegram was a ploy on behalf of the candidacy of an enemy of Sullivan, Mark Felt." Ungar, *FBI*, 545.

36 Ungar, *FBI*, 556; Ruckelshaus interview, 12 June 2007; Felt, *FBI Pyramid*, 296.

37 Richard M. Cohen and Jules Witcover, *A Heartbeat Away: The Investigation and Resignation of Vice President Spiro T. Agnew* (New York: Viking Press, 1974), 78; Woodward, *Secret Man*, 40.

Cohen wrote that Woodward told him at the time the source for the tip was Deep Throat, but Woodward claimed he "did not identify the source at all." In *The Secret Man*, Woodward misdates the Agnew leak, writing as if it occurred in the spring of 1972 (or even earlier) when it almost certainly occurred no earlier than April/May 1973. The mistake, moreover, is repeated in Woodward's oral history for the Nixon Library, coupled with the interviewer's erroneous suggestion that Felt leaked stories adverse to the administration to the *Post* reporter while Hoover was still alive—which was certainly not the case. In an October 2011 interview, Woodward affirmed that the chronology of the Agnew leak as presented in *The Secret Man* "looks like it's not right." Bob Woodward Oral History, 14 December 2010, RMNL; e-mail to author from Richard M. Cohen, 30 April 2011; author interview with Bob Woodward, 12 October 2011.

38 Woodward, *Secret Man*, 40, 150; Cohen and Witcover, *Heartbeat Away*, 78–79.

On April 10, Agnew had called Haldeman to seek his assistance in contacting U.S.

Senator Glenn Beall (R-Maryland), who was the brother of the chief federal prosecutor looking into the allegations. The vice president wanted the White House to express concern about the course of the investigation, hoping that would steer prosecutors away from making Agnew a target. H. R. Haldeman, *The Haldeman Diaries: Inside the Nixon White House* (New York: G. P. Putnam's Sons, 1994), 629–630.

39 Richard M. Cohen and Bill Richards, "Jury Investigating Baltimore County Executive," *WP*, 22 May 1973, A1.

40 Felt also leaked to *Time* magazine information about the illicit payments to Agnew. John Stacks, "The Man Who Was Deep Throat: Chasing Mark Felt," http://www.time .com/time/politics/article/0,8599,1868043,00.html, 19 December 2008.

41 Bob Woodward and Carl Bernstein "Wiretaps Put on Phones of 2 Reporters," *WP*, 3 May 1973, A1; Bernstein and Woodward, *All the President's Men*, 271.

42 Felt learned about the details of the wiretapping operation on October 20, 1971, from a memo Edward S. Miller (Sullivan's successor) prepared at Felt's direct request. Memo, Miller to Rosen, "Sensitive Coverage Placed at Request of the White House," 20 October 1971, WCS, FBI FOIA; FD-302, "Edward S. Miller," 12 May 1973, WCS, FBI FOIA.

43 Author interview with Donald E. Santarelli, 2 June 2011.

44 Gray, *In Nixon's Web*, 298; typewritten notes, "Interview w[ith] X," 5 March [1973], Series I, 75.18, WBWP, HRC; typewritten notes, "Meeting" 24 March [1973], Series I, 75.18, WBWP, HRC; Bernstein and Woodward, *All the President's Men*, 271.

   Woodward's typewritten notes dated 24 March 1973 were initially released as part of the Mark Felt file by the Ransom Center in 2007, which houses the Woodward and Bernstein collection. But as Ed Gray (son of Pat Gray) was the first to discern, the one-page document dated March 24 could not have reflected an interview *with* Felt. The notes twice refer to Felt in the third person, and there is no mention of a meeting around this date with Deep Throat either in *All the President's Men* or *The Secret Man*. Meanwhile, Felt's name is not mentioned in the third person in any interview notes from verified meetings that took place between Woodward and Deep Throat. In an October 2011 interview, Woodward agreed that "there's no way [the March 24 typewritten notes are from] a conversation with Mark Felt." He thought the document had simply been misfiled at some point. Gray, *In Nixon's Web*, 298–300; Woodward interview, 12 October 2011.

45 The article, for example, cited the *Time* magazine story of February 26, but erroneously stated it was published on March 12.

46 Woodward and Bernstein, "Wiretaps Put on Phones of 2 Reporters," A1; typewritten notes, "Interview w[ith] X," 5 March [1973], Series I, 75.18, WBWP, HRC.

47 Memo, Ruckelshaus to Felt, "Wiretaps on Newspapermen," 4 May 1973, WCS, FBI FOIA; Ungar, *FBI*, 546. Byrne dismissed the case against Ellsberg after it became known that Ellsberg had been overheard inadvertently on one of the wiretaps and the FBI could not produce the records promptly.

48 Memo, Jacobson to Walters, "Wiretaps on Newspapermen," 11 May 1973, WCS, FBI FOIA.

49 John Dean, *Lost Honor* (Los Angeles: Stratford Press, 1982), 68–69; Felt, *FBI Pyramid*, 140–141; Ray Wannall, *The Real J. Edgar Hoover: For the Record* (Paducah, KY: Turner Publishing Company, 2000), 147.

   Sullivan insisted on putting his answers in a written memo to Ruckelshaus rather than submit to an FBI interview. Memo, Sullivan to Ruckelshaus, "Sensitive Coverage Placed at Request of the White House," 11 May 1973, WCS, FBI FOIA.

50 Kutler, *Abuse of Power*, 460–466; author transcript, tape recording, Nixon and Haig, conversation no. 916-11, 11 May 1973, RMNL.

51 Author transcript, conversation no. 916-11, 11 May 1973, RMNL.

52 Ibid.

53 Ibid. By "reforms" Haig meant the Huston plan.

54 Ungar, *FBI*, 557.

    Crewdson's article was not the only one to come out after Ruckelshaus initiated the investigation but before he could make its results public. *Time*'s Sandy Smith also contributed to a May 7 cover story that shed more light on the Nixon administration's wiretapping since 1969. "Nixon's Nightmare: Fighting to Be Believed," *Time*, 14 May 1973 (published May 7), 17–26, 30–32.

55 Kutler, *Abuse of Power*, 463.

56 Author transcript, tape recording, Nixon and Haig, conversation no. 165-10, 12 May 1973, RMNL.

57 Felt, *FBI Pyramid*, 303.

58 Bernstein and Woodward, *All the President's Men*, 316–317; Carl Bernstein and Bob Woodward, "Vast GOP Undercover Operation Originated in 1969," *WP*, 17 May 1972, A1; typewritten notes, "Interview w[ith] X," 5 March [1973], Series I, 75.18, WBWP, HRC.

59 Bernstein and Woodward, *All the President's Men*, 317.

60 Ibid., 318; Woodward, *Secret Man*, 98; William Claiborne, "Nixon Name Used to Pressure CIA," *WP*, 17 May 1973, A1.

    Among the untruths Felt told Woodward on May 16 were these assertions:

- that Dean had talked to Senator Howard Baker, the ranking member of the Senate Watergate Committee, and that Baker was "in the bag completely";
- that President Nixon had personally threatened John Dean;
- that Haldeman, Ehrlichman, Mitchell, Mardian, and Dean had contributed their own personal funds to support the cover-up, and that Mitchell had supposedly been "cut loose" after he did not meet his quota.

    See John W. Dean, "Why the Revelation of the Identity of Deep Throat Has Only Created Another Mystery," http://writ.news.findlaw.com/dean/20050603.html, 3 June 2005, and Exchange of Letters to the Editor, "'A G-Man's Life,'" *NYT Book Review*, 11 June 2006, F6.

61 Bernstein and Woodward, *All the President's Men*, 317–320; Woodward, *Secret Man*, 98–99.

62 Woodward, *Secret Man*, 101.

63 Woodward Oral History, 14 December 2010; Dean, "Why the Revelation of the Identity of Deep Throat Has Only Created Another Mystery."

    Although Woodward acknowledged his report was overwrought, he has nonetheless asserted that Felt was probably referring to the CIA's alleged involvement in domestic espionage, elements of which would become public in 1975. But neither the Commission on CIA Activities within the United States (Rockefeller Commission) nor the Senate Select Committee to Study Governmental Operations with Respect to Intelligence Activities (Church Committee) found any evidence that newspapers or reporters had ever been put under CIA surveillance for printing stories about White House misconduct.

See, for example, Commission on CIA Activities within the United States, *Report to the President* (Washington, DC: Government Printing Office, 1975), 199–203.

64 Gray, *In Nixon's Web*, 51.

65 Jeremiah O'Leary, "Hoover Feud Figure Leaving Justice Post," *WS*, 24 June 1973, A2.

CHAPTER 11. THE MAKING OF DEEP THROAT: 1973–1981

1 Jeremiah O'Leary, "Veteran Agent May Head FBI," *WS*, 27 May 1973, A1.

2 Leonard Garment Oral History, 5 October 2007, RMNL, 9–10; Aaron Latham, "How the *Washington Post* Gave Nixon Hell," *New York*, 14 May 1973, 56; Leonard Downie, Jr., *The New Muckrakers: An Inside Look at America's Investigative Reporters* (Washington, DC: New Republic Books, 1976), 43; Memo, Gergen to the President, "Conversations with Bob Woodward on Watergate," 28 April 1973, Watergate Issues File, Box 106, SMOF, WHCF, RMNL.

   During one panel discussion in the late 1990s, Sam Dash, the Senate Watergate Committee's majority counsel, was asked about disclosures to the press. "Leak?" he responded. "I leaked all the time. Everybody did." Stanley I. Kutler, "Watergate Misremembered: The Shallow Debate about Deep Throat," http://www.slate.com/id/2067123/, 18 June 2002.

3 An outline of the book had been due as early as the previous October. Carl Bernstein and Bob Woodward, *All the President's Men* (New York: Simon & Schuster, 1974), 182; Downie, *New Muckrakers*, 42; Alicia B. Shepard, *Woodward and Bernstein: Life in the Shadow of Watergate* (Hoboken, NJ: John Wiley & Sons, 2007), 59–61, 65, 68.

4 "Watergate on Film," *Time*, 29 March 1976 (published March 22), 54–58, 63; John W. Dean, *Lost Honor* (Los Angeles: Stratford Press, 1982), 78–79.

5 As Woodward put it in 1976, when the film version came out, "Redford was a factor in getting us to write the kind of book we wrote." Robert Brent Toplin, *History by Hollywood: The Use and Abuse of the American Past* (Urbana: University of Illinois Press, 1996), 182–183; Shepard, *Woodward and Bernstein*, 75–76; David Greenberg, "Throat Clearing: Watergate Conspiracy Theories That Still Won't Die," http://www.slate.com/id/2119989/, 1 June 2005; Eric Pace, "Film Rights on Watergate Book Sold," *NYT*, 7 March 1974, 33; Amy Laskowski, "She Made Hollywood Stars Shine," *Boston (MA) BU Today*, 5 February 2010; W. Joseph Campbell, *Getting It Wrong: Ten of the Greatest Misreported Stories in American Journalism* (Berkeley, CA: University of California Press, 2010), 119.

6 Bob Woodward Oral History, 14 December 2010, RMNL.

   After reading the first few chapters, the S&S editor decided that the new approach worked well. Ibid.

7 Timothy Crouse, *The Boys on the Bus* (New York: Random House, 2003), 292.

   Woodward disclosed to Crouse that "somebody at the Justice Department" was the source for the October 30, 1972, quote that alleged the "whole damn [Watergate] thing [was] a Haldeman operation." When *All the President's Men* was published in June 1974, an astute reporter might have noticed that a quote directly attributed to Deep Throat in the book had also been linked to an official in the Justice Department—which, of course, encompassed the FBI. Bernstein and Woodward, *All the President's*

Men, 198; Crouse, *Boys on the Bus*, 296; Carl Bernstein and Bob Woodward, "Magazine Says Nixon Aide Admits Disruption Effort," *WP*, 30 October 1972, A1.

8 AP, "Hugh Sloan Called Major Source for News Articles on Watergate," *NYT*, 8 April 1974, 25; Shepard, *Woodward and Bernstein*, 102.

9 Woodward Oral History, 14 December 2010, RMNL.

10 Latham, "How the *Washington Post* Gave Nixon Hell," 49.

11 Richard Harwood, "Laurence Stern, Prize-Winning *Post* Editor, Dies at 50," *WP*, 12 August 1979, C7.

12 Laurence Stern, "Bureau Hurt by Watergate," *WP*, 17 June 1973, A1.

13 Ibid.; see also John M. Crewdson, "FBI Warns Staff on Leaking Data," *NYT*, 26 August 1973, 1.

14 Bernstein and Woodward were asked in 2008 via e-mail if either recalled being interviewed by Stern in 1973 for his story on the FBI. Bernstein did not respond, and Woodward wrote that the article "Does not ring a bell with me. Remember by June 1973 the *Post* had a dozen or more reporters on the story." While the second sentence is true, it ignores the fact that Bernstein and Woodward had an almost proprietary interest in the topic at the *Post*—one that was respected as such by the paper's editors and reporters, starting with Bradlee. More to the point, Stern was clearly writing about press coverage of the scandal in the months immediately following the break-in. That was precisely when Woodward and Bernstein so dominated Watergate coverage that in and outside the paper they became the seamless reportorial team known by the contraction "Woodstein." E-mail to author from Bob Woodward, 26 June 2008.

15 Stern, "Bureau Hurt by Watergate," A1; W. Mark Felt, *The FBI Pyramid: From the Inside* (New York: G. P. Putnam's Sons, 1979), 221.

16 James McCartney, "The *Washington Post* and Watergate: How Two Davids Slew Goliath," *Columbia Journalism Review*, July/August 1973, 15, 16.

17 Crewdson, "FBI Warns Staff on Leaking Data," 1; see also John M. Crewdson, "A Saddened Witness," *NYT*, 6 August 1973, 22.

18 Bob Woodward, *The Secret Man: The Story of Watergate's Deep Throat* (New York: Simon & Schuster, 2005), 110, 113.

19 Author interview with Roger L. Depue, 19 May 2011.

20 Memo, "Mr. Kelley," 29 November 1973, WMF, FBI FOIA; Felt, *FBI Pyramid*, 12; John D. O'Connor, "I'm the Guy They Called Deep Throat," *Vanity Fair*, July 2005, 133; author interview with Paul V. Daly, 25 May 2011.

21 Carl Bernstein and Bob Woodward, "Parts 'Inaudible,'" *WP*, 8 November 1973, A1. How Felt knew about the tampering remains a mystery to this day. Woodward wrote in *The Secret Man* that Felt "was in touch with many friends [at the White House]" even after he left the Bureau, and also that "once you're in the FBI you never truly leave it." It was true that Felt had developed good contacts in the White House after serving as the FBI's liaison for three years. But knowledge of the erasure was very limited initially; only Nixon, his three lawyers, presidential secretary Rose Mary Woods, chief of staff Alexander Haig, and presidential aide Stephen Bull knew about the gap. But Woods's brother, Joseph I. Woods, was a former FBI agent, and she had also remained friends with former FBI executive Louis Nichols. Either connection might explain how Felt learned about the erasure and/or acquired gossip about the White House. (Hays Gorey), "'Deep Throat': Narrowing the Field," *Time*, 3 May 1976 (published April 26),

17–18; William B. Anderson Oral History, 14 February 2008, SOCXFBI, 14; Woodward, *Secret Man*, 103; Woodward Oral History, 14 December 2010.

22 Bernstein and Woodward, "Parts 'Inaudible,'" A1. Stephen Bull, who maintained the taping system, later suggested that the gap was caused by the Uher transcription machine used by Rose Mary Woods. The machine, according to Bull, was known to malfunction from time to time. Stephen Bull Oral History, 25 June 2007, RMNL, 25–26.

23 Typewritten notes, "Interview with X," 9 October [1972], Series I, 75.18, WBWP, HRC.

Despite all that was left out, when a leading "profiler," Roger L. Depue, the former unit chief of the FBI's Behavioral Sciences Unit, was retained by NBC's *Dateline* program in 2002, he determined, on the basis of all the remarks contained in *All the President's Men*, that Deep Throat was a "white male, about 50 years of age, from the Midwest or West Coast, of blue-collar upbringing . . . [in] law enforcement . . . [and] he did not work in the White House." This was nearly a spot-on identification of Mark Felt, except that he was fifty-nine years old in 1972, and from Idaho. Roger L. Depue Oral History, 15 February 2006, SOCXFBI, 12.

24 AP, "Hugh Sloan Called Major Source for News Articles on Watergate," 25; Crewdson, "A Saddened Witness," 22.

Woodward called Pat Gray's attorney, Stephen Sachs, to inform him the blackmail allegation was going to be included in the book about Watergate he was writing with Bernstein. When Sachs asked Gray about the charge on January 30, 1974, Gray said, "That is false. *Insanely* false. . . . Tell those bastards that that is horribly, palpably false." Despite the vehemence of Gray's denial, and the fact that he risked being proven a liar by the Nixon tape recordings, the allegation was nonetheless included a few months later in *All the President's Men*. When Gray read that the source for the allegation was Deep Throat, it contributed greatly to his lasting conviction that Woodward's secret man did not really exist. He was a fabrication, designed, in part, to shield the authors from legitimate libel suits. L. Patrick Gray III with Ed Gray, *In Nixon's Web: A Year in the Crosshairs of Watergate* (New York: Times Books, 2008), 180–181.

25 Campbell, *Getting It Wrong*, 117.

26 David Von Drehle, "FBI's No. 2 Was 'Deep Throat,'" *WP*, 1 June 2005, A6; AP, "Hugh Sloan Called Major Source for New Articles on Watergate," 25; Harry Rosenfeld, "Don't Expect Dean to Solve It," *ATU*, 2 June 2002, B5.

27 John Limpert, "Deep Throat: If It Isn't Tricia It Must Be . . . ," *Washingtonian*, June 1974, 17; Timothy Noah, "Another Bulletin from the Deep Throat Desk," http://www.slate.com/id/1003283/, 26 July 1999.

Waldrop, who began covering Washington in 1933, was editor of the *Washington Times-Herald* before it was bought out by the *Post* in 1954.

28 Dennis Farney, "If You Drink Scotch, Smoke, Read, Maybe You're 'Deep Throat,'" *WSJ*, 25 June 1974, 1; John Limpert, "Deeper into Deep Throat," *Washingtonian*, August 1974, 17–18.

Another telling clue that was widely overlooked appeared in a book by Richard Cohen and Jules Witcover about the resignation of Vice President Agnew. Entitled *A Heartbeat Away*, the book revealed that Deep Throat was the source of the tip that Woodward shared with Cohen in the spring of 1973 about an investigation of Agnew. It tended to point the finger in the direction of the FBI, since the tip was that "FBI files contained apparently unverified allegations that Agnew had accepted a bribe while vice president." Cohen later recalled that he would never have referred to Deep Throat "without [Woodward's] permission." Richard M. Cohen and Jules Witcover, *A Heartbeat Away* (New York: Viking Press, 1974), 78; e-mail to author from Richard M. Cohen, 15 May 2011.

29 Limpert, "Deeper into Deep Throat," 17–18. Asked in 2009 if he could recall the identity of his Justice Department source, Limpert said he could not.

30 Edward Jay Epstein, "Did the Press Uncover Watergate?" *Commentary*, July 1974, 24.

31 Rob Modic, "Ex-Official Wants FBI Put under Senate Control," *Elyria (OH) Chronicle-Telegram*, 25 October 1973, F1; Mike Wolk, "'White House Meddled with FBI,'" *Camden (NJ) Courier Post*, 11 October 1973, 33.

32 Wolk, "'White House Meddled with FBI,'" 33; Modic, "Ex-Official Wants FBI Put under Senate Control," F1; Joan Mitchell, "Felt Flaunts FBI Fibre," *University of New Haven (CT) News*, 19 April 1974, 1.

33 Joseph A. Lastelic, "Mark Felt Recommends FBI Changes," *Kansas City (MO) Star*, 1 October 1975, 14.

Epstein's article in *Commentary* was the first to point out that *All the President's Men* unfairly elevated the press's role in uncovering the scandal. To the late Katharine Graham's credit, the *Washington Post* publisher tried to correct this misinterpretation. "Sometimes people accuse us of bringing down a president, which, of course, we didn't do," she said in 1997. "The processes that caused [Nixon's] resignation were constitutional." The public's refusal to entertain (or remember) the complexities of the matter is largely responsible for this false perception. Epstein, "Did the Press Uncover Watergate?" 21–24; Campbell, *Getting It Wrong*, 122.

34 Woodward, *Secret Man*, 120–121.

35 Kathleen Patterson, "Former FBI Man Denies Role in Watergate Leaks," *Kansas City (MO) Times*, 18 November 1974, 3A; Epstein, "Did the Press Uncover Watergate?" 24; Farney, "If You Drink Scotch, Smoke, Read," 1; Woodward, *Secret Man*, 117.

36 John M. Crewdson, "Sabotaging the GOP's Rivals: Story of a $100,000 Operation," *NYT*, 9 July 1973, 1; John M. Crewdson, "Sabotage by Segretti: Network of Amateurs," *NYT*, 10 July 1973, 1.

37 Memo, Jacobson to Director, "Watergate—Alleged Leak to *New York Times* re Donald Segretti Matter," 23 July 1973, WIDI, FBI FOIA; Jacobson to Director, "Watergate—Alleged Leak to *New York Times* re Donald Segretti Matter," 2 October 1973, WIDI, FBI FOIA; Ronald J. Ostrow, "FBI Investigating Its Former No. 2 Official," *LAT*, 17 November 1974, A1; Memo, Legal Counsel to Jacobson, "Watergate—Alleged Leak to the *New York Times* re Donald Segretti Matter," 31 May 1974, WMF, FBI FOIA.

38 Ruckelshaus did not tell Kelley the true story about how he learned that Felt had allegedly leaked to Crewdson, viz., via a phone call from a man who introduced himself as "Crewdson." Instead, Ruckelshaus said that Jack Conmy investigated the matter after publication of the May 11 article, and that Conmy learned from Crewdson that Felt was the chief source. Memo, Jacobson to Callahan, "Watergate—Alleged Leak to *New York Times* re Donald Segretti Matter," 4 April 1974, WIDI, FBI FOIA; FD-302, "Jack L. Conmy," 19 August 1974, WIDI, FBI FOIA; FD-302, "William D. Ruckelshaus," 27 August 1974, WIDI, FBI FOIA; Memo, Bassett to Callahan, "Watergate—Alleged Leak to *New York Times* re Donald Segretti Matter," 5 September 1974, WIDI, FBI FOIA; Memo, Jacobson to Director, "Watergate—Alleged Leak to *New York Times* re Donald Segretti Matter," 12 October 1973, WIDI, FBI FOIA.

39 Author interview with confidential source, 6 November 2010; Memo, Jacobson to Director, "Watergate—Alleged Leak to *New York Times* re Segretti Matter," 23 July 1973, WIDI, FBI FOIA; Memo, Jacobson to Director, "Watergate—Alleged Leak to *New York Times* re Donald Segretti Matter," 24 July 1973, WIDI, FBI FOIA; FD-302, "Jack L. Conmy," 19 August 1974, WIDI, FBI FOIA.

John Crewdson declined to talk about this matter when approached; William Ruckelshaus could not recall the incident. E-mail to author from John Crewdson, 23 May 2011; e-mail to author from William D. Ruckelshaus, 4 October 2011.

40 Memo, Jacobson to Director, "Watergate—Alleged Leak to *New York Times* re Donald Segretti Matter," 13 August 1973, WIDI, FBI FOIA; Memo, Kelley to Callahan, et al., "Information Appearing in *The New York Times*," 13 August 1973, WIDI, FBI FOIA; Robert H. Phelps, *God and the Editor: My Search for Meaning at the* New York Times (Syracuse, NY: Syracuse University Press, 2009), 216–217; Memo, Jacobson to Director, "Watergate—Alleged Leak to *New York Times* re Donald Segretti Matter," 12 October 1973, WIDI, FBI FOIA.

41 Bryce Nelson, "Two Nixon Aides Helped Break Watergate Story, Reporters Say," *LAT*, 8 April 1974, A1; Crewdson, "FBI Warns Staff on Leaking Data," 1.

42 Memo, Jacobson to Callahan, "Watergate—Alleged Leak to *New York Times* re Segretti Matter," 4 April 1974, WIDI, FBI FOIA.

43 Author interview with Angelo J. Lano, 4 November 2010.

In an infamous episode only partially depicted in *All the President's Men*, Bernstein and Woodward suggested that Lano was one of their sources, and threatened to expose him as such. In point of fact, SAC Robert Kunkel authorized Lano to be in contact with Bernstein but only for the purpose of having "Bernstein identify his source of information for numerous stories he has written" about Watergate. Angelo J. Lano, "Sworn Statement," 26 October 1972, WG, FBI FOIA; Memo, Acting Director to Attorney General, "James W. McCord Jr., et al.," 26 October 1972, WG, FBI FOIA; Paul P. Magallanes Oral History, 25 August 2005, SOCXFBI, 15.

44 FD-302, "Mark Felt," 17 June 1974, WIDI, FBI FOIA; Letter, Felt to Webster, "Leak of Confidential FBI Documents to *New York Times* Reporter [John Crewdson], FOIA Request," 19 June 1978, WMF, FBI FOIA; Memo, Legal Counsel to Jacobson, "Watergate—Alleged Leak to the *New York Times* re Donald Segretti Matter," 31 May 1974, WMF, FBI FOIA.

45 FD-302, "Mark Felt," 17 June 1974, WIDI, FBI FOIA; Letter, Felt to Webster, "Leak of Confidential FBI Documents to *New York Times* Reporter [John Crewdson], FOIA Request," 19 June 1978, WMF, FBI FOIA; Memo, Legal Counsel to Jacobson, "Watergate—Alleged Leak to the *New York Times* re Donald Segretti Matter," 31 May 1974, WMF, FBI FOIA.

46 Lano interview, 4 November 2010.

47 FD-302, "Mark Felt," 17 June 1974, WIDI, FBI FOIA.

48 FD-302, "Carol R. Tschudy," 14 June 1974, WIDI, FBI FOIA.

49 Memo, Legal Counsel to Jacobson, "Watergate—Alleged Leak to the *New York Times* re Donald Segretti Matter," 31 May 1974, WMF, FBI FOIA; FD-302, "William C. Sullivan," 17 June 1974, WIDI, FBI FOIA.

50 Letter, Felt to Kelley, "Dear Clarence," 20 June 1974, WMF, FBI FOIA; Felt, *FBI Pyramid*, 55; Clarence M. Kelley and James Kirkpatrick Davis, *Kelley: The Story of an FBI Director* (Kansas City, MO: Andrews, McMeel & Parker, 1987), 63.

51 Letter, Kelley to Felt, "Dear Mark," 3 July 1974, WMF, FBI FOIA.

Felt's protestations about being fingered as Deep Throat had an impact on Kelley, if not in 1974, then later. He wrote in his memoir that "Not long ago many people thought Deep Throat might have been my old friend Mark Felt. . . . This is nonsense." Kelley, *Story of an FBI Director*, 154–155.

52 AP, "Hugh Sloan Called Major Source for News Articles on Watergate," 25; Eric Pace, "'Gulag,' in Huge Quantity, Goes to the Stores Early," *NYT*, 7 June 1974, 24; Michael Schudson, *Watergate in American Memory: How We Remember, Forget, and Reconstruct the Past* (New York: Basic Books, 1992), 112.

As Woodward acknowledged in his Nixon Library oral history, *All the President's Men* only left out Felt's name and that he worked at the FBI. Woodward Oral History, 14 December 2010.

53 "Covering Watergate: Success and Backlash," *Time*, 8 July 1974 (published July 1), 68–73; Woodward, *Secret Man*, 116; Woodward Oral History, 14 December 2010, RMNL.

54 FD-302, "William D. Ruckelshaus," 18 July 1974, WIDI, FBI FOIA; Memo, Bassett to Callahan, "Alleged Leak to *New York Times* re Donald Segretti Matter," 31 July 1974, WMF, FBI FOIA.

55 "Source of Leaks Sought by FBI," *NYT*, 26 September 1974, 17; Ostrow, "FBI Investigating Its Former No. 2 Official," A1; Patterson, "Former FBI Man Denies Role in Watergate Leaks," 3A.

56 Ostrow, "FBI Investigating Its Former No. 2 Official," A1.

57 Sanford J. Ungar, *FBI* (Boston: Atlantic Monthly Press, 1976), 557.

58 Downie, *New Muckrakers*, 39; Schudson, *Watergate in American Memory*, 104.

The film's treatment of Simons and Sussman led to a lot of hard feelings (although Sussman had already stopped talking to Woodward, once a good friend, years before because he had been cut out of the book project that resulted in *All the President's Men*). Sussman was not even a character in the movie, and Simons was portrayed in a way that trivialized his role, and made him seem a "mere functionary" under Bradlee. Simons became so "embittered by the movie version co-opting the truth" that his friendship with Bradlee was never the same afterwards. Shepard, *Woodward and Bernstein*, 83, 142.

59 William E. Lenchtenburg, "All the President's Men," in Mark C. Carnes, ed., *Past Imperfect: History According to the Movies* (New York: Henry Holt, 1995), 290.

60 Von Drehle, "FBI's No. 2 Was 'Deep Throat,'" A6; Frank Rich, "Don't Follow the Money," *NYT*, 12 June 2005, C14.

The film, moreover, underscored one clue about Felt's identity, though it was not recognized as such at the time. "But we talked about [George] Wallace," Woodward pleads with Deep Throat early on. The connection to the Wallace disclosure had first been mentioned in Barry Sussman's 1974 Watergate history; undoubtedly, it was a good clue, the disclosure of which discomfited Woodward. Dean, *Lost Honor*, 94; Barry Sussman, *The Great Cover-up: Nixon and the Scandal of Watergate* (Arlington, VA: Seven Locks Press, 1992), 102.

61 Shepard, *Woodward and Bernstein*, 147–149; Richard Reeves, "Lots of Footwork, No Footnotes," *NYT Book Review*, 18 April 1976, 174; Schudson, *Watergate in American Memory*, 114–115; (Hays Gorey), "'Deep Throat': Narrowing the Field," *Time*, 3 May 1976 (published April 26), 17–18.

62 Bradlee's knowledge of Deep Throat had been previously limited to his "job, expe-

rience, access, and expertise." He knew in which agency Felt worked, and that the information he provided was "consistently right." Although it was often assumed that managing editor Howard Simons knew or eventually learned Deep Throat's identity, he did not. Bernstein and Woodward, *All the President's Men*, 145–146; Ben Bradlee, *A Good Life: Newspapering and Other Adventures* (New York: Simon & Schuster, 1995), 365; Ben Bradlee Oral History, 14 December 2010, RMNL; Woodward Oral History, 14 December 2010, RMNL; Leon Friedman and William F. Levantrosser, eds., *Watergate and Afterward: The Legacy of Richard M. Nixon* (Westport, CT: Greenwood Press, 1992), 178, 185.

63 (Hays Gorey), "Woodward on the Record—Sort Of," *Time*, 3 May 1976 (published April 26), 17.

64 John M. Crewdson, "Ex-FBI Aide Sees 'Scapegoat' Role," *NYT*, 30 August 1976, 20.

65 Dean, *Lost Honor*, 2–3, 191.

66 Dean, *Lost Honor*, 2–3, 47, 84, 191, 219, 292–295; John Stacks, "The Man Who Was Deep Throat," http://www.time.com/time/politics/article/0,8599,1868043,00.html, 19 December 2008.

67 Anthony Marro, "Gray and 2 Ex-FBI Aides Deny Guilt as 700 at Court Applaud Them," *NYT*, 21 April 1978, 17.

68 Felt, *FBI Pyramid*, 226.

De Toledano had advised Nixon to burn the secret tape recordings "on the White House lawn" during Watergate. He received half the proceeds from Felt's memoir, although he was not listed as a coauthor and his name appeared only on the copyright page. In 2003, Felt's son paid de Toledano $10,000 for rights to any augmentation of the book; two years later, when Felt came forward as Deep Throat, de Toledano sued the son on the basis that this revelation was of commercial value and had been withheld. De Toledano also was scorching in his criticism of Felt after the disclosure. Douglas Martin, "Ralph de Toledano, 90, Writer Known as a Nixon Friend, Dies," *NYT*, 6 February 2007, D8; Joe Holley, "Ralph de Toledano, 90; Ardent Conservative," *WP*, 7 February 2007, B7; Ralph de Toledano, "Deep Throat's Ghost," *American Conservative*, 4 July 2005, 14–15.

69 Felt, *FBI Pyramid*, 12–13, 213.

70 Ibid., 225–226, 294.

71 Ibid., 226.

72 David Wise, "Apologia by No. 2," *WP*, 27 January 1980, BR3.

73 Monica Crowley, *Nixon in Winter* (New York: Random House, 1998), 298; Robert Sam Anson, *Exile: The Unquiet Oblivion of Richard M. Nixon* (New York: Simon & Schuster, 1984), 233–235.

74 Robert Pear, "Nixon Willing to Testify at Ex-FBI Officials' Trial," *NYT*, 20 September 1980, 70; Laura A. Kiernan, "Nixon's Account: Final Chapter in FBI Aides' Trial," *WP*, 2 November 1980, A14; Robert Pear, "Testimony by Nixon Heard in FBI Trial," *NYT*, 30 October 1980, A1; Stephen E. Ambrose, *Nixon: Ruin and Recovery, 1973–1990* (New York: Simon & Schuster, 1991), 536–537.

75 Woodward, *Secret Man*, 144.

76 "Reagan Pardons Ex-FBI Agents in Break-in Case," *WSJ*, 16 April 1981, 2; Letter, Reagan to Miller, 28 April 1981, RWRL; Letter, Felt to Reagan, 9 May 1981, RWRL; Michael Dobbs, "Watergate and the Two Lives of Mark Felt," *WP*, 20 June 2005, A1; Anson, *Unquiet Oblivion*, 235; Christopher Hitchens, "Minority Report," *The Nation*, 5 March 1988, 294.

According to Anson, Nixon sent a magnum of champagne in addition to or instead of his book. As of this writing, Nixon's postpresidential papers are not open so it is not possible to research his role vis-à-vis the Felt trial or pardon.

EPILOGUE: 1982–2011

1 W. Joseph Campbell, *Getting It Wrong: Ten of the Greatest Misreported Stories in American Journalism* (Berkeley, CA: University of California Press, 2010), 117, 125–126.

2 Curtis Prendergast with Geoffry Colvin, *The World of Time, Inc.: The Intimate History of a Changing Enterprise, 1960–1980* (New York: Atheneum, 1986), 366.

3 Leonard Garment, *Crazy Rhythm: My Journey from Brooklyn, Jazz, and Wall Street to Nixon's White House, Watergate, and Beyond* (New York: Times Books, 1997), 250; Eleeza V. Agopian, "Acclaimed Journalist Entertains Questions, Provokes Political Ideas," *California Aggie*, 29 February 2000, 1.

4 Bob Woodward, *The Secret Man: The Story of Watergate's Deep Throat* (New York: Simon & Schuster, 2005), 40, 150; Richard M. Cohen and Jules Witcover, *A Heartbeat Away* (New York: Viking Press, 1974), 78; Richard Cohen, "A Brave Friend," *WP*, 1 June 2005, A19; e-mail to author from Richard M. Cohen, 30 April 2011; Mark Memmott, "'Deep Throat' Revelation Raises New Questions," *USA Today*, 1 June 2005, A6.

5 Richard Reeves, "Lots of Footwork, No Footnotes," *NYT Book Review*, 18 April 1976, 174; ABC News, transcript, "Watergate Revisited," *Nightline*, 17 June 1982, 6–7.

6 Stanley I. Kutler, "Watergate Misremembered: The Shallow Debate about Deep Throat," http://www.slate.com/id/2067123/, 18 June 2002; Fred Emery, "So Who Was Deep Throat?" *Guardian*, 20 April 1994, T2.

7 James Mann, "Deep Throat: An Institutional Analysis," *Atlantic*, May 1992, 106–112.

8 Howard Kurtz, "Tracking Deep Throat: Watergate Anniversary Spurs Search for Source," *WP*, 18 April 1992, C1; Woodward, *Secret Man*, 154–155.

9 Author interview with Roger L. Depue (chief of the FBI's Behavioral Sciences Unit from 1980 to 1989), 19 May 2011; Ben Bradlee, *A Good Life: Newspapering and Other Adventures* (New York: Simon & Schuster, 1995), 365.

In his memoir, Bradlee wrote, "I had accepted Woodward's desire to identify [Deep Throat] to me only by job, experience, access, and expertise. That amazes me now, given the high stakes. I don't see how I settled for that, and I would not settle for that now." Bradlee, *A Good Life*, 365.

10 *CBS News* transcript, "Watergate: The Secret Story," 17 June 1992, 12; Kurtz, "Tracking Deep Throat," C1.

11 Pincus's research during this period also resulted in an insightful article regarding a second Deep Throat, i.e., Edward Bennett Williams. Walter Pincus, "A Watergate Mystery: Was There a Second 'Deep Throat'?" *WP*, 28 June 1992, C3; Kurtz, "Tracking Deep Throat," C1; Karlyn Barker and Walter Pincus, "Watergate Revisited: 20 Years after the Break-in, the Story Continues to Unfold," *WP*, 14 June 1992, A1; *CBS News*, "Watergate: The Secret Story," 10; Monica Crowley, *Nixon in Winter* (New York: Random House, 1998), 303; National Security Archive, "The Deep Throat File," http://www.gwu.edu/~nsarchiv/NSAEBB/NSAEBB156/index2.htm, 22 June 2005.

12 *CBS News*, "Watergate: The Secret Story," 11; Bradlee, *A Good Life*, 365.

The first person to point out that Deep Throat's information was sometimes "dead wrong" was John Dean in his 1982 memoir, *Lost Honor*. Leonard Garment, in his 1997 memoir, also pointed out that Deep Throat got a lot of things wrong; he "clearly had only a 'hallway' familiarity with Watergate's complicated evidence." The truth of this observation never gained traction, perhaps because the bad information did not make it into the *Washington Post*'s Watergate coverage for the most part; it appeared primarily in *All the President's Men*. Ben Bradlee Oral History, 14 December 2010, RMNL; John W. Dean, *Lost Honor* (Los Angeles: Stratford Press, 1982), 34, 300, 316–322; John W. Dean, "Why the Revelation of the Identity of Deep Throat Has Only Created Another Mystery," http://writ.news.findlaw.com/dean/20050603, 3 June 2005; Garment, *Crazy Rhythm*, 249.

13 David Daley, "Deep Throat: 2 Boys Talking Politics at Summer Camp May Have Revealed a Watergate Secret," *Hartford Courant*, 28 July 1999, A1; W. Mark Felt and John O'Connor, *A G-Man's Life: The FBI, Being "Deep Throat," and the Struggle for Honor in Washington* (New York: PublicAffairs, 2006), 292, 294.

14 Felt and O'Connor, *A G-Man's Lfe*, 298; Daley, "Deep Throat: 2 Boys Talking Politics," A1.

15 Timothy Noah, "Deep Throat Revealed (Again)," http://www.slate.com/id/1003033/, 17 June 1999; Timothy Noah, "Deep Throat Revealed (One Last Time)," http://www.slate.com/id/1003088/, 24 June 1999; Timothy Noah, "Another Bulletin from the Deep Throat Desk," http://www.slate.com/id/1003283/, 26 July 1999; Timothy Noah, "Deep Throat: The Game Is Afoot," http://www.slate.com/id/1003301/, 29 July 1999; Timothy Noah, "The Final Word on Deep Throat (So Far)," http://www.slate.com/id/1003363/, 9 August 1999; Timothy Noah, "Nixon: I Am Not an Anti-Semite," http://www.slate.com/id/1003783/, 7 October 1999; Timothy Noah, "Len Garment Kills the Messenger," http://www.slate.com/id/1005766/, 28 July 2000; Timothy Noah, "Salon and John Dean's Deep Throat Candidate Revealed!" http://www.slate.com/id/2065193/, 1 May 2002; Timothy Noah, "Why Did Bob Woodward Lunch with Mark Felt in 1999?" http://www.slate.com/id/2065299/, 2 May 2002; Timothy Noah, "Yes, Virginia, There Is a Deep Throat," http://www.slate.com/id/2065560/, 8 May 2002; Timothy Noah, "John Dean Says Deep Throat Was Not a G-Man," http://www.slate.com/id/2067081/, 17 June 2002; Timothy Noah, "Was Fred Fielding Deep Throat?" http://www.slate.com/id/2082179/, 8 May 2003; Timothy Noah, "Was Fred Fielding Deep Throat? Part 2," http://www.slate.com/id/2082752/, 8 May 2003; Timothy Noah, "Was Fred Fielding Deep Throat? Part 3," http://www.slate.com/id/2082905/, 13 May 2003; Timothy Noah, "Rehnquist Wasn't Deep Throat," http://www.slate.com/id/2113517/, 14 February 2005.

16 Timothy Noah, "The Final Word on Deep Throat (So Far)."

17 John D. O'Connor, "I'm the Guy They Called Deep Throat," *Vanity Fair*, July 2005, 88; Ronald Kessler, *Bureau: The Secret History of the FBI* (New York: St. Martin's Press, 2002), 178, 180; Woodward, *Secret Man*, 161, 167, 173–174.

O'Connor and Kessler both wrote incorrectly that Woodward visited the Felt home in August 1999; the visit occurred in February 2000, the day after Woodward delivered a lecture at UC-Davis. Agopian, "Acclaimed Journalist Entertains Questions," 1.

18 O'Connor, "I'm the Guy They Called Deep Throat," 89.

19 Todd S. Purdum, "'Deep Throat' Unmasks Himself: Ex-No. 2 at FBI," *NYT*, 1 June 2005, A1; Woodward, *Secret Man*, 136, 144, 201, 204; O'Connor, "I'm the Guy They

Called Deep Throat," 133; Vicki Haddock, "The Bay Area's 'Deep Throat' Candidate," *San Francisco Chronicle*, 16 June 2002, D1.

20 Alicia C. Shepard, *Woodward and Bernstein: Life in the Shadow of Watergate* (Hoboken, NJ: John Wiley and Sons, 2007), 258.

21 Evan Thomas, "Understanding Deep Throat," *Newsweek*, 13 June 2005, 22–23; John Stacks, "The Man Who Was Deep Throat: Chasing Mark Felt," http://www.time.com/ time/politics/article/0,8599,1868043,00.html, 19 December 2008; Evan Thomas with Karen Breslau, "Shopping a Big Secret," *Newsweek*, 13 June 2005, 30; Joe Hagan and Katherine Rosman, "How a Lawyer Finally Unveiled 'Deep Throat,'" *WSJ*, 2 June 2005, B1; O'Connor, "I'm the Guy They Called Deep Throat," 86; Edward Wyatt, "'Deep Throat' Sells Rights to His Story," *NYT*, 16 June 2005, A22.

22 Woodward, *Secret Man*, 223; Katharine Q. Seelye, "Disclosure by Magazine Catches *Post* by Surprise," *NYT*, 1 June 2005, A16; Shepard, *Woodward and Bernstein*, 251–255, 260–263.

The main story in the *New York Times* reported that Woodward and Bernstein "initially declined to confirm the *Vanity Fair* article, believing *they had promised* [emphasis added] Mr. Felt unconditional confidentiality till his death." In the *Post*, Howard Kurtz suggested that it was Bernstein's and Woodward's fidelity to their source that cost the newspaper the scoop of the year. Purdum, "'Deep Throat' Unmasks Himself: Ex-No. 2 at FBI," A1; Alessandra Stanley, "Woodward and Bernstein, Dynamic Duo, Together Again," *NYT*, 3 June 2005, A16; Howard Kurtz, "A 33-Year-Old Pledge Was Kept at a Price: The *Post*'s Lost Scoop," *WP*, 2 June 2005, A13; Graydon Carter, "Mr. Felt Goes to Washington," *Vanity Fair*, August 2005, 52.

23 Ruth Marcus, "'It Was Not I,'" *WP*, 5 June 2005, B7; Stephen Amidon, "It's All Relative," *WP*, 5 June 2005, B1; Carol Benfell, "A Family Secret: Joan Felt Explains Why Family Members Urged Her Father, Watergate's 'Deep Throat,' to Reveal His Identity," *Santa Rosa (CA) Press Democrat*, 5 June 2005, A1; Carol Benfell, "Woodward-Felt Meeting Yielded No Answers," *Santa Rosa (CA) Press Democrat*, 7 July 2005, A1.

24 Spencer Soper, "Watergate's 'Deep Throat' Identified as Santa Rosa Man," *Santa Rosa (CA) Press Democrat*, 1 June 2005, A1; Dan Balz and R. Jeffrey Smith, "Conflicted and Mum for Decades," *WP*, 1 June 2005, A1; Dan Morgan, "Contemporaries Have Mixed Views," *WP*, 1 June 2005, A9; T. Christian Miller, "Source Reflected the Era," *LAT*, 1 June 2005, A1; Thomas, "Understanding Deep Throat," 22–32; David Johnston, "Used to Hoover's Imperious Demands, but Troubled by 'Switchblade Mentality,'" *NYT*, 1 June 2005, A17; Nina J. Easton, "Insiders' Parlor Game Takes Surprising Twist," *BG*, 1 June 2005, A6; Michael Kranish, "Tipster Had Access, Motive to Help Make History," *BG*, 1 June 2005, A6; Dan Eggen, "At FBI, Reflections on Felt and Loyalty," *WP*, 2 June 2005, A21; Hagan and Rosman, "How a Lawyer Finally Unveiled 'Deep Throat,'" B1; "William Greider, "Lies, Guts and Deep Throat," *The Nation*, 20 June 2005, 4.

Dissenting views on the Left were presented by *Slate*'s Jack Shafer, who called Felt "just another vigilant protector of Washington turf," and Victor Navasky, who stressed Felt's pre-Watergate history, as did John Nields, one of the government lawyers who prosecuted Felt. Besides Buchanan on the Right, Ralph de Toledano, the ghost writer on Felt's memoir, argued that Felt acted mostly out of "personal pique." Jack Shafer, "Why Did Deep Throat Leak?" http://www.slate.com/id/2120148/, 2 June 2005; Victor Navasky, "Deep Threat," *The Nation*, 27 June 2005, 4–5; John W. Nields, "The Contradiction of 'Deep Throat,'" *WP*, 12 June 2005, B9; Ralph de Toledano, "Deep Throat's Ghost," *American Conservative*, 4 July 2005, 14–15; Michael Miner, "Deception in the Name of Truth," *Chicago Reader*, 10 June 2005, 4.

A few weeks later, the *Post*'s Michael Dobbs, after reviewing thousands of declassified documents and interviewing dozens of people who dealt with Felt, wrote more insightfully, "It is impossible to disentangle Felt's sense of outrage over what was happening to the country from his own desire to scramble to the top of 'the FBI Pyramid.'" Dobbs, "Watergate and the Two Lives of Mark Felt," A1; Michael Dobbs, "Revenge Was Felt's Motive, Former Acting FBI Chief Says," *WP*, 27 June 2005, A4.

Deep Throat's revised memoir adds "conjecture to speculation about Felt's motives," John Dean wrote in the *New York Times Book Review*. Yet the revision, if anything, was even more self-serving than the original work. Felt and O'Connor, *A G-Man's Life*; John Dean, "The Source Runs Dry," *NYT Book Review*, 7 May 2006, H18.

25 "'Deep Throat' Ex-Boss Shocked by Revelation," http://abcnews.go.com/ThisWeek/politics/story?id-853440&page-1, 26 June 2006; Michael Kranish, "Tipster Had Access, Motive," A6; David Johnston, "Ex-FBI Chief Calls Deep Throat's Unmasking a Shock," *NYT*, 27 June 2005, A11; David Stout, "FBI Chief's Book Revisits Watergate," *NYT*, 9 March 2008, A27.

26 Dobbs, "Revenge Was Felt's Motive," A4.

27 Dan Eggen, "At FBI, Reflections on Felt and Loyalty," A21.

28 Kessler, *Bureau*, 179.

Not all the agents who worked on the Watergate case took a dim view of Felt. In his 2007 oral history with the Society of Former FBI Agents, John W. Mindermann said, "I believe Mark Felt deserves very special mention for the lonely, dangerous but essential, even critical role he played as Deep Throat, the secret, timely provider of inside information to Woodward and Bernstein. . . . Without Felt's feeding, confirming, and guiding those reporters, who published information which stoked the public and drove political and public demands to keep the investigation alive, it['s] quite possible that we would not have made it as far as we eventually did. In my view as a participatory insider, Mark Felt is another real, genuine American hero and a tremendous credit to the FBI."

"All that said, the investigators of the Watergate came away from the experience scarred and, to some small degree, tainted. It is simply not possible to roll in the muck and come out cleanly. Because of the duplicity, rule-breaking, threats, political intrigue, and struggle up to and including the highest levels, we all were engulfed in an unseemly, embarrassing historical event. . . . But none of us who experienced Watergate will forget or ever be trusting of political authority/leadership in our Republic again." John W. Mindermann Oral History, 7 March 2007, SOCXFBI, 27.

29 Author interview with John J. McDermott, 17 November 2010; Letter, McDermott to Craig Detlo, 1 November 2006, courtesy of the author.

30 McDermott interview, 17 November 2010; author interview with Scott Erskine, 17 May 2011.

Although Erskine could not identify who sponsored Felt's application, in all likelihood it was Edward S. Miller, the former assistant director of the Domestic Intelligence Division, who had been prosecuted along with Felt in the late 1970s. Miller had also been a prominent member of the Felt faction at the Bureau and aware of his role as Deep Throat by 1977. "Nothing new" was Miller's reaction to the 2005 *Vanity Fair* article. Author interviews with Edward S. Miller, 17 May and 27 October 2011.

31 Timothy Noah, "Oedipus Bob," http://www.slate.com/id/2122163/, 7 July 2005; Shepard, *Woodward and Bernstein*, 237.

32 Brendan Lyons, "Deep Throat's Tale Revealed," *ATU*, 5 June 2005, A1; Brendan Lyons, "Account Adds Intrigue to Deep Throat Story," *ATU*, 7 June 2005, A1.

Although these stories did not receive the attention they deserved, Ben Bradlee did send a complimentary e-mail to Brendan Lyons, the *Times Union* reporter who wrote the articles. Rex Smith, "When Big News Is Met with Shrugs," *ATU*, 11 June 2005, A7.

In April 1982, Woodward and John Dean were lecturing at the University of Massachusetts. Woodward took the occasion to ask Dean if the story about Gray blackmailing President Nixon was accurate. "No, not really," said Dean. Gray received the nomination because Attorney General Richard Kleindienst "had gone to bat for [him]." Woodward's response was, "[I] got that story from a source at the White House, usually a pretty good source." Dean, *Lost Honor*, 300.

33 Woodward, *Secret Man*, 85–87; Ronald J. Ostrow, "FBI Investigating Its Former No. 2 Official," *LAT*, 17 November 1974, A1; Sanford J. Ungar, *FBI* (Boston: Atlantic Monthly Press, 1976), 556–557.

34 Author interview with William D. Ruckelshaus, 8 December 2010; William Ruckelshaus Oral History, 12 April 2007, RMNL, 8; Bob Woodward Oral History, 14 December 2010, RMNL.

Ruckelshaus's call to Woodward occurred just a few days after he had been contacted by the *Post*'s Michael Dobbs, who was writing a long article about Felt for the newspaper; indeed, Ruckelshaus's call may have been prompted by second thoughts following his conversation with Dobbs; the former FBI director had "decline[d] to detail the evidence against Felt" for Dobbs, even though most of the story had already appeared in Sanford Ungar's history of the Bureau published thirty years earlier.

According to Ruckelshaus, Woodward thought enough of the information he was given on June 21 to contact Crewdson immediately. Woodward subsequently reported back to Ruckelshaus that Sullivan had succeeded in getting Felt blamed for something he (Sullivan) did. Michael Dobbs, "Watergate and the Two Lives of Mark Felt," *WP*, 20 June 2005, A1; Ruckelshaus interview, 8 December 2010; Ruckelshaus Oral History, 12 April 2007, 8.

35 Author interview with Bob Woodward, 12 October 2011.

36 Benfell, "Woodward-Felt Meeting Yielded No Answers," A1; Carl Bernstein and Bob Woodward, *All the President's Men* (New York: Simon & Schuster, 1974), 130.

37 Joan Didion, "The Deferential Spirit," *New York Review of Books*, 19 September 1996, 18.

38 Laura Norton, "Woodward and Bernstein Laud Felt's Courage," *Santa Rosa (CA) Press Democrat*, 16 January 2009, A1.

39 CBS News, transcript, *Face the Nation*, 5 June 2005, 5, 6.

40 Harry Rosenfeld, "Confidential Sources Still Vital to Free Press," *ATU*, 2 June 2005, A13.

41 Earl Silbert Oral History, 17 September 2008, RMNL; David Binder, "George E. MacKinnon, 89, Dies; Was Appeals Judge for 25 Years," *NYT*, 3 May 1995, D21; *U.S. v John N. Mitchell, Harry R. Haldeman, John D. Ehrlichman*, 559 F.2d 31 (181 U.S. App D.C. 254, 1976), 91, 92, 93.

MacKinnon, during his one term in the U.S. House of Representatives from 1946 to 1948, had worked with then-Congressman Nixon in investigating the Alger Hiss case.

42 *U.S. v John N. Mitchell, Harry R. Haldeman, John D. Ehrlichman*, 559 F.2d 31 (181 U.S. App D.C. 254, 1976), 93.

Bibliography and Sources

INTERVIEWS AND CORRESPONDENCE

Daniel M. Armstrong
David Beckwith
Carl Bernstein
Benjamin C. Bradlee
Samuel C. Butler
Joseph A. Califano, Jr.
Donald E. Campbell
Robert P. Campbell
Stanley Cloud
John J. Clynick
Richard M. Cohen
Patrick Collins
Len Colodny
Charles W. Colson
Jack L. Conmy
John M. Crewdson
Paul V. Daly
John W. Dean III
Cartha D. "Deke" DeLoach
Roger L. Depue
Michael Dobbs
Leonard Downie, Jr.
Mel Elfin
Scott A. Erskine
William C. Gaines
J. Alan Galbraith
Leonard Garment
Robert E. Gebhardt
Irwin F. Gellman
Seymour Glanzer
Ed Gray
Barbara L. Herwig
Nicholas M. Horrock
Robert L. Jackson
David D. Kinley

Egil "Bud" Krogh
John B. Kuhns
Angelo J. Lano
Stephan Lesher
John Limpert
Brendan J. Lyons
Frank McCulloch
John J. McDermott
Daniel C. Mahan
James Mann
Philip T. Mellinger
Lawrence Meyer
Edward S. Miller
John D. O'Connor
Ronald J. Ostrow
Richard D. Rogge
Harry M. Rosenfeld
Susan Rosenfeld
William D. Ruckelshaus
Stephen H. Sachs
Donald E. Santarelli
Martin Schram
Earl J. Silbert
Hugh W. Sloan, Jr.
Edward L. Smith
John F. Stacks
Barry Sussman
Nina Totenberg
Ray Wannall
John L. Wilhelm
Bob Woodward

SOCIETY OF FORMER FBI AGENTS (SOCXFBI)

Oral History Collection
Thomas E. Bishop, 13 January and 3 February 2004
Daniel F. Bledsoe, 19 August 2009
Charles Bolz, 25 September 2009
Homer A. Boynton, 2 March 2006
Paul V. Daly, 10 February 2005
Roger L. Depue, 15 February 2006
Graham J. Desvernine, 4 October 2006; 8–9 March 2007
Paul P. Magallanes, 25 August 2005
Edward S. Miller, 23 May 2008
John W. Mindermann, 7 March 2007
Leonard M. "Bucky" Walters, 4 March 2003

ARCHIVAL COLLECTIONS

Federal Bureau of Investigation (FBI via Freedom of Information Act)
W. Mark Felt Main File (WMF)
L. Patrick Gray III Main File (LPG)
Henry E. Petersen Main File (HEP)
William C. Sullivan Main File (WCS)
Watergate Inspection Division Investigation (WIDI)
Watergate Main File (WG)

Jimmy E. Carter Library (JECL)
White House Staff Files
    Robert J. Lipshutz Papers

National Archives (NARA)
Watergate Special Prosecution Force (WSPF)
    Dirty Tricks Task Force
    Nixon Grand Jury Records

Richard M. Nixon Library (RMNL)
Richard M. Nixon Tape Recordings
White House Staff Files
    H. R. Haldeman Papers
    John W. Dean Papers
    David R. Young Papers

ORAL HISTORIES
Carl Bernstein, 22 October 2007
Benjamin C. Bradlee, 14 December 2010
Stephen B. Bull, 25 June 2007
Dwight L. Chapin, 2 April 2007
John J. Chester, 30 July 2002
Charles W. Colson, 12 January 1973; 15 June and 21 September 1988; 17 August 2007
Leonard Garment, 6 April and 5 October 2007
H. R. "Bob" Haldeman, 13 August 1987; 11–13 April 1988
Egil "Bud" Krogh, 18 December 1972; 5 September 2007
Terry F. Lenzner, 4–5 December 2008
Jeb Stuart Magruder, 23 March 2007
Elliot L. Richardson, 31 May 1988
William D. Ruckelshaus, 12 April 2007
William Safire, 27 March 2008
Earl J. Silbert, 17 September 2008
Jerrold L. Schecter, 24 February 1988
Lowell P. Weicker, Jr., 23 October 2008
Bob Woodward, 14 December 2010

National Security Archive
The Deep Throat File, http://www.gwu.edu/~nsarchiv/NSAEBB/NSAEBB156/index2 .htm, 22 June 2005.

Ronald W. Reagan Library (RWRL)
White House Office of Records Management (WHORM) Alphabetical File
White House Office of Records Management (WHORM) Subject File
Presidential Pardons and Sentence Commutations
White House Staff Files
 Office of Speechwriting

University of Texas at Austin
Harry Ransom Center (HRC)
Bob Woodward and Carl Bernstein Watergate Papers (WBWP)

Wheaton College, Wheaton, IL
Charles W. Colson Papers

U.S. GOVERNMENT BOOKS AND DOCUMENTS

Chu, Vivian S., and Henry B. Hogue. "FBI Directorship: History and Congressional Action," Congressional Research Service, 7 June 2011.

Commission on CIA Activities within the United States. *Report to the President* (Washington, DC: Government Printing Office, 1975).

Ford, Harold P. *William E. Colby as Director of Central Intelligence, 1973–1976* (Washington, DC: CIA Center for the Study of Intelligence, 1993).

Hathaway, Robert M., and Russell Jack Smith. *Richard Helms as Director of Central Intelligence, 1966–1973* (Washington, DC: CIA Center for the Study of Intelligence, 1993).

The Public Papers of the Presidents of the United States, 1969–1974 Richard Nixon, 6 vols. (Washington, DC: Government Printing Office, 1970–1975).

U.S. Congress, House of Representatives, Committee on the Judiciary. *Hearings, Impeachment of Richard M. Nixon, President of the United States*, 93rd Cong., 2nd sess., 39 vols. (Washington, DC: Government Printing Office, 1974).

———. *Report, Impeachment of Richard M. Nixon, President of the United States*, 93rd Cong., 2nd sess. (Washington, DC: Government Printing Office, 1974).

U.S. Congress, House of Representatives, Special Subcommittee on Intelligence of the Committee on Armed Services. *Report, Inquiry into the Alleged Involvement of the Central Intelligence Agency in the Watergate and Ellsberg Matters*, 93rd Cong., 1st sess. (Washington, DC: Government Printing Office, 1973).

———. *Hearings, Inquiry into the Alleged Involvement of the Central Intelligence Agency in the Watergate and Ellsberg Matters*, 94th Cong., 1st sess. (Washington, DC: Government Printing Office, 1975).

U.S. Congress, Senate, Committee on Foreign Relations. *Hearings, Dr. Kissinger's Role in Wiretapping*, 93rd Cong., 2nd sess. (Washington, DC: Government Printing Office, 1974).

———. *Hearings, Nomination of Richard Helms to Be Ambassador to Iran and CIA International and Domestic Activities*, 93rd Cong., 1st sess. (Washington, DC: Government Printing Office, 1974).

U.S. Congress, Senate, Committee on the Judiciary. *Hearings, Louis Patrick Gray III*, 93rd Cong., 1st sess. (Washington, DC: Government Printing Office, 1973).

U.S. Congress, Senate, Select Committee on Presidential Campaign Activities (SCPCA). *Hearings, Presidential Campaign Activities of 1972*, 93rd Cong., 1st sess., 27 vols. (Washington, DC: Government Printing Office, 1973).

———. *Final Report*, 93rd Cong., 2nd sess. (Washington, DC: Government Printing Office, 1974).

U.S. Congress, Senate, Select Committee to Study Governmental Operations with Respect to Intelligence Activities. *Hearings*, 94th Cong., 2nd sess., 7 vols. (Washington, DC: Government Printing Office, 1975).

———. *Final Report*, 94th Cong., 2nd sess., 6 vols. (Washington, DC: Government Printing Office, 1976).

Watergate Special Prosecution Force. *Report* (Washington, DC: Government Printing Office, 1975).

NEWSPAPERS AND PERIODICALS

Boston Globe
Los Angeles Times
Manchester Union Leader
The Nation
The New Republic
New York Times
Newsday
Newsweek
Time
Times Union (Albany, New York)
Vanity Fair
Wall Street Journal
Washington Daily News
Washington Post
Washington Star
The Washingtonian

ARTICLES (PERIODICALS AND ONLINE)

Barker, Karlyn, and Walter Pincus. "Watergate Revisited: 20 Years after the Break-in, the Story Continues to Unfold," *WP*, 14 June 1992, A1.

(Beckwith, David). "The Spy in the Cold," *Time*, 29 January 1973, 17, 20.

Bernstein, Carl, and Bob Woodward. "Bugging 'Participant' Gives Details," *WP*, 11 September 1972, A1.

————. "Spy Funds Linked to GOP Aides," *WP*, 17 September 1972, A1.

————. "2 Linked to Secret GOP Fund," *WP*, 18 September 1972, A1.

————. "FBI Finds Nixon Aides Sabotaged Democrats," *WP*, 10 October 1972, A1.

————. "Testimony Ties Top Nixon Aide to Secret Fund," *WP*, 25 October 1972, A1.

————. "Magazine Says Nixon Aide Admits Disruption Effort," *WP*, 30 October 1972, A1.

————. "Parts 'Inaudible,'" *WP*, 8 November 1973, A1.

Carter, Graydon. "Mr. Felt Goes to Washington," *Vanity Fair*, August 2005, 52.

Collins, Patrick. "Gun, Bug, Map of Democratic HQ Found in Desk of White House Aide," *WDN*, 30 June 1972, 1, 3.

Corn, David, and Jeff Goldberg. "How Mark Felt Fooled the FBI," *The Nation*, 4 July 2005, 19–23.

Crewdson, John M. "'69 Phone Taps Reported on Newsmen at 3 Papers," *NYT*, 11 May 1973, 18.

————. "Sabotaging the GOP's Rivals: Story of a $100,000 Operation," *NYT*, 9 July 1973, 1.

————. "Sabotage by Segretti: Network of Amateurs," *NYT*, 10 July 1973, 1.

————. "FBI Warns Staff on Leaking Data," *NYT*, 26 August 1973, 1.

Daley, David. "Deep Throat: 2 Boys Talking Politics at Summer Camp May Have Revealed Watergate Secret," *Hartford Courant*, 28 July 1999.

Dean, John W. "Why the Revelation of the Identity of Deep Throat Has Only Created Another Mystery," http://writ.news.findlaw.com/dean/20050603.html, 3 June 2005.

Didion, Joan. "The Deferential Spirit," *New York Review of Books*, 19 September 1996, 14–19.

Dobbs, Michael. "Watergate and the Two Lives of Mark Felt: Roles as FBI Official, 'Deep Throat' Clashed," *WP*, 20 June 2005, A01.

Epstein, Edward Jay. "Did the Press Uncover Watergate?" *Commentary*, July 1974, 21–24.

Feldstein, Mark. "Watergate Revisited," *American Journalism Review*, August/September 2004, 60–68.

Gaines, William, and Max Holland. "Deep Throat 3.0," http://www.washingtondecoded.com/site/2007/05/wtrgte.html, 11 May 2007.

Garrow, David J. "A Revealing Look Back at Deep Throat," *CT*, 7 August 2005, 14-1.

(Gorey, Hays). "'Deep Throat': Narrowing the Field," *Time*, 3 May 1976, 17–18.

————. "Woodward on the Record—Sort Of," *Time*, 3 May 1976, 17.

Holland, Max. "The Secret That Wasn't: Deep Throat Exposed in 1973," http://www.washingtondecoded.com/site/2008/09/deep-throat-exposedin-1973.html, 11 September 2008.

Latham, Aaron. "How the *Washington Post* Gave Nixon Hell," *New York*, 14 May 1973, 49–56.

Limpert, John. "Deep Throat: If It Isn't Tricia It Must Be . . . ," *The Washingtonian*, June 1974, 17.

————. "Deeper into Deep Throat," *The Washingtonian*, August 1974, 17–18.

Lyons, Brendan. "Deep Throat's Tale Revealed," *ATU*, 5 June 2005, A1.

————. "Account Adds Intrigue to Deep Throat Story," *ATU*, 7 June 2005, A1.

McCartney, James. "The *Washington Post* and Watergate: How Two Davids Slew Goliath," *Columbia Journalism Review*, July/August 1973, 8–22.

McGuire, Mark. "Revelation Troubles Watergate Veteran," *ATU*, 1 June 2005, A5.

Mann, James. "Deep Throat: An Institutional Analysis," *Atlantic*, May 1992, 106–112.

————. "All the Bureaucracy's Men," *WP*, 5 June 2005, B1.

Mellinger, Philip T. "Deconstructing Deep Throat," http://www.washingtonian.com/articles/capitalcomment/21589.html

Noah, Timothy. "Mark Felt, RIP," http://www.slate.com/id/2207159/, 19 December 2008.

O'Connor, John D. "'I'm the Guy They Called Deep Throat,'" *Vanity Fair*, July 2005, 86–89, 129–133.

Ostrow, Ronald J. "FBI Investigating Its Former No. 2 Official," *LAT*, 17 November 1974, A1.

Pincus, Walter. "A Watergate Mystery: Was There a Second 'Deep Throat'?" *WP*, 28 June 1992, C3.

Rosenfeld, Harry. "Don't Expect Dean to Solve It," *ATU*, 2 June 2002, B5.

(Smith, Sandy). "The Bugs at the Watergate," *Time*, 3 July 1972, 10–11.

———. "Watergate, Contd.," *Time*, 14 August 1972, 21–22.

———. "The Watergate Issue," *Time*, 28 August 1972, 20.

———. "More Fumes from the Watergate Affair," *Time*, 23 October 1972, 23.

———. "Denials and Still More Questions," *Time*, 30 October 1972, 18–19.

———. "The FBI: Political Orders," *Time*, 6 November 1972, 48, 50.

———. "How High?" *Time*, 6 November 1972, 50.

———. "'Tattletale Gray,'" *Time*, 15 January 1973, 20.

———. "Questions about Gray," *Time*, 5 March 1973, 14–15.

———. "The Fight over the Future of the FBI," *Time*, 26 March 1973, 17–20, 25–26, 28.

Stern, Laurence. "Bureau Hurt by Watergate," *WP*, 17 June 1973, A1.

Stacks, John. "The Man Who Was Deep Throat: Chasing Mark Felt," http://www.time.com/time/politics/article/0,8599,1868043,00.html, 19 December 2008.

Sussman, Barry. "Kenneth Dahlberg's Role in Watergate," http://www/niemanwatchdog.org/index.cfm?fuseaction-showcase.view&showcaseide=00161, 11 October 2011.

———. "Watergate, 25 Years Later: Myths and Collusion," http://watergate.info.sussman/25th.shtml, June 1997.

———. "Why Deep Throat Was an Unimportant Source and Other Reflections on Watergate," http://www.niemanwatchdog.org/index.cfm?fuseaction=background.view&backgroundid=51&forumaction=post, 29 July 2005.

Woodward, Bob. "Bremer's Car Called Motel on Wheels," *WP*, 18 May 1972, A17.

Woodward, Bob, and Carl Bernstein. "$100,000 Gift to Nixon Campaign Is Traced to Texas Corporation," *WP*, 6 October 1972, A1.

———. "Wiretaps Put on Phones of 2 Reporters," *WP*, 3 May 1973, A1.

BOOKS

Aitken, Jonathan. *Nixon: A Life* (Lanham, MD: Regnery Publishing, 1993).

———. *Charles W. Colson: A Life Redeemed* (New York: Doubleday, 2005).

Ambrose, Stephen E. *Nixon: The Triumph of a Politician, 1962–1972* (New York: Simon & Schuster, 1989).

———. *Nixon: Ruin and Recovery, 1973–1990* (New York: Simon & Schuster, 1991).

Anson, Robert Sam. *Exile: The Unquiet Oblivion of Richard Nixon* (New York: Simon & Schuster, 1984).

Ben-Veniste, Richard, and George Frampton, Jr. *Stonewall: The Real Story of the Watergate Prosecution* (New York: Simon & Schuster, 1977).

Bernstein, Carl. *Loyalties: A Son's Memoir* (New York: Simon & Schuster, 1989).

Bernstein, Carl, and Bob Woodward. *All the President's Men* (New York: Simon & Schuster, 1974).

Bok, Sissela. *Secrets: On the Ethics of Concealment and Revelation* (New York: Pantheon Books, 1982).

———. *Lying: Moral Choice in Public and Private Life* (New York: Vintage Books, 1999).

Bradlee, Ben. *A Good Life: Newspapering and Other Adventures* (New York: Simon & Schuster, 1995).

Bray, Howard. *The Pillars of the Post: The Making of a News Empire in Washington* (New York: W. W. Norton, 1980).

Broder, David S. *Behind the Front Page: A Candid Look at How the News Is Made* (New York: Simon & Schuster, 1987).

Califano, Joseph A., Jr. *Inside: A Public and Private Life* (New York: PublicAffairs, 2004).

Campbell, W. Joseph. *Getting It Wrong: Ten of the Greatest Misreported Stories in American Journalism* (Berkeley: University of California Press, 2010).

Carnes, Mark C., ed. *Past Imperfect: History According to the Movies* (New York: Henry Holt, 1995).

Cohen, Richard M., and Jules Witcover. *A Heartbeat Away* (New York: Viking Press, 1974).

Colodny, Len, and Robert Gettlin. *Silent Coup: The Removal of a President* (New York: St. Martin's Press, 1991).

Colson, Charles W. *Born Again* (Old Tappan, NJ: Chosen Books, 1976).

Crouse, Timothy. *The Boys on the Bus* (New York: Random House, 2003).

Crowley, Monica. *Nixon Off the Record* (New York: Random House, 1996).

———. *Nixon in Winter* (New York: Random House, 1998).

Dash, Samuel. *Chief Counsel: Inside the Ervin Committee—The Untold Story of Watergate* (New York: Random House, 1976).

Davis, James Kirkpatrick. *Spying on America: The FBI's Domestic Counterintelligence Program* (Westport, CT: Praeger, 1992).

———. *Assault on the Left: The FBI and the Sixties Antiwar Movement* (Westport, CT: Praeger, 1997).

Dean, John W., III. *Blind Ambition: The White House Years* (New York: Simon & Schuster, 1976).

———. *Lost Honor: The Rest of the Story* (Los Angeles: Stratford Press, 1982).

———. *Unmasking Deep Throat: History's Most Elusive News Source* (San Francisco: Salon.com Books, 2002).

———. *Blind Ambition: The End of the Story* (Palm Springs, CA: Polimedia Publishers, 2009).

DeLoach, Cartha D. "Deke." *Hoover's FBI: The Inside Story by Hoover's Trusted Lieutenant* (Washington, DC: Regnery, 1995).

Dickinson, William B., Jr., ed. *Watergate: Chronology of a Crisis*, vol. 1 (Washington, DC: Congressional Quarterly, 1973).

Downie, Leonard, Jr. *The New Muckrakers: An Inside Look at America's Investigative Reporters* (Washington, DC: New Republic Books, 1976).

Doyle, James. *Not above the Law: The Battles of Watergate Prosecutors Cox and Jaworski* (New York: William Morrow, 1977).

Ehrlichman, John. *Witness to Power: The Nixon Years* (New York: Simon & Schuster, 1982).

Eisler, Kim. *Masters of the Game: Inside the World's Most Powerful Law Firm* (New York: Thomas Dunne Books, 2010).

Emery, Fred. *Watergate: The Corruption of American Politics and the Fall of Richard Nixon* (New York: Simon & Schuster, 1994).

Epstein, Edward Jay. *Between Fact and Fiction: The Problem of Journalism* (New York: Vintage Books, 1975).

Feldstein, Mark. *Poisoning the Press: Richard Nixon, Jack Anderson, and the Rise of Washington's Scandal Culture* (New York: Farrar, Straus and Giroux, 2010).

Felt, W. Mark. *The FBI Pyramid: From the Inside* (New York: G. P. Putnam's Sons, 1979).

Felt, Mark, and John O'Connor. *A G-Man's Life: The FBI, Being "Deep Throat," and the Struggle for Honor in Washington* (New York: PublicAffairs, 2006).

Friedman, Leon, and William F. Levantrosser, eds. *Watergate and Afterward: The Legacy of Richard M. Nixon* (Westport, CT: Greenwood Press, 1992).

Garment, Leonard. *Crazy Rhythm: My Journey from Brooklyn, Jazz, and Wall Street to Nixon's White House, Watergate, and Beyond* (New York: Times Books, 1997).

———. *In Search of Deep Throat: The Greatest Political Mystery of Our Time* (New York: Basic Books, 2000).

Garza, Hedda, compiler. *The Watergate Investigation Index: Senate Select Committee Hearings and Report on Presidential Campaign Activities* (Wilmington, DE: Scholarly Resources, 1982).

———. *The Watergate Investigation Index: House Judiciary Committee Hearings and Report on Impeachment* (Wilmington, DE: Scholarly Resources, 1985).

Gellman, Irwin F. *The Contender: Richard Nixon, the Congress Years, 1946–1952* (New York: Free Press, 1999).

Goldman, William. *Adventures in the Screen Trade: A Personal View of Hollywood and Screenwriting* (New York: Warner Books, 1983).

Goldstein, Janice L. *Watergate: Chronology of a Crisis*, vol. 2 (Washington, DC: Congressional Quarterly, 1974).

Graff, Garrett M. *The Threat Matrix: The FBI at War in the Age of Global Terror* (New York: Little, Brown, 2011.

Graham, Katherine. *Personal History* (New York: Alfred A. Knopf, 1997).

Gray, L. Patrick, III, with Ed Gray. *In Nixon's Web: A Year in the Crosshairs of Watergate* (New York: Times Books, 2008).

Greenberg, David. *Nixon's Shadow: The History of an Image* (New York: W. W. Norton, 2003).

Haig, Alexander M., Jr., with Charles McCarry. *Inner Circles: How America Changed the World—A Memoir* (New York: Warner Books, 1992).

Halberstam, David. *The Powers That Be* (New York: Alfred A. Knopf, 1979).

Haldeman, H. R. *The Haldeman Diaries: Inside the Nixon White House* (New York: G. P. Putnam's Sons, 1994).

Haldeman, H. R., with Joseph DiMona. *The Ends of Power* (New York: Times Books, 1978).

Havill, Adrian. *Deep Truth: The Lives of Bob Woodward and Carl Bernstein* (Secaucus, NJ: Birch Lane Press, 1993).

Helms, Richard, with William Hood. *A Look over My Shoulder: A Life in the Central Intelligence Agency* (New York: Random House, 2003).

Hoff, Joan. *Nixon Reconsidered* (New York: Basic Books, 1994).

Holland, Max. *The Kennedy Assassination Tapes: The White House Conversations of Lyndon B. Johnson Regarding the Assassination, the Warren Commission, and the Aftermath* (New York: Alfred A. Knopf, 2004).

Hougan, Jim. *Secret Agenda: Watergate, Deep Throat, and the CIA* (New York: Random House, 1984).

Hunt, E. Howard, with Greg Aunapu. *American Spy: My Secret History in the CIA, Watergate, and Beyond* (Hoboken, NJ: John Wiley & Sons, 2007).

Jaworski, Leon. *The Right and the Power: The Prosecution of Watergate* (New York: Reader's Digest Press, 1976).

Kelley, Clarence M., and James Kirkpatrick Davis. *Kelley: The Story of an FBI Director* (Kansas City, MO: Andrews, McMeel & Parker, 1987).

Kelly, Tom. *The Imperial Post: The Meyers, the Grahams and the Paper That Rules Washington* (New York: William Morrow, 1983).

Kessler, Ronald. *The FBI: Inside the World's Most Powerful Law Enforcement Agency* (New York: Pocket Books, 1993).

———. *Bureau: The Secret History of the FBI* (New York: St. Martin's Press, 2002).

———. *The Secrets of the FBI* (New York: Crown, 2011).

Kindred, Dave. *Morning Miracle: Inside the* Washington Post (New York: Doubleday, 2010).

Kleindienst, Richard G. *Justice: The Memoirs of Attorney General Richard Kleindienst* (Ottawa, IL: Jameson Books, 1985).

Krogh, Egil "Bud," with Matthew Krogh. *Integrity: Good People, Bad Choices and Life Lessons from the White House* (New York: PublicAffairs, 2007).

Kutler, Stanley I. *The Wars of Watergate: The Last Crisis of Richard Nixon* (New York: Alfred A. Knopf, 1990).

———. *Abuse of Power: The New Nixon Tapes* (New York: Free Press, 1997).

Liddy, G. Gordon. *Will: The Autobiography of G. Gordon Liddy* (New York: St. Martin's Press, 1980).

Liebovich, Louis W. *Richard Nixon, Watergate, and the Press: A Historical Perspective* (Westport, CT: Praeger, 2003).

Lukas, J. Anthony. *Nightmare: The Underside of the Nixon Years* (New York: Viking Press, 1976).

McCord, James W., Jr. *A Piece of Tape: The Watergate Story—Fact and Fiction* (Rockville, MD: Washington Media Services, 1974).

McGee, Jim, and Brian Duffy. *Main Justice: The Men and Women Who Enforce the Nation's Criminal Laws and Guard Its Liberties* (New York: Simon & Schuster, 1996).

Magruder, Jeb Stuart. *An American Life: One Man's Road to Watergate* (New York: Atheneum, 1974).

Malcolm, Janet. *The Journalist and the Murderer* (New York: Vintage, 1990).

Mollenhoff, Clark R. *Game Plan for Disaster: An Ombudsman's Report on the Nixon Years* (New York: W. W. Norton, 1976).

Nixon, Richard M. *RN: The Memoirs of Richard Nixon* (New York: Grosset & Dunlap, 1978).

———. *In the Arena: A Memoir of Victory, Defeat, and Renewal* (New York: Simon & Schuster, 1990).

Novak, Robert D. *The Prince of Darkness: 50 Years Reporting in Washington* (New York: Crown Forum, 2007).

O'Brien, Lawrence F. *No Final Victories: A Life in Politics from John F. Kennedy to Watergate* (Garden City, NY: Doubleday, 1974).

Obst, David. *Too Good to Be Forgotten: Changing America in the '60s and '70s* (New York: John Wiley & Sons, 1998).

Olson, Keith W. *Watergate: The Presidential Scandal That Shook America* (Lawrence: University Press of Kansas, 2003).

Oudes, Bruce, ed. *From: The President: Richard Nixon's Secret Files* (New York: Harper & Row, 1989).

Pack, Robert. *Edward Bennett Williams for the Defense* (New York: Harper & Row, 1983).

Perlstein, Rick. *Nixonland: The Rise of a President and the Fracturing of America* (New York: Scribner, 2008).

Perry, James M. "Watergate Case Study," in Tom Rosenstiel and Amy S. Mitchell, *Thinking Clearly: Cases in Journalistic Decision-Making* (New York: Columbia University Press, 2003).

Phelps, Robert H. *God and the Editor: My Search for Meaning at the* New York Times (Syracuse, NY: Syracuse University Press, 2009).

Powers, Thomas. *The War at Home: Vietnam and the American People, 1964–1968* (New York: Grossman Publishers, 1973).

———. *The Man Who Kept the Secrets: Richard Helms and the CIA* (New York: Knopf, 1979).

Prendergast, Curtis, with Geoffrey Colvin. *The World of Time, Inc.: The Intimate History of a Changing Enterprise, 1960–1980* (New York: Atheneum, 1986).

Richardson, Elliot. *The Creative Balance: Government, Politics, and the Individual in America's Third Century* (New York: Holt, Rinehart, 1976).

Riebling, Mark. *Wedge: The Secret War between the FBI and CIA* (New York: Alfred A. Knopf, 1994).

Roberts, Chalmers M. *The* Washington Post: *The First 100 Years* (Boston: Houghton Mifflin, 1977).

Rosen, James. *The Strong Man: John Mitchell and the Secrets of Watergate* (New York: Doubleday, 2008).

Rudenstine, David. *The Day the Presses Stopped: A History of the Pentagon Papers Case* (Berkeley: University of California Press, 1996).

Schudson, Michael. *Watergate in American Memory: How We Remember, Forget, and Reconstruct the Past* (New York: Basic Books, 1992).

Shepard, Alicia C. *Woodward and Bernstein: Life in the Shadow of Watergate* (Hoboken, NJ: John Wiley & Sons, 2007).

Shepard, Geoff. *The Secret Plot to Make Ted Kennedy President: Inside the* Real *Watergate Conspiracy* (New York: Sentinel, 2008).

Sirica, John J. *To Set the Record Straight: The Break-in, the Tapes, the Conspirators, the Pardon* (New York: W. W. Norton, 1979).

Small, Melvin. *The Presidency of Richard Nixon* (Lawrence: University Press of Kansas, 1999).

Society of Former Special Agents of the FBI, Inc. *Society of Former Special Agents of the FBI*, 2nd ed. (Paducah, KY: Turner Publishing Company, 1998).

Stans, Maurice H. *The Terrors of Justice: The Untold Side of Watergate* (New York: Everest House, 1978).

Strober, Deborah Hart, and Gerald S. Strober. *The Nixon Presidency: An Oral History of the Era* (Washington, DC: Brassey's, 2003).

Sullivan, William C., with Bill Brown. *The Bureau: My Thirty Years in Hoover's FBI* (New York: W. W. Norton, 1979).

Summers, Anthony, with Robbyn Swan. *The Arrogance of Power: The Secret World of Richard Nixon* (New York: Viking, 2000).

Sussman, Barry. *The Great Cover-up: Nixon and the Scandal of Watergate* (Arlington, VA: Seven Locks Press, 1992).

Theoharis, Athan G. *Spying on Americans: Political Surveillance from Hoover to the Huston Plan* (Philadelphia: Temple University Press, 1978).

Theoharis, Athan G., ed., with Tony Poveda, Susan Rosenfeld, and Richard Gid Powers. *The FBI: A Comprehensive Reference Guide* (Phoenix, AZ: Oryx Press, 1999).

Thomas, Evan. *The Man to See: Edward Bennett Williams* (New York: Simon & Schuster, 1991).

Thompson, Fred D. *At That Point in Time: The Inside Story of the Senate Watergate Committee* (New York: Quadrangle, 1975).

Toplin, Robert Brent. *History by Hollywood: The Use and Abuse of the American Past* (Urbana: University of Illinois Press, 1996).

Ulasewicz, Tony, with Stuart A. McKeever. *The President's Private Eye: The Journey of Detective Tony U. from NYPD to the Nixon White House* (Westport, CT: MACSAM Publishing, 1990).

Ungar, Sanford J. *FBI* (Boston: Little, Brown, 1976).

Walters, Vernon A. *Silent Missions* (Garden City, NY: Doubleday, 1978).

Wannall, Ray. *The Real J. Edgar Hoover: For the Record* (Paducah, KY: Turner Publishing Company, 2000).

White, Theodore H. *Breach of Faith: The Fall of Richard Nixon* (New York: Atheneum, 1975).

Wicker, Tom. *One of Us: Richard Nixon and the American Dream* (New York: Random House, 1991).

Witcover, Jules. *The Making of an Ink-Stained Wretch: Half a Century Pounding the Political Beat* (Baltimore, MD: Johns Hopkins University Press, 2005).

Woodward, Bob. *Shadow: Five Presidents and the Legacy of Watergate* (New York: Simon & Schuster, 1999).

———. *The Secret Man: The Story of Watergate's Deep Throat* (New York: Simon & Schuster, 2005).

Woodward, Bob, and Carl Bernstein. *The Final Days* (New York: Simon & Schuster, 1976).

MULTIMEDIA

Haldeman, H. R. *The Haldeman Diaries: Inside the Nixon White House*, CD-ROM (Los Angeles: Sony Imagesoft, 1994).

Index